ADMINISTRATIVE LAW AND JUDICIAL DEFERENCE

In recent years, the question whether judges should defer to administrative decisions has attracted considerable interest amongst public lawyers throughout the common law world. This book examines how the common law of judicial review has responded to the development of the administrative state in three different common law jurisdictions—the United Kingdom, the United States of America, and Canada—over the past 100 years. This comparison demonstrates that the idea of judicial deference is a valuable feature of modern administrative law, because it gives lawyers and judges practical guidance on how to negotiate the constitutional tension between the democratic legitimacy of the administrative state and the judicial role in maintaining the rule of law.

Volume 10 in the series Hart Studies in Comparative Public Law

Hart Studies in Comparative Public Law
Recent titles in this series:

The Scope and Intensity of Substantive Review
Traversing Taggart's Rainbow
Edited by Hanna Wilberg and Mark Elliott

Entick v Carrington
250 Years of the Rule of Law
Edited by Adam Tomkins and Paul Scott

Administrative Law and Judicial Deference
Matthew Lewans

Soft Law and Public Authorities
Remedies and Reform
Greg Weeks

Legitimate Expectations in the Common Law World
Edited by Matthew Groves and Greg Weeks

The Dynamics of Exclusionary Constitutionalism
Mazen Masri

Constitutional Courts, Gay Rights and Sexual Orientation Equality
Angioletta Sperti

Principled Reasoning in Human Rights Adjudication
Se-Shauna Wheatle

Human Rights and Judicial Review in Australia and Canada
Janina Boughey

The Foundations and Traditions of Constitutional Amendment
Edited by Richard Albert, Xenophon Contiades and Alkmene Fotiadou

The Federal Idea
Public Law Between Governance and Political Life
Edited by Amnon Lev

Comparative Federalism
Constitutional Arrangements and Case Law
Francesco Palermo and Karl Kössler

Governance by Numbers
The Making of a Legal Model of Allegiance
Alain Supiot

Administrative Law and Judicial Deference

Matthew Lewans

·HART·
PUBLISHING
OXFORD AND PORTLAND, OREGON
2018

Hart Publishing
An imprint of Bloomsbury Publishing Plc

Hart Publishing Ltd
Kemp House
Chawley Park
Cumnor Hill
Oxford OX2 9PH
UK

Bloomsbury Publishing Plc
50 Bedford Square
London
WC1B 3DP
UK

www.hartpub.co.uk
www.bloomsbury.com

Published in North America (US and Canada) by
Hart Publishing
c/o International Specialized Book Services
920 NE 58th Avenue, Suite 300
Portland, OR 97213-3786
USA

www.isbs.com

First published in hardback, 2016
Paperback edition, 2018

British Library Cataloguing-in-Publication Data
A catalogue record for this book is available from the British Library.

ISBN: PB: 978-1-50992-113-3
HB: 978-1-84946-277-8

Library of Congress Cataloging-in-Publication Data

Lewans, Matthew, author.
Administrative law and judicial deference / Matthew Lewans.

pages cm. — (Hart studies in comparative public law ; 10)

Includes bibliographical references and index.

ISBN 978-1-84946-277-8 (hardback : alk. paper) 1. Judicial review of administrative acts—United States. 2. Judicial review of administrative acts—Canada. 3.Judicial review of administrative acts—Great Britain. 4. Administrative law—United States. 5. Administrative law—Canada. 6. Administrative law—Great Britain. I. Title.

K3175.L49 2016 342'.06–dc23
2015036602

Typeset by Compuscript Ltd, Shannon

For Lila and Nicholas

Acknowledgements

This book began as a dissertation for my Doctorate of Juridical Science degree, which has been revised and rewritten since I defended it. I want to thank David Dyzenhaus (my SJD supervisor, whose scholarship in administrative law and jurisprudence provided a source of inspiration and whose comments greatly improved my understanding of these subjects), Michael Taggart (my mentor, whose energy and enthusiasm for administrative law convinced me to pursue graduate studies in the first place), and Dimitrios Kyritsis (my friend, who has generously shared his insights on many of the issues I have attempted to address in this book).

I also benefited greatly from suggestions made by members of my examination committee: Lorne Sossin, Sujit Choudhry, Mark Aronson, Jennifer Nedelsky, and Markus Dubber. Professor Aronson's detailed report, in particular, prompted me to explore the rich history of American administrative law, and consider how it might explain intellectual developments in other common law jurisdictions.

The University of Toronto and the Social Sciences and Humanities Research Council of Canada provided me with financial support throughout my doctoral studies. Without this support, I would never have been able to pursue a career in academia.

When I was struggling to complete the manuscript, I often looked to my family and friends for guidance and support. While I have many debts in this regard, I particularly want to thank my siblings—Julia, Cindy, Billy, Carmen, Mary, Audrey, and Stephanie—and my extended family, Nikos Daskalakis and Maria Kantonidou, for providing me with much needed encouragement and motivation to finish the project. I also want to thank my academic colleagues Eric Adams, TRS Allan, Ryan Arcand, Rueban Balasubramaniam, Paul Daly, Martin Hevia, Cam Hutchison, Hudson Janisch, Eran Kaplinsky, Matthew Kramer, Paul McHugh, James Muir, Erin Nelson, Zoran Oklopcic, Charles-Maxime Pannacio, Amanda Perreau-Saussine, Jacob Rowbottom, Barry Sullivan, Rayner Thwaites, Eddy Ventose, Lars Vinx, Mark Walters, and Bruce Ziff for generously offering their time, assistance, and camaraderie.

My father, Paul Lewans, QC, has always been a quiet source of wisdom and strength. Among other things, he has shown how lawyers can sustain a sense of justice and fair play in our communities. I still have much to learn from him.

Finally, I want to thank my wife, Lila, for listening and understanding from near and afar; and my favourite kid, Nicholas, for keeping it real. Σας αγαπώ από εδώ ως τον ουρανό.

Table of Contents

Table of Cases

Canada

Israel

New Zealand

South Africa

United Kingdom

United States of America

Table of Legislation

Canada

South Africa

United Kingdom

United States of America

Table of Conventions, Treaties, etc

1

A Question about Administrative Law

ONE OF THE most puzzling questions in public law concerns the status of administrative law: do administrative officials have legitimate authority to interpret the law? Surprisingly, common law jurists have only addressed this issue indirectly when responding to a different question concerning the legitimacy of judicial review: when are judges entitled to quash an administrative decision? Over the last century, much ink has been spilt discussing the legitimacy of judicial review without much regard for the legitimacy of administrative law.

Nevertheless, there is broad consensus that the administrative state plays a vital role in contemporary society. Scholars agree that administrative institutions have pervasive legal influence,[1] but only modest attempts have been made to explore the normative foundations of these institutional arrangements and how other legal officials, including judges, should respond to administrative decisions. At best, the question regarding the administrative law has been relegated to a sidebar in persistent debates regarding the proper ambit of judicial review.[2] Hence, public law scholarship tends to focus on legislative intent or the parameters of administrative 'jurisdiction', which are determined by legislatures or courts, rather than articulating why administrative decisions are worthy of respect in a democracy committed to the rule of law. This preoccupation generates a hollow conception of administrative law, because it is portrayed merely as a species of political power that emerges when the law runs out.[3]

[1] Peter Strauss, 'The Place of Agencies in Government: Separation of Powers and the Fourth Branch' (1984) 84 *Columbia Law Review* 573; Paul Craig, *Administrative Law*, 6th edn (London, Sweet & Maxwell, 2008) chs 2 and 4; SA de Smith, Lord Woolf and JL Jowell, *Judicial Review of Administrative Action*, 5th edn (London, Sweet & Maxwell, 1995) ch 1; HWR Wade and Christopher Forsyth, *Administrative Law*, 10th edn (Oxford, Oxford University Press, 2009) ch 1.

[2] See, eg Christopher Forsyth (ed), *Judicial Review and the Constitution* (Oxford, Hart Publishing, 2000).

[3] See, eg Ronald Dworkin's doughnut analogy, which has been used frequently as a starting point for analysing administrative discretion. Ronald Dworkin, *Taking Rights Seriously* (London, Duckworth, 1977) 31; Denis Galligan, *Discretionary Powers: a legal study of official discretion* (Oxford, Clarendon Press, 1986) ch 1; TRS Allan, 'Doctrine and Theory in Administrative Law: An Elusive Quest for the Limits of Jurisdiction' [2003] *Public Law* 429, 435.

In this book, I will argue that administrative law should be approached from a different direction, one which aims to explain its constitutional legitimacy from the ground up rather than attempting to identify the point at which judicial review is triggered. Thus, instead of focusing our attention on jurisdictional parameters, we should ask more directly whether administrative officials have legitimate authority to interpret the law, what the normative basis of that legitimacy is, and how it ought to be incorporated into a constitutional framework unified by the rule of law.

The contrast between these different approaches underscores a conspicuous doctrinal schism within the common law world. The schism divides administrative lawyers in the United Kingdom and other Commonwealth countries from their counterparts in the United States of America and Canada. Much of this book examines the history behind this schism, but the basic differences can be gleaned from a brief overview of three landmark cases.

I. JURISDICTIONAL ERROR

Anisminic Ltd was a British corporation which owned a manganese mine located in the Sinai Peninsula. Prior to the Suez-Sinai war, Anisminic estimated the value of its mine to be £4.5 million, but Israeli forces damaged approximately £500,000 worth of property during the war and the Egyptian government expropriated the remaining assets after the Israeli army withdrew. Anisminic subsequently mounted a public relations campaign to dissuade its former clients from purchasing manganese from the Egyptian authority which took over the mine. In order to placate Anisminic, the Egyptian government agreed to purchase all of the remaining assets for £500,000, but the agreement stated that the settlement did not prejudice Anisminic's ability to seek compensation from any other state.

Almost two years later, the United Arab Republic paid £27.5 million to the United Kingdom as compensation for property damage incurred by its citizens during the war. This fund was to be distributed by the Foreign Compensation Commission, pursuant to the Foreign Compensation Act 1950 and its related regulations.[4] Among other things, the Act declared that any 'determination by the commission of any application made to them … shall not be called into question in any court of law'.[5] Anisminic applied for compensation, but after a four-day hearing the Commission rejected the bulk of its claim on the basis that Anisminic had failed to prove that the Egyptian economic authority was not its 'successor in title' within the meaning of the

[4] Foreign Compensation Act 1950 (UK), 14 Geo VI, c 12.
[5] ibid s 4(4).

regulations.[6] Anisminic then brought an application for judicial review to overturn the Commission's decision.

The House of Lords held that the Commission had exceeded its jurisdiction by misconstruing the 'successor in title' provision.[7] However, the majority opinions in *Anisminic* advanced two very different conceptions of 'jurisdictional' error. In the lead judgment for the Court, Lord Reid drew a distinction between jurisdiction in its 'narrow and original' sense and jurisdiction in its 'wider' sense. The narrow sense of jurisdiction referred to whether the legislature had empowered an administrative decision-maker to 'enter on the inquiry in question'.[8] In this sense, the Commission was authorised to decide whether Anisminic was entitled to compensation, because it had been expressly empowered by an Act of Parliament to decide that question. If further support for this conclusion was needed, it could be drawn from the privative clause in the statute, which stated that the Commission's decisions could not be challenged in court.

Nevertheless, Lord Reid concluded that the Commission's authority was subject to additional legal constraints, which he associated with administrative jurisdiction in its 'wider' sense.[9] He stated that:[10]

> there are many cases where, although the tribunal had jurisdiction to enter on the inquiry, it has done or failed to do something in the course of the inquiry which is of such a nature that its decision is a nullity. It may have given its decision in bad faith. It may have made a decision which it had no power to make. It may have failed in the course of the inquiry to comply with the requirements of natural justice. It may in perfect good faith have misconstrued the provisions giving it power to act so that it failed to deal with the question remitted to it and decided some question which was not remitted to it. It may have refused to take into account something which it was required to take into account … If it is entitled to enter on the inquiry and does not do any of those things which I have mentioned in the course of the proceedings, then its decision is equally valid whether it is right or wrong subject only to the power of the court in certain circumstances to correct an error of law.

Even though he thought the Commission had jurisdiction in the narrow sense, Lord Reid held that the Commission had exceeded its jurisdiction in the wider sense because it had deviated from what he considered to be the 'true construction' of the regulation. The result is that, even though Lord Reid recognised that there were two different conceptions of jurisdiction in play, he asserted that both sets of parameters had been established by Parliament. Thus, Lord Reid and the other judges who sided with the

[6] Foreign Compensation (Egypt) (Determination and Registration of Claims) Order 1962 (SI 1962/2187), s 4(1).

[7] *Anisminic Ltd v Foreign Compensation Commission* [1969] 2 AC 147 (HL).

[8] ibid 171.

[9] ibid 195 (Lord Pearce).

[10] ibid 170.

majority claimed that they were not, in fact, disregarding parliamentary intent by quashing the decision, despite the privative clause which signalled Parliament's desire to insulate the Commission's decision from judicial interference.[11]

Lord Reid's opinion in *Anisminic* highlights three chronic problems with the doctrine of jurisdictional error. The first concerns a point I made earlier: that administrative law is perceived primarily in terms of its outer limits. Lord Reid's opinion focuses exclusively upon the parameters of the Commission's jurisdiction, which he assumes are established by either Parliament or via judicial interpretation of Parliament's will. As a result, Lord Reid's approach involves a hollow conception of administrative law that does not adequately explain the legitimate authority of administrative officials.

The second problem is that this framework for judicial review is incoherent. This incoherence is rooted in the fact that the term 'jurisdiction' trades upon conflicting conceptions of law. Lord Reid's 'narrow' conception identifies the parameters of administrative jurisdiction by reference only to positive law established by Parliament, whereas his 'wider' conception asserts additional legal parameters established through judicial interpretation of what the law (understood more broadly than legislative commands) requires. So in addition to being hollow, the doctrine of jurisdictional error in *Anisminic* is radically unstable because it incorporates conflicting ideas regarding the nature of jurisdictional parameters.

This confusion is particularly acute when judges attempt to grapple with the interpretive problem posed by privative clauses. If judges disagree with an administrative decision, they can circumvent the privative clause by assuming that Parliament intended for courts to enforce unwritten limits associated with jurisdiction in the 'wider' sense; conversely, they can justify judicial quiescence by adopting the 'narrow' sense of jurisdiction and interpreting the enabling legislation and privative clause strictly.

The third problem concerns the constitutional legitimacy of judicial review. If the doctrine of jurisdictional error were only hollow and incoherent, it might be possible to defend it as a rhetorical veneer which enables judges to achieve outcomes that are consistent with their own sense of equity or justice. But that argument is usually regarded as a poor one. Generally speaking, we expect that judges will respect the law instead of manipulating legal analysis to secure outcomes they personally prefer, especially when judicial interpretation of the law conflicts with decisions made

[11] See, eg ibid 208 (Lord Wilberforce): 'The courts, when they decide that a "decision" is a "nullity", are not disregarding the preclusive clause. For, just as it is their duty to attribute autonomy of decision of action to the tribunal within the designated area, so, as the counterpart of this autonomy, they must ensure that the limits of that area which have been laid down are observed ... In each task they are carrying out the intention of the legislature, and it would be misdescription to state it in terms of a struggle between the courts and the executive'.

by other legal officials who have been authorised through the democratic process to decide a particular question on behalf of the community. This belief is shared by judges who, like Lord Reid, attempt to justify their decisions by invoking express or implied notions of parliamentary intent instead of mounting the bolder claim that judges are entitled to prioritise their own assessments regarding the substantive merits of an administrative decision.

If we accept the idea that administrative officials have legitimate authority to interpret the law and that judges should not interfere with an administrative decision merely because they disagree with its substance, then we have good reasons for exploring an alternative theory of administrative law to guide the practice of judicial review. More particularly, we have good reasons to consider whether the doctrine of judicial deference, which prevails in Canada and the United States, provides a sounder account of the constitutional relationship between the judiciary and the administrative state.

II. JUDICIAL DEFERENCE

In 1977, the Canadian Union of Public Employees (CUPE) commenced a legal labour strike directed against the New Brunswick Liquor Corporation. During the strike, the Corporation began using management personnel to operate its retail stores. This tactic provoked the union to picket stores owned by the company throughout the province. The union also lodged a complaint with the Public Service Labour Relations Board, alleging that the Corporation had violated section 102(3)(a) of the Public Service Labour Relations Act, which stated that 'the employer shall not replace the striking employees or fill their position with any other employee'.[12] The Board agreed, and ordered the Liquor Corporation to stop using managers as replacement employees. The Corporation challenged the Board's decision by applying for judicial review, even though section 101 of the Act stated that 'every order, award, direction, decision, declaration, or ruling of the Board … is final and shall not be questioned or reviewed in any court'.[13]

The Canadian Supreme Court unanimously upheld the Board's decision. However, Dickson J did not rely upon the jurisdictional rationale set out in *Anisminic*.[14] Instead, he began by observing that the provincial legislature had not determined the meaning of section 102(3)(a). Although an interpretation of the provision was a question of law, he declined to characterise it as a 'jurisdictional' issue, saying that 'courts, in my view, should not be alert to brand as jurisdictional, and therefore subject to broader curial

[12] Public Service Labour Relations Act, RSNB 1973, c P-25.

[13] ibid s 101(1).

[14] *Canadian Union of Public Employees, Local 963 v New Brunswick Liquor Corporation* [1979] 2 SCR 227.

review, that which may be doubtfully so'.[15] Because the dispute fell within the Board's statutory mandate and the legislation stated that judges should not interfere with the Board's decision, Dickson J held that it was inappropriate for the Court to intervene, saying:[16]

> Section 101 constitutes a clear statutory direction on the part of the Legislature that public sector labour matters be promptly and finally decided by the Board. Privative clauses of this type are typically found in labour relations legislation. The rationale for protection of a labour board's decisions within jurisdiction is straightforward and compelling. The labour board is a specialized tribunal which administers a comprehensive statute regulating labour relations. In the administration of that regime, a board is called upon not only to find facts and decide questions of law, but also to exercise its understanding of the body of jurisprudence that has developed around the collective bargaining system, as understood in Canada, and its labour relations sense acquired from accumulated experience in the area.
>
> The usual reasons for judicial restraint upon review of labour board decisions are only reinforced in a case such as the one at bar. Not only has the Legislature confided certain decisions to an administrative board, but to a separate and distinct Public Service Labour Relations Board. That Board is given broad powers—broader than those typically vested in a labour board—to supervise and administer the novel system of collective bargaining created by the Public Service Labour Relations Act. The Act calls for a delicate balance between the need to maintain public services, and the need to maintain collective bargaining. Considerable sensitivity and unique expertise on the part of Board members is all the more required if the twin purposes of the legislation are to be met. Nowhere is the application of those skills more evident than in the supervision of a lawful strike by public service employees under the Act.

Accordingly, Dickson J held that the Court could not intervene merely because it disagreed with the Board's interpretation of the statute. Instead, he concluded that judicial intervention could only be justified where the Board's decision was 'so patently unreasonable that its construction cannot be rationally supported by the relevant legislation and demands intervention by the court upon review'.[17] After considering the Board's rationale for its decision, which was to prevent labour disputes from escalating in a manner which compromised the public interest, Dickson J held that the Board's interpretation of the provision was not patently unreasonable, and upheld the Board's decision.

A similar approach is apparent in *Chevron USA v Natural Resources Defense Council*, a case in which the Supreme Court of the United States held that judges should defer to reasonable administrative interpretations

[15] ibid 233.
[16] ibid 235–36.
[17] ibid 237.

of law.[18] The case concerned the legality of the Environmental Protection Agency's interpretation of the Clean Air Act. In 1977, Congress amended the Act in order to impose more demanding air quality standards in States which had not attained national ambient air quality standards.[19] The amendments aimed to reduce air emissions by requiring noncompliant States to implement stringent permit requirements for 'new or modified major stationary sources' of air pollution.[20] However, the legislation did not determine the meaning of the term 'stationary source'—it was ambiguous whether 'stationary source' referred to a discrete apparatus within an industrial plant or whether it applied to the industrial complex as a 'bubble' or integrated whole.[21] Ultimately, the EPA adopted the 'bubble' definition of 'stationary source', and its decision was challenged by environmental action groups on the ground that it was contrary to Congress's objective of accelerating State compliance with national air quality standards.

As in *CUPE*, the Supreme Court of the United States upheld the EPA's decision without resorting to jurisdictional analysis.[22] Instead, Stevens J held that the meaning of the Act was ambiguous, because neither the statute nor the legislative history determined how the Act should be construed. In his view, Congress had adopted an open-ended definition of 'stationary source' in order to strike a compromise between conflicting interest groups.[23] In light of the circumstances, Stevens J held that the Court should respect the EPA's interpretation of the Act, saying:[24]

> In these cases the Administrator's interpretation represents a reasonable accommodation of manifestly competing interests and is entitled to deference: the regulatory scheme is technical and complex, the agency considered the matter in a detailed and reasoned fashion, and the decision involves reconciling conflicting policies. Congress intended to accommodate both interests, but did not do so itself on the level of specificity presented by these cases. Perhaps that body consciously desired the Administrator to strike the balance at this level, thinking that those

[18] *Chevron USA Inc v Natural Resources Defense Council, Inc* 467 US 837 (1984).

[19] Clean Air Act Amendments of 1977 Pub L No 95-95, 91 Stat 685.

[20] ibid s 129; 42 USC § 7502.

[21] ibid: '(i) "Stationary sources" means any building, structure, facility, or installation which emits or may emit any air pollutant subject to regulation under the Act. (ii) "Building, structure, facility, or installation" means all of the pollutant emitting activities which belong to the same industrial grouping, are located on one or more continuous or adjacent properties, and are under the control of the same person (or persons under common control) except the activities of any vessel'.

[22] *Chevron* (n 18 above) 842–43. Instead of asking whether the issue under review is jurisdictional in nature, *Chevron* set out a two-step process for determining the legality of an administrative decision. Under step one, the reviewing court asks whether Congress has directly addressed the precise question at issue. If Congressional intent is clear, the court must give effect to Congress's intent regardless of the administrative interpretation of the statute. However, if Congressional intent is not clear, the court must proceed to step two, which requires the court to defer to an administrative interpretation provided that it is reasonable.

[23] ibid at 851.

[24] ibid at 865–66.

> with great expertise and charged with responsibility for administering the provision would be in a better position to do so; perhaps it simply did not consider the question at this level; and perhaps Congress was unable to forge a coalition on either side of the question, and those on each side decided to take their chances with the scheme devised by the agency. For judicial purposes, it matters not which of these things occurred.
>
> Judges are not experts in the field, and are not part of either political branch of the Government. Courts must, in some cases, reconcile competing political interests, but not on the basis of the judges' personal policy preferences. In contrast, an agency to which Congress has delegated policymaking responsibilities may, within the limits of that delegation, properly rely upon the incumbent administration's views of wise policy to inform its judgments. While agencies are not directly accountable to the people, the Chief Executive is, and it is entirely appropriate for this political branch of the Government to make such policy choices—resolving the competing interests which Congress itself either inadvertently did not resolve, or intentionally left to be resolved by the agency charged with the administration of the statute in light of everyday realities.

Therefore, Stevens J concluded that in situations where Congressional intent is unclear, courts should not simply impose their own construction of the statute.[25] Rather, they should defer to an administrative decision, provided that the decision is not 'arbitrary, capricious, or manifestly contrary to the statute'.[26] When Stevens J assessed the EPA's reasons for adopting the plant-wide definition of 'stationary source', which was to give States more flexibility while attempting to balance federal environmental standards with the desire to promote economic growth,[27] he concluded that it was not unreasonable and therefore upheld the decision.

The main distinction between the doctrine of jurisdictional error set out in *Anisminic* and the doctrine of judicial deference outlined in *CUPE* and *Chevron* is the way in which administrative law is conceived. Instead of defining administrative law by reference to jurisdictional limits, Dickson and Stevens JJ both emphasise the constitutional legitimacy of administrative institutions and decisions. Among other things, they highlight the democratic pedigree of administrative institutions and the fact that the legislature had given administrative officials the authority to interpret the law regarding a controversial legal question. In addition, they both point out that administrative officials have experience and expertise regarding the implementation of legislative policies which warrants a degree of judicial respect. Thus, both *CUPE* and *Chevron* provide a more elaborate account of the

[25] ibid at 843.

[26] ibid at 844–45.

[27] Thomas Merrill, 'The Story of *Chevron USA Inc v Natural Resources Defense Council, Inc*: Sometimes Great Cases Are Made Not Born' in William Eskridge, Philip Frickey and Elizabeth Garrett (eds), *Statutory Interpretation Stories* (New York, Foundation Press, 2011) 165, 175.

reasons which legitimate administrative legal authority than Lord Reid's judgment in *Anisminic*, which focuses merely upon parameters derived from a positivistic understanding of legislative intent.

Furthermore, because both *CUPE* and *Chevron* avoid the confusion associated with conflicting notions of jurisdictional parameters, the doctrine of judicial deference seems more coherent—at least at a theoretical level. Instead of simultaneously asserting 'narrow' and 'broad' jurisdictional parameters based upon conflicting conceptions of law, the doctrine of judicial deference asks judges to consider whether an administrative decision is reasonable in light of the circumstances. Thus, the conflicting notions of administrative jurisdiction are replaced by a unified standard of legality.

However, history shows that judicial deference in Canadian and American administrative law has been anything but straightforward. In Canada, much confusion stems from the fact that the Supreme Court has never made a decisive break from the language of jurisdictional error.[28] However, even if the doctrine of judicial deference were not corrupted in this way, the complex analytical framework which has emerged in Canada would still raise serious questions about its integrity.[29] Thus, one prominent academic observed as early as 1996 that '*CUPE* has run into the sand, and a reformulation is needed urgently',[30] a plea recently echoed by various members of the Canadian Supreme Court.[31]

Similar concerns about the doctrine of judicial deference have been expressed in the United States. Even though *Chevron* is easily the most cited decision in American administrative law, it seems to have raised more questions than it has resolved. For example, even though the concept of jurisdiction is noticeably absent from American common law, a similar confusion arises because *Chevron* deference is contingent upon whether Congress 'has directly spoken to the precise question at issue'.[32] Thus, there has been significant controversy over what constitutes a sufficiently 'clear' expression

[28] See, eg David Mullan, 'The Re-emergence of Jurisdictional Error' (1985) 14 *Administrative Law Reports* 326; David Mullan, 'The Supreme Court of Canada and Jurisdictional Error: Compromising *New Brunswick Liquor*' (1987) 1 *Canadian Journal of Administrative Law & Practice* 71; David Mullan, 'A Blast from the Past: A Surreptitious Resurgence of *Metropolitan Life*?' (1992) 5 Administrative Law Reports (2d) 117; David Mullan, 'Recent Developments in Administrative Law: The Apparent Triumph of Deference!' (1999) 12 *Canadian Journal of Administrative Law & Practice* 192.

[29] See, eg David Mullan, 'Deference from *Baker* to *Suresh* and Beyond: Interpreting the Conflicting Signals' in David Dyzenhaus (ed), *The Unity of Public Law* (Oxford, Hart Publishing, 2004) 21.

[30] Michael Taggart, 'Outside Canadian Administrative Law' (1996) 46 *University of Toronto Law Journal* 649, 652.

[31] *Toronto (City) v Canadian Union of Public Employees, Local 79* [2003] 3 SCR 77, 113–48 (LeBel J); *Dunsmuir v New Brunswick* [2008] 1 SCR 190.

[32] *Chevron* (n 18 above) 842.

of Congressional intent.[33] Additional confusion has been caused by uncertainty over the scope of the *Chevron* doctrine—whether it applies to all administrative interpretations of law, or whether it is limited to some smaller subset of administrative action.[34] These and other concerns have prompted one prominent American scholar to argue that 'as a legal doctrine, [*Chevron*] has proven to be a complete and total failure, and thus the Supreme Court should overrule it at the first possible opportunity'.[35]

III. THE ARGUMENT IN BRIEF

In this book, I will examine how jurists in the United Kingdom, the United States of America, and Canada have conceptualised administrative law. In addition to highlighting important doctrinal differences and similarities concerning judicial review of administrative decisions, the comparative analysis also serves as a prelude to a theoretical account of the legitimacy of administrative law and the related issue of judicial deference towards administrative decisions.

While this comparative analysis might be enriched by examining how other legal cultures—including civilian jurisdictions—consider administrative law, I will focus my attention on the common law perspective. The doctrine of jurisdictional error in the United Kingdom serves as a baseline for my analysis, because it outlines the traditional common law approach to administrative law. This approach also crops up periodically in American and Canadian public law doctrine, and it continues to be a central feature in other Commonwealth countries. However, the law pertaining to judicial review of administrative decisions in the United States and Canada has since broken away from jurisdictional error in favour of a doctrine of judicial deference towards administrative decisions. In order to better understand the historical basis for this doctrinal schism, its normative underpinnings, and its practical consequences, I will juxtapose the intellectual history of jurisdictional error with that of judicial deference in the United States and Canada, which emerged in the wake of the *Lochner* era and the rise of the modern administrative state in North America.

33 Antonin Scalia, 'Judicial Deference to Administrative Interpretations of Law' (1989) 38 *Duke Law Journal* 511, 520–21; Note, '"How Clear is Clear" in *Chevron*'s Step One?' (2005) 118 *Harvard Law Review* 1687; Matthew Stephenson and Adrian Vermeule, '*Chevron* Has Only One Step' (2009) 95 *Virginia Law Review* 597; Kenneth Bamberger and Peter Strauss, '*Chevron*'s Two Steps' (2009) 95 *Virginia Law Review* 611.

34 *United States v Mead Corp* 533 US 218 (2001); Cass Sunstein, '*Chevron* Step Zero' (2006) 92 *Virginia Law Review* 187.

35 Jack Beerman, 'End the *Chevron* Experiment Now: How *Chevron* Has Failed and Why It Can and Should Be Overruled' (2009–10) 42 *Connecticut Law Review* 779, 782.

In Chapter two, I investigate why the traditional constitutional theory fails to provide an adequate account of administrative law in a constitutional democracy. I will argue that this blind spot has been inherited from AV Dicey's constitutional theory. Dicey famously argued that there was no such thing as administrative law in the United Kingdom, and claimed that his conclusion followed logically from the constitutional principles of parliamentary sovereignty and the rule of law. However, I will argue that Dicey's theory is unfounded as a matter of historical fact, contestable as a matter of principle, and rests on an incoherent theoretical foundation. From an historical perspective, the United Kingdom had an established system of administrative law long before Dicey published his constitutional treatise, so it is a mistake to accept the validity of his historical assertions regarding administrative law. I will argue that instead of treating Dicey's claim as axiomatic, it is better understood as a controversial ideological argument—one which is hostile to the political aims of the modern administrative state. When this rhetorical veneer is stripped away, we can see that Diceyan constitutional theory is both incoherent and dialectical because it involves an attempt to marry Jeremy Bentham's legal positivism (which emphasises the sovereignty of Parliament) with Blackstone's natural law theory (which emphasises the supremacy of judges over legal interpretation) within the same constitutional theory. Once the underpinnings of Dicey's theory have been exposed, we can begin to develop a more forthright theory about the legitimacy of administrative law.

In Chapter three, I examine the legacy of Diceyan constitutional theory through case-law analysis regarding the doctrine of jurisdictional error and, more recently, proportionality review in the United Kingdom. I will argue that judicial reasoning in these cases reflects the deeply rooted problems with Diceyan constitutional theory set out in Chapter two. The primary problem in this respect is that the practice of judicial review is fundamentally incoherent, whether it is conceived in terms of jurisdictional error or proportionality. More specifically, this overview reveals two conflicting lines of authority: one line of cases holds that administrative officials are entitled to wield an unrestrained form of political discretion that can be shielded from judicial review by legislative fiat; the other line of cases holds that judges always retain the licence to quash administrative decisions which do not comply with their own substantive interpretations of the law. In light of the incoherence of jurisdictional error and proportionality review, a debate has now emerged within the United Kingdom regarding the merits of judicial deference as an organising doctrine. I argue that in order to fully assess this proposal, one should consider the American and Canadian experience with this doctrinal framework.

In Chapter four, I will examine the intellectual history behind the doctrine of judicial deference by contrasting Diceyan common law constitutionalism with an alternative, protestant conception of constitutionalism which emerged in the United States of America by the end of the nineteenth century and attracted influential adherents over the course of the *Lochner* era. By examining the work of James Thayer, Oliver Wendell Holmes Jr, Louis Brandeis, and Felix Frankfurter, I will argue that this conception of constitutionalism rests on normative premises which are democratic, pragmatic, contextual, and functional in character. Thus, instead of instructing judges to extrapolate jurisdictional parameters directly from the statutory text or common law values, the judicial role is portrayed as relatively limited because interpretive authority over the law is shared with administrative officials. So instead of enabling judges to construe the Constitution or legislation in a manner which obstructed the emergence of the administrative state, proponents of judicial restraint urged judges to accommodate legislative reform and statutory delegations of authority to administrative officials.

However, it is important to point out that proponents of judicial restraint did not advocate judicial abdication: they still asserted that judges still have a constitutional obligation to ensure that administrative decisions are fair and reasonable, and that the intensity of judicial oversight should be calibrated according the nature of the interest affected by a governmental decision. Accordingly, governmental decisions which seriously impacted civil liberties were subjected to more onerous burdens of due process and substantive justification than decisions which impacted economic interests. Nevertheless, because this tradition of judicial restraint still co-exists alongside another constitutional perspective which allocates supremacy over law-creation to the legislature and supremacy over legal interpretation to the judiciary, the *Chevron* doctrine remains plagued by quixotic quests for legislative intent before judges will consider deferring to an administrative decision.

In Chapter five, I will examine how the intellectual movement in American legal culture at the beginning of the twentieth century had a ripple effect on the practice of judicial review in Canada. During the first half of the twentieth century, the law of judicial review in Canada was organised around the doctrine of jurisdictional error and a formal conception of the separation of powers, two doctrines which were received from the United Kingdom via decisions from the Judicial Committee of the Privy Council. However, over the course the twentieth century, Canadian jurists began developing a doctrine of deference inspired by the American discourse on judicial restraint outlined in Chapter four. While influential judges like Ivan Rand and Bora Laskin did not rely directly on American sources or case authority, they both employed reasoning which resonates strongly with the jurisprudence of Thayer, Holmes, Brandeis, and Frankfurter. As in the United States, the Canadian doctrine of judicial deference does not entail judicial submission to administrative decisions—judges are entitled to intervene if an administrative decision is procedurally unfair or substantively unreasonable. But by the same token, it remains plagued by frequent attempts to extrapolate the parameters of judicial review directly from the statutory text or conceptual analysis of the issue at stake, because the doctrine of judicial deference has been grafted onto a pre-existing framework informed by the doctrine of jurisdictional error and a formal conception of the separation of powers.

In the concluding chapter, I will respond to the question of administrative law by developing a theoretical account of administrative law and judicial deference organised around three interrelated issues in jurisprudence and political theory: authority, legitimacy, and legality. I will argue that administrative officials do have legitimate authority to interpret the law if they have been legally empowered by a democratically responsible branch of government to decide a question of law on behalf of the community, and their decision conveys concern and respect for the persons affected by their decision in both a procedural and substantive sense. The legitimacy of administrative law is rooted partly in the fairness of democratic decisions to authorise administrative officials to resolve interpretive disputes about the law. However, I will argue that the legitimacy of an administrative decision also depends on whether it complies with procedural and substantive standards entailed by the rule of law. More specifically, I will argue that the legitimacy of administrative law is conditioned by a principle of legality which requires administrative officials to treat individuals who are subject to their decisions as self-governing moral agents whose views regarding how the law ought to be interpreted should be taken into consideration. Furthermore, I will argue that the procedural rights associated with the rule of law have substantive bite on the content of administrative law, because administrative officials have a duty to provide decisions which respond to the arguments tendered by the parties and to justify their decision in light of more basic legal standards such as enabling legislation and constitutional values.

If my theoretical argument regarding the legitimacy of administrative law is sound, it has important implications for the practice of judicial review in a constitutional democracy. Contrary to Diceyan constitutional theory, it suggests that judges share responsibility for maintaining the rule of law with administrative officials. Therefore, the fact that a judge disagrees with an administrative interpretation of the law is not a sufficient justification for interfering with it, because that would defy the democratic basis for delegating authority to administrative officials in the first place. However, it is equally problematic for judges to defer submissively to an administrative decision simply because an administrative official was authorised by statute, because the legitimacy of administrative authority also depends on how it is exercised. The upshot of this is that judges should respect or defer to administrative decisions which are fair and reasonable, instead of substituting their interpretation of the law when it deviates from the substance of an administrative decision. In sum, my aim is to explain and justify the conjunction of administrative law and judicial deference.

2

Rethinking the Diceyan Dialectic

TO UNDERSTAND BETTER why the question about administrative law has been neglected in the common law tradition, it is worth revisiting Albert Venn Dicey's theory of the English constitution. Dicey famously claimed that administrative law, which he regularly associated with French *droit administratif*, was utterly foreign to the English legal system. He deduced this from two principles he took to be the foundation of the constitution: parliamentary sovereignty and the rule of law. According to Dicey, these two principles occupied the entire constitutional field, and ensured the primary status of Parliament and the judiciary. But the consequence of this assumption was that there was no distinct form of legal authority left to be exercised by administrative institutions. The persistence of the Diceyan perspective in public law doctrine and scholarship thus explains, to a large extent, why the idea of administrative legal authority remains undeveloped in most common law legal systems.

There are two very different ways to understand Dicey's theory. The first assumes that the principles of parliamentary sovereignty and the rule of law are a priori constitutional axioms locked in a zero-sum contest for supremacy within the constitutional order. This binary understanding of the constitution pits Parliament's monopoly on law-making against the judiciary's monopoly on law interpretation.[1] By definition, Diceyan constitutionalism can only perceive administrative authority as either an unrestrained exercise of political discretion, akin to delegated legislative power,[2] or it achieves legal status by virtue of its substantive congruence with judicial standards of correct procedure or judgement.[3] Moreover, Diceyan constitutionalism

[1] David Dyzenhaus, 'Formalism's Hollow Victory' [2002] *New Zealand Law Review* 525.

[2] See, eg the manner in which the Donoughmore Committee describes the essence of an administrative decision: 'In the case of the administrative decision, there is no legal obligation upon the person charged with the duty of reaching the decision to consider and weigh submissions and arguments, or to collate any evidence, or to solve any issue. The grounds upon which he acts, and the means which he takes to inform himself before acting, are left entirely to his discretion'. United Kingdom, *Committee on Ministers' Powers Report* (Cmd 4060) (London, HMSO, 1932) 81. By contrast, a judicial decision involves 'an application of the law of the land': ibid 73.

[3] See, eg Coke J's sweeping dictum in *James Bagg's Case* (1615) 11 Co Rep 93b, 98a, 77 ER 1271, 1277–78, where he held: 'that to this Court of King's Bench belongs authority, not only to correct errors in judicial proceedings, but other errors and misdemeanors extra-judicial,

appears to pivot on an insoluble dialectic between parliamentary sovereignty and the rule of law, because it incorporates two conflicting conceptions of law. Dicey's principle of parliamentary sovereignty is inspired by John Austin's positivist theory of law, in which Parliament plays the role of an uncommanded commander;[4] and his principle of the rule of law is inspired by William Blackstone's natural law theory, in which 'the judges in the several courts of justice' serve as 'the depositaries of the laws; the living oracles, who must decide in all cases of doubt'.[5] While this conflict explains much of the confusion associated with judicial review, for now I just want to identify the Diceyan dialectic simply as a matter of constitutional theory.

There is, however, a second and more elaborate explanation of Dicey's theory that recognises it as an illustration of a central problem in political liberalism. I argue that Dicey's theory helps us to understand the tension between the liberal commitments to democratic government (on the one hand) and to substantive limitations on the extent to which government may interfere with personal liberty (on the other).[6] This explanation tracks the same tension in Dicey's theory between parliamentary sovereignty and the rule of law but, unlike the Diceyan dialectic, it does not exclude the idea of administrative authority by stipulation. Rather, it understands the tension as an outcrop of the same friction that Isaiah Berlin identified between 'positive' and 'negative' liberty almost 50 years ago.[7] To borrow Berlin's terminology, Dicey was wedded to the notion of negative liberty, and this is revealed by the substantive limits he incorporated into his version of the English constitution. He thought these limits would promote maximum protection for individual liberty and (by extension) a limited role for government.[8] Conversely, Dicey was disturbed by constitutional reforms that extended the franchise because they culminated in new, redistributive government policies. These policies were legitimised by the notion of positive liberty, the idea that all citizens should be free to exercise self-government and (by extension) participate in the democratic process in order to decide

tending to the breach of peace, or oppression of the subjects, or to the raising of faction, controversy, debate or to any manner of misgovernment; so that no wrong or injury, either public or private, can be done but that it shall be reformed or punished by due course of law'.

[4] John Austin, *The Province of Jurisprudence Determined* (Cambridge, Cambridge University Press, 1995) 192–96.

[5] William Blackstone, *Commentaries on the Laws of England* (London, Cavendish Publishing, 2001) vol I, *69.

[6] David Dyzenhaus, 'Dicey's Shadow' (1993) 43 *University of Toronto Law Journal* 127; David Dyzenhaus, 'Form and Substance in the Rule of Law: A Democratic Justification for Judicial Review?' in Christopher Forsyth (ed), *Judicial Review and the Constitution* (Oxford, Hart Publishing, 2000) 141.

[7] Isaiah Berlin, 'Two Concepts of Liberty' in Isaiah Berlin, *Four Essays on Liberty* (Oxford, Oxford University Press, 1969) 118.

[8] Friedrich Hayek held similar views about the rule of law. However, he constructed his conception as an explicit political theory rather than wrapping it in the mantle of 'legal science'. See FA Hayek, *The Road to Serfdom* (London, Routledge, 1944).

how to govern their political community. Dicey was reluctant to recognise the legality of the modern welfare state, and this is reflected in the fact that his constitutional theory does not contemplate any role for administrative legal authority.

This chapter examines both accounts of Dicey's constitutional theory. I will argue that the first account is both reductive and unhelpful, because it obscures the political foundations of Dicey's constitutional principles and distorts the reality of legal practice. The result is that lawyers who invoke this account are unable to explain administrative authority as a valuable characteristic of modern government or to explain how judges can respect the autonomy of administrative judgement while at the same time rendering it consistent with values associated with the rule of law. These opportunities emerge only when one adopts the second, more substantive, account of Dicey's constitutional theory, which enables us to engage with its political and institutional arguments more directly. I will argue that, by doing so, we can begin to address the question about administrative law in a more transparent and intelligent manner.

Section I below offers a brief sketch of the Diceyan dialectic which highlights the essential features of his constitutional model and exposes its inadequate portrayal of legal practice. Section II develops the more elaborate account of Dicey's theory in order to demonstrate that these weaknesses can be ascribed to Dicey's political ideology. I argue that, in order to grapple with the Diceyan dialectic, one must recognise that this political debate does not raise any a priori objections to the concept of legitimate administrative authority. Rethinking the Diceyan dialectic in this way is important because it allows us to engage in the fruitful enterprise of revealing a principled basis for the complex systems of administrative regulation that exist in modern democratic societies. By engaging with the issue in this fashion, we can better justify arguments regarding judicial review or restraint.

I. THE DICEYAN DIALECTIC

Before Dicey, very few lawyers recognised constitutional law as a domain distinct from the more general principles of the common law. One of Dicey's express aims in writing his *Introduction to the Study of the Law of the Constitution* was to carve out a coherent system of constitutional law so that it might become a subject of sustained legal scholarship.[9] To put it

[9] AV Dicey, *Introduction to the Study of the Constitution*, 10th edn (London, Macmillan & Co, 1959) ch 1. Dicey's famous treatise was first published in 1885, and the last edition Dicey edited personally was the seventh in 1908. However, the text itself remained unaltered in subsequent editions, save for an extended introduction by ECS Wade. I will refer to the 10th edition throughout.

simply, Dicey wanted to identify the 'rules which directly or indirectly affect the distribution or exercise of the sovereign power in the state' so that they could be examined and expounded through legal analysis.[10]

When Dicey was appointed Vinerian Professor at Oxford, English universities were advocating an undergraduate course to prepare students for the legal profession.[11] At the time, English law appeared to be a chaotic mass of precedent. Earlier attempts to lend the law a sense of structure like Coke's *Institutes* or Blackstone's *Commentaries* could not dispel the confusion inherent in the common law. Instead, legal practice was organised around the different forms of action, but when this framework (which had significant deficiencies of its own) was abolished in 1875 the need to bring some sense of order to the common law was acute. This period marked the revival of 'legal science' in both England and the United States of America, as law professors on both sides of the Atlantic began to portray law as a subject that could only be rationalised if it were taught alongside the natural sciences in universities.[12]

Throughout his career, Dicey employed the language of legal science to advocate a curriculum devoted to the principled study of law.[13] In his view, the current system of pupils reading law in chambers was inadequate because it was fragmentary and unsystematic: pupils only learned random, particular points of law without developing an appreciation for the grand legal principles that unified the law of tort, contract, and the common law as a whole. This myopia was also symptomatic of many textbook writers, who tended to portray a legal subject in terms of formal rules and exceptions rather than a coherent body of legal principle.[14] Dicey argued that

[10] ibid 23.

[11] See generally, Richard A Cosgrove, *The Rule of Law: Albert Venn Dicey, Victorian Jurist* (London, Macmillan, 1980) ch 3.

[12] David Sugarman, 'The Legal Boundaries of Liberty: Dicey, Liberalism and Legal Science' (1983) 46 *Modern Law Review* 102, 107. The notion of legal science stretches back at least to Roman Law, but it resurfaces at important intersections in the history of the common law. See Robert Gordon, 'Book Review of *Tort Law in America: An Intellectual History* by G Edward White' (1981) 94 *Harvard Law Review* 903; Howard Schweber, 'The "Science" of Legal Science: The Model of the Natural Sciences in Nineteenth-Century American Legal Education' (1999) 17 *Law & History Review* 421. One such resurgence occurred in the late nineteenth century as legal training became increasingly formalised. Thus, Sugarman argues that Dicey was part of an Anglo-American movement (centred in the Harvard and Oxford law faculties) which included Christopher Langdell, Oliver Wendell Holmes Jr, James Barr Ames, Samuel Williston, Sir Henry Maine, James Bryce, Sir Frederick Pollock, Sir Thomas Erskine Holland and Sir William Anson.

[13] AV Dicey, *Can English Law be Taught at the Universities?* (London, MacMillan & Co, 1883). Dicey wrote a series of articles on the subject of legal education in which he repeatedly invoked the 'scientific' nature of law. See also AV Dicey, 'Legal Education' (1871) 25 *MacMillans* 115; 'The Teaching of English Law at Harvard' (1899) 76 *Contemporary Review* 742; 'The Study of Jurisprudence' (1880) 5 *Law Magazine & Review* 382; 'Law-Teaching, Oral and Written' in Herbert Hensley Henson (ed), *A Memoir of the Right Honourable Sir William Anson* (Oxford, Clarendon Press, 1920) 84.

[14] Dicey, *Can English Law be Taught?* (n 13 above) 10–14.

professors dedicated to the notion of legal science could provide an antidote to this problem by analysing and defining basic legal concepts, organising these concepts according to the rules of logic, and using the method of legal science to identify an agenda for legal reform. In Dicey's words:[15]

> It is for professors to set forth the law as a coherent whole—to analyse and define legal conceptions—to reduce the mass of legal rules to an orderly series of principles, and to aid, stimulate and guide the reform or renovation of legal literature.

This latter task was particularly important because by reforming the available legal literature, law professors could improve both the form and the substance of the common law.[16]

These considerations provide the backdrop for Dicey's constitutional theory, in which he expressly sought to enhance the prestige of constitutional law by extricating it from other domains of inquiry.[17] Like Blackstone, Dicey believed in the wisdom and dignity of the common law as a cultural artefact that revealed the noble character of the English nation.[18] The difference, according to Dicey, was that his conception of constitutional law was realistic, contemporary, and detached from moral or political argument, whereas Blackstone's *Commentaries* tended to mythologise the common law. Thus, Dicey professed to be neither a critic, nor an apologist, nor a eulogist, but simply an 'expounder' of the constitution[19] whose task was 'to state what are the laws which form part of the constitution, to arrange them in their order, to explain their meaning, and to exhibit where possible their logical connection'.[20]

Although he recognised the contributions of lawyers, historians, and political theorists who had addressed the topic before him, Dicey argued that previous attempts to identify the law of the constitution had failed to capture its distinct legal nature. Lawyers (especially Blackstone) were prone to 'unreal language' that obscured the meaning of the constitution;[21]

[15] ibid 18. See also Dicey, 'The Study of Jurisprudence' (n 13 above).

[16] Dicey, *Can English Law be Taught?* (n 13 above) 23–24: 'The rules of law which are supposed to be so inflexible are, for the most part, in fact enactments of judicial legislation, and nothing is more remarkable or more intelligible than the ease with which judicial legislation is swayed by the pressure of authoritative opinion. Busy magistrates, dealing with cases as they occur, take their principles from text-writers. Particular authors have notoriously, even in recent times, modeled, one might almost say brought into existence, whole departments of law'.

[17] See Stefan Collini, *Public Moralists: Political Thought and Intellectual Life in Britain 1850–1930* (Oxford, Clarendon Press, 1991) ch 7.

[18] Julia Stapleton, 'Dicey and his Legacy' (1995) *History of Political Thought* 234.

[19] Dicey, *Introduction* (n 9 above) 4.

[20] ibid 32.

[21] ibid 11: 'We have all learnt from Blackstone, and writers of the same class, to make such constant use of expressions which we know not to be strictly true to fact, that we cannot say for certain what is the exact relation between the facts of constitutional government and the more or less artificial phraseology under which they are concealed'.

historians had cured this defect by paying attention to hard facts, but their 'antiquarianism' or excessive reverence for historical curiosities made their treatises unsuitable for contemporary legal analysis;[22] and while political theorists examined issues of significant parliamentary importance, those issues were matters of conventional morality, not law.[23] 'Law', insofar as Dicey defined it, merely meant 'any rule which will be enforced by the courts',[24] whether it was written (in the case of statutes) or unwritten (in the case of common law principles).[25] So Dicey trained his sights on accepted sources of law—statutes, the common law, solemn agreements (eg the Bill of Rights), treaties and quasi-treaties—in order to unearth the true nature of the English constitution.[26] The two central principles or 'legal facts'[27] that emerged from Dicey's exegesis were parliamentary sovereignty and the rule of law.

The principle of parliamentary sovereignty means that Parliament has 'the right to make or unmake any law whatever; and, further, that no person or body is recognised by the law of England as having a right to override or set aside the legislation of Parliament'.[28] In other words, Parliament has a monopoly over law-making under the constitution, and no other institution (ie the executive, the judiciary, the electorate, or either House acting alone) can limit this privilege through de jure means. The only de facto limitations on Parliament's legislative function derive from political or popular morality, which constitutes both 'external' and 'internal' constraints. Popular morality is an external constraint on Parliament's law-making function, because statutes that are radically at odds with public opinion are likely to undermine parliamentary authority by inciting civil disobedience; and it is an internal constraint, because Members of Parliament are a product of, and therefore highly responsive to, public opinion.[29] Because the Members

[22] ibid 14: 'Let us eagerly learn all that is known, and still more eagerly all that is not known about the Witenagemót. But let us remember that antiquarianism is not law, and that the function of a trained lawyer is not to know what the law of England was yesterday, still less what is was centuries ago, or what it ought to be to-morrow, but to know and be able to state what are the principles of law which actually and at the present day exist in England'.

[23] ibid 20–21: 'The truth is that Bagehot and Professor Hearn deal and mean to deal mainly with political understandings or conventions and not with rules of law ... These inquiries are, many of them, great and weighty; but they are not inquiries that will ever be debated in the law court'.

[24] ibid 40.

[25] ibid 27–28.

[26] ibid 6, fn 1. The terms 'solemn agreements' and 'quasi-treaties' are Dicey's. Although Dicey did discuss various constitutional conventions in his treatise, it was clear that he did not consider them to be 'law' by virtue of the fact that they were enforced by popular sentiment rather than the courts. See W Ivor Jennings, 'In Praise of Dicey' (1935) 13 *Public Administration* 123, 130.

[27] Dicey's characterisation of legal principles as matters of 'fact' is symptomatic of the legal science movement. See, eg Dicey, *Introduction* (n 9 above) 11, 68.

[28] Dicey, *Introduction* (n 9 above) 40.

[29] ibid 76–85.

of Parliament are themselves steeped in the popular sentiment of the times, they are likely to enact laws that were more or less sympathetic to public opinion.

By contrast, the rule of law deals with the common law enforced by 'ordinary' courts. According to Dicey, the rule of law has three interrelated aspects. First, it establishes 'the absolute supremacy or predominance of regular law as opposed to the influence of arbitrary power, and excludes the existence of arbitrariness, of prerogative, or even of wide discretionary authority on the part of government'.[30] Secondly, it establishes[31]

> equality before the law, or the equal subjection of all classes to the ordinary law of the land administered by the ordinary law courts; the 'rule of law' in this sense excludes the idea of any exemption of officials or others from the duty of obedience to the law which governs other citizens or from the jurisdiction of the ordinary tribunals.

Finally, Dicey emphasised that the rule of law is entrenched at common law as part of the constitution, rather than a legislative code. In this sense, the law of the constitution is not the source of individual rights, but the consequence of multiple judicial decisions that define those rights. This was an important point for Dicey, because he thought this feature of the rule of law conferred a special advantage: if individual rights were deduced from codified principles, they could be suspended as easily as they had been enacted, but if liberty were diffused through the customary law of the land, it could only be suspended or amended through wholesale revolution.[32]

Dicey's conception of the rule of law is significant because, by definition, it excludes the possibility that administrative institutions might wield legal authority under the constitution.[33] The most fundamental problem, according to Dicey, is that *droit administratif* threatens the principle of formal equality which is essential to the rule of law, because it judges transactions between citizens and the state according to 'principles essentially different from those rules of private law which govern the rights of private persons towards their neighbours'.[34] This danger was reflected by the doctrine of the separation of powers prevailing in France that prevented 'the government, the legislature, and the courts from encroaching on one another's province'.[35] Dicey distinguished the French doctrine of the separation of powers from the principle of judicial independence underlying the English constitution. In France, the separation of powers established reciprocal principles, namely that ordinary judges ought to be independent and

[30] ibid 202–3.
[31] ibid.
[32] ibid 201.
[33] ibid ch 12.
[34] ibid 388.
[35] ibid 337.

irremovable *and* that the government and its officials 'ought (whilst acting officially) to be independent of and to a great extent free from the jurisdiction of the ordinary courts'.[36] This latter addendum, which contains the germ of administrative legal authority, is anathema to Dicey's conception of the rule of law, because it exposes citizens to what he regarded as arbitrary executive action and immunises public officials from liability in tort.[37] Unless government officials remain subject to the 'fixed' certainty of private law administered by the ordinary courts, formal equality and the rule of law will be undermined.

Ironically, even at the time Dicey published his first edition, his analysis was prone to the same defects he attributed to the previous generations of lawyers, historians and political theorists who took an interest in the English constitution. Despite his rhetoric of legal science, Dicey did not discover his principles through rigorous induction, but rather 'found what he hoped or expected to find'.[38] Dicey merely adopted the concept of sovereignty he inherited from Hobbes via Blackstone and John Austin's positivist theory of law.[39] The idea of an uncommanded commander was the orthodox political doctrine of the period, and Dicey rather took it for granted as a pillar of his constitutional theory.[40] And although his conception of the rule of law was innovative by comparison, Dicey did not draw its content from established case law. It is more accurate to say that the rule of law principle, like that of parliamentary sovereignty, was stipulated by the author.

The catalogue of errors attributed to Dicey is well documented, so there is no need to delve into great detail here.[41] Nevertheless, I want to briefly examine three particular defects, because they illustrate the dissonance

[36] ibid 338.

[37] Dicey frequently refers to allied notions of 'discretion', 'arbitrariness', 'executive prerogative' and 'despotism' to characterise the concept of *droit administratif*. See, eg ibid 335–50, where Dicey examines the historical lineage of *droit administratif*. Dicey thought *droit administratif* was bound to be uncertain and arbitrary in its application because it remained under the control of the executive branch of government, which was motivated by the preferences or opinion of politicians rather than the wisdom of independent judges.

[38] Bernard Hibbits, 'The Politics of Principle: Albert Venn Dicey and the Rule of Law' (1994) 23 *Anglo-American Law Review* 1, 30.

[39] Dicey, *Introduction* (n 9 above) 70–76; Martin Loughlin, *Public Law and Political Theory* (Oxford, Clarendon Press, 1992) ch 7; FH Lawson, 'Dicey Revisited' (1959) 7 *Political Studies* 109, 113; O Hood Phillips, 'Dicey's *Law of the Constitution:* A Personal View' [1985] *Public Law* 587.

[40] AWB Simpson, 'The Common Law and Legal Theory' in AWB Simpson (ed), *Oxford Essays in Jurisprudence*, 2nd series (Oxford, Clarendon Press, 1973) 77, 96: 'Dicey announced that it was the law that Parliament was omnicompetent, explained what this meant, and never devoted so much as a line to fulfilling the promise he made to demonstrate that this was so. The oracle spoke, and came to be accepted'.

[41] HW Arthurs, 'Rethinking Administrative Law: A Slightly Dicey Business' (1979) 17 *Osgoode Hall Law Journal* 1, 6–7; PP Craig, *Public Law and Democracy in the United Kingdom and the United States of America* (Oxford, Clarendon Press, 1990) 26–27; Henry Parris, *Constitutional Bureaucracy: The Development of British Central Administration since the Eighteenth Century* (London, George Allen & Unwin Ltd, 1969) ch 9.

between Dicey's theory and common legal practice when the first edition of *The Law of the Constitution* rolled off the presses. These defects belie the factual basis Dicey claimed for the pillars of his constitutional theory and provide sufficient justification for revising it in light of the reality of the modern administrative state.[42]

First, Dicey did not acknowledge the extent to which the English legal system already utilised administrative institutions—boards, commissions, inspectorates, ministries, etc—to deliver public goods and services.[43] Although the elaborate system of the courts of local and special jurisdiction was becoming obsolete by the mid-nineteenth century, their decline coincided with the emergence of new administrative institutions that formed the basis of the modern administrative state.[44] Beginning with the introduction of the Factory and Mines Inspectorates in 1833, the central government began administering national policies through various forms of delegated authority. While this practice evolved over the next 40 years, one can say with confidence that the blueprint for the modern system of administration had been laid out well before 1870, the year Dicey identified with the emergence of unorthodox 'collectivist' legislation.[45] So although Dicey was keenly aware of the battle between the Crown and Parliament over conciliar courts like the Star Chamber in the seventeenth century, he was either ignorant or unduly dismissive of the emanations of administrative authority in the nineteenth century.[46]

[42] As Ivor Jennings puts it, 'the criticism of Dicey is not that his politics were wrong, but that his constitution did not exist. It is not that the Rule of Law is undesirable, but that it was not correct analysis of the British Constitution of 1885 and has become even more incorrect since'. W Ivor Jennings, 'Book Review of *Introduction to the Study of the Law of the Constitution* by AV Dicey' (1940) 3 *Modern Law Review* 321, 322.

[43] HW Arthurs, '*Without the Law*': *Administrative Justice and Legal Pluralism in Nineteenth-Century England* (Toronto, University of Toronto Press, 1985) ch 4–6; Parris, *Constitutional Bureaucracy* (n 41 above); W Ivor Jennings, *The Law and the Constitution*, 5th edn (London, University of London Press, 1959) 308–11. Some prominent examples from this era include the Factory and Mines Inspectorates (1833), the Education inspectorate (1833), the Poor Law Commission (1834), the Board of Health (1848), and the Railway and Canal Commission (1873).

[44] These ancient modes of governance, administered by local and communal courts and justices of the peace, might also be characterised as a form of administrative authority. See Edith G Henderson, *Foundations of English Administrative Law: Certiorari and Mandamus in the Seventeenth Century* (Cambridge MA, Harvard University Press, 1963).

[45] Arthurs, *Without the Law* (n 43 above) 95, 183–87; Parris, *Constitutional Bureaucracy* (n 41 above).

[46] Dicey, *Introduction* (n 9 above) 369–73; AV Dicey, *The Privy Council: The Arnold Prize Essay 1860* (London, Whittaker, 1860). While Dicey did recognise the importance of factory legislation, education reform and the new Poor Laws, he dismissed their significance for a period he characterised (perhaps too hastily) as the zenith of Benthamite individualism. See AV Dicey, 'Fifty Years of Reform in England' (1882) 35 *Nation* 49; *Lectures on the Relation Between Law and Public Opinion in England During the Nineteenth Century*, 2nd edn (London, Macmillan & Co Ltd, 1962) 237ff; Dicey, *Introduction* (n 9 above) 387, 397. Parris, *Constitutional Bureaucracy* (n 41 above) 266 aptly notes that 'Dicey's erroneous beliefs about Benthamism and its influence on legislation have helped to perpetuate a myth about

Secondly, even if we assume that Dicey recognised the extent of administrative law in 1885, his theory distorts the manner in which it was supervised through judicial review. The most glaring omissions in this respect are (1) the failure to recognise the concept of administrative 'jurisdiction', which was the central hypothesis for judicial supervision of public power, and (2) the importance of the prerogative writs, which provided a remedy distinct from private law claims for damages against public officials who had exceeded their authority.[47] Already by the sixteenth century, litigants began seeking redress by claiming prerogative relief, because common law actions against public officials were impractical and ineffective modes of redress.[48] Assuming that the aggrieved citizen had the means to pursue such an action, lawsuits targeted only low-ranking public officials, who usually were not capable of satisfying a judgment even if the action was successful. The unhappy result was that private law remedies were doubly flawed: they did not adequately vindicate a citizen's grievance *and* they imposed an inordinate burden on persons who, although not responsible for issuing warrants, were liable to be prosecuted if they refused to execute them.[49] Neither citizens nor the state benefited from this state of affairs. This framed a dilemma for common law courts: whether to grant relief to the citizen or some form of public interest immunity to the official. The result was relentless confusion.[50] Gradually the courts began restricting recovery to situations where the defendant had acted 'without jurisdiction', a term that implies (*contra* Dicey) that the legality of decisions made by public officials should be judged according to standards that deviate from the ordinary private law;[51] the Privy Council began imprisoning plaintiffs until they abandoned their cause of action;[52] and punitive costs were imposed on unsuccessful plaintiffs for wrongful vexation.[53] All these reactions were

nineteenth-century government—the myth that between 1830 and 1870 or thereabouts, central administration in Great Britain was stationary, if not actually diminishing, and that this state of affairs ended when a new current of opinion, collectivism, superseded individualism'.

[47] Jennings, 'In Praise of Dicey' (n 26 above) 236–38.

[48] Henderson, *Foundations* (n 44 above) c 1.

[49] ibid 13–18.

[50] Amnon Rubinstein, *Jurisdiction and Illegality* (Oxford, Clarendon Press, 1965) ch 4.

[51] *Case of the Marshalsea* (1598) 5 Co Rep 99b; Rubinstein, *Jurisdiction and Illegality* (n 50 above) 56–61. This explains why, from its very inception, the concept of administrative jurisdiction developed an affinity for what Murray Hunt calls the 'spatial metaphor'. Jurisdiction served to delimit the boundaries of liability. If a public official acted within his jurisdiction, he was exempt; if he acted without jurisdiction, he was liable. See Murray Hunt, 'Sovereignty's Blight: Why Contemporary Public Law Needs the Concept of "Due Deference"' in Nicholas Bamforth and Peter Leyland (eds), *Public Law in a Multi-Layered Constitution* (Oxford, Hart Publishing, 2003) 337.

[52] For example, when William Headley sued the Sewer Commissioners for false imprisonment, the Privy Council imprisoned him until he relinquished his action. *Headley v Sir Anthony Mildmay* (1617) 1 Rolle 395, 81 ER 560. See *Acts of the Privy Council*, 1616–17, 240; Henderson, *Foundations* (n 44 above) 25–35.

[53] Henderson, *Foundations* (n 44 above) 17.

motivated by the desire to curb the use of tort as the means for prosecuting grievances against public officials.

Thus, steady recourse to the prerogative writs began in the early seventeenth century as an alternate means for checking public power.[54] This point, insofar as it relates to Dicey's constitutional theory, is important. It demonstrates, contrary to Dicey's claims about the rule of law, that the common law had developed a means for supervising administrative authority that recognised the special status of administrative officials. The development of prerogative relief enabled common law courts to supervise the exercise of public power while still recognising the special status of public officials who owed public, not private, duties and obligations. In short, the prominence of prerogative relief in English public law supports the claim Dicey was so keen to falsify, namely, 'that the relation of individuals to the State is governed by principles essentially different from those rules of private law which govern the rights of private persons towards their neighbours'.[55]

Dicey's omission regarding the role of prerogative relief in securing liberty is all the more striking since they were widely celebrated as prizes secured by judicial champions of the common law like Sir Edward Coke and Sir John Holt. Moreover, the relationship between *habeas corpus*, which was one of Dicey's favourite constitutional devices,[56] and the other prerogative writs is unmistakable: it secured freedom without resorting to an action in damages.[57] The modern development of the different prerogative writs occurred more or less in tandem during the seventeenth century precisely because common law actions in damages were hobbled by inherent defects.[58] By the middle of the eighteenth century, Lord Mansfield recognised the close affinity between the different 'prerogative writs',[59] a classification echoed by Blackstone.[60] So by the time Dicey wrote his first edition, prerogative relief had been well established and was rapidly becoming the preferred avenue for reviewing administrative decisions,[61] so much so that even by the end of the

[54] ibid, chs 2–5; Rubinstein, *Jurisdiction and Illegality* (n 50 above) c 4. See, eg *James Bagg's Case* (n 3 above); *Commins v Massam* (1643) March NC 196, 82 ER 473; *Groenvelt v Burwell* (1700) 1 Ld Raym 454, 91 ER 1202.

[55] Dicey, *Introduction* (n 9 above) 388.

[56] ibid ch 6. The fact that a scholar of Dicey's calibre only recognised *habeas corpus* suggests that his disregard of the other prerogative writs was somewhat disingenuous.

[57] SA de Smith, 'The Prerogative Writs' (1951) 11 *Cambridge Law Journal* 40; JH Baker, *An Introduction to English Legal History*, 4th edn (London, Butterworths, 2002) ch 9; Lawson, 'Dicey Revisited' (n 39 above) 116.

[58] Henderson, *Foundations* (n 44 above) 94–95.

[59] *R v Cowle* (1759) 2 Burr 834, 97 ER 587.

[60] Blackstone, *Commentaries on the Laws of England* (n 5 above) vol III *131–*134.

[61] Henderson, *Foundations* (n 44 above) chs 4–5. De Smith, 'Prerogative Writs' (n 57 above) 48 observes that after Holt's sweeping reformulation of *certiorari* in *Groenvelt* (n 54 above) that: 'the King's Bench became inundated with motions for *certiorari* to quash rates and orders made by Justices and other bodies exercising administrative functions under semi-judicial forms. It became what Gneist has called an *Oberverwaltungsgericht*, a supreme court of

seventeenth century, Parliament began enacting privative clauses in order to limit or exclude it altogether.[62]

Privative clauses pose a final problem for Dicey's theory, because they seem to pit parliamentary sovereignty directly against the rule of law. These provisions purport to limit or exclude judicial review in order to immunise administrative action from judicial oversight. Although Dicey ignored or (at the very least) largely discounted the prevalence of administrative institutions and did not address the widespread legislative practice of resorting to privative clauses, he did acknowledge the apprehension that his constitutional principles might conflict, at least in theory. This potential conflict frames the Diceyan dialectic between the principles of parliamentary sovereignty and the rule of law.

Dicey argued that the apprehension of a constitutional dialectic was 'delusive', because the principles of parliamentary sovereignty and the rule of law were mutually supportive.[63] On closer inspection, however, it seems that Dicey's resolution is more problematic than he lets on. Dicey claims that the rule of law supports parliamentary sovereignty by insisting on a narrow judicial construction of parliamentary will. He argues that since the resolutions of either House have no independent juridical significance, a bi-cameral legislature must express its will through determinate legislative acts that are always subject to judicial interpretation. In this situation, judges can only give effect to the precise wording of each statute. According to Dicey, this interpretive approach greatly contributes 'to the authority of the judges and to the fixity of the law',[64] because parliamentary legislation regarding matters historically governed by the common law would be strictly construed. Therefore, the timeless rationale of the common law, and its constitutive values, would largely remain undisturbed by parliamentary incursions.[65]

> Parliament is supreme legislator, but from the moment Parliament has uttered its will as lawgiver, that will becomes subject to the interpretation put upon it by the judges of the land, and the judges, who are influenced by the feelings of magistrates no less than by the general spirit of the common law, are disposed to construe statutory exceptions to common law principles in a mode which would not commend itself either to a body of officials, or to the Houses of Parliament, if the

administration, supervising much of the business of local government by keeping subordinate bodies within their legal limitations by writs of *certiorari* and prohibition, and ordering them to perform their duties by writs of *mandamus*'.

62 Rubinstein, *Jurisdiction and Illegality* (n 50 above) 71–73. See, eg An act to prevent and suppress seditious conventicles, 22 Car II, c 1, s 6: 'no other court whatsoever shall intermeddle with any cause or causes of appeal upon this act, but they shall be finally determined in the quarter-sessions only'.

63 Dicey, *Introduction* (n 9 above) ch 13.

64 ibid 408.

65 ibid 413–14.

> Houses were called upon to interpret their own enactments ... In England judicial notions have modified the action and influenced the ideas of the executive government. By every path we come round to the same conclusion, that Parliamentary sovereignty has favoured the rule of law, and that the supremacy of the law of the land both calls forth the exertion of Parliamentary sovereignty, and leads to its being exercised in a spirit of legality.

The upshot is that Dicey resolved the problem by prioritising the judicial role in interpreting legislative will. And the mode of interpretation Dicey had in mind was anchored by common law values that were, by their very nature, conservative and opposed to the exercise of executive discretion, which he thought was bound to be determined by arbitrary political opinion. Thus, Dicey argued that the configuration of the English constitution precluded the emergence of administrative law, because it was sceptical of any form of administrative legal authority.

Unfortunately, Dicey's theory cannot address the problem posed by privative clauses, because these instruments bring the contest between parliamentary sovereignty and the rule of law into stark relief. When Parliament issues a clear directive that it wants judges to abstain from reviewing certain administrative decisions, Dicey's resolution is unhelpful because judges have to choose which constitutional principle will prevail. This explains why the doctrine of jurisdictional error, which enables judges to grapple with the problem posed by privative clauses, is so volatile and erratic.[66] Judges have historically adopted different notions of jurisdictional error in order to justify very different postures towards privative clauses, ranging from total abstention from judicial review to determining correct answers for administrative institutions to implement. In the former case, administrative action is treated as an extra-legal exercise of political power because it is wholly beyond the reach of judicial review; in the latter case, the court ignores Parliament's will and administrative action is brought to heel in accordance with judicially determined standards of judgement. So Dicey's resolution is both illusory and irrelevant, at least insofar as privative clauses are concerned.

This point cannot be marginalised as an extraordinary phenomenon that Dicey could have otherwise accommodated within his theory. On the contrary, it shows that Dicey's theory cannot provide an adequate rationale of administrative legal authority at all, even in situations where Parliament does not resort to a privative clause, because there is simply no room for independent administrative judgement in his binary constitution. In situations where Parliament delegates a decision-making power to an administrative

[66] For accounts of the confusion regarding jurisdictional error at common law, see DM Gordon, 'The Relation of Facts to Jurisdiction' (1929) 45 *Law Quarterly Review* 459; PP Craig, *Administrative Law*, 5th edn (London, Sweet & Maxwell, 2003) ch 15; Paul Craig, 'Ultra Vires and the Foundations of Judicial Review' (1998) 57 *Cambridge Law Journal* 63, 66.

institution, Dicey envisages only two options where it exercises 'judicial or quasi-judicial powers'.[67] First, the decision-maker must 'conform precisely to the language of any statute by which the power is given' or else 'the courts of justice may treat its action as a nullity'.[68] Secondly, it must comport with 'the spirit of judicial fairness and equity' which English courts ultimately enforce through judicial review. In either case, an administrative institution would not possess any measure of legal authority under the constitution, because its decisions would be determined by another branch of government.[69]

II. RETHINKING THE DICEYAN DIALECTIC

If Dicey's theory is demonstrably flawed, is there an alternative way to explain his conception of the English constitution? The answer to that question, I argue, is best tackled by looking through the lens that Dicey claimed to eschew, namely that of political theory. While Dicey's theory was clearly at odds with legal practice, it was a seamless extension of the political principles which he espoused. Put bluntly, 'Dicey saw the constitution of 1885 through Whig spectacles. His [constitutional] principles were Whig principles'.[70]

But in order to gain a better view of the political terrain on which Dicey's theory is pitched, I will briefly review Isaiah Berlin's famous essay regarding a central tension in liberal political theory between 'positive' and 'negative' conceptions of liberty.[71] This framework contributes to two important tasks in the more general project of rethinking the Diceyan dialectic. First, it shows that Dicey's terms of reference are political in nature, as opposed to scientific or immutable constitutional axioms. This is not to say that the principles of parliamentary sovereignty and the rule of law are unimportant or fanciful legal fictions. On the contrary, they have been so persistent in constitutional theory because they tap into widely held convictions

[67] It is revealing that Dicey could only envisage a species of delegated power that was 'judicial' or 'quasi-judicial' rather than 'administrative' in nature. AV Dicey, 'The Development of Administrative Law in England' (1915) 31 *Law Quarterly Review* 148.

[68] ibid 151.

[69] ibid. Although Dicey recognised that, by 1915, Parliament was clearly delegating some kind of authority to administrative institutions, he never recanted his view that the English constitution could not accommodate the notion of administrative law, because 'the fact that the ordinary law courts can deal with any actual and provable breach of the law committed by any servant of the Crown still preserves that rule of law which is fatal to the existence of true *droit administratif*'. See also Cosgrove, *Rule of Law* (n 11 above) 98–102.

[70] Jennings, 'In Praise of Dicey' (n 26 above) 128. In many ways, Dicey's constitutional scholarship is an example of what Herbert Butterfield famously dubbed 'the whig interpretation of history': Herbert Butterfield, *The Whig Interpretation of History* (Harmondsworth, Penguin, 1973) 9.

[71] Berlin, 'Two Concepts' (n 7 above).

regarding legal legitimacy and democratic constitutionalism. Rather, I want to show that the particular political content that Dicey imported into his constitutional framework, especially his revulsion for administrative law, is contestable. This interpretive task prefaces the second, constructive endeavour to advance an alternative constitutional theory that is more defensible in light of liberal and democratic values. While I will not address this second task in this chapter, it is important to acknowledge that the two projects are interrelated, and that any attempt to move beyond the Diceyan dialectic should still respect the important political values that underpin it.

A. Berlin's Dilemma

In his essay 'Two Concepts of Liberty', Berlin examines two recurrent, often conflicting, conceptions of liberty that frequently emerge in debates concerning the question of obedience and coercion in political philosophy. The first, 'negative' conception of liberty concerns 'the area within which a man can act unobstructed by others'.[72] This conception of liberty is generally opposed to social constraints on the grounds that they are likely to suffocate individual originality, energy, the pursuit of truth, social progress, and so forth.[73] But Berlin also recognises that negative liberty is not a supreme ideal, and is often strained by the political controversies it provokes. At the very least, negative liberty cannot be unlimited, because that would entail a Hobbesian state of nature which would preclude the emergence of civil society. Naturally, proponents of negative liberty prefer only those constraints that provide minimal conditions for social interaction, such as the enforcement of criminal law—any further trade-offs between negative liberty and other political ideals (such as equality, justice, happiness, or security) are prone to disagreement.[74] These controversies are liable to be compounded by the fact that certain social policies, such as ameliorating poverty, might be both justified and criticised on the grounds of negative liberty (eg, whether poverty should be regarded as attributable to human agency and socio-economic arrangements that are morally or politically significant).[75]

Berlin does not take sides in any of these particular debates in the essay, in part because he takes a relatively uncritical stance on negative liberty compared to its counterpart. His only comment is that these sorts of issues

[72] ibid 122.

[73] John Stuart Mill, *On Liberty* (London, JW Parker & Son, 1859).

[74] Berlin, 'Two Concepts' (n 7 above) 122–31.

[75] ibid 122–23. However, in his later writings Berlin does suggest that, to the extent that negative liberty is harnessed in service of *laissez-faire* economic arguments, such arguments pervert the value of liberty. See Isaiah Berlin, 'My Intellectual Path', *New York Review of Books* (14 May 1998) 53, 58; reprinted in Isaiah Berlin, *The First and the Last* (London, Granta, 1999) 61.

are likely to remain a matter of 'infinite debate'.[76] But he makes one further point that is worth noticing: that negative liberty is not logically related to any particular form of government, including democracy. In his words,

> [j]ust as a democracy may, in fact, deprive the individual citizen of a great many liberties which he might have in some other form of society, so it is perfectly conceivable that a liberal-minded despot would allow his subjects a large measure of personal freedom.[77]

Thus, negative liberty is threatened by *any* form of government, including a democratic one.

The second, 'positive', conception of liberty concerns the freedom of self-direction: to participate in the act of self-governance by conceiving goals and realising them of one's own accord.[78] Berlin is noticeably more critical of this idea because he thinks it leads one down a slippery slope towards authoritarian or totalitarian governance, the principal targets of his essay. This supposed tendency stems from the way in which the individual personality is frequently bifurcated in political thought, namely by distinguishing between the 'authentic' or 'rational' self, associated with conceiving long-term goals and purposes, and the 'empirical' or 'spontaneous' self, governed by irrational impulses and desires.[79] Historically speaking, this distinction has been exploited by despots and tyrants who justify their oppression by claiming to possess a better understanding of their subjects' 'authentic' personalities. In other words, despotism was justified on the basis that citizens cannot be trusted to govern in their true interests, because they are blinded by their 'empirical' or irrational personalities. Thus, the idea of positive liberty could be perverted by despotic governments, even benign ones.[80]

This explains why Berlin is also suspicious of popular governments premised on the ideal of positive liberty. Although positive liberty demands that an individual be recognised as an agent of free will, Berlin is wary of this idea in its 'socialised' form of collective self-direction.[81] Of course, humans are social creatures and it is only logical that they should engage in common enterprises, the most obvious being government. If citizens could govern themselves by affording equal participation in popular government, it might

[76] ibid 126.

[77] ibid 129–31.

[78] ibid 131: 'I wish, above all, to be conscious of myself as a thinking, willing, active being, bearing responsibility for my choices and able to explain them by references to my own ideas and purposes. I feel free to the degree that I believe this to be true, and enslaved to the degree that I am made to realize that it is not'.

[79] ibid 132.

[80] ibid 145–54.

[81] ibid 154–62. Berlin recoils from calling this an extension of positive liberty, saying that it bears an equally close relationship to the distinct ideals of equality and fraternity. Nevertheless, he also refuses to dismiss the case for social recognition from positive liberty as confusion, because the two ideas are still intimately connected.

seem that such an arrangement is justified by positive liberty. But Berlin, in keeping with his pluralist convictions, was reluctant to subscribe to this view, because he apprehended that popular government might regress into monism—the same tendency that characterised tyrants and despots who believed they had exclusive insight into how to construct social harmony. Just as positive liberty might be perverted to justify tyranny of the few, it might be perverted to justify tyranny of the majority.[82]

While this concern might explain why Berlin is reluctant to wholeheartedly endorse democratic government, it does not rebut the strong moral relationship between the 'positive' conception of liberty and claims regarding the legitimacy of democratic decisions. Rather, Berlin's reticence highlights a central dilemma for democratic theory: how to reconcile the tension between the 'positive' value of liberty associated with democratic government and the 'negative' value of liberty associated with legal limits on the coercive power of the state. This dilemma is particularly challenging because, as Berlin's essay shows, the tension is rooted in different conceptions of liberty,[83] which virtually all participants in political debates will invoke (either directly or implicitly) in order to justify arguments about enforcing democratic outcomes, inviolable legal rights or some more sophisticated synthesis of the two.[84] Moreover, this type of moral tension is ripe for what Ronald Dworkin calls 'theoretical disagreements' in law, because it is implicated in many contemporary debates about the proper role of judicial review under a democratic constitution.[85]

But despite his suspicions about democratic government, Berlin offers some tentative ideas on how to negotiate the dilemma. The key to avoiding the excesses of popular sovereignty, in Berlin's view, is to remain vigilant against 'the accumulation of power itself ... since liberty [is] endangered by the mere existence of absolute authority as such'.[86] At the very least, this requires the establishment of certain minimum, inviolable frontiers of negative liberty to restrain the exercise of sovereignty. Once again, Berlin declines to give specific content to these limits, other than to say that they preserve

[82] ibid 162–66.

[83] David Dyzenhaus makes a similar claim when he argues that: 'even radical democratic proceduralism seems to presuppose some protected liberal substance so that all involved in the great debates of political theory are part of one big, though sometimes rancorous family. The various positions in that debate no longer seem greatly at odds with each other. Rather, they look like points along a continuum marked by the extent of protected liberal substance. The less the extent of protected substance, the more faith is put in the outcomes of procedures, and vice versa'. See Dyzenhaus, 'Form and Substance' (n 6 above) 144. See also David Dyzenhaus, 'The Politics of Deference: Judicial Review and Democracy' in Michael Taggart (ed), *The Province of Administrative Law* (Oxford, Hart Publishing, 1997) 279, 280.

[84] See, eg Ronald Dworkin, 'Hart's Postscript and the Character of Political Philosophy' (2004) 24 *Oxford Journal of Legal Studies* 1; Ronald Dworkin, *Justice in Robes* (Belknap Press, Cambridge, 2006) ch 4.

[85] Ronald Dworkin, *Law's Empire* (London, Fontana, 1986).

[86] Berlin, 'Two Concepts' (n 7 above) 163.

'an essential part of what we mean by being a normal human being'. But later in the same section, Berlin suggests that these frontiers are related to something like the rule of law, since they include rules prohibiting conviction without trial or punishment under a retroactive law.[87]

This strategy of fragmenting state power and establishing inviolable rules to protect negative liberty is broadly consistent with two legal concepts that are strongly implicated in Dicey's constitutional theory: the separation of powers and the rule of law. But, as Berlin's essay suggests, these issues are frequently contested by virtue of their political nature. Therefore, we must unpack Dicey's views on these matters in order to ascertain whether they can be reconciled with our current understanding of modern democratic government and the role that administrative decision-makers actually play within that framework.

B. Dicey's Dilemma

It is not difficult to recognise the relationship between Dicey's constitutional principles and Berlin's analytical framework. At a very general level, Dicey's idea of the rule of law was meant to provide a bulwark against parliamentary action. Nevertheless, it is important to follow through with the analysis, because only by revealing the political content of Dicey's theory will we be able to engage in a forthright discussion about the character of the Diceyan dialectic. As Berlin aptly noted, 'to understand such movements or conflicts is, above all, to understand the ideas or attitudes to life involved in them, which alone make such movements part of human history, and not mere natural events'.[88] This advice is equally germane when probing the 'scientific' prestige Dicey claimed for his constitutional theory and its place in public law more generally.

At the beginning of the nineteenth century, English politics were marked by at least three important influences.[89] The first concerned the ongoing transition from monarchical to parliamentary government. While this process was set in motion by the Civil War and formalised by the Bill of Rights in 1689 and the Act of Settlement in 1701, it was not until the early nineteenth century that Parliament secured its independence from the Crown's influence. The transition to parliamentary government, however, did not entail full democratic reform. That process would take another century, culminating in 1928 when women were granted an equal vote in parliamentary elections.

[87] ibid 166.
[88] ibid 121.
[89] See Jennings, 'In Praise of Dicey' (n 26 above).

The second influence concerned the profound impact of the industrial revolution, which began in the latter half of the eighteenth century. The enormous social, technological, and economic changes associated with the industrial revolution spilled over into the political arena. This age of national prosperity lent considerable force to laissez-faire capitalism, but it also invigorated political movements amongst the landed gentry, the newly propertied, and the working classes. Unsurprisingly, the rapid technological advances sparked by the industrial revolution also caused a significant political upheaval throughout England.

Finally, popular optimism and economic prosperity in Britain gave an imperialist edge to political scholarship during the nineteenth century.[90] The rhetoric of Blackstone and Burke regarding the felicitous nature of English law, as compared with its continental counterparts, was a recurrent device in both legal and political discourse. As Ivor Jennings noted, 'British economic supremacy in the nineteenth century was not likely to extinguish the notion that Englishmen had an inherent capacity for government which other nations did not possess'.[91]

Dicey, like many other intellectuals of his period, took an avid interest in the politics of the nineteenth century and his scholarship reflects a curious amalgam of these influences. Among other things, he was a staunch individualist; a proponent of laissez-faire economic policy; a great admirer of Jeremy Bentham and the utilitarian reform movement (although he was less enthusiastic about democratic constitutional reform); and, like Blackstone, he was prone to eulogise the distinct Englishness latent in the common law and traditional legal institutions. But at times, these sentiments led Dicey to make some rather peculiar claims, among them that 'Benthamism was … little else than the logical and systematic development of those individual rights, and especially of that individual freedom which has always been dear to the common law of England'.[92] Of course, this is absurd. Bentham made a career of lampooning the common law and its chief expositor, Blackstone. He regarded the common law as nothing more than an irrational or 'fictional' impediment to utilitarian reform and sought to relieve his readers from the delusion (induced by Blackstone) that the common law was, in fact, law at all.[93] Moreover, Dicey's suggestion of a common law ground

[90] Collini, *Public Moralists* (n 17 above).

[91] Jennings, 'In Praise of Dicey' (n 26 above) 127. See also Stapleton, 'Dicey and His Legacy' (n 18 above); Hugh Tulloch, 'A.V. Dicey and the Irish Question: 1870–1922' (1980) 15 *Irish Jurist (NS)* 137, 145.

[92] Dicey, *Law and Public Opinion* (n 46 above) 176.

[93] Jeremy Bentham, *A Fragment on Government* (Cambridge, Cambridge University Press, 1988). Strangely enough, Dicey still married Bentham to the common law, even though he thought Bentham's critique of Blackstone had 'achieved complete success'. See AV Dicey, 'Blackstone's Commentaries' (1909–10) 54 *National Review* 653, 657.

for individual rights does not square easily with Bentham's contempt for the notion of natural rights.[94]

In order to understand why Dicey forced this marriage between Bentham and the common law, we have to gain a better understanding of his political predilections. Dicey's political theory hinged on individualism, an ideology he ascribed to Bentham.[95] Dicey revered Bentham's utilitarian principle—that legislation should promote the greatest happiness of the greatest number—and held that it was contingent upon the idea that the individual was the best judge of his own happiness. But, unlike Bentham, Dicey was sceptical of the legislature's role in promoting utility. Given the diversity and complexity of individual desires, Dicey thought that the legislature could not orchestrate individual happiness; it could only aspire to establish the conditions under which citizens might prosper.[96] Thus, Dicey claimed that 'though *laissez-faire* is not an essential part of utilitarianism it was practically the most vital part of Bentham's legislative doctrine'.[97]

In reality, it seems that the utilitarians were themselves more divided on this issue. Even John Stuart Mill, the great author of the liberal manifesto *On Liberty*, significantly qualified his views over his lifetime.[98] But Dicey remained throughout an undaunted supporter of laissez-faire.[99] While he advocated legal reforms which repealed unnecessary laws, he was deeply sceptical of proactive legislative measures. In his mind, individualism was the only political creed worthy of being called 'legal science', because its principles established logical and systematic parameters for both parliamentary and judicial legislation.[100] This enthusiasm is underlined by the fact that Dicey extolled Bentham by comparing him to the great mechanical inventors of the industrial revolution, such as James Watt and Richard Arkwright,[101] suggesting that legislation constructed along individualist lines was characteristic of an advanced, prosperous and technological civilisation.

Dicey's dilemma concerned the social implications of his brand of individualism. On the one hand, he could understand how institutions like trade unions and democratic government could be reconciled with individualism;

[94] Jeremy Bentham, 'Anarchical Fallacies; Being an Examination of the Declaration of Rights Issued During the French Revolution' in J Bowring (ed), *The Works of Jeremy Bentham* (Edinburgh, W Tait, 1843) 489.

[95] Dicey, *Law and Public Opinion* (n 46 above), Lecture VI. See also AV Dicey, 'Modern English Law' (1876) 23 *Nation* 273; AV Dicey, 'Bentham' (1878) 27 *Nation* 352.

[96] ibid 137.

[97] ibid 147.

[98] Shirley Robin Letwin, *The Pursuit of Certainty* (Cambridge, Cambridge University Press, 1965) chs 24–25.

[99] In fact, at various points in *Law and Public Opinion*, Dicey takes Mill to task for corrupting the utilitarian creed by importing notions of egalitarianism. See, eg Dicey, *Law and Public Opinion* (n 46 above), xxviii (fn 2).

[100] ibid 135–36, Lecture IV.

[101] ibid 130. See also Dicey, 'Bentham' (n 95 above).

he was also wary, however, that such developments might undermine his preference for laissez-faire. At the micro level of social interaction, individualism entailed the expansion of freedom of contract, but Dicey was troubled by the problem posed by trade combines (a conglomeration of individual contracts) for laissez-faire economic policy. He thought this 'speculative paradox'[102] revealed an important gap in Benthamite philosophy: 'the tendency of all individualists to neglect the social aspect of human nature'.[103] In retrospect, this observation applies equally to Dicey's constitutional theory, because he could not rationalise a valuable proactive role for a democratically elected government.

This same dilemma played out at the macro level of social interaction. While Dicey could see how individualism might aid movements for democratic reform, he recognised that a democratic government could not guarantee individualist legislation since its actions would be dictated by public opinion, not legal science.[104] Public opinion was the antithesis of Dicey's scientific legislative rationale, because it consists of the volatile 'speculative views' held by the electorate instead of an enlightened theory of legislation.[105] It has no intrinsic preference for individualism, logicality or coherence because at bottom it is driven by the accumulation of irrational self-interest and prejudice, manipulated by party factions and cobbled together through ad hoc political compromises to result in legislation.[106] It was all too predictable that the chickens hatched through democratic reform would come home to roost in a manner worrisome to the Victorian compromise, whereby an elite governing class passed laissez-faire legislation through Parliament. No sooner had the Radicals begun repealing old law and introducing constitutional reforms than the opponents of laissez-faire began mobilising political support for new government programmes premised on the conflicting ideal of 'collectivism' that state intervention should enhance common welfare.[107] The interesting point here is that although

[102] *Law and Public Opinion* (n 46 above) 155. See also AV Dicey, 'The Legal Limits of Liberty' (1868) 3 *Fortnightly Review (NS)* 1.

[103] *Law and Public Opinion* (n 46 above) 158.

[104] ibid 158–68. Like Berlin, Dicey recognised that individualism did not logically entail democratic government (or vice versa), but that there was still a strong kinship between these political values.

[105] ibid 3. It is no accident that Dicey begins his discussion on public opinion by reciting Hume's paradox and refers to public opinion as various forms of vulgar irrationality (ie, the manifestation of feelings, beliefs, sentiments, inclinations and speculations), in contrast to the rational logic of individualism.

[106] ibid 12. See also AV Dicey, 'The Social Movement in England' (1884) 38 *Nation* 29; 'The Social Movement in England—II' (1884) 38 *Nation* 49; 'The Social Movement in England—III' (1884) 38 *Nation* 272. Dicey clearly recognised the anti-democratic tendencies of the party system. See *Law and Public Opinion* (n 46 above), Introduction; AV Dicey, 'A Sign of the Times in England' (1883) 37 *Nation* 30.

[107] *Law and Public Opinion* (n 46 above) 259.

the collectivist rationale conflicted with laissez-faire, it remained strictly compatible with the utilitarian principle Bentham preached.[108]

But compatibility with utilitarianism did not redeem collectivist initiatives in Dicey's estimation. Throughout his *Lectures on Law and Public Opinion*, he makes a series of thinly veiled attacks on various collectivist legislative policies. For instance, in Lecture VIII he derides publicly funded education (for compelling uninterested individuals to bear the expense);[109] workmen's compensation schemes (for eroding freedom of contract, personal responsibility and forcing employers to pay for insurance);[110] and welfare reform and old age pensions (for comforting undeserving individuals).[111] Dicey's tone is even more strident in his Introduction to the second edition, where he advocates the disenfranchisement of persons in receipt of social assistance[112] in addition to lamenting the advent of labour standards legislation and progressive taxation.[113]

Against this background, it is easy to see where Dicey's political theory fits in terms of Berlin's typology. If Berlin was a tad sympathetic towards negative liberty, Dicey was a true believer. Whereas Berlin thought laissez-faire was a perversion of negative liberty and was prepared to allow room for other values (like equality or justice), Dicey's vision was more one sided: negative liberty was the ultimate value and its epitome was laissez-faire economic policy. If a legislative proposal could not be justified on the grounds that it enhanced the scope of individual freedom, it was automatically suspect. This largely explains Dicey's antipathy for redistributive social programmes. And like Berlin, Dicey understood that democratic government does not guarantee negative liberty, because it is ultimately contingent upon the ebb and flow of public opinion. Since public opinion was characterised by irrationality and prone to manipulation by party factions, parliamentary government posed a constant threat to Dicey's preferred ideological equilibrium.

Both Berlin and Dicey opted for similar escapes from their respective dilemmas, namely to establish guaranteed frontiers of negative liberty as a bulwark against the exercise of popular sovereignty. For a short period (at least in retrospect), it seemed to Dicey that an enlightened Parliament inspired by the doctrine of individualism was capable of maintaining such limits, but as the electorate became increasingly heterogeneous these limits became confused by ideological conflict. So Dicey resorted to other devices to constrain legislative adventures.

[108] ibid xxx at fn 1 and Lecture IX.
[109] ibid 278–79.
[110] ibid 282–83.
[111] ibid 292–96.
[112] ibid xxxiv, li.
[113] ibid li–lii.

One device was the referendum or 'nation's veto', whereby all amendments to any important piece of legislation, including (but not necessarily limited to) constitutional reform, were contingent upon popular approval.[114] Toward the end of the nineteenth century, when democratic constitutional reform was becoming politically entrenched, Dicey began advocating the referendum as a means of limiting the extent to which Parliament could exercise legislative power. Sir Henry Maine, speaking of the Swiss experience, declared that the referendum 'can only be considered thoroughly successful by those who wish that there should be as little legislation as possible' because most citizens, when confronted with an actual legislative proposal, were apt to find some reason for preferring the status quo.[115] Dicey conceded this observation, but dismissed its critical aspect by saying 'no one has a right to complain of an effective bridle that it is not a spur'.[116] At other times, he cast the referendum in a more positive light by comparing it to the role of a jury.[117] This analogy is loaded, because Dicey idealised the jury system as the means by which individual liberty could be vindicated by fellow citizens who were apt to deflect the coercive power of the state.[118] The same reasoning applied to the referendum: if you were going to have a democratic government, warts and all, it was best to fashion a democratic constraint to prevent political parties from imposing rash legislative policies on society in general.[119] Thus, the referendum was consistent with Dicey's political beliefs, not because he was a proponent of popular sovereignty (as I have already noted, Dicey was at best ambivalent about public opinion), but because it fostered a minimalist role for the legislative branch.[120]

[114] See AV Dicey, 'The Referendum' (1894) 23 *National Review* 65; AV Dicey, 'The Referendum and its Critics' (1910) 212 *Quarterly Review* 538; AV Dicey, 'The United States and the Swiss Confederation' (1885) 41 *Nation* 297. Hugh Tulloch points out that, in addition to the question of home rule for Ireland, Dicey wanted to subject the Old Age Pensions Act of 1908 and female suffrage to the test of a referendum in the hopes that both initiatives would be thwarted by conservative public opinion. See Tulloch, 'Irish Question' (n 91 above) 155.

[115] Sir Henry Maine, *Popular Government* (London, John Murray, 1885) 96–98.

[116] Dicey, 'The Referendum and its Critics' (n 114 above) 543.

[117] ibid 548.

[118] AV Dicey, 'Judicial Policy' (1874) 29 *Macmillan's* 473, 481: 'When an unreformed Parliament failed to represent large masses of the people, the jury-box became a representative institution, and popular sentiment expressed itself through the voice of the jury, when it could find no utterance within the walls of the House of Commons'.

[119] Dicey, 'Referendum and Its Critics' (n 114 above), 543. The main problem with democratic government, according to Dicey, was the advent of party factions that tended to give modern legislation an extremist bent: 'The point in debate is whether the English democracy now established in power requires to be spurred on towards rapid legislation by the factitious and by no means disinterested agitation that forms the life of the party system, or rather needs some strong check on the tendency to yield at once to the prevalent idea, sentiment, or passion of the moment'. See also Dicey, 'The Referendum' (n 114 above); Cosgrove, *Rule of Law* (n 11 above) 108–9.

[120] See Tulloch, 'Irish Question' (n 114 above); Mads Qvortrup, 'AV Dicey: The Referendum as the People's Veto' (1999) 20 *History of Political Thought* 531. For a contrary argument that Dicey was in fact 'an ardent supporter of popular sovereignty', see Rivka Weill, 'Dicey was not Diceyan' (2003) 62 *Cambridge Law Journal* 474.

The second, more subtle, strategy was to reserve a prominent role for the judiciary under the constitution in the hope that it would limit parliamentary incursions along lines mandated by legal science. Dicey regarded the judiciary as 'the best and soundest of English institutions'[121] and the common law or 'judicial legislation' as the most important aspect of the English legal system.[122] It accounted for nearly all law governing interpersonal relationships (contract and tort); some of the better examples of parliamentary legislation, like the Sale of Goods Act, were in reality a codification of common law rules; and even those statutes that were not premised on the common law were subjected to judicial interpretation, which endowed them with 'nearly all their real significance'.[123] It is difficult to overstate Dicey's admiration for the Bench. In his mind, public reverence for judicial character guaranteed compliance with its decisions,[124] in contrast with public contempt for parliamentary legislation.[125]

Dicey attributed this institutional superiority to the character of the English courts. Although judicial temperament was (to a limited extent) influenced by public opinion, Dicey thought judges made up an independent social caste with its own distinct motives. Members of the judiciary were an elite group of legally trained professionals who were well remunerated and shared the sentiments of the higher social classes.[126] Judicial independence ensured that English courts remained insulated from political manoeuvring, and the traditions of common law practice favoured the rigorous application of legal science to discrete cases, especially in the face of popular opposition.[127] By contrast, he suggested that Members of Parliament were likely to adopt more sweeping, haphazard remedies in order to ingratiate themselves to a fickle electorate.[128] Thus, the nature of the judicial role was, insofar as possible, to mould legislation in accordance with the tenets of legal science[129] and had the extra advantage of restricting the use of state coercion to enforcing discrete judicial decisions.

[121] Dicey, 'Judicial Policy' (n 118 above) 473.
[122] Dicey, *Law and Public Opinion* (n 46 above) 361.
[123] ibid 362.
[124] Dicey, 'Judicial Policy' (n 118 above) 474.
[125] AV Dicey, 'The Prevalence of Lawlessness in England' (1883) 37 *Nation* 95.
[126] Dicey, 'Judicial Policy' (n 118 above) 478.
[127] ibid. See also AV Dicey, 'Sir George Bramwell and the English Bench' (1881) 33 *Nation* 468.
[128] Dicey, *Law and Public Opinion* (n 46 above) 370 (fn 1): 'Parliament in most instances pays little regard to any general principle whatever, but attempts to meet in the easiest and most off-hand manner some particular grievance or want. Parliament is guided not by considerations of logic but by the pressure which powerful bodies can bring to bear on its action. Ordinary parliamentary legislation then can at best be called only tentative. Even ordinary judicial legislation is logical, the best judicial legislation is scientific'.
[129] In this regard, Dicey's theory bears strong resemblances to John Austin's concept of authority and utilitarian epistemology. Austin argued that because the masses were incapable of assessing the utility of alternative courses of conduct for themselves, they should defer to the

III. REVISITING THE QUESTION ABOUT ADMINISTRATIVE LAW

Having said all this, what are we to make of Dicey's constitutional theory and its aversion to administrative legal authority? From a distance, Dicey's theory seems utterly confused and unstable. On the one hand, it is anchored by Austinian legal positivism and the notion of legislative sovereignty; on the other hand, it prescribes an anti-positivist judicial role that ultimately determines the content of legislation by common law standards, usually with the aim of stifling popular legislative projects.[130] In practice, the principles of parliamentary sovereignty and the rule of law are seen to be locked in a contest for supremacy within the constitution, and this contest effectively excludes any independent, constructive legal role for administrative institutions.

But we might better understand it as an attempt, albeit controversial and confused, to come to grips with the central tension between 'negative' and 'positive' liberty in democratic society. From this point of view, it was designed to set what Dicey thought were the legitimate limits of state authority. The gloss of legal science lent it the necessary leverage to 'define as precisely as possible the boundaries which delineated permissible self-regarding behaviour ("rights") from activities which interfered with the "self-regarding" activities of others'.[131] This strategy has important institutional implications, since legal science was reserved for judges, lawyers and law professors who would remain faithful to laissez-faire ideals. Parliamentary legislation was tolerated only to the letter, with the residue accruing to the judiciary. By elimination, there was no room for administrative authority, because there was no scenario in which judges should defer to administrative interpretations of law.

The fact that Dicey's political ideology caused him to preclude administrative authority in this way should be cause for concern amongst constitutional theorists, because it skews our understanding of how to resolve questions

judgement of an elite class of 'inquirers' who were capable of applying the utilitarian science to human affairs. This argument explains, to some extent, Austin's apology for the common law, which deviates from Bentham. See Austin, *The Province of Jurisprudence Determined* (n 4 above), Lecture III; John Austin, *Lectures on Jurisprudence or the Philosophy of Positive Law*, 5th edn, Robert Campbell (ed) (London, John Murray, 1885) vol I, Lecture III; RB Friedman, 'An Introduction to Mill's Theory of Authority' in JB Schneewind (ed), *Mill: A Collection of Critical Essays* (London, Macmillan, 1968) 379.

[130] This confusion may be symptomatic of a deeper problem in traditions of political thought. For instance, while Thomas Hobbes' political philosophy reserves pride of place for a sovereign legislator and positive law, it also preserves an important role for the judiciary and natural law reasoning. See, eg David Dyzenhaus, 'Hobbes and the Legitimacy of Law' (2001) 20 *Law & Philosophy* 461. Likewise, while John Austin's command theory of law revolves around an uncommanded commander, it also preserves a significant role for judicial elites for fear that the legislative branch may fall under the control of the masses. See above n 129.

[131] Sugarman, 'Legal Boundaries' (n 12 above) 108.

of legal authority as between different legal institutions or officials. These questions have traditionally been addressed through debates regarding a separation or division of legal powers, but in responding to that debate by simply asserting the doctrine of judicial independence, Dicey underestimated the complex normative interrelationship between the executive, legislative, and judicial institutions. The result is that, although Dicey's theory does attempt to grapple with questions of how to resolve disagreements between Parliament and the courts, his resolution is problematic because it appears to give judges a broad licence to emaciate enabling legislation. It is just as problematic from the perspective of administrative law that Dicey's theory does not afford any degree of legal authority for administrative officials, since they play such an important role in deciding how best to interpret and implement legislative policies on a daily basis.

However, even today there is a persistent tendency to divorce Dicey's constitutional theory from its controversial political foundations. The most telling evidence of this is the tendency amongst both public lawyers and historians to venerate Dicey's *description* of the constitution, while ignoring the *normative* political foundation Dicey laid for it in his other writings. For instance, in their landmark textbook on administrative law, Sir William Wade and Christopher Forsyth preface their discussion of Dicey's constitutional theory by observing that 'most students of public law feel no need to explore the theory which forms its background; or, if they do, they find little illumination'.[132] This statement is both ambiguous and problematic. If Wade and Forsyth mean to promote the constitutional principles of parliamentary sovereignty and the rule of law *as Dicey conceived them*, then they are assuming a constitutional theory that cannot be reconciled with the complex institutional practices associated with the reality of the modern administrative state. If, however, they mean to advance a conception of Diceyan constitutionalism which can be reconciled with the modern administrative state, then the substantive content of that conception should be articulated. By simply venerating Dicey's theory without probing its political foundations, Wade and Forsyth perpetuate the Diceyan dialectic which tends to obscure important questions regarding administrative authority. This tendency explains the seemingly intractable nature of current debates about judicial review which remain trapped by the Diceyan dialectic.[133]

One way of grappling with this problem is to acknowledge that descriptions of orthodox constitutional theory rooted in the Diceyan tradition contain an important blind-spot regarding the question of administrative authority. Instead of treating administrative institutions as alien or hostile

[132] HWR Wade & Christopher Forsyth, *Administrative Law*, 10th edn (Oxford, Oxford University Press, 2009) 7. See also chs 1–2, more generally.

[133] TRS Allan, 'The Constitutional Foundations of Judicial Review: Conceptual Conundrum or Interpretative Inquiry?' (2002) 61 *Cambridge Law Journal* 87.

to the rule of law per se, public lawyers should look for additional resources to explain why administrative judgments are important and valuable from a legal perspective. In doing so, they would be exploring an avenue of inquiry which Dicey recognised (but did not pursue) in his later years when he softened his criticism regarding *droit administratif*. Although Dicey never altered his essential ideas about the rule of law and the English constitution, his perception of *droit administratif* changed dramatically between the first and the seventh edition of his treatise. These revisions, which were prompted by Dicey's engagement with French public lawyers, reveal 'a distinct change of tone, and indeed a very handsome acknowledgment of the way in which *droit administratif* had become a stable body of law administered by tribunals which were now almost completely judicialized'.[134] Hence, in describing the character of *droit administratif* in 1908, Dicey rendered a more optimistic assessment:[135]

> To any person versed in the judicial history of England, it would therefore appear to be possible, or even probable, that *droit administratif* may ultimately, under the guidance of lawyers, become, through a course of evolution, as completely a branch of the law of France (even if we use the word 'law' in its very strictest sense) as Equity has for more than two centuries become an acknowledged branch of the law of England.

Nevertheless, Dicey ruled out the possibility of a similar development in England because he thought that the logic of *droit administratif*, which judges the relationship between citizen and state essentially different from the rule of private law, was simply incompatible with English constitutional tradition.[136]

I want to revive this line of inquiry in subsequent chapters by examining the doctrine of judicial deference towards administrative decisions. That doctrine requires judges to consider various reasons for deferring to administrative decisions, and to ensure that administrative decisions are in fact generally faithful to those values. This analysis provides a better foundation for understanding administrative authority and a principled way to revise our understanding of traditional constitutional theory in light of the modern administrative state. Nevertheless, it is also important to recognise that the doctrine of deference has problems of its own that require attention.[137] Although it has greatly benefited from the piecemeal method of the common

[134] Lawson, 'Dicey Revisited' (n 39 above), 111. See also, Dicey, *Introduction* (n 9 above) ch 12; AV Dicey, '*Droit Administratif* in Modern French Law' (1901) 17 *Law Quarterly Review* 302.

[135] Dicey, *Introduction* (n 9 above) 382–83.

[136] ibid 389–91.

[137] See, eg Michael Taggart, 'Outside Canadian Administrative Law' (1996) 46 *University of Toronto Law Journal* 649.

law, it needs to be further refined as a matter of principle. This more theoretical endeavour, which will be undertaken in the last chapter, reveals the normative basis of the interrelationship between courts and administrative institutions within complex constitutional arrangements. In other words, it reveals a possibility that Dicey rejected too hastily: the possibility of developing a constitutional theory that is capable of explaining and justifying how administrative decision-makers contribute to the modern democratic ideal of good governance.

3

The Legacy of the Diceyan Dialectic

DESPITE ITS DRAWBACKS, Diceyan constitutionalism continues to exert a powerful influence over judicial review in the United Kingdom. The most telling testament to the resiliency of this paradigm is the fact that both friends and foes of the administrative state have been unable to articulate another model to rival it.[1] Instead, debates regarding judicial review have typically been characterised by reiterations of the Diceyan dialectic with little or no discussion about whether administrative officials have legitimate authority to interpret the law, whether judges have a constitutional duty to respect administrative decisions, and how that duty can be reconciled with the rule of law.[2]

While the persistence of Diceyan constitutionalism is problematic, it also has significant merits. One reason it remains so influential is that it conveys the compelling idea that legitimate governmental authority is constituted by law—it derives its legitimacy from the law as opposed to its sheer ability to exert its will over those subject to its decisions. Although Dicey did employ the notion of sovereignty, that authority was couched within a theory of constitutional law. Dicey maintained that parliamentary sovereignty was constituted by the legal interrelationship between democratic and aristocratic institutions, an arrangement he called 'democracy tempered by snobbishness'.[3] The consequence of this arrangement was that the Crown, Lords, and Commons could only produce binding legislation when they cooperated to issue statutes which were public, general, stable, and prospective

[1] P McAuslan, 'Administrative Law and Administrative Theory: The Dismal Performance of Administrative Lawyers' (1978) 9 *Cambrian Law Review* 40; RW Blackburn, 'Dicey and the Teaching of Public Law' [1985] *Public Law* 679, 687; C Harlow, 'Changing the Mindset: The Place of Theory in English Public Law' (1994) 14 *Oxford Journal of Legal Studies* 419.

[2] See generally, Christopher Forsyth (ed), *Judicial Review and the Constitution* (Oxford, Hart Publishing, 2000).

[3] AV Dicey, *Lectures on the Relation between Law and Public Opinion in England during the Nineteenth Century*, 2nd edn reissued with a preface by ECS Wade (London, Macmillan & Co Ltd, 1962) 57.

in character.[4] In addition, Dicey argued that disputes regarding the legality of government action and interpretation of parliamentary legislation were to be adjudicated by an independent judiciary. Taken together, these ideas express powerful and enduring sentiments about how legitimate authority is constituted by law, employs law to achieve political ends, and is held to account for its decisions in the public domain.

Nevertheless, these insights are often confounded in practice. As I argued in Chapter two, the confusion associated with the Diceyan dialectic stems from the way in which Dicey married a positivist conception of law (which assigns sovereign, unreviewable legislative authority to Parliament) with a conception of natural law which reserves pride of place for the judiciary (which retains exclusive interpretive authority over the law). This confusion is acute in hard cases, where judges and lawyers tend to gravitate to one of the two poles in the Diceyan dialectic. On the one hand, judges sometimes lose their grip on the idea that administrative authority is constituted by law and substitute, in its place, the idea that administrative power is validated in a merely formal sense. This subtle slip has significant repercussions, because instead of ensuring that governmental decisions are fair and substantively justifiable in the light of constitutional values, judges truncate their role to inquire simply whether an administrative decision has an adequate statutory pedigree. Hence, this approach to judicial review results in 'submissive deference' towards administrative decisions, whereby judges 'submit to the intention of the legislature, on a positivist understanding of intention' by rubber stamping governmental decisions.[5]

On the other hand, judges who are inclined to impose more substantial rule of law constraints are drawn to heavy handed 'correctness review', whereby judges substitute their own interpretation of the law for an existing administrative decision whenever the two diverge on the merits. In the previous chapter, I argued that Dicey preferred this approach, which is corroborated by the prominent role he reserved for the judiciary in his constitutional theory.[6] But I also demonstrated how Dicey's political ideology caused him to promote a controversial conception of the rule of law, which actively opposed the emergence of the modern administrative state. Thus, Dicey simultaneously held that administrative law was constitutionally untenable, and recommended a robust form of judicial review which would stifle redistributive policies enacted by a democratically elected legislature.

[4] While Dicey did recognise the formal validity of Acts of Indemnity which operated retrospectively, he regarded this as an exceptional use of legislative power. See AV Dicey, *Introduction to the Study of the Constitution*, 10th edn (London, Macmillan & Co, 1959) 412–13. Furthermore, by requiring Acts of Indemnity to be validated through the regular parliamentary legislative process, the government still remained subject to law despite the fact that the statute compromised the aspect of prospectivity.

[5] David Dyzenhaus, 'The Politics of Deference: Judicial Review and Democracy' in Michael Taggart (ed), *The Province of Administrative Law* (Oxford, Hart Publishing, 1997) 279, 286.

[6] Dicey, *Introduction* (n 4 above) 188, 413–14.

In this chapter I will demonstrate how, despite Dicey's claim that administrative law is unconstitutional, the modern administrative state has become entrenched in the United Kingdom. In doing so, I will examine how the deep tension associated with the Diceyan dialectic—the normative tension between the constitutional principles of parliamentary sovereignty and the rule of law—has been perpetuated by the common law doctrines of jurisdictional error and, more recently, proportionality.

I. JURISDICTIONAL ERROR AND THE DICEYAN DIALECTIC

Before the introduction of the Human Rights Act 1998 (the HRA),[7] judicial scrutiny of administrative decisions in the United Kingdom revolved around the doctrine of jurisdictional error.[8] At bottom, the doctrine is inspired by a formal conception of the separation of powers, in which the legislature has exclusive jurisdiction over law-creation, the judiciary has exclusive jurisdiction over law-interpretation, and administrative officials are responsible for implementing law laid down by Parliament and interpreted by judges. Thus, the doctrine of jurisdictional error hinges on a distinction between 'jurisdictional' issues and the 'merits' of an administrative decision.[9] This distinction is formal because it assumes that the scope of judicial review is determined by sources of law which mark a particular issue as jurisdictional, obviating the need for judges to weigh relevant moral or political reasons that might otherwise justify judicial intervention.[10] Put differently, jurisdictional review is formal because it enables judges to determine the scope and intensity of judicial review by identifying an issue as jurisdictional instead of engaging in a more controversial assessment of whether the principles of political morality justify judicial intervention in a given case.

According to the doctrine of jurisdictional error, 'jurisdictional' issues are questions of law and, since legal interpretation is the exclusive province of the judiciary, should be determined exclusively by judges.[11] Therefore, when reviewing an administrative decision a judge is entitled to reassess

[7] Human Rights Act 1998 (UK), c 42.

[8] Amnon Rubinstein, *Jurisdiction and Illegality* (Oxford, Clarendon Press, 1965); HWR Wade and Christopher Forsyth, *Administrative Law*, 10th edn (Oxford, Oxford University Press, 2009) ch 7.

[9] Wade and Forsyth, *Administrative Law* (n 8 above) ch 8; Paul Craig, *Administrative Law*, 6th edn (London, Sweet & Maxwell, 2008) ch 14; Lord Woolf, Jeffrey Jowell and Andrew Le Sueur, *De Smith's Judicial Review*, 6th edn (London, Sweet & Maxwell, 2009) ch 4.

[10] See, eg F Schauer, 'Formalism' (1987) 97 *Yale Law Journal* 509; David Dyzenhaus, 'Formalism's Hollow Victory' (2002) *New Zealand Law Review* 526; Christopher Forsyth, 'Showing the Fly the Way Out of the Flybottle: The Value of Formalism and Conceptual Reasoning in Administrative Law' (2007) 66 *Cambridge Law Journal* 325.

[11] Traditionally, jurisdictional issues include questions like whether an administrative decision-making body has been properly constituted, whether it has embarked upon proper lines of inquiry, or whether its decision falls within the scope of its legal authority.

any jurisdictional assessments on a de novo basis. As Farwell LJ puts it in *R v Shoreditch Assessment Committee*, '[n]o tribunal of inferior jurisdiction can by its decision finally decide on the question of the existence or extent of such jurisdiction; such question is always subject to review by the High Court'.[12]

By contrast 'non-jurisdictional' issues or the 'merits' of an administrative decision are, by their nature, political; and since the legislature has sovereign authority in the political realm, it is entitled to delegate decision-making authority over political matters to administrative officials. Therefore, administrative officials are entitled to determine the outcome through the exercise of discretion, and judges are not entitled to intervene merely because they would have decided the matter differently. As Lord Denman puts it in *R v Bolton*, '[e]ven if [a] decision should on the merits be unwise or unjust, on these grounds we cannot reverse it'.[13]

The primary difficulty with this framework is that the analytical distinction between jurisdictional and non-jurisdictional issues has proven to be incoherent.[14] When introducing the topic of jurisdictional review in 1929 DM Gordon observed 'that in no branch of English law is there more confusion and conflict',[15] an assessment that has been echoed by every major administrative law treatise in the United Kingdom. William Wade and Christopher Forsyth observe candidly that judges 'can make the doctrine mean almost anything they wish by finding implied limitations in Acts of Parliament'.[16] Similarly, Lord Woolf, Jeffrey Jowell, and Andrew Le Sueur observe that jurisdictional review 'calls for analytical distinctions which have, as judicial review has developed, become difficult if not impossible to sustain'.[17] Likewise, Paul Craig points out that the case law reveals a variety of conflicting methods for jurisdictional review ranging from the 'collateral fact' approach, to 'limited review', to 'extensive review' of questions of law.[18] The chequered history of jurisdictional review has prompted at least one prominent legal theorist to observe that 'in so far as *theories* of jurisdiction and nullity draw chiefly on conceptual analysis for their contribution to doctrinal clarification, their practical value and philosophical status are alike open to question'.[19]

[12] *R v Shoreditch Assessment Committee* [1910] 2 KB 859, 880.

[13] *R v Bolton* (1841) 1 QB 66; [1835–42] All ER 71, 73.

[14] HW MacLauchlan, 'Judicial Review of Administrative Interpretations of Law: How Much Formalism Can We Reasonably Bear?' (1986) 36 *University of Toronto Law Journal* 343; TRS Allan, 'Doctrine and Theory in Administrative Law: An Elusive Quest for the Limits of Jurisdiction' [2003] *Public Law* 429.

[15] DM Gordon, 'The Relation of Facts to Jurisdiction (1929) 45 *Law Quarterly Review* 459.

[16] Wade and Forsyth, *Administrative Law* (n 8 above) 37.

[17] Woolf, Jowell, and Le Sueur, *Judicial Review* (n 9 above) 178.

[18] Craig, *Administrative Law* (n 9 above) c 14; Paul Craig, 'Ultra Vires and the Foundations of Judicial Review' (1998) 57 *Cambridge Law Journal* 63.

[19] Allan, 'Doctrine and Theory in Administrative Law' (n 14 above) 435.

In what follows, I will briefly examine the history of judicial review in the United Kingdom in order to demonstrate how the doctrinal incoherence of jurisdictional error is rooted in the Diceyan dialectic. A review of the case law shows that the judges have adopted conflicting conceptions of jurisdictional error.[20] The first approach, anchored by the principle of parliamentary sovereignty, asserts that judges can only enforce jurisdictional parameters established by positive facts about legislative intent so that administrative officials are subject to the rule of law only to the extent provided for by Parliament. Beyond these jurisdictional parameters, administrative officials are entitled to exercise a non-justiciable form of political discretion free from judicial scrutiny. Because this approach assumes that judges should submit to administrative decisions so long as those decisions are compatible with a positivist understanding of legislative intent,[21] I will refer to it as 'submissive deference' towards administrative decisions.[22]

The second approach, which recommends open-ended 'correctness review' of administrative decisions, is underpinned by a thicker conception of the rule of law and asserts that judges are entitled to enforce jurisdictional parameters which derive from a broader array of common law principles and values. While correctness review adopts a sanguine attitude towards judicial intervention, it continues to pay lip service to the principle of parliamentary sovereignty by asserting that Parliament relies implicitly upon judges to determine the content of the law through interpretation and adjudication. Like those judges who defer submissively to administrative decisions, judges who engage in correctness review claim that their primary concern is to identify whether Parliament in fact intended an issue to be 'jurisdictional'. However, because correctness review enables judges to draw upon an array of common law resources, it broadens the scope for judicial intervention significantly and reduces the latitude for administrative action.

[20] A privative clause is a statutory provision that purports to exclude or otherwise limit judicial review. While privative clauses may take on a variety of different forms (eg finality clauses, time limitation clauses, no *certiorari* clauses, subjective opinion clauses, etc) they all share the same general purpose: to consolidate the power of executive officials by preventing judicial interference with administrative decisions. See Craig, *Administrative Law* (n 9 above) ch 27.

[21] While I recognise that legal positivism has become a broad church, encompassing a variety of different views united by the belief that the existence of law is contingent upon social facts, deference as submission is most closely aligned with the philosophical views espoused by HLA Hart. Put simply, deference as submission assumes the following propositions: (1) the separation thesis, which hinges on an analytical distinction between 'law as it is' and 'law as it ought to be', is valid; (2) judges have a legal duty to enforce the law as it is, as opposed to how they believe it ought to be; (3) the content of the law is determined by linguistic conventions regarding the semantic properties of legal rules; and (4) in cases where the semantic properties of a legal rule are unsettled or uncertain, legal officials are empowered to determine the meaning of the law through an exercise of legislative discretion: HLA Hart, 'Positivism and the Separation of Law and Morals' (1958) 71 *Harvard Law Review* 593.

[22] Lord Reid famously referred to this approach in *Anisminic* as jurisdiction in the 'narrow and original sense' of the word. See *Anisminic Ltd v Foreign Compensation Commission* [1969] 2 AC 147, 171 (HL).

And, as the House of Lords decision in *Anisminic* shows, when correctness review is taken to its logical conclusion it collapses the distinction between jurisdictional issues and the merits altogether so that all questions of law are ultimately determined by judges.

Lord Sumner's opinion in *Rex v Nat Bell Liquors Ltd* provides an example of how the common law of judicial review conflates these two notions of jurisdictional error.[23] In that case, a company was fined CAN$200 and had its entire inventory of liquor seized when, contrary to provincial prohibition laws, one of its employees sold 12 bottles of whisky to a police informant. The company sought *certiorari* on the ground that the conviction could not be supported by the testimony of the police informant, who had a previous criminal record.

Writing for the Privy Council, Lord Sumner noted that the company's application was unusual because the conviction 'was on its face correct, sufficient and complete' and there was no allegation of fraud or bias.[24] He went so far as to say:[25]

> A justice who convicts without evidence is doing something that he ought not to do, but he is doing it as a judge, and if his jurisdiction to entertain the charge is not open to impeachment, his subsequent error, however grave, is a wrong exercise of a jurisdiction which he has, and not a usurpation of a jurisdiction which he has not ... To say that there is no jurisdiction to convict without evidence is the same thing as saying that there is jurisdiction if the decision is right, and none if it is wrong; or that jurisdiction at the outset of a case continues so long as the decision stands, but that, if it is set aside, the real conclusion is that there never was any jurisdiction at all.

Thus, Lord Sumner held that the Court could not reweigh the evidence because such an inquiry would intrude upon the merits.[26]

However, in the same judgment Lord Sumner also opined that the function of judicial review 'goes to two points: one is the area of the inferior jurisdiction and the qualifications and conditions of its exercise; the other is the observance of law in the course of its exercise'.[27] In saying this, he suggests that even if an administrative official is properly seised with jurisdiction at the outset of a hearing, a court is nevertheless entitled to scrutinise the legality of the hearing process and the substantive justification for the outcome. In 1957, the Court of Appeal cited Lord Sumner's opinion as authority for the proposition that a court is entitled to reach beyond a privative clause to correct any error of law or fact (jurisdictional or non-jurisdictional) so long as the error is apparent on the face of the record.[28] Thus,

[23] *Rex v Nat Bell Liquors Ltd* [1922] 2 AC 128 (JCPC).
[24] ibid 140–41.
[25] ibid 151–52.
[26] ibid 165.
[27] ibid 156.
[28] *R v Medical Appeal Tribunal, Ex parte Gilmore* [1957] 1 QB 574 (CA).

Lord Sumner's opinion simultaneously supports two conflicting conceptions of jurisdictional error. His decision recommends submissive deference, insofar as he conceives that the judicial role is limited to verifying whether Parliament has in fact given an administrative decision-maker power to decide a particular question; however, he also suggests that the court is entitled to ascertain whether the decision-maker observed the law during the course of that inquiry.

Because the doctrine of jurisdictional review incorporates conflicting models of judicial review, it is fundamentally incoherent or unstable.[29] Murray Hunt makes a similar observation when he says '[t]his is the contemporary manifestation of our Diceyan inheritance: a constitutional discourse that selectively invokes democratic positivism and liberal constitutionalism in order to justify or explain a particular [judicial] decision'.[30] In what follows, I will argue that Hunt accurately describes the Janus-faced nature of judicial review in the United Kingdom. One face—which is typified by cases like *Liversidge v Anderson*,[31] *Associated Provincial Picture Houses v Wednesbury Corporation*,[32] *Nakkuda Ali v Jayaratne*,[33] *R v Home Secretary, ex parte Hosenball*,[34] *Secretary of State for the Home Department v Rehman*,[35] *R (SB) v Governors of Denbigh High School*,[36] and *Belfast City Council v Miss Behavin' Ltd*[37]—asserts that administrative law is essentially the exercise of political discretion that can be immunised from judicial review by legislative fiat. The other face—which is typified by cases like *Roberts v Hopwood*,[38] *Ridge v Baldwin*,[39] *Anisminic Ltd v Foreign Compensation Commission*,[40] *Pearlman v Keepers and Governors of Harrow School*,[41] and *Huang v Secretary of State for the Home Department*[42]—asserts that the legality of administrative decisions is ultimately contingent

[29] Thus, it appears that the law of judicial review is vulnerable to what Ronald Dworkin calls the 'semantic sting': when lawyers and judges debate the proper ambit of judicial review, their disagreement appears at first glance to be about the meaning of central concepts like 'jurisdiction' or 'merits'. However, when these disagreements are unpacked, it appears that the participants are actually engaged in a more fundamental, theoretical disagreement about the nature of law. See Ronald Dworkin, *Law's Empire* (Oxford, Hart Publishing, 1998) ch 2.

[30] Murray Hunt, 'Sovereignty's Blight: Why Contemporary Public Law Needs the Concept of "Due Deference"' in Nicholas Bamforth and Peter Leyland (eds), *Public Law in a Multi-Layered Constitution* (Oxford, Hart Publishing, 2003) 337, 344.

[31] *Liversidge v Anderson* [1942] AC 206 (HL).

[32] *Associated Provincial Picture Houses v Wednesbury Corporation* [1948] 1 KB 223 (CA).

[33] *Nakkuda Ali v Jayaratne* [1951] AC 66 (JCPC).

[34] *R v Home Secretary, ex parte Hosenball* [1977] 1 WLR 766 (CA).

[35] *Secretary of State for the Home Department v Rehman* [2003] 1 AC 153 (HL).

[36] *R (SB) v Governors of Denbigh High School* [2007] 1 AC 100 (HL).

[37] *Belfast City Council v Miss Behavin' Ltd* [2007] 1 WLR 1420 (HL).

[38] *Roberts v Hopwood* [1925] AC 578 (HL).

[39] *Ridge v Baldwin* [1964] AC 40 (HL).

[40] *Anisminic* (n 22 above).

[41] *Pearlman v Keepers and Governors of Harrow School* [1979] QB 56 (CA).

[42] *Huang v Secretary of State for the Home Department* [2007] 2 AC 167 (HL).

upon whether they comport with judicial interpretation of the law, even when an administrative decision is protected by a privative clause.

A. Deference as Submission

An outline of submissive deference can be found in the writings of Lord Hewart, who in 1929 wrote a polemical critique of the administrative state.[43] Hewart, who had been both a politician and a judge, was a vocal critic of what he called administrative 'lawlessness'. Following Dicey, Hewart asserted that the rule of law required citizens and public officials to be subject to the ordinary law administered by judges; and the purpose of the rule of law was to preserve the bulwark of negative liberty which he thought had been created and sustained by the common law up until the twentieth century.[44] Hence, Hewart's response mirrored Dicey's—he argued that the administrative state had been constructed in a manner which undermined both parliamentary sovereignty and the rule of law.[45] Parliamentary sovereignty was undermined by the fact that the political party which controlled a majority of elected representatives could grant administrative officials broad discretionary powers which could be exercised without parliamentary oversight; and the rule of law was undermined by the fact that privative clauses allowed administrative officials to wield these powers without being supervised by the judiciary. Thus, Hewart concluded that administrative law 'is simply the exercise of arbitrary power in relation to certain matters which are specified or indicated by statute ... and left to the uncontrolled discretion of the Executive and its servants'.[46]

However, Hewart's assault on the administrative state was hypocritical. First, during his political career as a Member of Parliament, Solicitor-General, and Attorney-General from 1913–22, Hewart supported legislation which established the same type of broad administrative discretionary powers that he condemned in *The New Despotism*.[47] Secondly, in his capacity as Lord Chief Justice, Hewart wrote an opinion which stunted the reach of judicial review so that large swathes of administrative decisions were deemed to be immune from judicial oversight.[48] In *R v Legislative Committee of the*

[43] Lord Hewart, *The New Despotism* (London, Ernest Benn Ltd, 1929).

[44] ibid ch 2.

[45] ibid 17.

[46] ibid 46.

[47] Robert Jackson, *The Chief: The Biography of Gordon Hewart Lord Chief Justice of England 1922–40* (London, George G Harrap & Co Ltd, 1959) 214–16. Interestingly, it seems that Hewart himself returned to this view in his later years, because he recognised that the welfare state could not be realised without employing the delegated authority he had railed against in *The New Despotism*.

[48] David Dyzenhaus, *The Constitution of Law: Legality in a Time of Emergency* (Cambridge, Cambridge University Press, 2006) 123.

Church Assembly, Lord Hewart held that an administrative decision-maker must not only have the statutory authority to affect an individual's legal rights, but also have a 'superadded' duty to act judicially in order to be subject to judicial review.[49] This decision stood for the proposition that judges were powerless to check a wide array of 'administrative' functions which accompanied the rise of the welfare state.

This line of thinking culminated in *Nakkuda Ali v Jayaratne*, a case in which the Judicial Committee of the Privy Council held that a textile dealer was not entitled to a hearing prior to the revocation of his business licence.[50] In that case, the Court held that because the Controller of Textiles was not required to act 'judicially', he had no legal duty to hold a hearing. Thus, despite issuing grave warnings about the risk of arbitrary administrative power, Hewart's decision exacerbated that risk by establishing an analytical distinction which enabled judges to rubber-stamp administrative decisions even when those decisions lacked any semblance of fairness.

On this score, Hewart's assumption that administrative officials operate largely without the rule of law shares common ground with DM Gordon's 'pure' theory of jurisdictional review.[51] However, unlike Hewart, Gordon's theory was not driven by deep-seated suspicions regarding the constitutional legitimacy of the administrative state. Rather, Gordon's project was driven by his belief that the common law of judicial review could be rationalised along coherent, conceptual lines which could be determined without considering the procedural or substantive propriety of administrative action in context.[52] He argued that the law of judicial review would be improved if judges adhered to a consistent, categorical distinction between law and politics, which could be mapped onto the analytical distinctions familiar to judicial review like the distinction between judicial and administrative functions or the distinction between jurisdictional and non-jurisdictional issues.[53]

In order to discipline the practice of judicial review, Gordon proposed a 'pure' theory which revolved around a 'sane, coherent, and self-consistent theory of jurisdiction'.[54] Gordon claimed that as long as an administrative

[49] *R v Legislative Committee of the Church Assembly* [1928] 1 KB 411, 415.

[50] *Nakkuda Ali* (n 33 above). This decision has since gained notoriety as one of the low points in the history of judicial review in the United Kingdom. See HWR Wade, 'The Twilight of Natural Justice?' (1951) 67 *Law Quarterly Review* 103; Wade and Forsyth, *Administrative Law* (n 8 above) 411–12.

[51] K Roach, 'The Administrative Law Scholarship of DM Gordon' (1989) 34 *McGill Law Journal* 1; Paul Craig, *Administrative Law* (n 9 above) 441–44.

[52] Roach, 'The Administrative Law Scholarship of DM Gordon' (n 51 above) 2–6.

[53] ibid 34.

[54] DM Gordon, 'The Relation of Facts to Jurisdiction' (1929) 45 *Law Quarterly Review* 459, 460. Gordon built his theory upon a series of cases from the early nineteenth century that were sceptical of any attempt to review the process or substance of administrative decisions. See, eg *Brittain v Kinnaird* (1819) 1 B & B 432; *Cave v Mountain* (1840) 1 Mon & G 257; *R v Bolton* [1841] 1 QB 66; *R v Rotherham (Inhabitants)* [1842] 3 QB 776; *R v Buckinghamshire JJ* [1843] 3 QB 800.

official was empowered by statute to decide a particular matter, her decision should be treated as conclusive regardless of whether the decision was fair or justifiable. Gordon argued that, by virtue of its sovereign authority, Parliament alone is entitled to create legal rights and obligations and delegate fragments of that power to administrative officials. In doing so, Parliament delegates *complete* adjudicative and remedial authority to the administrative agency.[55] Once an administrative official's jurisdiction or 'capacity to take cognisance' of an issue has been established, she cannot lose jurisdiction by acting unfairly or committing a substantive error of judgement. Since all decision-makers (including superior courts) are fallible, Gordon claims that it is futile to speak of standards of correctness because 'there is no means of dealing with facts in the absolute, and the legislature knows this'.[56] Hence, the best the common law can achieve is finality, whereby '[a]n untrue finding must be just as conclusive as a true one'.[57]

In effect, Gordon's theory treats administrative officials as mini-sovereigns that project their unconstrained will within the scope of their statutory mandate. Thus, he claims that administrative tribunals 'are not concerned with pre-existing rights and liabilities, but themselves create the rights and liabilities that they enforce'; and that 'the discretion of an "administrative" tribunal, as opposed to judicial discretion, is a "pure", "complete", or "unfettered" discretion'.[58] Since there are no pre-existing rights and liabilities in the administrative realm, a party has no legal rights—they can only be disappointed, but not injured, by an administrative decision.[59] Gordon's theory thus leaves very little scope for judicial review, because no other institution is entitled to scrutinise the process or substance of administrative action.[60]

Although Gordon's pure theory did not attract support from other scholars,[61] his approach to jurisdictional review is reflected in cases like

[55] Although Gordon acknowledges the possibility that Parliament might divide authority amongst different tribunals, he argues that this result should be avoided wherever possible because it results in inconvenience and inefficiency. See Gordon, 'The Relation of Facts to Jurisdiction' (n 54 above) 463–66.

[56] DM Gordon, 'Conditional or Contingent Jurisdiction of Tribunals' (1960) 1 *University of British Columbia Law Review* 185, 200. It is difficult to overestimate Gordon's enthusiasm for finality. Elsewhere he remarks that 'every tribunal with power to investigate an alleged offence is quite within its jurisdiction in finding the accused guilty, however complete his innocence'. See Gordon, 'The Relation of Facts to Jurisdiction' (n 54 above) 462.

[57] ibid.

[58] DM Gordon, '"Administrative" Tribunals and the Courts' (1933) 49 *Law Quarterly Review* 94, 107–8. For a similar distinction, see United Kingdom, *Committee on Ministers' Powers Report* (Cmd 4060) (London, HMSO, 1932) 73–81.

[59] ibid. See also DM Gordon, 'Case Comment' (1933) 11 *Canadian Bar Review* 510.

[60] DM Gordon, 'The Observance of Law as a Condition of Jurisdiction' (1931) 47 *Law Quarterly Review* 386.

[61] Stanley de Smith worried that Gordon's theory would reduce judicial review 'almost to the vanishing point'; Louis Jaffe characterised Gordon's theory as 'barrenly semantic'; and Wade and Forsyth reject Gordon's theory, because it ignores the judicial role in maintaining

Liversidge[62] and *Wednesbury*.[63] The issue in *Liversidge* concerned the legality of an executive detention order during wartime. In that case, the Emergency Powers (Defence) Act, 1939 empowered Cabinet to make such regulations 'as appear … to be necessary or expedient for securing the public safety, the defence of the realm, the maintenance of public order and the efficient prosecution of any war'.[64] Cabinet subsequently approved Regulation 18B of the Defence (General) Regulations, 1939, which stated:

> If the Secretary of State has reasonable cause to believe any person to be of hostile origin or associations or to have been recently concerned in acts prejudicial to the public safety or the defence of the realm or in the preparation or instigation of such acts and that by reason thereof it is necessary to exercise control over him, he may make an order against that person directing that he be detained.

Robert Liversidge was subsequently detained without charge after the Home Secretary deemed him to be a threat to public safety, and he sued for false imprisonment to compel the Home Secretary to provide 'reasonable cause' for his detention.

However, the House of Lords held that even though the statute required the Home Secretary to have reasons for issuing the order, neither the statute nor the regulation entitled the Court to discover what those reasons were. Viscount Maugham, who wrote the lead judgment for the majority, rejected Liversidge's argument that the Court ought to interpret Regulation 18B in light of a common law presumption which favoured liberty, saying that 'we should prefer a construction which will carry into effect the plain intention of those responsible for the Order in Council rather than one which will defeat that intention'.[65] He held that the regulation gave the Home Secretary unreviewable discretionary power to detain Liversidge, saying:[66]

> I cannot myself believe that those responsible for the Order in Council could have contemplated for a moment the possibility of the action of the Secretary of State being subject to the discussion, criticism and control of a judge in a court of law.

Viscount Maugham buttressed this point by noting that the Home Secretary was not required to act 'judicially'—he could receive hearsay evidence, was not required to give notice, and did not have any duty to respond to objections to his order. Moreover, because the Home Secretary had to assess classified information, it would be dangerous for the Court to examine the basis

'constitutional fundamentals'. See SA de Smith, *Judicial Review of Administrative Action*, 3rd edn (London, Stevens & Sons Ltd, 1973) 98; L Jaffe, 'Judicial Review: Constitutional and Jurisdictional Fact' (1957) 70 *Harvard Law Review* 953, 961–63; Wade and Forsyth, *Administrative Law* (n 8 above) 300–301.

62 *Liversidge* (n 31 above).
63 *Wednesbury* (n 32 above).
64 Emergency Powers (Defence) Act 1939 (UK), 2 & 3 Geo VI, c 62, s 1.
65 *Liversidge* (n 31 above) 219.
66 ibid 220.

for the order. Finally, any lingering concerns about the legality of the Home Secretary's decision were assuaged by the fact that the Home Secretary was a member of the Cabinet, responsible directly to Parliament on matters of state security. Thus, Viscount Maugham upheld the order merely because the Home Secretary had stipulated he had reasonable grounds for issuing it. So even though the Home Secretary did not give any reasons or supporting evidence for the detention order, Viscount Maugham invoked the maxim *omnia esse rite acta*—'all acts are presumed to have been rightly and regularly performed'.[67]

A similar approach is employed in *Wednesbury*,[68] a case concerning the legality of a licence condition imposed by a municipal council. The condition prohibited a cinema from admitting children under the age of 15 to Sunday performances. The owner sought judicial review, but Lord Greene rejected the owner's argument saying '[t]he effect of the legislation is not to set up the court as an arbiter of the correctness of one view over another'.[69] Like Viscount Maugham in *Liversidge*, Lord Greene emphasised that the council was exercising a discretionary power, as opposed to a 'judicial' one, and therefore the Court could only interfere if the council had 'contravened the law'.[70] He then stated:[71]

> a person entrusted with a discretion must … direct himself properly in law. He must call his own attention to the matters which he is bound to consider. He must exclude from his consideration matters which are irrelevant to what he has to consider. If he does not obey those rules, he may truly be said … to be acting 'unreasonably.' Similarly, there may be something so absurd that no sensible person could ever dream that it lay within the powers of the authority.

In order to illustrate his point, Lord Greene cited the example of a 'red haired teacher, dismissed because she has red hair' in order to clarify the level of absurdity required to justify judicial intervention. Thus, he concluded that 'once it is conceded … that the particular subject-matter dealt with by this condition was one which it was competent for the authority to consider, there, in my opinion, is an end of the case'.[72]

The main point is that even though both *Liversidge* and *Wednesbury* recognise that administrative authority is subject to the rule of law, both cases perceive it to be a relatively flimsy constraint that does not enable the court to scrutinise a particular administrative decision. In *Liversidge*, this meant that even though the statute expressly required the Home Secretary to have reasonable cause for detaining Liversidge, the Court could not require him

[67] ibid 224.
[68] *Wednesbury* (n 32 above).
[69] ibid 230–31.
[70] ibid 228.
[71] ibid 229.
[72] ibid 230.

to disclose his reasons for issuing the detention order; and although the Court in *Wednesbury* recognised that it could scrutinise the basis for an administrative decision, this meant that the Court would only intervene if the administrative decision was 'so absurd that no sensible person could ever dream that it lay within the powers of the authority'.[73] In either case, the approach to judicial review enables the government to establish what David Dyzenhaus calls 'grey holes' of legality: situations where the legal constraints on administrative action 'are so insubstantial that they pretty well permit government to do as it pleases'.[74]

B. Correctness Review

The second, conflicting approach to jurisdictional review holds that even though administrative officials have been empowered by Parliament to implement legislation, their decisions must comport with common law principles and values whose content is determined exclusively by the judiciary. The underlying assumption is that since judges are the guardians of the rule of law, they are entitled to intervene whenever an administrative decision deviates from judicial interpretation of what the law requires. Thus, this approach to judicial review assumes that judges are entitled to intervene even if the enabling statute purports to exclude judicial review altogether. In this respect, Byles J seems to support correctness review in *Cooper v Wandsworth Board of Works* when he asserts that 'although there are no positive words in a statute ... yet the justice of the common law will supply the omission of the legislature'.[75]

However, because judicial interpretation of the common law in the early twentieth century was strongly influenced by nineteenth-century political values, the notion of correctness review provided judges who were suspicious of Parliament's redistributive policies with means to oppose the operation of the administrative state. As I argued in the previous chapter, Dicey himself advocated this strategy. He believed that as long as judges had the final word on legal interpretation they could preserve the rule of law by interpreting new legislation narrowly so as to minimise the impact of legislative policy. Similarly, when judges began to grapple with the expansion of the administrative state during the first half of the twentieth century,

[73] *Wednesbury* (n 32 above) 229. See also *Council of Civil Service Unions v Minister for the Civil Service* [1985] AC 374, 410, where Lord Diplock declared that an administrative decision would only be quashed for *Wednesbury* unreasonableness where the decision 'is so outrageous in its defiance of logic or of accepted moral standards that no sensible person who had applied his mind to the question could have arrived at it'.

[74] Dyzenhaus, *The Constitution of Law* (n 48 above) 42.

[75] *Cooper v Wandsworth Board of Works* (1863) 14 CBNS 180, 194.

correctness review was sometimes employed to undermine administrative decisions because they believed the substance of those decisions was at odds with laissez-faire economics.[76]

For instance, when the House of Lords overturned the Poplar Borough Council's wage policy in *Roberts v Hopwood*, the Court invoked a rule of law justification. The issue in the case concerned section 62 of the Metropolis Management Act 1855, which gave borough councils power to pay their employees 'such salaries and wages the board ... may think fit'.[77] From 1 May 1920, the Poplar borough in London adopted a minimum wage of £4 a week for municipal employees in order to offset post-war inflation. However, even after inflation began to subside in 1921 the council kept the policy on the basis that it was the minimum wage the council ought to pay as a model employer. At the end of the fiscal year, the district auditor disallowed £5000 in wages on the ground that he deemed them to be excessive and therefore 'contrary to law'.[78] He then levied a surcharge on the borough councillors personally, seeking to recoup the money he thought had been distributed illegally as wages. The councillors sought judicial review, arguing that the enabling legislation enabled them to adopt such a wage policy.

The House of Lords held that the wages were illegal because the council's wage policy was tainted by jurisdictional error. One of the more interesting aspects of the decision is that, as in *Wednesbury*, the Court thought the council's statutory discretion had to be exercised reasonably even though the statute itself did not mention such a qualification. Thus, Lord Atkinson stated that '[m]any things are contrary to law though not prohibited by any statute'.[79] But unlike *Wednesbury*, the Court thought the reasonableness constraint had substantially more bite: it held that the rule of law required the council to adopt a wage policy based upon laissez-faire, free market principles. As Lord Wrenbury puts it:[80]

> Wages in a particular service are such sum as a reasonable person, guiding himself by an investigation of the current rate in fact found to be paid in the particular industry, and acting upon the principle that efficient service is better commanded by paying an efficient wage, would find to be the proper sum ... It is a figure which is not to be based upon or increased by motives of philanthropy nor even of generosity stripped of commercial considerations. It is such figure as is the reasonable pecuniary equivalent of the service rendered. Anything beyond this is not wages. It is an addition to wages, and is a gratuity.

Since the council had based its wage policy upon other considerations, Lord Wrenbury held it to be contrary to law and therefore it had been proper for

[76] John Griffiths, 'Judges in Politics: England' (1968) 3 *Government and Opposition* 485; JAG Griffiths, *The Politics of the Judiciary*, 5th edn (London, Fontana Press, 1997).

[77] Metropolis Management Act 1855 (UK), 18 & 19 Vict, c 120, s 62.

[78] Public Health Act 1875 (UK), 38 & 39 Vict, c 55, s 247.

[79] *Roberts* (n 38 above) 596.

[80] ibid 612.

the auditor to impose the surcharge. Lord Atkinson went further, saying that the council acted unreasonably because its policy was driven 'by some eccentric principles of socialistic philanthropy or by a feminist ambition to secure the equality of the sexes in the matter of wages'.[81]

But this line of cases also includes decisions like *Ridge v Baldwin*, which trumpet the value of fairness in an administrative context.[82] The case concerned a decision by the local watch committee of the Brighton Police to dismiss its Chief Constable. Prior to the committee's decision, Ridge and two other detectives were charged with conspiracy to obstruct the course of justice. At trial, Ridge was acquitted by the jury, but the two detectives were convicted. Nevertheless, during the sentencing hearing, the trial judge criticised Ridge for failing to provide professional and moral leadership to his fellow officers. Shortly after the trial, the watch committee unanimously dismissed Ridge under section 191(4) of the Municipal Corporations Act, which stated that the committee could suspend or dismiss 'any borough constable whom they think negligent in the discharge of his duty'.[83] Ridge sought a declaration that the committee's decision was void, arguing that the committee had exceeded its jurisdiction by failing to provide him with notice and an opportunity to respond.

The House of Lords' decision in *Ridge v Baldwin* is widely celebrated as a decision which establishes a common law foundation for an individual's right to fair process. In the leading opinion for the Court, Lord Reid assumed that there was no statutory requirement to comply with the principles of natural justice.[84] Nevertheless, he held that the committee had breached its common law duty to hold a hearing. On this point, Lord Reid held that there was 'an unbroken line of authority to the effect that an officer cannot lawfully be dismissed without first telling him what is alleged against him and hearing his defence or explanation'.[85] In addition, he rejected Lord Hewart's analytical distinction between judicial and administrative functions[86] and the *Nakkuda Ali* case, saying that the decision 'was given under a serious misapprehension of the effect of the older authorities and therefore cannot be regarded as authoritative'.[87] Thus, he concluded that the watch committee had exceeded its jurisdiction by failing to hold a hearing.[88]

[81] ibid 594. For further commentary on the decision, see P Fennell, '*Roberts v. Hopwood*: The Rule Against Socialism' (1986) 13 *Journal of Law & Society* 401.

[82] *Ridge v Baldwin* (n 39 above).

[83] Municipal Corporations Act 1882 45 & 46 Vict, c 50, s 191(4).

[84] *Ridge v Baldwin* (n 39 above) 64.

[85] ibid 66.

[86] ibid 75.

[87] ibid 79.

[88] Because Lord Reid concluded that the committee's decision was void, the clear inference is that he regarded breach of natural justice as a jurisdictional error. See Wade and Forsyth, *Administrative Law* (n 8 above) 417–18.

Despite the ebb and flow of jurisdictional error in the United Kingdom, one gets the sense that the tide was shifting in favour of correctness review by the mid-1950s. Early signs of this can be seen when the Court of Appeal in *Shaw* expanded judicial review to correct any error on the face of the record, a proposition that was later extended in *R v Medical Appeal Tribunal, ex parte Gilmore* to allow the Court to correct non-jurisdictional errors even when an administrative decision was protected by a privative clause.[89] This trend was also spurred onward by the Franks Committee Report which recommended that Parliament restrain the use of privative clauses, a recommendation that was later implemented by the Tribunals and Inquiries Act 1958 when Parliament repealed most privative clauses enacted prior to 1958.[90] These developments gave judges more confidence in asserting a robust supervisory role.[91] Consequently, when ECS Wade wrote the preface to the tenth edition of Dicey's *An Introduction to the Study of the Constitution* in 1959, he observed that '[t]wenty years ago [Dicey's] concept of the rule of law was challenged more vigorously than the principle of parliamentary sovereignty. To-day we find that position has been reversed'.[92]

Nevertheless, the formal justification for judicial review continued to be grounded in the principle of parliamentary sovereignty, even though judges conflated conflicting conceptions of legislative intent. The consequence of this rhetorical device was that judges could resort to either submissive deference or correctness review without having to confront deeper questions of political principle or regulatory context, and the doctrine of jurisdictional error lost much of its explanatory power.

Anisminic provides an excellent case study in this regard, because it shows how the House of Lords could simultaneously engage in correctness review while purporting to heed the will of Parliament. Even though the Foreign Compensation Act 1950 included a privative clause stating that any 'determination by the commission ... shall not be called into question in any court of law', the House of Lords overturned the Foreign Compensation Commission's decision on the basis that it had exceeded its jurisdiction by misconstruing an Order in Council.[93] Lord Reid famously observed:[94]

> It has sometimes been said that it is only where a tribunal acts without jurisdiction that its decision is a nullity. But in such cases the word 'jurisdiction' has been used in a very wide sense, and I have come to the conclusion that it is better not to use the term except in the narrow and original sense of the tribunal being entitled to enter on the inquiry in question. But there are many cases where, although

89 *Gilmore* (n 28 above).

90 Tribunals and Inquiries Act 1958 (UK), 6 & 7 Eliz II, c 66, s 11.

91 HWR Wade, *Administrative Law*, 2nd edn (Oxford, Clarendon Press, 1967) 84–93.

92 AV Dicey, *An Introduction to the Study of the Constitution*, 10th edn (London, MacMillan, 1959) cxciii.

93 *Anisminic* (n 40 above).

94 ibid 171, 173–74.

> the tribunal had jurisdiction to enter on the inquiry, it has done or failed to do something in the course of the inquiry which is of such a nature that its decision is a nullity. It may have given its decision in bad faith. It may have made a decision which it had no power to make. It may have failed in the course of the inquiry to comply with the requirements of natural justice. It may in perfect good faith have misconstrued the provisions giving it power to act so that it failed to deal with the question remitted to it and decided some question that was not remitted to it. It may have refused to take into account something which it was required to take into account. Or it may have based its decision on some matter which, under the provisions setting it up, it had no right to take into account. I do not intend this list to be exhaustive. But if it decides a question remitted to it for decision without committing any of these errors it is as much entitled to decide that question wrongly as it is to decide it rightly.

Lord Pearce similarly asserts that '[l]ack of jurisdiction may arise in various ways': failing to observe 'conditions precedent', issuing remedies that the tribunal 'has no jurisdiction to make', departing from the rules of natural justice, asking the wrong questions, and taking irrelevant considerations into account.[95] Such a broad characterisation of jurisdictional error explodes the distinction between jurisdictional issues and the merits altogether. If one adopts the logic of Lord Reid and Lord Pearce, there is no reason for judges to exercise any restraint at all when reviewing an administrative decision. So when Lord Reid states that 'the question is whether on a true construction of the Order the applicants did or did not have to prove anything with regard to successors in title',[96] he is boldly asserting that judges are entitled to run roughshod over an administrative decision any time they disagree with it.

II. JUDICIAL REVIEW AND PUBLIC LAW THEORY

Despite the chequered history of jurisdictional error, it is tempting to conclude that *Anisminic* ultimately resolved the doctrinal tension in favour of correctness review. However, subsequent developments show that *Anisminic*'s triumph is more myth than reality, because when either judges or academics attempt to articulate a basis for judicial review they continue to shuttle between submissive deference and correctness review in different regulatory contexts. Thus, while scholars in the textbook tradition report the triumph of correctness review, the claim appears to be a hasty generalisation because it ignores or discounts prominent examples of submissive deference which continued to surface in the post-*Anisminic* era. And while functionalist scholars argue that correctness review disregards the democratic legitimacy of the administrative state, they do not reject judicial review

[95] ibid 195.
[96] ibid 174.

outright. Consequently, functionalist scholars usually retain an ambiguous role for judges in their constitutional theory, but fail to articulate a normative rationale for that role for fear it might be exploited by judges attracted to correctness review. Hence, the debate about judicial review in the United Kingdom has gone stale: as the recent ultra vires debate demonstrates, scholarly discussions regarding the constitutional foundations of judicial review in the United Kingdom remain trapped by the Diceyan dialectic.

A. The Textbook Tradition

Despite the rapid expansion of the administrative state during the twentieth century, the textbook tradition in the United Kingdom continues to revolve around Diceyan constitutional theory.[97] Like Dicey and Gordon, writers in the textbook tradition are unified by the belief that the doctrine of jurisdictional error can be rationalised as unfolding logically from axiomatic principles. But unlike Gordon, these writers sympathise with Dicey's argument that the rule of law is best ensured when judges review administrative decisions according to a correctness standard.

The convergence of opinion amongst textbook writers regarding correctness review is best illustrated by their treatment of decisions like *Ridge v Baldwin* and *Anisminic*. The challenge in the wake of these decisions was to explain and justify the expansion of correctness review—to articulate a constitutional argument which justifies a decision to impose a legal duty to provide a hearing when the legislation failed to provide for such a duty, or to overturn an administrative decision protected by a privative clause.

William Wade's response to this challenge follows the lead of Dicey and the House Lords in *Anisminic*: while he attempts to straddle the dialectic between parliamentary sovereignty and the rule of law at a theoretical level, as a practical matter he prefers judges to have an open-ended licence for correctness review. While Wade acknowledges parliamentary sovereignty as the predominant constitutional principle, he is generally suspicious of the democratic process.[98] Thus, in his Hamlyn lectures Wade claims that the electoral process 'fails to provide for fair distribution of seats, for fair results in elections and for fair selection of candidates'.[99] Similar concerns pervade his assessment of the law-making process, which he claims is beholden to party factions, truncates parliamentary oversight, diminishes ministerial

[97] David Sugarman, 'Legal Theory, the Common Law Mind and the Making of the Textbook Tradition' in William Twining (ed), *Legal Theory and Common Law* (Oxford, Blackwell, 1986) 26; DJ Galligan, 'Judicial Review and the Textbook Writers' (1982) 2 *Oxford Journal of Legal Studies* 257.

[98] HWR Wade, 'The Basis of Legal Sovereignty' [1955] *Cambridge Law Journal* 172.

[99] HWR Wade, *Constitutional Fundamentals* (London, Stevens & Sons, 1980) 20.

responsibility, and produces substandard legislation.[100] These observations underlie Wade's conclusion that 'we have allowed the constitution to become an elective dictatorship'.[101]

In light of these deficiencies, Wade advocates a prominent role for judges. He argues that parliamentary sovereignty is ultimately contingent upon judicial recognition. Following Hans Kelsen and John Salmond, Wade argues that parliamentary sovereignty is the ultimate legal rule which validates subordinate laws but cannot validate itself. Thus, he concludes that the principle of parliamentary sovereignty 'lies in the keeping of the courts, and no Act of Parliament can take it from them'.[102] The implications of this conclusion are apparent in his famous claim that:[103]

> [a]ll law students are taught that Parliamentary sovereignty is absolute. But it is the judges who have the last word. If they interpret an Act to mean the opposite of what it says, it is their view which represents the law.

So while Wade derives the authority of legislation from the principle of parliamentary sovereignty, that principle depends upon what he calls the 'political fact' of judicial recognition.[104]

Similar themes permeate Wade's administrative law scholarship. According to Wade, 'the rule of law demands proper legal limits on the exercise of power', and those limits extend beyond the terms of the statute to include common law values like natural justice.[105] The justification for common law limits is that if judges fail to control administrative officials they would be free to exercise 'dictatorial'[106] or 'arbitrary' power.[107] In order to prevent this, Wade asserts that judges are entitled to quash an administrative decision 'if it breaks one of the many judge-made rules'.[108] However, the extent of judicial review contemplated by Wade is unlimited. Although he frequently asserts that there is a viable distinction between jurisdictional review and an appeal on the merits, the distinction quickly collapses as he sifts through the case law:[109] he argues the that the scope of jurisdictional review is unpredictable, because enabling legislation often does not indicate whether an issue should be treated as jurisdictional;[110] even if the impugned

[100] ibid 22–23. See also HWR Wade, *Administrative Law*, 3rd edn (Oxford, Clarendon Press, 1971) ch 1; Wade and Forsyth, *Administrative Law* (n 8 above) 24–27.

[101] ibid 23.

[102] Wade, 'The Basis of Legal Sovereignty' (n 98 above) 189.

[103] Wade, *Constitutional Fundamentals* (n 99 above) 65.

[104] Wade (n 102 above) 188.

[105] HWR Wade, *Administrative Law* (n 100 above) 51; Wade and Forsyth, *Administrative Law* (n 8 above) 18, 30–33.

[106] Wade, *Constitutional Fundamentals* (n 99 above) 65.

[107] Wade, *Administrative Law* (n 100 above) 6.

[108] ibid 1. See also Wade and Forsyth, *Administrative Law* (n 8 above) 5.

[109] ibid 53–55, 70–73.

[110] ibid 90.

error is non-jurisdictional, judges are entitled to intervene if the error is apparent on the face of the record;[111] and even if the error is one of fact (traditionally seen to be a non-jurisdictional error) Wade sees no reason to prevent judges from intervening.[112]

But the full extent of Wade's theory appears in his treatment of *Anisminic*. Even though he concedes that Parliament intended to exclude judicial review in that case,[113] he praises what he calls 'the wisdom of the judicial casuistry' by which the Court reversed the Commission's decision.[114] In his view, a privative clause which excludes judicial review is 'repugnant to a coherent legal system' and judges are entitled to reach beyond it 'by looking at what the intention of Parliament ought to be rather than at what it is'.[115] The corollary to this proposition, which Wade points out elsewhere, is that 'statutory tribunals have in effect been stripped of all power to give final decisions on points of law'.[116]

While Stanley de Smith agrees that the common law of judicial review had become 'fairly coherent' in the wake of *Anisminic*, he recognises that judicial application of those principles remained complex, conflicted, and contingent upon context.[117] Like Wade, de Smith traces the common law development of judicial review to a series of foundational decisions 'which have survived into the modern age and have been applied in entirely new situations'.[118] However, unlike Wade, de Smith is more inclined to highlight the erratic nature of judicial review. In the third edition of his book, published five years after *Anisminic*, he observes:[119]

> During the last few years judicial review has become less technical, less compartmentalised, more imaginative, but no easier to expound in a consecutive and coherent form. For the loosening of analytical concepts and the modification of the doctrine of binding precedent at the highest level has reduced legal certainty and left individual judges with a wider discretion to do what seems fair and reasonable in the circumstances of a particular case. And some concepts that used to be dominant (*e.g.* the principle that a duty to act judicially in accordance with natural justice arose only in the exercise of a judicial-type function) are not dead but cataleptic. When evoked they are apt to emerge disconcertingly from the tomb.

111 ibid 94–98.

112 ibid 97–98.

113 HWR Wade, 'Constitutional and Administrative Aspects of the Anisminic Case' (1969) 85 *Law Quarterly Review* 198, 199. See also Wade, *Constitutional Fundamentals* (n 99 above) 64.

114 Wade, 'Constitutional and Administrative Aspects' (n 113 above) 201.

115 ibid.

116 Wade, *Administrative Law* (n 100 above) 97.

117 SA de Smith, *Judicial Review of Administrative Action*, 3rd edn (London, Stevens & Sons, 1973) 18.

118 ibid 25.

119 ibid 38.

Thus, de Smith concludes that '[a]t bottom ... the problem of defining the concept of jurisdiction for the purposes of judicial review has been one of public policy rather than one of logic',[120] and that '[t]he rules of natural justice are not rigid norms of unchanging content ... [but] may vary according to context'.[121]

De Smith's contextual emphasis helps explain two decisions, both written by Lord Denning, during the post-*Anisminic* period. The first decision, *R v Home Secretary, ex parte Hosenball*, provides an example of submissive deference reminiscent of *Liversidge* and *Wednesbury*.[122] The issue in *Hosenball* concerned an order of the Home Secretary to deport Mark Hosenball, an American journalist who had published a provocative article regarding a domestic surveillance programme. The original deportation order alleged that Hosenball was a threat to public safety, but failed to provide any materials to support this allegation. So although Hosenball was given a hearing before a special advisory panel, he could not respond to the substance of the allegation. Accordingly, he sought judicial review on the ground that the Home Secretary had failed to comply with the principles of natural justice laid out in *Ridge v Baldwin*.

At the outset of his judgment, Lord Denning seemed to sympathise with Hosenball's plight. He noted that 'if this were a case in which the ordinary rules of natural justice were to be observed, some criticism could be directed upon it'.[123] However, he immediately qualified this statement by saying 'this is no ordinary case ... and our history shows that, when the state itself is endangered, our cherished freedoms may have to take second place'.[124] After citing *Liversidge*, Lord Denning stated it would be inappropriate for the Court to require the Home Secretary to state his reasons for issuing the order, because it would jeopardise confidential sources of information. But the most telling passages in Lord Denning's judgment concern the nature of judicial review in the context of national security.[125]

> There is a conflict here between the interests of national security on the one hand and the freedom of the individual on the other. The balance between these two is not for a court of law. It is for the Home Secretary. He is the person entrusted by Parliament with the task.

Lord Lane echoed this sentiment, stating that 'in the end it is the Secretary of State who must ... be trusted to speak the last word'.[126]

[120] ibid 98.
[121] ibid 141. See also SA de Smith, 'The Right to a Hearing in English Administrative Law' (1955) 68 *Harvard Law Review* 569, 581–96.
[122] *Hosenball* (n 34 above).
[123] ibid 778.
[124] ibid.
[125] ibid 783.
[126] ibid 786.

The second decision rendered by Lord Denning came only a year later in *Pearlman v Keepers and Governors of Harrow School.*[127] Under the Leasehold Reform Act 1967, Parliament gave tenants the right to purchase the freehold on favourable terms, so long as the rateable value of the freehold did not exceed £1,500. Sidney Pearlman wanted to purchase his leasehold property, but was barred by statute because its rateable value was £1,597. In order to purchase the property, Pearlman applied under the Housing Act 1974 to reduce the rateable value of the property to reflect the value of improvements he had made to the property. However, the County Court judge held that the central heating system Pearlman had installed was not a 'structural alteration, extension or addition' within the meaning of the Housing Act. Pearlman then sought judicial review, even though the Housing Act contained a privative clause stating that the decision of the County Court 'shall be final and conclusive'.

Despite the privative clause, the Court of Appeal quashed the decision on the ground that the County Court judge had misconstrued the provision. Lord Denning pointed out that even though the decision was protected by a privative clause 'certiorari can still issue for excess of jurisdiction, or for error of law on the face of the record'.[128] Moreover, he pointed out that the distinction between jurisdictional and non-jurisdictional issues was 'rapidly being eroded' after *Anisminic*, saying that '[s]o fine is the distinction that in truth the High Court has a choice before it whether to interfere with an inferior court on a point of law'. At that point, Lord Denning stated:[129]

> I would suggest that this distinction should now be discarded. The High Court has, and should have, jurisdiction to control the proceedings of inferior courts and tribunals by way of judicial review. When they go wrong in law, the High Court should have power to put them right ... The way to get things right is to hold thus: no court or tribunal has any jurisdiction to make an error of law on which the decision of the case depends. If it makes such an error, it goes outside its jurisdiction and certiorari will lie to correct it.

After considering the facts, Lord Denning found that the judge had erred in deciding that the heating system was not a 'structural alteration, extension or addition'; and since the outcome hinged upon that issue, the privative clause could not prevent the Court from overturning the decision.

Reading *Hosenball* and *Pearlman* in isolation, one might conclude that they exemplify results-oriented adjudication by a judge with a cavalier approach to judicial review. In this respect, de Smith's point about the importance of context is suggestive—the fact that Lord Denning defers submissively in a case regarding national security, but boldly employs correctness oversight on economic matters is consistent with trends from other

[127] *Pearlman* (n 41 above).
[128] ibid 68.
[129] ibid 70.

common law jurisdictions. But as I have shown throughout this chapter, the manner in which Lord Denning fudges the reasoning between *Hosenball* and *Pearlman* is the norm, not the exception, insofar as the doctrine of jurisdictional error is concerned. Even in the wake of *Anisminic*, *Hosenball* and *Pearlman* the law pertaining to judicial review was clearly unstable. In *South East Asia Fire Bricks Sdn Bhd v Non-Metallic Products Manufacturing Employees Union* the Judicial Committee of the Privy Council rejected Lord Denning's claim that the distinction between jurisdictional and non-jurisdictional issues was obsolete;[130] however, that same year Lord Diplock endorsed *Pearlman* by saying that '[t]he break-through made by *Anisminic* … was that, as respects administrative tribunals and authorities, the old distinction between errors of law that went to jurisdiction and errors of law that did not, was for practical purposes abolished'.[131] In the midst of this, Wade remarked that '[a]ll that can be said with certainty at the present stage is that there is a medley of contradictory opinions in the appellate courts and the conflict between the rival interpretations of *Anisminic* is unresolved'.[132]

Finally, even when the House of Lords attempted to clarify jurisdictional review in *R v Hull University Visitor, ex parte Page*, it spoke equivocally in favour of both submissive deference and correctness review.[133] That case concerned the legality of a decision by the University of Hull to dismiss Edgar Page, a senior lecturer in its Philosophy Department. According to the termination letter, Page was being dismissed for redundancy; however, the university statutes stated that no member of the teaching staff could be removed from office except for good cause. Page petitioned the Queen, who was visitor responsible for the university, to declare his termination to be void. When the Lord President of the Privy Council rejected his petition, Page applied for judicial review.

As in so many other cases, the House of Lords' decision in *Page* incorporates two different conceptions of jurisdictional error. On the one hand, *Page* represents the triumph of correctness review, because the Court unanimously endorses Lord Denning's suggestion in *Pearlman* that the judges are entitled to quash any administrative decision containing an error of law. Thus, Lord Browne-Wilkinson states that 'in general any error of law made by an administrative tribunal or inferior court in reaching its decision can be quashed for error of law',[134] and Lord Griffiths says that '[i]n the case of bodies other than courts, in so far as they are required to apply the law

[130] *South East Asia Fire Bricks Sdn Bhd v Non-Metallic Mineral Products Manufacturing Employees Union* [1981] AC 363 (JCPC).

[131] *In Re Racal Communications Ltd* [1981] AC 374, 383 (HL). See also *O'Reilly v Mackman* [1983] 2 AC 237, 279 (HL).

[132] William Wade, *Administrative Law*, 5th edn (Oxford, Clarendon Press, 1982) 266–67.

[133] *R v Hull University Visitor, ex parte Page* [1993] AC 682 (HL).

[134] ibid 702, 706 (Lord Slynn).

they are required to apply the law correctly'.[135] According to this logic, it appeared that the Court would proceed to determine whether the visitor had misconstrued the university statutes.

Nevertheless, the majority held that the visitor was entitled to apply 'domestic law' without regard for common law principles. In a key passage, Lord Browne-Wilkinson declares that:[136]

> the visitor is applying not the general law of the land but a peculiar, domestic law of which he is the sole arbiter and of which the courts have no cognisance. If the visitor has power under the regulating documents to enter into the adjudication of the dispute (i.e., is acting within his jurisdiction in the narrow sense) he cannot err in law in reaching this decision since the general law is not the applicable law. Therefore he cannot be acting ultra vires and unlawfully by applying his view of the domestic law in reaching his decision. The court has not jurisdiction either to say that he erred in his application of the general law (since the general law is not applicable to the decision) or to reach a contrary view as to the effect of the domestic law (since the visitor is the sole judge of such domestic law).

The point is that while on its face *Page* asserts that correctness review should apply to 'ordinary' administrative decisions, it relies upon the idea of submissive deference when explaining why Page was not entitled to *certiorari* on the facts. Thus, the Diceyan dialectic is perpetuated in *Page*: judges are entitled to engage in correctness review when reviewing 'ordinary' administrative decisions,[137] but defer submissively when reviewing the decisions of 'special' or 'domestic' tribunals.[138]

B. Functionalism and the Political Constitution

While the textbook tradition gravitates towards a Diceyan perspective of the administrative state, that perspective has been challenged by scholars writing in the 'functionalist' style.[139] Whereas textbook writers emphasise individualism and the importance of rule of law constraints on government, functionalism rejects the notion that individual interests are fundamentally at odds with the public interest. Put simply, the disagreement between functionalists and the textbook tradition involves a deeper debate over political values like liberty and equality—whereas textbook scholars subscribe to a

[135] ibid 693.

[136] ibid 702–3, 693–94 (Lord Griffiths).

[137] See, eg *Boddington v British Transport Police* [1999] 2 AC 143 (HL). However, as we saw in *Hosenball*, whether an administrative decision is 'ordinary' remains a controversial question.

[138] See, eg *R v Visitors to the Inns of Court, ex parte Calder* [1994] QB 1 (CA).

[139] Martin Loughlin, *Public Law and Political Theory* (Oxford, Clarendon Press, 1992) ch 6–7; Martin Loughlin, 'The Functionalist Style in Public Law' (2005) 55 *University of Toronto Law Journal* 361, 367, 378–82.

conception of negative liberty and regard the administrative state with fear and hostility, functionalists welcome the emergence of the administrative state as the progressive and liberating realisation of a society in which the state secures the well-being of its subjects, promotes social solidarity, coordinates behaviour, and formulates policy through law.

However, neither neo-Diceyans nor functionalists are apt to describe their disagreement in these terms. If anything, they often appear to be talking at cross purposes about the nature of law. Instead of isolating and defining legal concepts (eg 'sovereignty', 'rule of law', 'jurisdiction'), functionalist scholars attempt to re-establish important connections between law and the social sciences. In rejecting conceptual analysis, the functionalist approach aims to occupy empirical high ground by observing what law actually 'is' or 'does'[140] in order to critique the application of legal doctrines which undermine social policy objectives.[141]

This brief summary displays both the negative and positive elements within the functionalist style of public law.[142] The negative element, which tends to be the primary focus of functionalist scholarship, consists of exposing and eradicating 'the classical theological jurisprudence of concepts'.[143] In this respect, functionalism shares some common ground with utilitarians who debunked the notion that the state was necessarily constrained by 'natural rights',[144] as well as American jurists like Oliver Wendell Holmes Jr who famously derided conceptual analysis by saying '[t]he life of law has not been logic; it has been experience'.[145] This negative element is particularly critical of rule of law justifications for judicial review, because functionalists argue that the concept provides cover for conservative attacks

[140] Hence, functionalists restrict their inquiries to 'sociological jurisprudence' or manifestations of 'law-in-action' (ie what causes judges to arrive at particular decisions or how legal rules actually influence human behaviour) instead of entertaining more philosophical questions about the nature or essence of law or legal normativity. See, eg Felix Cohen, 'Transcendental Nonsense and the Functional Approach' (1935) 35 *Columbia Law Review* 809; Felix Cohen, 'The Problems of a Functional Jurisprudence' (1937) 1 *Modern Law Review* 5, 7–8; John Willis, 'Three Approaches to Administrative Law: The Judicial, the Conceptual, and the Functional' (1935) 1 *University of Toronto Law Journal* 53; John Willis, 'Statute Interpretation in a Nutshell' (1938) 16 *Canadian Bar Review* 1; Carol Harlow and Richard Rawlings, *Law and Administration*, 3rd edn (Cambridge, Cambridge University Press, 2009).

[141] Loughlin, *Public Law and Political Theory* (n 139 above) 105.

[142] David Dyzenhaus, 'The Left and the Question of Law' (2004) 17 *Canadian Journal of Law and Jurisprudence* 7.

[143] Cohen, 'Transcendental Nonsense and the Functional Approach' (n 140 above) 821.

[144] Loughlin, *Public Law and Political Theory* (n 139 above) ch 6.

[145] Oliver Wendell Holmes, Jr, *The Common Law* (Boston MA, Little, Brown & Company, 1949) 1. On the relationship between American jurisprudence and functionalism, see Loughlin, *Public Law and Political Theory* (n 139 above) ch 6; Carol Harlow and Richard Rawlings, *Law and Administration* (n 140 above) 32–33; Robert Gordon, 'Willis's American Counterparts: The Legal Realists' Defence of Administration' (2005) 55 *University of Toronto Law Journal* 405.

on public regulation.[146] Thus, when Ivor Jennings examined the influence of judicial review on public housing reform during the inter-war period, he prefaced his analysis by saying that

> [t]he 'Rule of Law' is an unsound analysis because it is based on false assumptions about administrative jurisdiction; and it is irrelevant because it assumes that the legal system which has to be regulated is the legal system of *laissez faire.*[147]

At a more concrete level, the negative element highlights the habitually erratic manner in which judges apply common law doctrines, which impedes the operation of the administrative state. Thus, functionalists frequently deride the concept of administrative 'jurisdiction' as a 'weasel word'[148] or 'comforting conceptualism',[149] because judges can expand or retract the meaning of jurisdictional error while maintaining the façade that they are vindicating parliamentary intent. John Willis's famous essay on statutory interpretation is a classic example of this critique: he illustrates how common law maxims of statutory interpretation enable judges to either adopt a broad or narrow reading of enabling legislation. But the main thrust of his argument is to show how this doctrinal rhetoric enables judges to undermine the implementation of important legislative reforms while purporting to uphold the rule of law.[150]

By contrast, the positive element in functionalism shifts attention away from abstract logic towards the democratic process and a practical assessment which aims to identify which institutions are best equipped to implement social policy.[151] Like Bentham, functionalists argue that the democratisation of the legislative branch yields social policies consistent with the maximisation of social welfare. However, unlike Bentham, the functionalist conception of democracy is not purely instrumental—it contains what Martin Loughlin calls an 'ethical' dimension which gives rise to some tension vis-à-vis its negative attitude towards judicial review.[152]

An example of this tension can be seen in the scholarship of JAG Griffith. The negative element is front and centre in his famous book, *The Politics*

[146] Harold Laski, 'Judicial Review of Social Policy in England: A Study of *Roberts v. Hopwood*' (1925–26) 39 *Harvard Law Review* 832; Harry Arthurs, 'Protection against Judicial Review' (1983) 43 *Revue du Barreau* 277.

[147] WI Jennings, 'The courts and administrative law—the experience of English housing legislation' (1936) 49 *Harvard Law Review* 426, 430.

[148] John Willis, 'Canadian Administrative Law in Retrospect' (1974) 24 *University of Toronto Law Journal* 225, 244.

[149] Bora Laskin, 'Certiorari to Labour Boards: The Apparent Futility of Privative Clauses' (1952) 30 *Canadian Bar Review* 986, 994.

[150] Willis, 'Statute Interpretation in a Nutshell' (n 140 above). With respect to statutory interpretation, functionalists assert a strong preference for a purposive interpretation; however they are sceptical whether judges possess either the practical resources or the personal inclination to undertake a genuinely purposeful approach.

[151] Willis, 'Three Approaches to Administrative Law' (n 140 above).

[152] Loughlin, *Public Law and Political Theory* (n 139 above) 119.

of the Judiciary.[153] By exposing the inconsistent manner in which judges exercise the power of judicial review, he challenges the assumption that judges are merely engaged in conceptual analysis or enforcing parliamentary intent. He argues that by tracking the 'creative function' of the judiciary one can unmask its true political character.[154] Thus, Griffith demonstrates how judges in the early twentieth century frequently invalidated expropriations of private property through compulsory purchase orders,[155] but were reluctant to intervene in cases where local authorities refused to provide public housing to the homeless.[156] Similarly, he shows how judges frequently turned a blind eye toward executive detention orders issued on national security grounds, but actively opposed trade union activity.[157] Griffith's point is not that judges, as a group, act in concert to promote a particular political agenda, but rather that individual judges act according to their own controversial conception of the public interest, which often fails to afford adequate respect for individual interests (in cases involving national security) or public welfare (in cases involving public housing and collective bargaining).[158]

This type of critique explains why Griffith is generally critical of judicial review relative to the democratic political process. Griffith argues that 'law is not and cannot be a substitute for politics',[159] and derides attempts to construct a grand theory of judicial review.[160] Instead, he urges political engagement to resolve important issues of social policy. In his view, 'the best we can do is to enlarge the areas for argument and discussion'[161] and 'to create situations in which groups of individuals may make their political claims and seek to persuade governments to accept them'.[162] Among other things, this means that disputes should be resolved by politicians who are accountable to the electorate, that access to information should be enlarged to 'force government out of secrecy and into the open', and that greater efforts be made to ensure freedom of the press.[163] In short, Griffith suggests that courts should retire from the field so as to enable democratic channels of accountability to correct abuses of public authority.

153 JAG Griffith, *The Politics of the Judiciary*, 5th edn (London, Fontana, 1997).

154 ibid 6–7. Griffith defines political disputes as 'those cases which arise out of controversial legislation or controversial action initiated by public authorities, or which touch important moral or social issues'.

155 ibid 103–4.

156 ibid 137–45.

157 ibid ch 3.

158 ibid 297.

159 JAG Griffith, 'The Political Constitution' (1979) 42 *Modern Law Review* 1, 16.

160 JAG Griffith, 'The Brave New World of Sir John Laws' (2000) 63 *Modern Law Review* 160.

161 Griffith, 'The Political Constitution' (n 159 above) 20.

162 ibid 18.

163 ibid 16.

But despite his trenchant criticism of judicial review, Griffith stops short of recommending its abolition. For example, after rehearsing his deconstruction of English case law in his Pritt Lecture, Griffith cautions that

> if, in light of all these decisions, we direct our efforts simply to diminishing the power of the courts, we shall find ourselves in no better case. Seeking to resist judicial authoritarianism, we shall find that we have merely increased executive authoritarianism.[164]

Similarly, although John Willis was sceptical of judicial modes of reasoning,[165] he still recognised '[a]n administrator is no less liable to err in applying standards of policy than a judge is to err in applying standards or law, and he should be equally liable to correction'.[166] At the time he made this statement, Willis and his fellow functionalists argued that a system of expert administrative courts could act as a sufficient corrective,[167] provided that the civil service adopted a culture which imbued judicial habits of mind.[168] But when these checks failed to materialise, functionalists developed a grudging acceptance of judicial review, provided that it was exercised with restraint.[169]

This ambivalence reveals that, despite its negative attitude towards overly abstract or conceptual accounts of the rule of law, functionalism nevertheless retains an interest in exploring how judicial review can be reconciled with democratic values.[170] However, because functionalist scholars adopt such a sceptical posture towards value-based reasoning while advancing the case against judicial review, they are often inhibited from developing an evaluative, constructive account of the interrelationship between legal institutions. The fact that functionalism continues to project this sense of ambivalence, rather than unmitigated hostility, towards judicial review holds out some hope that functionalism might yet be capable of being reconciled with the rule of law.[171]

164 JAG Griffith, *Administrative Law and the Judges: The Pritt Memorial Lecture 1978* (London, Haldane Society of Socialist Lawyers, 1978) 20. Earlier in the lecture, Griffith conceded that '[i]t is by no means clear to me what role would be played by the judiciary in a socialist society'. For similar comments see John Willis, 'Correspondence: More on the Nolan Case' (1951) 29 *Canadian Bar Review* 580, 584–85.

165 John Willis, 'The McRuer Report: Lawyers' Values and Civil Servants' Values' (1968) 18 *University of Toronto Law Journal* 351.

166 John Willis, 'Three Approaches to Administrative Law' (n 140 above) 80.

167 ibid. See also Willis, *The Parliamentary Powers of English Government Departments* (Cambridge MA, Harvard University Press, 1933).

168 William Robson, *Justice and Administrative Law*, 3rd edn (London, Stevens & Sons, 1951) ch 5.

169 Willis, 'Canadian Administrative Law in Retrospect' (n 148 above) 244–45. See also Michael Taggart, 'Prolegomenon to an Intellectual History of Administrative Law in the Twentieth Century: The Case of John Willis and Canadian Administrative Law' (2005) 43 *Osgoode Hall Law Journal* 223, 248–50.

170 See, eg Adam Tomkins, 'The Role of the Courts in the Political Constitution' (2010) 60 *University of Toronto Law Journal* 1.

171 David Dyzenhaus, 'The Logic of the Rule of Law: Lessons from Willis' (2005) 55 *University of Toronto Law Journal* 691, 707.

C. Recycling the Dialectic: The Ultra Vires Debate

Unfortunately, the only major debate regarding judicial review at the turn of the twenty-first century—the ultra vires debate—does not provide a point for engagement between the textbook tradition and functionalism. Instead, the debate is restricted to scholars within the textbook tradition who, despite disagreeing intensely about the rhetorical justification for judicial review, share much the same perspective regarding its proper scope and intensity. Hence, the ultra vires debate is hollow because even though the parties appear to be disagreeing about the constitutional fundamentals, both camps endorse the holding in *Anisminic* that judges should review administrative decisions according to a correctness standard.[172]

On the one hand, proponents of the modified ultra vires model of judicial review—Christopher Forsyth and Mark Elliott—assert that judicial review is justified so long as judges pay lip service to parliamentary sovereignty when engaging in correctness review.[173] Their argument does not rely upon the traditional assumption that jurisdictional limits on administrative action have been determined by Parliament; they recognise that judges have played a creative role in expanding the scope of judicial review.[174] Nevertheless, Forsyth and Elliott assert that the judiciary lacks the constitutional authority to set these parameters on their own because this would destabilise a constitutional order which reserves supreme law-making authority for Parliament. Thus, they assert that parliamentary sovereignty is the central principle of judicial review in the sense that (1) judges should heed express statutory provisions which restrain judicial review; and (2) when judges impose constraints which are not expressly mentioned in the statute, they should invoke the presumption that Parliament generally intends for administrative officials to abide by the rule of law.[175] By grounding the justification of judicial review in this way, the modified ultra vires model anticipates the objection that judicial review is undemocratic: their riposte is that when Parliament delegates authority to administrative officials, it simultaneously gives judges tacit authorisation to interpret legislation 'in conformity with the rule of law'.[176]

[172] NW Barber, 'The Academic Mythologians' (2001) 21 *Oxford Journal of Legal Studies* 369.

[173] See, eg Christopher Forsyth, 'Of Fig Leaves and Fairy Tales: The Ultra Vires Doctrine, the Sovereignty of Parliament and Judicial Review' in Christopher Forsyth (ed), *Judicial Review and the Constitution* (n 2 above); Mark Elliott, 'The Ultra Vires Doctrine in a Constitutional Setting: Still the Central Principle of Administrative Law' in Christopher Forsyth (ed), *Judicial Review and the Constitution* (n 2 above) 83; Mark Elliott, *The Constitutional Foundations of Judicial Review* (Oxford, Hart Publishing, 2001).

[174] Elliott, 'The Ultra Vires Doctrine' (n 173 above), 101–102; Elliott, *Constitutional Foundations* (n 173 above), 125–27.

[175] Christopher Forsyth, 'Heat and Light: A Plea for Reconciliation' in Forsyth (ed), *Judicial Review and the Constitution* (n 2 above), 396–97.

[176] Elliott, 'The Ultra Vires Doctrine in a Constitutional Setting' (n 173 above) 95.

While Forsyth and Elliott ascribe primacy to parliamentary sovereignty, they both concede that the scope and intensity of judicial review is ultimately determined by judges.[177] Moreover, despite their concern that judges lack a constitutional licence to impose these constraints directly, they welcome the fact that judges have upheld these principles in the face of express attempts by Parliament to exclude or restrict judicial review. Even though the House of Lords in *Anisminic* discounted an express privative clause, Elliott argues that the decision was correct because 'it is the function of the judiciary to ensure that, so far as possible, legislation is interpreted in a manner which is consistent with the rule of law'.[178] Likewise, Forsyth claims that one of the main virtues of the modified ultra vires model is that it gives judges a general licence to circumvent privative clauses in order to uphold the rule of law.[179] The practical consequence, as Paul Craig points out, is that the modified ultra vires theory is 'capable only of performing a residual role by implicitly legitimating what the courts have chosen to do'.[180]

On the other hand, proponents of the common law model of judicial review—like Paul Craig and Sir John Laws—argue that judges have their own, independent constitutional warrant to enforce common law limits on administrative action, so long as judicial enforcement of those principles is not expressly excluded by Parliament.[181] Instead of relying upon the background assumption that Parliament intends to comply with the rule of law, Craig argues that judges are entitled to enforce rule of law values as part of their inherent common law jurisdiction.[182] Nevertheless, it is apparent that the common law model shares substantial common ground with the modified ultra vires theory because they both agree that judges have the ultimate power to determine how common law principles should be interpreted and imposed. As Sir John Laws points out, the common law model can be easily reconciled with the decision in *Anisminic* because it gives judges the final word on the legality of administrative action: he notes that administrative 'jurisdiction' is a protean word whose meaning is ultimately determined by

[177] Elliott, *Constitutional Foundations* (n 173 above) 100–104.

[178] ibid 124–25. See also Elliott, 'The Ultra Vires Doctrine in a Constitutional Setting' (n 173 above) 102–105.

[179] Christopher Forsyth, 'Of Fig Leaves and Fairy Tales' (n 173 above) 35–40.

[180] Paul Craig, 'Ultra Vires and the Foundations of Judicial Review' in Forsyth (ed), *Judicial Review and the Constitution* (n 2 above) 61. Christopher Forsyth seems to concede this point when he states that '...there is some truth in the charge that the modified doctrine is without content in that it provides little guidance to the actual reach or intensity of judicial review in a particular area'. Forsyth, 'Heat and Light: A Plea for Reconciliation' (n 175 above) 408.

[181] Paul Craig, 'Competing Models of Judicial Review' [1999] *Public Law* 428, 429. For Sir John Laws's contribution to the debate, see John Laws, 'Illegality: The Problem of Jurisdiction' in Michael Supperstone, James Goudie, and SirPaul Walker (eds), *Judicial Review*, 4th edn (London, LexisNexis, 2010).

[182] ibid 429.

courts, which means that 'the judges have, in the last analysis, the power they say they have'.[183]

While the ultra vires debate raises a variety of issues—whether the logic of parliamentary sovereignty entails the modified ultra vires justification or ignores an 'undistributed' or 'excluded' middle; whether implied parliamentary intent provides a meaningful guide for the development of legal principles relating to judicial review; whether the historical reliance on a common law justification for judicial review is consistent with the ultra vires rationale, etc—it raises three particular points which are relevant to our current discussion.

First, the debate provides a striking reminder of the powerful legacy of the Diceyan dialectic in the United Kingdom. The point here is not merely that the abstract terms of reference in the ultra vires debate—parliamentary sovereignty and the rule of law—resonate strongly with Dicey's theory, but rather that the debate assumes that the institutional roles of Parliament as the supreme legislator and the judiciary as the exclusive interpreter of the law exhaust the field of legitimate legal authority under the constitution. Hence, the debate perpetuates the notion that there is no such thing as administrative law.

Secondly, despite the apparent differences between ultra vires theorists and their common law counterparts, the debate makes no practical difference insofar as the actual practice of judicial review is concerned. As NW Barber points out, '[i]t is a remarkable feature of the debate over the modified ultra vires doctrine that there is not one judicial decision, rule, or principle of administrative law over which the supporters and opponents of the doctrine disagree'.[184] The upshot is that, despite their differences, both camps endorse a sweeping form of correctness review which is the hallmark of the textbook tradition.[185]

Finally, because the debate is pitched at an abstract, conceptual level, the participants seem to discount the importance of contextual analysis in determining the proper scope and intensity of judicial review in any given case.[186] Because modified ultra vires theorists adopt such a malleable definition of implied parliamentary intent as the *sine qua non* for judicial review, that notion cannot serve as a meaningful guide for judges. Because neither the modified ultra vires model nor the common law model account adequately

[183] Laws, 'Illegality' (n 181 above) 91.

[184] Barber, 'The Academic Mythologians' (n 172 above) 372. See also TRS Allan, 'The Rule of Law as the Foundation of Judicial Review' in Forsyth (ed), *Judicial Review and the Constitution* (n 2 above) 413; Michael Taggart, 'Ultra Vires as Distraction' in Forsyth (ed), *Judicial Review and the Constitution* (n 2 above) 427; Andrew Halpin, 'The Theoretical Controversy Concerning Judicial Review' (2001) 64 *Modern Law Review* 500; Timothy Endicott, 'Constitutional Logic' (2003) 53 *University of Toronto Law Journal* 201, 212–13.

[185] Galligan, 'Judicial Review and the Textbook Writers' (n 97 above).

[186] TRS Allan, 'The Constitutional Foundations of Judicial Review: Conceptual Conundrum or Interpretative Inquiry' (2002) 61 *Cambridge Law Journal* 87.

for the contextual complexity and diversity of the administrative state, they cannot grapple meaningfully with important questions regarding the legitimate scope and intensity of judicial review in particular cases.[187]

III. PROPORTIONALITY AND JUDICIAL DEFERENCE

The criticism regarding the relevance of context in judicial review has been blunted to a degree by the emergence of proportionality analysis in the United Kingdom. Whereas jurisdictional review hinges on an abstract, conceptual distinction, proportionality analysis focuses attention on whether the justification for an administrative decision is proportionate to its practical impact. Instead of stipulating an issue under review as jurisdictional or non-jurisdictional in order to determine the proper approach to judicial review, proportionality review provides an analytical framework which asks (1) whether a policy objective is sufficiently important to justify limiting individual rights; (2) whether the means employed by the state is rationally connected to its objective; and (3) whether the means employed by the state impairs individual rights more than necessary under the circumstances.[188] Thus, proportionality review does not guarantee that individual rights will trump the public interest, but provides a methodology for weighing competing claims of policy and principle in a particular context. However, as we will see, the character of proportionality review remains largely contingent upon the manner in which it is implemented.

The concept of proportionality has ancient philosophical roots,[189] and its pedigree can be traced to Aristotle[190] through the works Cicero,[191]

[187] Allan, 'The Constitutional Foundations of Judicial Review' (n 186 above).

[188] See *De Freitas v Permanent Secretary of Ministry of Agriculture* [1999] 1 AC 69 (PC); Paul Craig, 'Unreasonableness and Proportionality in UK Law' in Evelyn Ellis (ed), *The Principle of Proportionality in the Laws of Europe* (Oxford, Hart Publishing, 1999) 85, 99–100; Tom Hickman, *Public Law after the Human Rights Act* (Oxford, Hart Publishing, 2010) 179.

[189] Eric Engle observes that '[t]he *theory* of proportionality appears to have arisen rapidly, almost spontaneously, in Aristotle's thought, springing like Athena fully armed from his head': Eric Engle, 'The History of the General Principle of Proportionality: An Overview' (2012) 10 *Dartmouth Law Journal* 1.

[190] Aristotle, *Nicomachean Ethics* (Oxford, Oxford University Press, 2009) Book V, 85–86: 'This, then, is what the just is—the proportional; the unjust is what violates the proportion. Hence one term becomes too great, the other too small, as indeed happens in practice; for the man who acts unjustly has too much, and the man who is unjustly treated too little, of what is good. In the case of evil the reverse is true; for the lesser evil is reckoned a good in comparison with the greater evil, since the lesser evil is rather to be chosen than the greater, and what is worthy of choice is good, and what is worthier of choice a greater good'.

[191] MT Cicero, 'On the Commonwealth' in CD Yonge (ed), *The Treatises of M.T. Cicero on the Nature of the Gods; on Divination; on Fate; on the Republic; on the Laws; and on Standing for the Consulship* (London, Henry G Bohn, 1853) 367–68: 'No war can be undertaken by a just and wise state, unless for faith or self-defence. This self-defence of the state is enough to ensure its perpetuity, and this perpetuity is what all patriots desire ... All wars, undertaken without a proper motive, are unjust. And no war can be reputed just, unless it be duly announced and proclaimed, and if it be not preceded by a rational demand for restitution'.

Justinian,[192] and Thomas Aquinas.[193] However, scholars generally attribute the modern origins of the doctrine to German administrative law in the late nineteenth century.[194] Over the next century, this notion developed into a principle of West German constitutional law,[195] and was subsequently adopted by the European Court of Justice,[196] the European Court of Human Rights,[197] the Canadian Supreme Court,[198] the New Zealand Court of Appeal[199] and Supreme Court,[200] the South African Constitutional Court,[201] and the Israeli Supreme Court.[202]

While the notion of proportionality review was initially welcomed by both judges and scholars in the United Kingdom, its implementation has

[192] Theodor Mommsen and Paul Krueger (eds), Alan Watson (trans), *The Digest of Justinian* (Philadelphia PA, University of Pennsylvania Press, 1985) 291: 'Those who do damage because they cannot otherwise defend themselves are blameless; for all laws and all legal systems allow one to use force to defend oneself against violence. But if in order to defend myself I throw a stone at my attacker and I hit not him but a passerby, I shall be liable under the *lex Acquilia*; for it is permitted only to use force against an attacker and even then only so far as is necessary for self-defense and not for revenge'.

[193] Thomas Aquinas, *Summa Theologica, Treatise on Law* Alfred Freddoso (trans) (South Bend IN, St Augustine's Press, 2009) at 54: '[E]verything that exists for the sake of an end must be such that its form is proportioned to that end—in the way that the form of a saw is appropriate for cutting. In addition, everything that is rectified and measured must have a form proportioned to its rule and measure'.

[194] Alec Stone and Jud Mathews, 'Proportionality Balancing and Global Constitutionalism' (2008) 47 *Columbia Journal of Transnational Law* 72, 97–111. However, the authors acknowledge that German criminal law doctrine incorporated a principle of proportionality with respect to proportionate punishment and the defence of necessity long beforehand.

[195] ibid 104–11. See also Georg Nolte, 'General Principles of German and European Administrative Law—A Comparison in Historical Perspective' (1994) 57 *Modern Law Review* 191.

[196] Stone and Mathews (n 194 above) 139–45. See also Jürgen Schwarze, *European Administrative Law*, revised edn (London, Sweet & Maxwell, 2006) ch 5.

[197] Stone and Mathews (n 194 above) 145–52. Early cases include *Handyside v United Kingdom* (1976) 24 European Court of Human Rights (Series A); *Dudgeon v United Kingdom* (1981) (Series A No 45) ECtHR; Interestingly, Stone and Mathews assert that Strasbourg's adoption of proportionality analysis 'was heavily conditioned by its confrontation with cases coming from the U.K., where the "*Wednesbury* reasonableness" test—a type of highly deferential, "rational basis" standard—governed applications for judicial review of government acts': ibid 147.

[198] *R v Oakes* [1986] 1 SCR 103. Although the Court did not cite any foreign authority for its proportionality analysis, it is fair to say that '[t]he formula presented in *Oakes* is so close to the German version ... that we can presume the Court was familiar with German doctrine'. Stone and Mathews, 'Proportionality Balancing and Global Constitutionalism' (n 194 above) 117.

[199] *Ministry of Transport v Noort* [1992] 3 NZLR 260 (CA); *Moonen v Film & Literature Board of Review* [2000] 2 NZLR 9 (CA).

[200] *Hansen v The Queen* [2007] 3 NZLR 1 (SC).

[201] *State v Makwanyane*, 1995 (3) SA 391 (CC); *State v Williams & Others* 1995 (3) SA 632 (CC). Proportionality analysis is now entrenched more explicitly by s 36(1) of the Constitution of the Republic of South Africa, Act No 108 of 1996.

[202] *United Mizrachi Bank Ltd v Migdal Cooperative Village* (CA 6821/93) [1995] IsrSC 49(4) 221; *Beit Sourik Village Council v Government of Israel* (HC 2056/04) [2004] IsrSC 58(5) 807. See also Aharon Barak, 'Proportional Effect: The Israeli Experience' (2007) 57 *University of Toronto Law Journal* 369.

been marked by the same instability that plagued the doctrine of jurisdictional error.[203] When Lord Diplock summarised the law of judicial review in 1985, he opined that

> further development on a case by case basis may ... in the course of time add further grounds [of review]. I have in mind particularly the possible adoption in the future of the principle of 'proportionality' which is recognised in the administrative law of the European Economic Community.[204]

At the time, these comments resonated with a broader human rights movement in which scholars[205] and judges[206] advocated for domestic incorporation of the European Convention on Human Rights.[207] They were also buttressed by a smattering of cases which implied that judicial scrutiny would be augmented in cases where the individual interests were particularly pressing.[208] For instance, when the House of Lords reviewed the Home Secretary's decision to deport an asylum seeker in *Bugdaycay*, it did not ask simply whether he had rendered a decision 'so absurd that no sensible person could ever dream that it lay within the powers of the authority';[209] instead, the Court held that the Home Secretary's decision should be subjected to 'the most anxious [judicial] scrutiny' commensurate with 'the gravity of the issue which the decision determines'.[210]

However, the same court later rejected the proportionality standard in *Brind*, when it upheld the Home Secretary's directive which prohibited direct, unedited transmission of radio and television interviews with members of terrorist organisations.[211] After deciding that the directive was not unreasonable in the *Wednesbury* sense, Lord Ackner held it would be inappropriate for the Court to require the Home Secretary to provide a proportionate justification.[212] He declared that

> [u]nless and until Parliament incorporates the Convention into domestic law ... there appears to me to be at present no basis upon which the proportionality doctrine applied by the European Court can be followed by the courts of this country.[213]

[203] Hunt, 'Sovereignty's Blight' (n 30 above).

[204] *Council of Civil Service Unions* (n 73 above) 410.

[205] See, eg Wade, *Constitutional Fundamentals* (n 99 above).

[206] See, eg Leslie Scarman, *English Law—The New Dimension* (London, Stevens, 1974).

[207] Hickman, *Public Law after the Human Rights Act* (n 188 above) ch 2.

[208] John Laws, '*Wednesbury*' in Christopher Forsyth and Ivan Hare (eds), *The Golden Metwand and the Crooked Cord: Essays on Public Law in Honour of Sir William Wade* (Oxford, Oxford University Press, 1998) 185.

[209] *Wednesbury* (n 32 above) 229.

[210] *R v Secretary of State for the Home Department, ex parte Bugdaycay* [1987] AC 514, 531 (HL) (Lord Bridge).

[211] *R v Secretary of State for the Home Department, ex parte Brind* [1991] 1 AC 696 (HL).

[212] *Convention for the Protection of Human Rights and Fundamental Freedoms*, 4 November 1950, 213 UNTS 221, 224 ETS 5, art 10.

[213] ibid 763.

Nevertheless, the idea was revived by the European Court of Human Rights and the British Parliament. In 1999, the European Court of Human Rights held in *Smith & Grady v United Kingdom* that the traditional *Wednesbury* standard of review was an inadequate remedy for Convention rights.[214] The claimants in that case had challenged a military policy which prohibited homosexuals from serving in the armed forces, on the ground that the policy violated the claimants' right to privacy under the European Convention. Following *Brind*, both the Divisional Court and the Court of Appeal dismissed the claim, because the claimants had failed to demonstrate that the policy was unreasonable in the *Wednesbury* sense, and there was no basis for proportionality review under domestic law.[215] However, the European Court of Human Rights disagreed, saying that the policy constituted a disproportionate infringement of the claimants' right to privacy.[216] More importantly, the Court held that the application of the *Wednesbury* standard by the House of Lords was ipso facto a violation of article 13 of the Convention, because it failed to provide claimants with an 'effective remedy before a national authority'.[217]

While *Smith and Grady* was winding its way to Strasbourg, Tony Blair's Labour government initiated a plan to 'bring human rights home' to the United Kingdom by incorporating the European Convention on Human Rights into domestic law.[218] And when the final text of the Human Rights Act 1998 came into force on 2 October 2000, claimants had domestic access to the same remedies that were available under the jurisprudence of the European Court of Human Rights.[219] Hence, in the wake of *Smith and Grady* and the implementation of the HRA, proportionality review became the preferred mode of judicial review in cases where it was alleged that government action had infringed fundamental rights.

Any lingering doubts on this score were put to rest in *R (Daly) v Secretary of State for the Home Department*, when the House of Lords held that proportionality review was both conceptually distinct from the *Wednesbury* test and the appropriate mode of review where fundamental rights were at stake.[220] That case concerned a policy directive from the Home Secretary which required prison officials to exclude prisoners while searching their

[214] *Smith and Grady v United Kingdom* (2000) 29 EHRR 493.

[215] *R v Ministry of Defence, ex parte Smith* [1996] QB 517 (CA).

[216] *Smith & Grady* (n 214 above) [87]–[112].

[217] ibid [129]–[139].

[218] When Lord Irvine introduced the Human Rights Act 1998 to Parliament for its Second Reading, he stated: 'This Bill will bring human rights home. People will be able to argue for their rights and claim their remedies under the Convention in any court or tribunal in the United Kingdom'. Hansard HL Deb col 1228 (3 November 2007). See also, Secretary of State for the Home Department, 'Rights Brought Home: The Human Rights Bill' (Cm 3782, 1997).

[219] Human Rights Act (n 7 above) ss 2 and 6–7. See also, *R (Quark Fishing Ltd) v Secretary of State for Foreign and Commonwealth Affairs* [2006] 1 AC 529 [33]–[34] (HL).

[220] *R (Daly) v Secretary of State for the Home Department* [2001] 2 AC 532 (HL).

privileged legal correspondence. The House of Lords held that the policy was unlawful, because it constituted a disproportionate infringement of the prisoners' common law right to communicate confidentially with their lawyer: the Court held that the policy was too broadly conceived, and that the government's objective of ensuring prison order and security could be achieved through less invasive means.[221] In doing so, the Court held that proportionality review was required at common law and was not necessarily contingent upon the operation of the Convention.[222] Nevertheless, some members of the Court suggested that even though proportionality analysis required a more rigorous form of judicial scrutiny, it did not entail a departure from the traditional parameters of judicial review.[223] Hence, while Lord Steyn conceded that 'the proportionality approach may ... sometimes yield different results' from the *Wednesbury* test, he emphasised that '[t]his does not mean that there has been a shift to merits review'[224] and concluded by saying '[i]n law context is everything'.[225] This phrase frames a difficult problem for judges: how can one ensure that an administrative decision is proportionate without reweighing the merits of the case?

The upshot of this is that, while *Daly* provides a common law basis for proportionality review, the implementation of that approach has been marred by confusion.[226] This has been further complicated by judicial and academic commentary which asserts that while administrative decisions must be 'proportionate' to their effect on individual rights, administrative officials should be afforded a 'margin of appreciation'[227] or a degree of 'due deference'.[228] Like proportionality review, the 'margin of appreciation' doctrine derives from continental administrative law,[229] but has been invoked by the European Court of Human Rights to help explain whether state action is compatible with Convention rights.[230] Whereas proportionality

[221] ibid [21].
[222] ibid [23].
[223] ibid [28].
[224] ibid.
[225] ibid.
[226] Nicholas Blake, 'Importing Proportionality: Clarification or Confusion' [2002] *European Human Rights Law Review* 9.
[227] S Singh, M Hunt, and M Dennetriou, 'Is There a Role for the "Margin of Appreciation" in National Law After the HRA?' [1999] *European Human Rights Law Review* 15; Tom Bingham, 'Incorporation of the ECHR: The Opportunity and Challenge' [1998] 2 *Jersey Law Review* 257.
[228] See, eg Murray Hunt, 'Judicial Review after the Human Rights Act' (1999) 2 *Queen Mary Westfield College Law Journal* 14; Hunt, 'Sovereignty's Blight' (n 30).
[229] RSt Macdonald, 'The Margin of Appreciation' in RSt Macdonald, F Matscher and H Petzold (eds), *The European System for the Protection of Human Rights* (London, Martinus Nijhoff Publishers, 1993) 83.
[230] While some rights under the Convention are absolute, like the absolute prohibition of torture under Article 3, many rights under the Convention are subject to limitations which are 'prescribed by' or 'in accordance with' the law and are demonstrably 'necessary in a democratic society.' See, eg Article 8 (right to privacy and family life), Article 9 (freedom of thought, conscience, and religion), Article 10 (freedom of expression), and Article 11 (freedom of assembly and association).

analysis provides judges with a framework to help determine whether an administrative decision constitutes a justifiable limitation on individual rights, the margin of appreciation doctrine is used to identify the limits of judicial intervention. It is fitting, then, that the margin of appreciation has been referred to as 'the other side of the principle of proportionality'.[231]

Put simply, the margin of appreciation doctrine holds that judges should allow state institutions (legislatures, courts, and executive officials) some latitude in determining how to balance Convention rights with policy objectives. This idea was stated most clearly in *Handyside v United Kingdom*, where the European Court of Human Rights held that 'the machinery of protection established by the Convention is subsidiary to the national systems safeguarding human rights', which means that the Convention gives Contracting States primary responsibility for securing human rights.[232] Accordingly, the Court held that the Convention 'leaves to Contracting states a margin of appreciation', which ensures that national institutions have some space to determine how to reconcile public policies with Convention rights.[233] Practically speaking, this means that instead of attempting to strike the correct balance between Convention rights and domestic policy de novo, the court will only intervene if a governmental decision exceeds the margin of appreciation, which expands or contracts depending on the relative importance of the right in question.[234] Thus conceived, the margin of appreciation doctrine recognises that state institutions have a legitimate role to play in articulating the proper balance between human rights and policy concerns under the Convention.

Similar themes crop up in case law from the United Kingdom during the same period in which judges were experimenting with proportionality review. For instance, in *R v DPP, ex parte Kebilene*, the House of Lords upheld a decision by the Director of Public Prosecutions to prosecute three individuals under section 16A of the Prevention of Terrorism (Temporary

[231] Yutaka Arai-Takahashi, *The Margin of Appreciation Doctrine and the Principle of Proportionality in the Jurisprudence of the ECHR* (Oxford, Intersentia, 2002) 14: 'It is possible to consider the application of the proportionality principle as the other side of the margin of appreciation. The more intense the standard of proportionality becomes, the narrower the margin allowed to national authorities. If a reasonable or fair balance is found, the national authorities are considered to remain within the bounds of appreciation'.

[232] *Handyside v United Kingdom* (Application No 5493/72) [48]. Further support for this proposition is provided by Article 1 of the Convention, which gives assigns primary responsibility for securing Convention rights to the Contracting States.

[233] ibid.

[234] *Informationsverein Letina v Austria* (1993) 17 EHRR 91 [35]; *Dudgeon v United Kingdom* (1981) 4 EHRR 149 [52]. See also Michael Hutchinson, 'The Margin of Appreciation Doctrine in the European Court of Human Rights' (1999) 48 *International and Comparative Law Quarterly* 638, 640; Tom Lewis, 'What not to Wear: Religious Rights, the European Court, and the Margin of Appreciation' (2007) 56 *International and Comparative Law Quarterly* 395, 398–401.

Provisions) Act 1989.[235] The accused challenged the Director's decision on the basis that, even though the Human Rights Act 1998 was not yet in force, it gave rise to a legitimate expectation that the Director would not render a decision which infringed Convention rights; and since section 16A imposed a reverse onus of proof which violated the presumption of innocence under Article 6(2) of the Convention, they argued that the Director's decision was unlawful. In his majority opinion, Lord Steyn upheld the Director's decision on the basis that 'absent dishonesty or *mala fides* or an exceptional circumstance, the decision of the DPP to consent to the prosecution of the Respondents is not amenable to judicial review'.[236] However, in his concurring judgment, Lord Hope suggested that the Court should adopt a doctrine of judicial deference:[237]

> In this area difficult choices may have to be made by the executive or the legislature between the rights of the individual and the needs of society. In some circumstances it will be appropriate for the courts to recognise that there is an area of judgment within which the judiciary will defer, on democratic grounds, to the considered opinion of the elected body or person whose act or decision is said to be incompatible with the Convention. This point is well made at p. 74, para. 3.21 of *Human Rights Law and Practice* (Butterworths, 1999), of which Lord Lester of Herne Hill Q.C. and Mr David Pannick Q.C. are the General Editors, where the area in which these choices may arise is conveniently and appropriately described as the 'discretionary area of judgment.'

This reasoning is echoed in obiter passages in later cases, passages which assert that judges should recognise a 'discretionary area of judgment'[238] or provide administrative officials with a 'degree or margin of deference'.[239]

However, the question of judicial deference remains a highly controversial proposition. On the one hand, Lord Justice Laws endorsed the doctrine of deference in *International Transport Roth GmbH v Secretary of State for the Home Department*, and even set out criteria to help judges implement it on a case-by-case basis.[240] On the other hand, Lord Hoffmann rejected the

[235] *R v Director of Prosecutions (ex parte Kebilene)* [2000] 2 AC 326 (HL).

[236] ibid 371.

[237] ibid 381.

[238] *R (Mahmood) v Secretary of State for the Home Department* [2001] 1 WLR 840 [38] (CA); *Brown v Stott* [2003] 1 AC 681, 703 (PC).

[239] *International Transport Roth GmbH v Secretary of State for the Home Department* [2003] QB 728, 761 (CA). See also *Poplar Housing and Regeneration Community Association Ltd v Donoghue* [2002] QB 48 [69] (CA).

[240] ibid [83]–[87]. In his opinion, Laws LJ asserts: (1) that Acts of Parliament merit greater judicial deference than executive decisions or subordinate measures, (2) that greater judicial deference is owed in cases where the Convention contemplates a balance between individual rights and policy interests, (3) that greater judicial deference is owed where the subject matter falls within the traditional constitutional responsibility of Parliament or the executive, and (4) that greater judicial deference is owed where the subject matter implicates the actual or potential expertise of Parliament or the executive.

notion of deference in *R (Prolife Alliance) v BBC*, saying that 'I do not think its overtones of servility, or perhaps gracious concession, are appropriate to describe what is happening'.[241] Thus, it seems that even though the practice of judicial review in the United Kingdom has changed since the introduction of the HRA,[242] significant questions remain about how best to implement proportionality analysis in a manner which is both sensitive to contextual nuance and demonstrates respect for administrative decisions.

A closer examination of the recent case law reveals that, while the emergency of proportionality and deference has affected the practice of judicial review, those revisions have been rather modest. Even though there is a broad consensus that administrative decisions which affect fundamental rights should be subject to proportionality review, the case law reveals two distinct approaches which resemble submissive deference and correctness review.

A. Proportionality and Submissive Deference

The first approach—which follows the path taken in *Liversidge*, *Wednesbury*, and *Hosenball*—is outlined in cases like *Secretary of State for the Home Department v Rehman*,[243] *R (Begum) v Denbigh High School*,[244] and *Belfast City Council v Miss Behavin' Ltd*.[245] That approach holds that so long as the legislature intends to delegate discretionary authority over the matter to an administrative official, judges cannot compel them to justify their decisions or scrutinise the soundness of those justifications.[246] That this approach to judicial review persists in the wake of the HRA is surprising, and suggests that the guarantee given in *Daly*—that administrative decisions which affect fundamental rights will be subjected to anxious scrutiny—remains precarious.

As in *Hosenball*, *Rehman* concerns the legality of a deportation order. The claimant, Shafiq Ur Rehman, was a Pakistani citizen who had a four-year visa to work in the United Kingdom as a religious minister. During this period, Rehman married and had two children born in the United Kingdom. However, when he applied for indefinite leave to remain in the United Kingdom, the Home Secretary refused on the ground that Rehman was suspected of being involved with an overseas terrorist organisation.

Rehman appealed the Home Secretary's decision to the Special Immigration Appeals Commission [SIAC]. At the hearing, the Home Secretary

241 *R (ProLife Alliance) v British Broadcasting Corporation* [2004] 1 AC 185 [75] (HL).
242 Human Rights Act (n 7 above).
243 *Rehman* (n 35 above).
244 *Denbigh High School* (n 36 above).
245 *Miss Behavin' Ltd* (n 37 above).
246 Hickman, *Public Law after the Human Rights Act* (n 188 above) c 8.

asserted that 'while Mr. Rehman and his United Kingdom-based followers are unlikely to carry out any acts of violence in this country, his activities directly support terrorism in the Indian subcontinent and are likely to continue unless he is deported'. However, SIAC rejected the claim that the Home Secretary was the exclusive arbiter of whether someone was a threat to national security.[247] After reviewing the government's classified evidence *in camera*, SIAC concluded that the Home Secretary had failed to establish 'to a high civil balance of probabilities' that Rehman was involved in terrorist activities. Furthermore, it held that the Home Secretary had erred in his interpretation of what constituted a threat to national security. The SIAC panel held that a person could be considered a threat to national security only if (1) 'he engages in, promotes, or encourages violent activity which is targeted at the United Kingdom, its system of government or its people' or (2) if the person is involved in terrorist activities directed at a foreign government that is 'likely to take reprisals against the United Kingdom which affect the security of the United Kingdom or of its nationals'.[248]

The House of Lords overturned the SIAC's decision on the basis that it had overreached its statutory mandate. With respect to the evidentiary issue, the Court conceded that the Home Secretary's decision had to be both reasonable and proportionate in light of the available evidence.[249] However, it held that it was inappropriate for SIAC to require the Home Secretary to prove its case against Rehman. More specifically, the Court held that the Home Secretary was 'entitled to have regard to the precautionary and preventative principles'.[250] In this respect, Lord Hoffmann thought the Home Secretary wielded non-justiciable discretionary power:[251]

> What is meant by 'national security' is a question of construction and therefore a question of law within the jurisdiction of the Commission, subject to appeal. But there is no difficulty about what 'national security' means. It is the security of the United Kingdom and its people. On the other hand, the question of whether something is 'in the interests' of national security is not a question of law. It is a matter of judgment and policy. Under the constitution of the United Kingdom and most other countries, decisions as to whether something is or is not in the interests of national security are not a matter for judicial decision. They are entrusted to the executive. ... Accordingly it seems to me that the Commission is not entitled to differ from the opinion of the Secretary of State on the question of whether, for example, the promotion of terrorism in a foreign country by a United Kingdom resident would be contrary to the interests of national security.

Later, in a postscript written after 11 September 2001, Lord Hoffmann stated that 'such decisions, with serious potential results for the community,

[247] *Secretary of State for the Home Department v Rehman* [1999] INLR 517.
[248] ibid 528.
[249] *Rehman* (n 35 above) [11], [22].
[250] ibid [22].
[251] ibid [50], [53].

require a legitimacy which can be conferred only by entrusting them to persons responsible to the community through the democratic process'.[252] Accordingly, the Court held that SIAC had erred in requiring the Home Secretary to prove the allegation. Practically speaking, this means that SIAC could only question the Home Secretary's interpretation if it was 'one which no reasonable minister advising the Crown could in the circumstances reasonably have held'.[253] Thus, the House of Lords employed the same basic approach to judicial review modelled in *Liversidge*, *Wednesbury*, and *Hosenball*.

Similarly, in *R (SB) v Headteacher and Governors of Denbigh High School* the House of Lords held that administrative reasons are irrelevant insofar as proportionality review is concerned. The issue in *Begum* concerned the legality of a high school's dress code policy. Beginning in 1993, the Denbigh High School in Luton consulted with parents, school staff members, the school board of governors, and the Imams of three local mosques in order to formulate a new dress code for its multi-cultural student population. The consultations aimed to devise a policy which would balance respect for Muslim students' religious beliefs with the policy of 'securing high and improving standards, serving the needs of a diverse community, promoting a positive sense of community identity and avoiding manifest disparities of wealth and style'.[254] Ultimately, the school adopted a dress code which permitted female students to wear a shalwar-kameeze (a loose fitting tunic with tapered trousers) and headscarf—a policy which complied with the general consensus expressed by local religious leaders. However, when Shabina Begum arrived at the school wearing a jilbab (a full length, loose-fitting dress), a school official informed her that she would not be admitted. When Begum insisted that the dress code infringed her right to manifest her religious beliefs under article 9(2) of Convention, the school again consulted with Muslim leaders. When the school reaffirmed its policy, Begum sought judicial review on the ground that the school had imposed a disproportionate limitation on her Convention right.

Although Begum lost at first instance, the Court of Appeal held in her favour.[255] In his lead judgment, Brooke LJ held that dress code policy constituted a prima facie limitation on Begum's freedom to manifest her religion and, therefore, the Court had a duty to ensure that the policy was proportionate or 'necessary in a democratic society'.[256] He held that the school's 'decision-making structure' had to demonstrate adequate regard for the fact that the dress code limited a fundamental right. Furthermore, he set

[252] ibid [62].
[253] ibid [54].
[254] ibid [6].
[255] *R (SB) v Governors of Denbigh High School* [2005] 2 All ER 396 (CA).
[256] ibid [74].

out a detailed set of six questions that the school officials should consider when formulating its dress code policy, questions which highlighted the fact that a Convention right was at stake.[257] When the inquiry was framed in this manner, it was clear that the school had not approached its decision in this manner; in Brooke LJ's words, '[n]obody who considered the issues … started from the premise that the claimant had a right which is recognised by English law, and that the onus lay on the school to justify its interference with that right'.[258]

The House of Lords reversed this decision on the ground that the Court of Appeal had been too demanding of school officials. While the Court was divided over whether the dress code infringed Begum's right to manifest her religious beliefs, they all agreed that the policy constituted a proportionate limitation. In his opinion, Lord Bingham held that the Court of Appeal had erred in requiring school officials to consider how the dress code would impact Begum's Convention rights, saying 'what matters in any case is the practical outcome, not the quality of the decision-making process that led to it'.[259] In his view, the dress code was 'fully justified' because the school 'had taken immense pains to devise a uniform policy which respected Muslim beliefs but did so in an inclusive, unthreatening and uncompetitive way'. Thus, he concluded that it would be 'irresponsible of any court, lacking the experience, background and detailed knowledge of the head teacher, staff and governors, to overrule their judgment on a matter as sensitive as this'.[260] In a similar vein, Lord Hoffmann stated that the power of judicial review

> does not entitle a court to say that a justifiable and proportionate restriction should be struck down because the decision-maker did not approach the question in the structured way in which a judge might have done. Head teachers and governors cannot be expected to make such decisions with textbooks on human rights law at their elbows.[261]

The important point is that even though the school had never considered whether its policy objectives were sufficiently important to limit Begum's right to religious freedom or whether those objectives might be achieved through less invasive means, the House of Lords nevertheless concluded that the policy was proportionate.

The last case in this trilogy, *Belfast City Council v Miss Behavin' Ltd*, reinforces the Court's holding in *Denbigh High School*. The case concerned

[257] ibid [75].
[258] ibid [76].
[259] ibid [31].
[260] ibid [34].
[261] ibid [68].

Miss Behavin's application for a licence to operate a sex shop in the centre of Belfast. The application was referred to the City's Health and Environmental Services Committee, which recommended that City Council refuse the licence on the ground that 'nil' was the appropriate number of sex shops for that particular neighbourhood. In its recommendation, the Committee indicated that it had considered the character of the locality, the proximity of public services or places of worship, as well as the presence of other shops which would be of interest to families or children. The Council adopted the Committee's recommendation and refused the licence. However, Miss Behavin' applied for judicial review on the grounds that the refusal infringed his rights to peaceful enjoyment of property and freedom of expression under the Convention.

As in *Denbigh High School*, the Court of Appeal in Northern Ireland held that the Council had acted unlawfully by failing to consider the impact its decision would have on Miss Behavin's Convention rights.[262] However, the House of Lords overturned the Court of Appeal's decision, and cited *Begum* as authority for its conclusion. In her concurring opinion, Baroness Hale held that a reviewing court should only assess the proportionality of the outcome, rather than scrutinise the Council's reasons for refusing the licence:[263]

> The role of the court in human rights adjudication is quite different from the role of the court in an ordinary judicial review of administrative action. In human rights adjudication, the court is concerned with whether the human rights of the claimant have in fact been infringed, not with whether the administrative decision-maker properly took them into account.

Thus, the Council's failure to recognise the relevance of the Convention was irrelevant. What mattered was whether the Court could imagine a plausible, Convention-friendly justification for refusing the licence. So instead of holding administrative officials to account meaningfully for their decisions, the *Rehman* line of cases enables administrative officials to ignore or discount the relevance of fundamental legal rights to their decision-making discourse.[264] This seems to be Lord Rodger's point when he states that 'even if they [the Council] had had regard to the applicant's article 10 right in formulating their decision, it would still have been the same'.[265]

[262] *In the Matter of an Application by Misbehavin' Limited for Judicial Review* [2005] NICA 35 [57]–[58] and [63].

[263] *Miss Behavin'* (n 37 above) [31].

[264] As Tom Hickman points out, 'there is no *requirement* for decision-makers to make decisions well. They can take their chances. A sloppy, ill-reasoned or hasty decision might be perfectly consistent with the public authorities' obligations under the Human Rights Act if it *happens* to be the case that the outcome of the decision does not infringe a Convention right': Hickman, *Public Law after the Human Rights Act* (n 207 above) 238.

[265] *Miss Behavin'* (n 37 above) [28].

B. Proportionality and Correctness Review

By contrast *Huang v Secretary of State for the Home Department* applies a more demanding approach—one similar in material respects to the correctness standard employed in *Anisminic* and *Pearlman*.[266] The issue in *Huang* concerned a decision to deport a Chinese citizen. The Home Secretary denied Huang's application to remain in the United Kingdom because Immigration Rules only allowed 'the admission of a parent, grandparent, or other dependent relative of any person present and settled in the United Kingdom' if the relative was a widow who was at least 65 years old. Hence, even though Huang's ex-husband, daughter, son-in-law and two grandsons were lawful residents, her application was refused because she was neither a widow nor over the age of 65 at the time of her application.[267] Huang appealed the decision on the basis that it was a disproportionate infringement of her right to respect for her family life under Article 8 of the Convention. While Huang's initial appeal was successful, the Immigration Appeal Tribunal overturned the adjudicator's decision on the ground that the Secretary's decision did not rise to the level of *Wednesbury* unreasonableness.

However, the House of Lords overturned the Tribunal's decision because its proportionality analysis was incorrect. Lord Bingham, who wrote the majority opinion, held that the *Wednesbury* standard was inappropriate, because it was too relaxed and provided inadequate protection for Huang's Convention rights. He held that the Tribunal should have undertaken a de novo assessment of all relevant factors:[268]

> The first task of the appellate immigration authority is to establish the relevant facts. These may well have changed since the original decision was made. In any event, particularly where the applicant has not been interviewed, the authority will be much better placed to investigate the facts, test the evidence, assess the sincerity of the applicant's evidence and the genuineness of his or her concerns and evaluate the nature and strength of the family bond in the particular case. It is important that the facts are explored, and summarised in the decision, with care, since they will always be important and often decisive.
>
> The authority will wish to consider and weigh all that tells in favour of the refusal of leave which is challenged, with particular reference to justification under article 8(2). … The giving of weight to factors such as these is not, in our opinion, aptly described as deference: it is performance of the ordinary judicial task of weighing up the competing considerations on each side and according appropriate weight to the judgment of a person with responsibility for a given subject matter and access to special sources of knowledge and advice. That is how any rational judicial decision-maker is likely to proceed.

[266] *Huang* (n 42 above).

[267] At the time of her application, Huang was separated from her husband, who was also a British citizen.

[268] *Huang* (n 42 above) [15]–[16].

The difference between the *Rehman* line of cases and *Huang* is stark. Whereas the first line of cases holds that an administrative decision should not be disturbed unless the outcome is patently incompatible with Convention rights, *Huang* holds that the appellate tribunal should conduct a de novo assessment of 'all that tells in favour' of an administrative decision. Accordingly, the Court in *Huang* held that the Tribunal erred in asking whether the Home Secretary's decision fell within a range of proportionate outcomes—it should have gone through the evidence and reweighed the facts and relevant law to assess whether the decision was, in its view, correct. Today *Huang* is cited as authority for the proposition that administrative decisions are not generally entitled to any special regard or 'deference', and that judges should generally reassess a decision which affects fundamental rights on a de novo basis.[269]

IV. CONCLUSION

This chapter demonstrates how the law of judicial review in the United Kingdom remains anchored to Diceyan constitutionalism. Within this paradigm, Parliament has exclusive authority within the political realm to legislate, while the judiciary has exclusive authority to interpret the law, and administrative officials operate within a sphere of discretionary political power bounded at the margins by law set down by Parliament and interpreted by judges. This framework helps explain why the doctrine of jurisdictional error and the doctrine of proportionality have been applied in such an erratic fashion. On the one hand, cases like *Liversidge v Anderson*, *Wednesbury*, and *Nakkuda Ali* illustrate how judges tend to defer submissively to administrative decisions when they perceive that the rule of law merely requires them to verify that Parliament in fact intended for an administrative official to decide a particular issue. However, this approach is problematic because it turns the practice of judicial review into a sham exercise. Instead of scrutinising and evaluating the legality of administrative decisions in a meaningful fashion, judges declare that administrative functions are not subject to judicial scrutiny,[270] administrative officials do not have to abide by principles of fairness,[271] or that administrative officials are not required to provide reasons for their decisions.[272] At best, this approach enables judges to intervene when an administrative decision is 'so absurd that no sensible person could ever dream that it law within the powers

[269] Hickman, *Public Law after the Human Rights Act* (n 207 above) ch 5.
[270] *R v Legislative Committee of the Church Assembly* (n 49 above).
[271] *Nakkuda Ali* (n 33 above).
[272] *Liversidge* (n 31 above).

of the authority',[273] but this constraint is relatively toothless. Instead of holding administrative officials to account for their decisions in public, the *Wednesbury* standard incentivises government secrecy because judges will only intervene if a claimant can prove that the decision was patently foolish or ridiculous.

On the other hand, decisions like *Roberts v Hopwood*, *Ridge v Baldwin*, *Anisminic*, and *Pearlman* assert that the rule of law entitles judges to quash an administrative decision whenever it deviates from their interpretation of what the law requires. In some cases, like *Ridge v Baldwin*, this approach is attractive because it enables judges to ensure that administrative officials abide by fundamental values like fairness and reasonableness; however, in other cases, like *Roberts v Hopwood*, it seems that even when administrative officials abide by these values, this approach gives judges too broad a licence to gainsay the merits of an administrative decision. And when this approach is taken to its logical conclusion, as in *Anisminic*, it seems that judges are asserting an interpretive monopoly over the law which is difficult to reconcile with democratic values which underpin the legitimacy of the constitutional order and the administrative state. Among other things, these democratic values suggest that no particular class of legal officials should have a monopoly on determining the substantive content of the law.

Nevertheless, the law of judicial review in the United Kingdom seems to be turning towards a more contextual approach to judicial review.[274] This transition has emerged with the introduction of the HRA and the emergence of proportionality analysis which asks judges to probe the justification for administrative decisions in cases involving fundamental rights. Despite this, it seems that old habits die hard: proportionality analysis still tends to shuttle between submissive deference and correctness review. In *Rehman* the House of Lords resurrected the ghost of *Liversidge* by stating that the SIAC had erred in requiring the Home Secretary to prove that Rehman was a threat to the national security of the United Kingdom—the Home Secretary's decision to deport Rehman could only be impugned if the claimant could prove that the decision was irrational in the *Wednesbury* sense.[275] By contrast, in *Huang* the Court held that the Immigration Appeal Tribunal should 'consider and weigh all that tells in favour' of the decision under review, meaning that a reviewing court is entitled to exercise a plenary form of de novo reassessment.[276]

[273] *Wednesbury* (n 32 above) 229.

[274] Thomas Poole, 'The Reformation of English Administrative Law' (2009) 68 *Cambridge Law Journal* 142.

[275] *Rehman* (n 35 above).

[276] *Huang* (n 42 above).

More recent developments suggest that there may be changes on the horizon. In *R (Cart) v Upper Tribunal* the Supreme Court considered whether and to what extent common law judges could review decisions made by the specialist Upper Tribunal under the Tribunals, Court and Enforcement Act 2007.[277] While both the Divisional Court and the Court of Appeal sought to resurrect the doctrine of jurisdictional error defined by the pre-*Anisminic* case law, the Supreme Court rejected this approach. After noting 'several objections' to reviving the distinction between jurisdictional and non-jurisdictional errors,[278] Baroness Hale extended the criteria for an appeal set out in the enabling legislation. Thus, judicial review would lie if 'the proposed appeal would raise some important point of principle or practice' or if 'some other compelling reason' was apparent on the record.[279] In seeking to articulate an approach to judicial review which was more restrained than the doctrine of jurisdictional error, she sought to reconcile two constitutional principles. The first principle concerned 'the relative autonomy which Parliament had invested the tribunals as a whole and the Upper Tribunal in particular'; the second concerned 'the constitutional role of the High Court as guardian of the standard of legality and due process'.[280] Thus, it seems that the Supreme Court in the United Kingdom is embarking on a new mission—to develop a framework for judicial review which avoids the incoherent tendencies of jurisdictional error and confronts the need for judicial restraint in light of administrative expertise, but nevertheless preserves space for independent scrutiny in order to uphold the rule of law.

In this respect, it would be fruitful to examine whether the doctrine of judicial deference which holds sway in other common law jurisdictions might be employed productively in the United Kingdom.[281] In the next

[277] *R (Cart) v The Upper Tribunal* [2011] UKSC 28.

[278] ibid [39].

[279] Tribunals, Courts and Enforcement Act 2007, s 13(6).

[280] *R (Cart)* (n 277 above) [34].

[281] See, eg Jeffrey Jowell, 'Judicial deference: servility, civility or institutional capacity' [2003] *Public Law* 592; Jeffrey Jowell, 'Judicial Deference and Human Rights: A Question of Competence' in Paul Craig and Richard Rawlings (eds), *Law and Administration in Europe: Essays in Honour of Carol Harlow* (Oxford, Oxford University Press, 2003) 67; Jeffrey Jowell and Jonathan Cooper, 'Introduction' in Jeffrey Jowell and Jonathan Cooper (eds), *Delivering Rights: How the Human Rights Act is Working* (Oxford, Hart Publishing, 2003); TRS Allan, 'Human Rights and Judicial Review: A Critique of "Due Deference"' (2006) 65 *Cambridge Law Journal* 671; Aileen Kavanagh, 'Deference or Defiance? The Limits of the Judicial Role in Constitutional Adjudication' in Grant Huscroft (ed), *Expounding the Constitution: Essays in Constitutional Theory* (Cambridge, Cambridge University Press, 2008) 194; Jeff King, 'Institutional Approaches to Judicial Restraint' (2008) 28 *Oxford Journal of Legal Studies* 409; Aileen Kavanagh, *Constitutional Review under the UK Human Rights Act* (Cambridge, Cambridge University Press, 2009) ch 7; Aileen Kavanagh, 'Defending Deference in Public Law and Constitutional Theory: A Reply to TRS Allan' (2010) 126 *Law Quarterly Review* 236; AiAleen Kavanagh, 'Judicial Restraint in the Pursuit of Justice' (2010) 60 *University of Toronto Law Journal* 23; TRS Allan, 'Deference, Defiance, and Doctrine: Defining the Limits of Judicial Review' (2010) 60 *University of Toronto Law Journal* 41.

two chapters, I engage in a comparative study of the doctrines of judicial deference which animate American and Canadian administrative law. This comparative analysis demonstrates that the issues identified in this chapter are not peculiar to the public law of the United Kingdom—they tap into fundamental problems associated with constitutionalism, judicial review, and administrative law throughout the common law world.

4

Constitutionalism, Judicial Restraint, and Administrative Law

> 'This rule recognises that, having regard to the great, complex, ever-folding exigencies of government, much which will seem unconstitutional to one man, or body of men, may reasonably not seem so to another; that the constitution often admits of different interpretations; that there is often a range of choice and judgment; that in such cases the constitution does not impose upon the legislature any one specific opinion, but leaves open this range of choice; and whatever choice is rational is constitutional.'[1]

IN CHAPTER ONE, I briefly outlined the different doctrinal frameworks for judicial review of administrative decisions employed in the United Kingdom, the United States of America, and Canada. While the doctrine of jurisdictional error in the United Kingdom reserves pride of place for the judiciary as the exclusive arbiter of interpretive disputes about law, the doctrine of deference in the United States and Canada holds that because administrative officials have legitimate authority to interpret the law, judges should not interfere with an administrative decision merely because they disagree with it—they should only intervene if the decision is unfair or unreasonable. In this chapter, I will examine the intellectual history which precipitated the movement toward a doctrine of deference in the United States.

As in the United Kingdom, the controversy regarding judicial review in the United States has deep roots in common law constitutionalism. Although Marshall CJ famously declared in *Marbury v Madison* that the Supreme Court had the power to strike down Acts of Congress, stating that '[i]t is emphatically the province and duty of the Judicial Department to say what the law is',[2] the Court did not invoke that power again until 1856 when it struck down the Missouri Compromise on the ground that it deprived slave owners of property without due process.[3] And while the common law did allow for judicial review of administrative decisions, the scope of that form

[1] James Thayer, 'The Origin and Scope of the American Doctrine of Constitutional Law' (1893) 7 *Harvard Law Review* 129, 144.

[2] *Marbury v Madison* 5 US 137, 177 (1803).

[3] *Dred Scott v Sandford* 60 US 393 (1856). While the Supreme Court did strike down State legislation during this period, its decisions were often ignored or flouted by State governments.

of review was sharply limited for most of the nineteenth century.[4] Thus, in 1868 the Supreme Court declared that judicial review of administrative decisions was governed by a

> general doctrine, that an officer to whom public duties are confided by law, is not subject to the control of the courts in the exercise of the judgment and discretion which the law reposes in him as part of his official functions.[5]

However, judicial review of both legislation and administrative decisions quickly gained prominence in the aftermath to the American Civil War.[6] During Reconstruction, the Supreme Court declared military tribunals unconstitutional,[7] struck down amendments to the oath of loyalty,[8] and invalidated legislation authorising the use of legal tender.[9] This trend persisted into the Gilded Age when the Court struck down the Civil Rights Act of 1875[10] and the federal income tax,[11] setting the stage for the infamous *Lochner* period in American constitutional law.[12]

Judicial activism also obstructed efforts to lay the legal foundation for the modern administrative state. In 1876 the Supreme Court upheld the constitutionality of Granger laws—State legislation establishing maximum rates which could be charged by businesses affected with the public interest—noting that 'courts ought not to declare [a statute] to be unconstitutional, unless it is clearly so'.[13] However, only 10 years later the Court reversed its course by striking down an Illinois Granger law on the ground it infringed federal jurisdiction over interstate commerce, which prompted Congress to establish the first modern administrative agency—the Interstate Commerce Commission—in 1887 and endow it with rate-making powers.[14] This trend continued in 1890, when the Court struck down State legislation

See Barry Friedman, 'The History of the Countermajoritarian Difficulty, Part One: The Road to Judicial Supremacy' (1998) 73 *New York University Law Review* 333, 386–404.

[4] Jerry Mashaw, 'Federal Administration and Administrative Law in the Gilded Age' (2010) 119 *Yale Law Journal* 1362, 1399–1402; Jerry Mashaw, *Creating the Administrative Constitution: The Lost One Hundred Years of American Administrative Law* (New Haven CT, Yale University Press, 2012) 245.

[5] *Gaines v Thompson* 74 US 347, 352 (1868).

[6] Barry Friedman, 'The History of the Countermajoritarian Difficulty, Part II: Reconstruction's Political Court' (2002) 91 *Georgetown Law Journal* 1, 7–9. This struggle culminated in the impeachment of President Johnson by the House of Representatives on 24 February 1868.

[7] *Ex parte Milligan* 71 US 2 (1866).

[8] *Ex parte Garland* 71 US 333 (1866); *Cummings v Missouri* 72 US 277 (1867).

[9] *Hepburn v Griswold* 75 US 603 (1868). Two years later the Court overruled *Hepburn* in *Knox v Lee* 79 US 457 (1870).

[10] *Civil Rights Cases* 109 US 3 (1883). Among other things, this decision gave constitutional cover to Jim Crow laws which the Court later upheld under the infamous 'separate but equal' doctrine in *Plessy v Ferguson* 163 US 537 (1896).

[11] *Pollock v Farmers' Loan & Trust Co* 157 US 429 (1895).

[12] *Allgeyer v Louisiana* 165 US 578 (1897) is generally cited as the beginning of the *Lochner* period and *West Coast Hotel Co v Parrish* 300 US 379 (1937) as its end point.

[13] *Munn v Illinois* 94 US 113, 123 (1877).

[14] *Wabash, St Louis & Pacific Railway Company v Illinois* 118 US 557 (1886).

establishing a railway commission on the ground that the due process and equal protection clauses of the Fourteenth Amendment required a de novo judicial assessment of applicable freight charges.[15] Finally, in 1898 the Supreme Court held that federal courts were entitled to review ICC rate decisions on a de novo basis so as to determine whether they were confiscatory within the meaning of the Fourteenth Amendment.[16] The upshot of all these developments is that the Supreme Court's constitutional jurisprudence regarding federalism,[17] the separation of powers,[18] liberty,[19] property rights,[20] and due process[21] was deeply conservative, in the sense that it

[15] *Chicago, Milwaukee and St Paul Railway Company v Minnesota* 134 US 418, 458 (1890). One commentator later noted that this decision marked 'a complete volte-face on the part of the Court that fourteen years before pronounced the decision in *Munn v Illinois*'. See Edward Corwin, 'The Supreme Court and the Fourteenth Amendment' (1909) 7 *Michigan Law Review* 643, 660.

[16] *Smyth v Ames* 169 US 466 (1898). See Gerard Henderson, 'Railway Valuation and the Courts' (1919) 33 *Harvard Law Review* 902.

[17] See, eg *Wabash, St Louis & Pacific Railway Company* (n 14 above); *Hammer v Dagenhart* 247 US 251 (1918) (federal legislation prohibiting interstate trade of goods produced in factories which employed children struck down on the ground it infringed State jurisdiction under the Tenth Amendment); *Bailey v Drexel Furniture Co* 259 US 20 (1922) (federal legislation imposing an excise tax on employers using child labour struck down on the ground it infringed State jurisdiction under the Tenth Amendment); *United States v Butler* 197 US 1 (1936) (federal legislation imposing taxes on firms processing agricultural products and redistributing those proceeds to farmers struck down on the ground it infringed State jurisdiction under the Tenth Amendment); *Carter v Carter Coal Company* 298 US 238 (1936) (federal legislation establishing an administrative commission to set employment standards for the coal industry struck down on the ground it infringed State jurisdiction under the Tenth Amendment).

[18] See, eg *Panama Refining Co v Ryan* 293 US 388 (1935) (federal legislation delegating executive rule-making authority struck down on the ground it infringed the separation of powers between the legislative and executive branches of government); *Schecter Poultry Corp v United States* 295 US 495 (1935) (federal legislation delegating executive rule-making authority to struck down on the grounds it violated the separation of powers between the legislative and executive branches of government and infringed State jurisdiction under the Tenth Amendment).

[19] See, eg *Lochner v New York* 198 US 45 (1905) (State legislation prescribing maximum hours of work struck down on the ground that it infringed the rights to liberty and due process protected by the Fourteenth Amendment); *Adair v United States* 208 US 161 (1908) (federal legislation prohibiting employers from discriminating against employees belonging to a labour union struck down on the ground that it infringed the rights to liberty, property, and due process protected by the Fifth Amendment); *Coppage v Kansas* 236 US 1 (1915) (State legislation prohibiting employers from discriminating against employees belonging to a labour union struck down on the ground that it infringed the rights to liberty, property, and due process protected by the Fourteenth Amendment); *Adkins v Children's Hospital* 261 US 525 (1923) (federal legislation establishing an administrative board to set minimum wages for women and children in the District of Columbia struck down on the ground it infringed the rights to liberty and due process protected by the Fifth Amendment).

[20] See, eg *Smyth* (n 16 above); *Ohio Valley Water Co v Ben Avon Borough* 253 US 287 (1920); *Louisville Joint Stock Land Bank v Radford* 295 US 555 (1935) (federal legislation providing foreclosure relief to farmers struck down on the ground it infringed the rights to property protected by the Fifth Amendment).

[21] See, eg *Chicago, Milwaukee and St Paul Railway Company* (n 15 above); *Smyth* (n 16 above); *Lochner* (n 19 above); *Adair* (n 19 above); *Coppage* (n 19 above); *Adkins* (n 19 above); *Ben Avon* (n 20 above).

preserved antebellum social mores regarding race relations and frustrated attempts by Congress and State legislatures to redistribute wealth, rein in monopolistic trade practices, improve conditions of employment, introduce collective bargaining regimes, and delegate authority to administrative officials to achieve these policy objectives.

However, judicial activism during the *Lochner* period was offset by a counter-movement of judicial restraint[22] that served as the inspiration for doctrinal reforms that took place in the wake of the New Deal,[23] including the doctrine of judicial deference towards administrative decisions.[24] This counter-movement was animated by a protestant conception of constitutionalism in which the task of interpreting the Constitution was not the exclusive domain of judiciary, but a responsibility shared with citizens, legislatures, and administrative officials. Thus, proponents of judicial restraint staked out a *via media* between the conflicting jurisprudential traditions anchored by Jeremy Bentham's positivist theory of legislative sovereignty (on the one hand) and William Blackstone's natural law theory of judicial supremacy over legal interpretation (on the other). Over the next 50 years, the idea of judicial restraint attracted prominent scholars and judges, ultimately culminating in the doctrine of deference in cases like *Chevron USA v Natural Resources Defense Council*.[25]

Put briefly, the intellectual foundation of judicial restraint rests on premises that are *democratic* (ordinary citizens and their political representatives are entitled to participate in decisions regarding matters of common concern, including the interpretation of constitutional values), *pragmatic* (democratic and legal decision-making processes should not be conceived as a means for discovering metaphysical truths or original intent, but rather as a means for facilitating intelligent, principled inquiries to resolve social disputes in light of experience), *contextual* (the constitutional or legal justification for

[22] See, eg Thayer, 'The Origin and Scope of Constitutional Law' (n 1 above). However, the notion of judicial restraint in American constitutional law clearly predates 1893. See, eg *Munn* (n 13 above); Thomas Cooley, *A Treatise on the Constitutional Limitations Which Rest upon the Legislative Power of the States of the American Union* (Boston, Little, Brown, and Company, 1868) 164; Friedman, 'The Road to Judicial Supremacy' (n 3 above); Friedman, 'Reconstruction's Political Court' (n 6 above) 53.

[23] See, eg Bruce Ackerman, *We the People: Transformations* (Cambridge, Belknap Press, 1998) 360–82. Ackerman argues that '[t]he Court's transformative opinions of the early 1940's have served as the functional equivalents of Article Five amendments, establishing fixed points for legal reasoning during the next era'. See also Barry Cushman, *Rethinking the New Deal Court: The Structure of a Constitutional Revolution* (Oxford, Oxford University Press, 1998); William Leuchtenburg, *The Supreme Court Reborn: The Constitutional Revolution in the Age of Roosevelt* (Oxford, Oxford University Press, 1996).

[24] Reuel Schiller, 'The Era of Deference: Courts, Expertise, and the Emergence of New Deal Administrative Law' (2007) 106 *Michigan Law Review* 399. See, eg *Gray v Powell* 314 US 402, 413 (1941); *Dobson v Commissioner* 320 US 489, 501 (1943); *National Labor Relations Board v Hearst* 322 US 111 (1944); *Skidmore v Swift & Co* 323 US 134, 139–40 (1944).

[25] *Chevron USA Inc v Natural Resources Defense Council, Inc* 467 US 837 (1984).

a governmental decision should be proportionate to its impact or practical consequences), and *functional* (primary decision-making responsibility should reside with officials who possess relevant experience or expertise regarding a particular social problem).[26] Thus, instead of perceiving the modern administrative state as destabilising the existing social order or an incorrigible threat to constitutional rights, proponents of judicial restraint argued that state intervention can advance constitutional values like freedom and equality through legislative reform and administrative action.

Nevertheless, proponents of judicial restraint recognised that the Constitution requires judicial review to ensure that governmental decisions are 'reasonable' as opposed to 'arbitrary'. This is an important point, because it shows that proponents of judicial restraint were not blindly advocating the abolition of judicial power per se, but rather advancing a more nuanced argument regarding the legitimate distribution of political power amongst legislative, executive, and judicial institutions. So instead of asking whether they agree with the substance of an administrative decision, all things considered, judges should instead ask whether the individuals affected by the decision had an opportunity to participate in the decision-making process and whether the decision-maker articulated a reasonable justification for the outcome.

I. CONSTITUTIONALISM AND JUDICIAL RESTRAINT

A. Democratic Constitutionalism

In 1884, one year before Dicey published the first edition of his constitutional law treatise, a Harvard law professor wrote a comment in *The Nation* regarding the function of judicial review in a constitutional democracy. Whereas Dicey had argued in favour of giving judges licence to construe statutes narrowly so as to preserve negative liberty,[27] James Bradley Thayer argued that the purpose of judicial review is not to declare 'the true construction of the Constitution', but to ascertain 'whether another department has acted unreasonably'.[28] This idea forms the foundation of 'the most influential essay ever written on American constitutional law',[29] which Thayer published in the *Harvard Law Review* in 1893.[30]

[26] John Willis, 'Three Approaches to Administrative Law: The Judicial, the Conceptual, and the Functional' (1935) 1 *University of Toronto Law Journal* 53.

[27] AV Dicey, *Introduction to the Study of the Constitution*, 10th edn (London, Macmillan & Co, 1959) 413–14.

[28] James B Thayer, 'Constitutionality of Legislation: The Precise Question for a Court' (1884) 38 *Nation* 314 (10 April 1884).

[29] Henry Monaghan, '*Marbury* and the Administrative State' (1983) 83 *Columbia Law Review* 1, 7.

[30] Thayer, 'The Origin and Scope of Constitutional Law' (n 1 above).

James Thayer was born into a family of modest means in rural Massachusetts. His father had been a newspaper editor who supported temperance and abolition, but abandoned his trade in 1838 after a pro-slavery mob burned down the offices of John Greenleaf Whittier, a poet and abolitionist editor of the *Pennsylvania Freeman* who was living with the Thayers in Philadelphia at the time.[31] The family resettled in Massachusetts, where Thayer's father took up the cultivation of silk worms and his finances declined. Nevertheless, James and his childhood friend, Chauncey Wright, both developed into promising students.[32] After graduating Phi Beta Kappa from Harvard College in 1852, where he lived with Wright and enrolled in many of the same courses together,[33] Thayer taught in a private school for two years.[34]

Thayer enrolled at Harvard Law School in 1854, and graduated at the top of his class in 1856.[35] The topic of his gold medal dissertation, 'The Right of Eminent Domain', examines the constitutional legitimacy of governmental decisions to expropriate private property for public purposes.[36] Thayer argues that the power of eminent domain is an inalienable right of the state.[37] While he acknowledges that this right materialises only when 'public exigencies demand it', he does not set out any necessary conditions for exercising it.[38] His primary concern is to address who should decide whether the public interest justifies state expropriation, stating that 'it will be enough for the present purpose to indicate by whom this question is to be decided, without entering upon the principles which should govern the decision'.[39] In this respect, Thayer notes that 'the State itself must decide, as the final and only judge' or, alternatively, delegate this power to administrative officials.[40]

Nevertheless, Thayer argues that the right of eminent domain is subject to constitutional limitations. In countries like England, Thayer asserts that issues regarding the scope of eminent domain 'are for statesmen and the Houses of Parliament, but not for the judges or for Westminster Hall'.[41]

[31] Jay Hook, 'A Brief Life of James Bradley Thayer' (1993) 88 *Northwestern University Law Review* 1.

[32] James Bradley Thayer, *Letters of Chauncey Wright: with some account of his life* (Cambridge, John Wilson and Son, 1878) ch 1.

[33] James Parker Hall, 'James Bradley Thayer' in William Draper Lewis (ed), *Great American Lawyers* (Philadelphia PA, John C Winston Company, 1909) 345, 347–48.

[34] David Rabban, *Law's History: American Legal Thought and the Transatlantic Turn to History* (Cambridge, Cambridge University Press, 2013) 40.

[35] Hook, 'A Brief Life' (n 31 above) 2.

[36] JB Thayer, 'The Right of Eminent Domain' (1856) 9 *The Monthly Law Reporter* (New Series) 241.

[37] ibid.

[38] ibid 246.

[39] ibid 248.

[40] ibid 248–49.

[41] ibid 242–43.

But in countries with a written constitution, he argues that 'it falls to the judiciary to declare all legislative acts void that come in conflict with that instrument, or overstep the limits which it assigns to the legislative branch'.[42] Thus, Thayer acknowledges that judicial intervention is warranted when a public official seeks 'to appropriate private property … under cover of a public exigency, which clearly has no existence'.[43] However, in cases where there is reasonable disagreement regarding the weight of the evidence, he states that 'the judiciary may not substitute their discretion for that of the legislature, nor exercise it at all in a matter entrusted to the sole discretion to another department'.[44]

This early outline of Thayer's views reveals a basic tension in his constitutional theory similar to the Diceyan dialectic. On the one hand, Thayer derives the right of eminent domain from the social need for sovereign legislative authority, which he says 'originates in a necessity of the nature of man'.[45] However, he also argues that a written constitution 'qualifies, explains, and enunciates [sovereign] rights and powers, and then entrusts this high charter to the guardianship of its judicial representatives'.[46] Nevertheless, Dicey and Thayer offer contrasting strategies for negotiating this tension: whereas Dicey's conception of judicial review gives judges the licence to interpret legislation narrowly so as to preserve liberty and private property, Thayer argues that judges should generally defer to legislative or executive decisions unless those decisions clearly lack an evidentiary basis.

For the next 18 years, Thayer practised law in Boston. When the Civil War broke out, he joined the Loyal Publication Society, an abolitionist news agency which supported the Northern cause, while his brother and brother-in-law were killed while fighting in the Union Army.[47] When Thayer was appointed the Isaac Royall Professor at Harvard Law School in 1874, he revived his interest in judicial restraint as an organising theme in American constitutional law.[48] When the United States Supreme Court rendered its decision in the *Civil Rights Cases* on 8 October 1883, Thayer took the opportunity to elaborate his constitutional argument. The case concerned the constitutionality of the federal Civil Rights Act of 1875, which declared that 'all persons … shall be entitled to the full and equal enjoyment of the accommodations, advantages, facilities, and privileges of inns, public conveyances on land or water, theaters, and other places of public amusement', and prescribed penalties for anyone denying equal access to public facilities.

[42] ibid 249.
[43] ibid.
[44] ibid 249.
[45] ibid 242.
[46] ibid.
[47] G Edward White, 'Revisiting James Bradley Thayer' (1993–94) 88 *Northwestern University Law Review* 48, 64.
[48] Hook, 'A Brief Life' (n 31 above) 3.

The statute was part of a larger package of Reconstruction reforms to enlarge the constitutional rights of black citizens throughout the United States. In submissions defending the Act, the Solicitor General argued that the enforcement clause of the Fourteenth Amendment gave Congress the power to pass remedial legislation to ensure that citizens had equal access to the privileges of citizenship, including access to facilities (like railways and other public conveyances) which were charged with the public interest at common law.

By an 8-1 majority, the Supreme Court struck down the Act on the ground that the Fourteenth Amendment only applied to state action and therefore did not give Congress jurisdiction to regulate private relationships. In his majority opinion, Bradley J stated that 'the responsibility of an independent judgment is now thrown upon this court; and we are bound to exercise it according to the best lights we have'.[49] In his view, a plain reading of the Fourteenth Amendment revealed that 'the prohibitions of the amendment are against State laws and acts done under State authority',[50] meaning that Congress could only invoke it to strike down State legislation that was patently discriminatory. However, because the Civil Rights Act interfered with interpersonal relationships, Bradley J held that Congress had intruded upon State jurisdiction over civil rights. Despite recognising the social context in which the legislation had been passed, he noted that '[i]t would be running the slavery argument into the ground to make it apply to every act of discrimination which a person may see fit to make as to the guests he will entertain'.[51]

In a spirited dissent, Harlan J argued that 'the substance and the spirit of the recent amendments of the Constitution have been sacrificed by a subtle and ingenious verbal criticism'.[52] Responding to Bradley J's assertion that judges should exercise 'independent judgment' when assessing the constitutionality of legislation, Harlan J quoted a passage from the *Sinking Fund Cases*, in which the Court had declared that '[e]very possible presumption is in favour of the validity of a statute, and this continues until the contrary is shown beyond a rational doubt'.[53] He then asserted that the recent constitutional amendments should be interpreted in the same generous manner that the Court had used to construe Congressional jurisdiction prior to the Civil War, which enabled it to pass fugitive slave laws protecting

[49] *Civil Rights Cases* (n 10 above) 10.
[50] ibid 13.
[51] ibid 24.
[52] ibid 26.
[53] *Sinking Fund Cases* 99 US 718 (1878).

slave owners' proprietary claims over former slaves who had fled to another State.[54] Harlan J declared that

> the national legislature may, without transcending the limits of the Constitution, do for human liberty and the fundamental rights of American citizenship, what it did, with the sanction of this court, for the protection of slavery and the rights of the masters of fugitive slaves.[55]

In a letter to *The Nation*, written six months after the Court's decision, Thayer uses Bradley J's opinion to illustrate what he calls 'an erroneous view of the court's functions'.[56] For Thayer, the litmus test is not whether the substance of legislation aligns with the Court's interpretation of the constitutional text. Thayer argues that the Constitution was purposefully couched in broad language so that it could be adapted in light of unforeseen social problems. However, the nature of the constitutional text means that reasonable persons will disagree about how provisions like the Fourteenth Amendment should be interpreted. Thus, Thayer asserts that

> the function of the court is not that of fixing the construction of the Constitution which it believes to be the sound one, but that of determining whether another body, charged with an independent function … has discharged its office or exercised its judgment in an unreasonable manner.[57]

Thayer cites two different lines of authority to support his argument. The first line of authority derives from the *Sinking Fund Cases*, and Thayer reproduces the same passage which Harlan J had relied upon in his dissent. The second line of authority is a series of cases concerning judicial review of jury verdicts, which Thayer uses to show 'the difference between a case where the court has to exercise an "independent judgment," and a case where it merely passes on the reasonableness of the exercise of judgment by another body'.[58] In drawing this analogy, Thayer suggests that it is just as dangerous for judges to overturn Congress's interpretation of the Constitution as it is for them to second guess the verdict of one's peers.

Nine years later, Thayer expanded upon these ideas in his address to the World's Congress on Jurisprudence and Law Reform in Chicago. His speech, entitled 'The Origin and Scope of the American Doctrine of Constitutional Law', was published subsequently in the *Harvard Law Review* and provides the most detailed account of Thayer's constitutional theory. While Thayer asserts that judicial review of legislation and executive decisions has become commonplace, he points out that '[n]either the written [Constitution] nor the oath of the judges necessarily involves the right of reversing, displacing,

[54] See, eg *Prigg v Pennsylvania* 41 US 539 (1842); *Abelman v Booth* 62 US 506 (1858).
[55] *Civil Rights Cases* (n 10 above) 53.
[56] Thayer, 'Constitutionality of Legislation' (n 28 above) 315.
[57] ibid.
[58] ibid.

or disregarding any action of the legislature or the executive which these departments are constitutionally authorised to take'.[59] Further evidence for this assertion is drawn from salient constitutional signals: the Constitution incorporates a separation of powers between the different branches of government;[60] all members of Congress swear an oath to uphold the Constitution in performing their legislative functions; and the Founders considered, but rejected, a proposal which would have given judges the power to review the constitutionality of legislation prior to enactment.[61] Thayer marshals these points in aid of his argument that judicial review should not 'deprive another department of any of its proper power' or 'limit it in the proper range of its discretion',[62] because other officials share responsibility for upholding the Constitution and can be held accountable for their decisions through the political process.

Nevertheless, Thayer does not advocate judicial quiescence in the face of legislative or executive action.[63] He recognises that the Constitution entails some degree of judicial review, but argues that it is relatively limited. Unlike subsequent constitutional theorists, he does not rely upon a strict construction of the Constitution or an appeal to original intent in order to press his case.[64] In fact, he explicitly rejects strict constructionism and originalism as 'the mere and simple office of construing two writings, as two contracts or two statutes are construed and compared when they are said to conflict'.[65] For Thayer, this 'pedantic and academic treatment' of the Constitution lacks the 'combination of a lawyer's rigor with a statesmen's breadth of view which should be found in dealing with this class of questions in constitutional law'.[66] Even though he expresses reservations about some of the sweeping dicta in *Marbury v Madison*, he clearly approves of Marshall CJ's admonition in *McCulloch v Maryland* that one should 'never forget that it is a *constitution* we are expounding', one which is 'intended to endure for ages to come, and consequently, to be adapted to the various

[59] Thayer, 'The Origin and Scope of Constitutional Law' (n 1 above) 130.

[60] ibid 134–38.

[61] See, eg NY Const 1777 art III, which provided that 'whereas laws inconsistent with the spirit of this constitution, or with the public good, may be hastily and unadvisedly passed; Be it ordained, that the governor for the time being, the chancellor, and the judges of the supreme court, or any two of them, together with the governor' had the power to 'revise all bills about to be passed into laws by the legislature'.

[62] Thayer, 'The Origin and Scope of Constitutional Law' (n 1 above) 134–35.

[63] Alexander Bickel, *The Least Dangerous Branch: The Supreme Court at the Bar of Politics*, 2nd edn (New Haven CT, Yale University Press, 1986) 40; Sanford Gabin, 'Judicial Review, James Bradley Thayer, and the "Reasonable Doubt" Test' (1976) 3 *Hastings Constitutional Law Quarterly* 961, 974.

[64] See also James Thayer, 'Legal Tender' (1887) 1 *Harvard Law Review* 73.

[65] Thayer, 'The Origin and Scope of Constitutional Law' (n 1) 138.

[66] ibid.

crises of human affairs'.[67] Hence, Thayer recognises that the Constitution 'often admits of different interpretations', which leaves open 'a range of choice and judgment'.[68]

Given the prospect for reasonable disagreement in constitutional interpretation, Thayer advocates a 'rule of administration' which states that 'an Act of the legislature is not to be declared void unless the violation of the constitution is so manifest as to leave no room for reasonable doubt'.[69] In addition to authorities like the *Sinking Fund Cases*, Thayer offers two reasons for judicial restraint. The first reason is institutional—because other public officials have been given 'primary authority' to interpret the Constitution their decisions 'are entitled to a corresponding respect'.[70] Thayer emphasises that this respect is not premised 'on mere grounds of courtesy, but on very solid and significant grounds of policy and law' rooted in the democratic basis for the American Constitution.[71] Here again, he notes that if judges were supposed to be 'the chief protection against legislative violation of the constitution' the Constitution would have given judges plenary powers to revise legislation prior to enactment.[72]

The second reason is instrumental—in order to foster responsible democratic discourse about individual rights, judges should not arrogate exclusive interpretive authority over the Constitution. Instead, he notes:[73]

> If what I have been saying is true, the safe and permanent road towards reform is that of impressing upon our people a far stronger sense than they have of the great range of possible harm and evil that our system leaves open, and must leave open, to the legislatures, and of the clear limits of judicial power; so that responsibility may be brought sharply home where it belongs. The checking and cutting down of legislative power, by numerous detailed prohibitions in the constitution, cannot be accomplished without making the government petty and incompetent ... Under no system can the power of courts go far to save a people from ruin; our chief protection lies elsewhere. If this be true, it is of the greatest public importance to put the matter in its true light.

Thus, Thayer argues that his rule of administration helps to ensure that courts do not usurp the legislature's role as a forum for public discourse about justice. If the judiciary assumes that it has exclusive responsibility for upholding the Constitution, democratic deliberation will become sclerotic and focus upon narrow questions of 'mere legality, of what the constitution

[67] *McCulloch v Maryland* 17 US (4 Wheaton) 316, 407, 415 (1819), cited by Thayer in 'The Origin and Scope of Constitutional Law' (n 1 above) 138.

[68] Thayer, 'The Origin and Scope of Constitutional Law' (n 1 above) 144.

[69] ibid 140, citing Tilghman CJ in *Commonwealth v Smith*, 4 Bin 117 (1811).

[70] ibid 136.

[71] ibid.

[72] ibid.

[73] ibid 156.

allows' instead of considering broader 'questions of justice and right'.[74] In one of his last essays, Thayer zeroes in on this point by stating that the power of judicial review is accompanied by 'a serious evil', because

> the correction of legislative mistakes comes from the outside, and the people thus lose the political experience, and the moral education and stimulus that come from fighting the question out in the ordinary way, and correcting their own errors.[75]

Thayer's constitutional scholarship is important, because it represents one of the first systematic attempts to reconcile judicial deference towards governmental decisions with the rule of law.[76] Unlike other advocates of judicial restraint, Thayer does not argue from premises about the founder's intent or institutional competence. In fact, he objects to the notion that any person or class of public officials has a superior claim to define constitutional truths or determine how constitutional values should be balanced against the public interest. Instead, he asserts that constitutional values, by their nature, are subject to reasonable disagreement. Given this reality, he argues that the different branches of government share responsibility for interpreting the Constitution.[77] Nevertheless, he argues that all governmental determinations (legislative, judicial, and executive) remain subject to public scrutiny through the political process, judicial review, and jury trials—institutional checks which ensure that those decisions are both procedurally fair and rationally acceptable in light of a society's constitutional commitments. Thus, Thayer does not recommend either judicial quiescence or submission towards legislation or administrative decisions, but represents a sophisticated attempt to deal with problems posed by reasonable disagreement, democratic governance, and the rule of law.[78]

There are two plausible historical explanations for Thayer's scholarship. The first is that Thayer was a radical Republican at heart, who preferred the substantive policies pursued by Congress during Reconstruction over the Supreme Court's reactionary jurisprudence at the turn of the century.[79] The second, more elaborate explanation situates Thayer's scholarship within an older, Jeffersonian tradition which Larry Kramer calls 'popular constitutionalism'.[80] The democratic premise which inspires popular

[74] ibid 155.

[75] James Bradley Thayer, *John Marshall* (Boston MA, Houghton, Mifflin & Company, 1901) 106.

[76] 'One Hundred Years of Judicial Review: The Thayer Centennial Symposium' (1993) 88 *Northwestern University Law Review* 1.

[77] Gabin, 'Judicial Review' (n 63 above) 968.

[78] 'One Hundred Years of Judicial Review' (n 76 above) 1.

[79] Hook, 'A Brief Life' (n 31 above) 6.

[80] Larry Kramer, 'Judicial Supremacy and the End of Judicial Restraint' (2012) 100 *California Law Review* 621; Larry Kramer, *The People Themselves: Popular Constitutionalism and Judicial Review* (Oxford, Oxford University Press, 2004). See also White, 'Revisiting James Bradley Thayer' (n 47 above); G Edward White, 'Historicizing Judicial Scrutiny' (2005) 57 *South Carolina Law Review* 1.

constitutionalism is that 'primary authority to *interpret*, as well as to make, constitutional law' rests with ordinary citizens[81] as opposed to being the exclusive domain of any particular caste of officials. In this respect, popular constitutionalism resisted claims of judicial supremacy over constitutional interpretation which were advanced by Federalist lawyers.[82] Even though Jeffersonian democrats and their rivals agreed 'that the Constitution could and should be interpreted using the same, open-ended process of forensic argument that was employed across legal domains', they disagreed about *who* should have primary decision-making responsibility because of the controversial nature of constitutional interpretation.[83] Whereas influential Federalists, like James Kent, argued that judges should have the final word on constitutional interpretation in order to insulate property rights from legislative reform,[84] popular constitutionalists argue that the legislative, judicial, and executive branches of government share responsibility for interpreting the Constitution and those decisions should remain subject to popular supervision through the political process.[85] Nevertheless, popular constitutionalists also recognise that the judiciary has a role in assessing the constitutionality of governmental action. The point is that judicial review is 'at most, a subordinate, secondary check',[86] which means that while legislative and executive decisions are entitled to judicial respect, judicial intervention may be warranted when a governmental decision is arbitrary or unreasonable.[87]

While Thayer's life was cut short by heart failure on 14 February 1902, his theory is a landmark in discourse about judicial restraint in American constitutional law.[88] The cast of characters in this line of scholars, which David Luban calls an 'intellectual *Gemeinschaft* almost unparalleled in the history of juridical ideas', is impressive.[89] It includes judges like Oliver Wendell Holmes, Louis Brandeis, Learned Hand, Harlan Fiske Stone, Benjamin Cardozo, and Felix Frankfurter; it also includes constitutional

[81] Kramer, 'Judicial Supremacy' (n 80 above) 622.

[82] Friedman, 'The History of the Countermajoritarian Difficulty, Part One' (n 3 above) 371–81.

[83] Kramer, 'Judicial Supremacy' (n 80 above) 624–25.

[84] Kent's *Commentaries on American Law* was a highly influential digest, which 'envisaged the judiciary, through its protection of vested rights and its ability to determine the conditions permitting legislative abrogations of property holdings, as a buffer between established property holders and the people'. G Edward White, *The American Legal Tradition: Profiles of Leading American Judges* (Oxford, Oxford University Press, 2007) 51.

[85] Kramer, 'Judicial Supremacy' (n 80 above) 623. See also Kramer, *The People Themselves* (n 81 above) 105–14.

[86] ibid 628.

[87] ibid 629.

[88] Richard Posner, 'The Rise and fall of Judicial Self-Restraint' (2012) 100 *California Law Review* 519, 522.

[89] David Luban, 'Justice Holmes and the Metaphysics of Judicial Restraint' (1994) 44 *Duke Law Journal* 449, 452.

theorists like Henry Hart, Herbert Wechsler and Alexander Bickel as well as administrative law scholars like James Landis, Louis Jaffe, and Nathan Nathanialson.[90]

There is, however, one major problem that pervades this discourse: it requires the nebulous concept of reasonableness to carry a lot of freight regarding the tension between democratic governance and the rule of law.[91] At best, reasonableness seems ill-defined; at worst, fatuous. A lot depends on how it is unpacked in a particular case, because if it is employed in a robust manner it seems to collapse into an overweening form of correctness review; conversely, if it is employed in a flimsy manner it serves as an empty rhetorical device, which lends otherwise questionable governmental decisions a patina of constitutional legitimacy.

B. Pragmatic Constitutionalism

The legitimacy of judicial review was hotly contested during the *Lochner* era (1897–1937), a period in which the Supreme Court struck down swathes of federal and State legislation.[92] These decisions assumed that the Constitution gave judges a broad licence to enforce tight constraints on legislative and executive action.[93] First, the Court adopted an expansive interpretation of the rights to liberty and property protected by the Fifth and Fourteenth Amendments. For example, the Court held that the Fifth and Fourteenth Amendments generally prohibited both Congress and State legislatures from regulating employment relationships, because such legislation either constrained the freedom to contract for the provision of labour or compelled a transfer of property from employers to employees. The former principle was motivated by anti-slavery rhetoric that a worker had an inalienable natural right to dispose of his labour as he wished; the latter principle held that the existing market distribution of wealth and influence—which had been preordained by natural selection, transcribed into the common law, and entrenched by the Constitution—established a baseline of natural rights with which legislatures were powerless to interfere.

Secondly, the Court adopted an expansive interpretation of the due process clause contained in the Fifth and Fourteenth Amendments: instead of reading the due process clause as ensuring procedural rights in decisions

[90] ibid.

[91] While this is not the only problem that has been ascribed to Thayer's theory, it is the most significant one. See Gabin, 'Judicial Review' (n 63 above) 962–63.

[92] See, eg William Forbath, *Law and the Shaping of the American Labor Movement* (Cambridge, Harvard University Press, 1991) 177–92 and 199–203. Forbath estimates that State and federal courts struck down approximately 170 labour statutes during this period.

[93] Paul Kens, 'The Source of a Myth: Police Powers of the States and Laissez Faire Constitutionalism, 1900–1937' (1991) 35 *American Journal of Legal History* 70, 72.

affecting an individual's life, liberty, or property, the Court held repeatedly that these provisions imposed substantive limitations on legislative action. In short, any legislation which had the slightest effect on liberty or property was constitutionally suspect.[94]

Finally, the Court adopted a narrow interpretation of permissible justifications for legislative regulation of personal liberty or property rights. For instance, even though the Tenth Amendment gives State legislatures broad jurisdiction under the Constitution, the Court held that these powers were restricted to 'police powers'—matters specifically related to 'the peace, good order, morals and health of the community'.[95] While the parameters of the police powers were hotly contested during the *Lochner* era, this interpretive gloss ruled out many forms of redistribution and paternalism.[96] Furthermore, even when a legislative objective was clearly related to the public interest, the Court could strike down the statute if it was not convinced that the statutory means would ultimately achieve its ends.[97]

The majority opinion in *Coppage v Kansas* illustrates the confluence of these three trends.[98] In that case, the Supreme Court struck down State legislation prohibiting 'yellow dog' contracts: agreements by which an employer prohibited an employee from joining a labour union during the term of employment. Pitney J, writing for the Court, held that the legislation was repugnant to the Fourteenth Amendment, because it deprived 'employers of a part of their liberty of contract, to the corresponding advantage of the employed and the upbuilding [sic] of the labor organizations'.[99] He stated that the legislation constituted an 'arbitrary' or 'unreasonable' exercise of the police power, because it advanced the interests of labour unions, which in his view were 'not public institutions, charged by law with public or governmental duties, such as would render the maintenance of their membership a matter of direct concern to the general welfare'.[100]

Holmes J's dissenting opinion outlines a contrasting approach. He questions Pitney J's premise that the Constitution entrenches the status quo, and is deferential to the legislature's assessment of the public interest. Holmes J prefers a relatively 'thin' reading of the Fourteenth Amendment, which leaves substantial room for legislation based upon reasonable views about how to advance social welfare. Thus, he states that:[101]

> In present conditions a workman not unnaturally may believe that only by belonging to a union can he secure a contract that shall be fair to him … If that belief,

[94] Kens, 'The Source of a Myth' (n 93 above).
[95] *Munn* (n 13 above), 145 (Field J dissenting).
[96] Sunstein, 'Lochner's Legacy' (1987) 87 *Columbia Law Review* 873, 877.
[97] ibid 877–78.
[98] *Coppage* (n 19 above). See also *Adair* (n 19 above).
[99] *Coppage* (n 19 above) 16.
[100] ibid.
[101] ibid 26–27.

> whether right or wrong, may be held by a reasonable man, it seems to me that it may be enforced by law in order to establish the equality of position between the parties in which liberty of contract begins. Whether in the long run it is wise for the workingman to enact legislation of this sort is not my concern, but I am strongly of opinion that there is nothing in the Constitution of the United States to prevent it.

The important point is that, while both Pitney and Holmes JJ agree that the Constitution required legislatures to act 'reasonably', they disagree about the nature of that constraint. Unlike Pitney J, Holmes J rejects the idea that the Constitution implies a baseline of natural rights immune from regulation; and even though he personally doubts whether the statute's objective will be achieved in the long run, he thinks the legislation embodies a reasonably defensible belief that collective bargaining will advance the dignity and equality of employees in the workplace. In drawing this conclusion, Holmes J's employs ideas which resonate with Thayer's academic writings. But while there is strong evidence that Holmes J sympathised with Thayer's views, his work provides a complementary philosophical rationale for judicial restraint.

Oliver Wendell Holmes Jr was born into the upper-class, Brahmin subculture of Boston.[102] His father was a professor of medicine at Harvard, lectured on the Lyceum circuit, and wrote popular essays in the *Atlantic Monthly*; his mother was the daughter of a prominent member of Boston's mercantile class who also served on the Massachusetts Supreme Court.[103] Like Thayer, Holmes studied classics at Harvard, but left in his senior year to enlist in the Union Army. By this point, Holmes had admittedly been 'deeply moved by the Abolition cause'[104] through his friendship with Penrose Hallowell, a Quaker from Philadelphia and classmate at Harvard.[105] Through the intercession of his father, Holmes was eventually re-admitted to Harvard, graduated, and promptly joined the 20th Regiment which was preparing to march south in the fall of 1861.

Holmes's experience as a soldier shaped his personal philosophy, which in turn influenced his jurisprudential perspective. While he had been motivated initially to enlist by moral idealism—his belief that Southern society had been corrupted by slavery and that Union forces were engaged in a crusade—by the end of the Civil War his outlook had been tempered by doubt and disillusionment.[106] Out of two thousand Union Army regiments, only four

[102] G Edward White, *Justice Oliver Wendell Holmes: Law and the Inner Self* (New York, Oxford University Press, 1993) 20.

[103] ibid ch 1.

[104] Letter from Holmes to Arthur Garfield Hays 20 April 1928, Holmes Papers (Harvard Law School).

[105] White, *Justice Oliver Wendell Holmes* (n 102 above) 31–32.

[106] ibid ch 2; Louis Menand, *The Metaphysical Club: A Story of Ideas in America* (New York, Farrar, Strauss and Giroux, 2001); Saul Touster, 'In Search of Holmes from Within' (1964) 18 *Vanderbilt Law Review* 437.

suffered more casualties than Holmes's.[107] He was shot in the chest at the battle of Ball's Bluff on 21 October 1861, shot through the back of the neck at Antietam on 17 September 1862, survived the battle of the Wilderness, and was wounded by shrapnel near Chancellorsville.[108] These events were punctuated by 'the arbitrariness, drudgery, and myopia of war'—prolonged marching, bivouacking in harsh terrain, coping with severe weather conditions, and lingering images of combat in close quarters.[109] These personal experiences complicated Holmes's perspective of the Civil War. His moral idealism, which precipitated his enlistment, gave way to stoicism in the face of a social conflict that simultaneously threatened his survival and defied his comprehension. Thus, Holmes concluded that honourable self-sacrifice outweighed his personal desire to escape conflict, and that this duty was not justified by the immorality of slavery so much as a sense of loyalty to his regiment.[110]

In the fall of 1864, Holmes enrolled at Harvard Law School. Legal education at the time was relatively primitive by modern standards: there were only three faculty members, there were no mandatory examinations, and the only requirement was that students maintain enrolment for three semesters. After completing his degree and a brief sojourn in Europe, Holmes began his professional career working alongside James Thayer at a local law firm. In his spare time, he discussed philosophy with Chauncey Wright (Thayer's childhood friend), Charles Sanders Pierce, William James, and Nicholas St John Green.[111] Three members of this group—Wright, Pierce, and James—were the founders of American pragmatism, a philosophical movement which sought to separate philosophy from religion.[112] Holmes is also recognised as playing a critical role in the emergence of this school of thought.[113] At a very basic level, American pragmatism proceeds from the idea that philosophical inquiry should be driven by the scientific method so that even deeply held values, beliefs, and ideas remain subject to scrutiny, critique, and revision through applied practice and reflection upon experience. In this respect, American pragmatism was as revolutionary in philosophical circles as Charles Darwin's *Origin of Species* was in the natural sciences.[114] Whereas Darwin's thesis challenged the idea that the order of

[107] William Fox, *Regimental Losses in the American Civil War, 1861–1865* (Albany NY, Albany Publishing, 1889) 3.

[108] White, *Justice Oliver Wendell Holmes* (n 102 above) ch 2.

[109] ibid 50.

[110] Oliver Wendell Holmes, 'Memorial Day Address', 30 May 1895 in Max Lerner (ed), *The Mind and Faith of Justice Holmes* (Boston, Little, Brown and Company, 1946) ed: 'Most men who know battle know the cynic force with which the thoughts of common sense will assail them in times of stress; but they know that in their greatest moments faith has trampled those thoughts under foot'. See also White, *Justice Oliver Wendell Holmes* (n 102 above) 71.

[111] Menand, *The Metaphysical Club* (n 106 above) ch 9; Cheryl Misak, *The American Pragmatists* (Oxford, Oxford University Press, 2013) preface.

[112] Misak, *The American Pragmatists* (n 111 above) ch 2.

[113] ibid 77.

[114] ibid.

the natural world had been preordained by God, pragmatists challenged the idea that individuals could gain direct access to 'an ahistorical, transcendental, or metaphysical theory of truth' through divine revelation or Cartesian introspection.[115]

As Holmes immersed himself in the legal profession, he began cultivating a pragmatic account of legal reasoning.[116] At the time, American jurisprudence was riven by two conflicting traditions, both of which assumed that judges were exclusively concerned with the enforcement of legal rights as opposed to the advancement of public policy.[117] The natural law tradition asserted that the common law was built upon a foundation of natural rights, and attempted to identify and expound autonomous, value-neutral rules which could be deployed to vindicate those rights without being distracted by broader political or social considerations. The positivist tradition was inspired by scholars like Jeremy Bentham, and culminated in a movement to codify American law.[118] Bentham famously criticised the common law for flouting utilitarian ethics and advocated wide-ranging legislative reform to realign the law with public welfare.[119] John Austin buttressed Bentham's arguments by asserting that law was an autonomous system of rules which was distinguishable from morality. He famously argued that '[t]he existence of law is one thing; its merit or demerit is another', because the law derived exclusively from the commands of a sovereign legislator who had sufficient power to secure obedience by issuing sanctions for non-compliance.[120]

Throughout his career, Holmes sought to stake out a middle ground between the natural law tradition and nineteenth century legal positivism. In his response to the American codification movement, Holmes recasts the common law method as a pragmatic social inquiry the purpose of which is to resolve recurrent social problems in light of experience, saying:[121]

> It is the merit of the common law that it decides the case first and determines the principle afterwards. ... [L]awyers, like other men, frequently see well enough how they ought to decide on a given state of facts without being very clear as

[115] ibid 3.

[116] Frederic Kellogg, *Oliver Wendell Holmes, Jr., Legal Theory, and Judicial Restraint* (Cambridge, Cambridge University Press, 2007) ch 2; Thomas Grey, 'Holmes and Legal Pragmatism' (1989) 41 *Stanford Law Review* 787. While Holmes thought William James's version of pragmatism was 'an amusing humbug', his legal theory is consistent with the philosophical method employed by Chauncey Wright and Charles Sanders Pierce. See Misak, *The American Pragmatists* (n 111 above) ch 5.

[117] Morton Horwitz, *The Transformation of American Law 1870–1960: The Crisis of Legal Orthodoxy* (Oxford, Oxford University Press, 1992) 112.

[118] ibid ch 4.

[119] Jeremy Bentham, *A Fragment on Government* (Cambridge, Cambridge University Press, 1988).

[120] John Austin, *The Province of Jurisprudence Determined* (Cambridge, Cambridge University Press, 1995) 157.

[121] Oliver Wendell Holmes, Jr, 'Codes, and the Arrangement of the Law' (1870) 5 *American Law Review* 1.

> to the *ratio decidendi* ... It is only after a series of determinations on the same subject-matter, that it becomes necessary to 'reconcile the cases,' as it is called, that is, by a true induction to state the principle which has until then been obscurely felt. And this statement is often modified more than once by new decisions before the abstracted general rule takes its final shape. A well settled legal doctrine embodies the work of many minds, and has been tested in form as well as substance by trained critics whose practical interest it is to resist it at every step.

In this passage, Holmes espouses a 'bottom-up' theory of the common law, whereby the result is not deduced from natural law precepts or the commands of a sovereign legislator.[122] Rather, the law 'grows in a fallible way, where doubt, conflict, and disputes about what the law is are resolved under the force of experience'.[123] Only when a 'series of successive approximations' can be gleaned from jury verdicts or trial decisions can lawyers identify trends the rationale of which can be restated as general legal propositions.[124] Thus, the judicial role in Holmes's legal theory is secondary—the primary task of identifying the parameters of civil or criminal liability is performed by juries and trial judges acting as connoisseurs of community moral standards, while legal scholars and appellate judges deduce the policy rationale from these verdicts.[125] However, even general legal propositions are provisional, in the sense that they remain subject to revision in light of new experiences.[126] Holmes argued that the pragmatic approach is conducive to social order because it is more likely to generate a stable or 'well settled legal doctrine' than attempts to deduce law's content directly from a legislative text or appellate court decision.[127]

Despite his pragmatic leanings, Holmes was nevertheless attracted to aspects of legal positivism in order to deflect natural law arguments which assumed that individual rights invariably trumped the public interest. While Holmes concedes that any attempt to articulate a 'well-arranged body of the law' would be subject to 'infinite argument', he nevertheless asserts that 'it should be based on *duties* and not on *rights*'.[128] For Holmes, the natural rights tradition undermines social order, because it is built upon controversial, subjective impressions regarding the proper parameters of civil or

[122] Kellogg, *Oliver Wendell Holmes Jr* (n 116 above) ch 3.

[123] Misak, *The American Pragmatists* (n 111 above) 78.

[124] Holmes, 'Codes, and the Arrangement of the Law' (n 121 above) 2.

[125] Kellogg, *Oliver Wendell Holmes Jr* (n 116 above) 122–25.

[126] This orientation explains why Holmes characterises law as a 'prediction' or 'prophecy'. See Oliver Wendell Holmes, 'The Path of Law' (1897) 10 *Harvard Law Review* 457; Max Fisch, 'Justice Holmes, The Prediction Theory of the Law, and Pragmatism' in Kenneth Ketner and Christian Floesel (eds), *Peirce, Semeiotic and Pragmatism* (Bloomington IN, Indiana University Press, 1986) 6.

[127] Kellogg, *Oliver Wendell Holmes* (n 116 above) 33–34; White, *Justice Oliver Wendell Holmes* (n 102 above) 115. In this respect, Holmes's legal theory is remarkably similar to Pierce's version of pragmatism. See Misak, *The American Pragmatists* (n 111 above) ch 3.

[128] Holmes, 'Codes, and the Arrangement of the Law' (n 121 above) 3.

criminal liability instead of standards gleaned from objective community consensus.[129]

Nevertheless, Holmes did not accept Austin's assertion that legal duties emanate exclusively from sovereign commands. Thus, he 'hesitates to admit that only a definite body of political superiors can make what is properly called a law', because he says the locus and extent of political sovereignty are often 'questions of fact and of degree'.[130] He later clarifies this point in a book review by saying that 'other bodies not sovereign, and even [public] opinion, might generate law in a philosophical sense against the will of the sovereign' because

> in most states there has been a large number ... who have had no share in the political power; while at the same time their physical power, and consequently their desires, were not to be ignored, and in some cases were not to be disobeyed.[131]

Hence, Holmes concludes that Austin erred in arguing that 'all judge-made law is the creature of the sovereign or state'.[132] Instead, he contends that '[t]he judges have other motives for decision, outside their own arbitrary will, beside the commands of their sovereign' because '[a]ny motive ... be it constitution, statute, custom, or precedent, which can be relied upon as likely in the generality of cases to prevail, is worthy of consideration as one of the sources of law'.[133] Thus, Holmes's 'bottom-up' theory asserts that the content of the law is determined by judicial interpretation of positive law—the Constitution, legislation, and precedent—as well as experience, social practice, and popular opinion.

This line of thinking is apparent in Holmes's later writings. In his review of Christopher Columbus Langdell's casebook on contract law, Holmes sharpens his critique of the formalist style of legal reasoning,[134] which assumes that legal decisions are deduced from positive law without regard for the broader moral, political, social or economic context.[135] Holmes highlights what he calls a 'weak point in Mr. Langdell's habit of mind', which stems from an interest 'in the formal connection of things, or logic, as distinguished from the feelings which make the content of logic, and which have actually shaped the substance of the law'.[136] In a manner reminiscent of philosophical pragmatism's disdain for religious epistemology, Holmes refers to Langdell as 'the greatest living legal theologian' because

[129] Oliver Wendell Holmes, 'Natural Law' (1918) 32 *Harvard Law Review* 40.
[130] Holmes, 'Codes, and the Arrangement of the Law' (n 121 above) 4.
[131] Holmes, 'Book Notice' (1872) 6 *American Law Review* 723.
[132] Austin, *The Province of Jurisprudence* (n 120 above) 35.
[133] Holmes, 'Book Notice' (n 131 above).
[134] Oliver Wendell Holmes, 'Book Notice' (1880) 14 *American Law Review* 233, reviewing CC Langdell, *A Selection of Cases on the Law of Contracts*, 2nd edn (Boston MA, Little, Brown & Co, 1879).
[135] Frederick Schauer, 'Formalism' (1988) 97 *Yale Law Journal* 509.
[136] Holmes, 'Book Notice' (n 131 above) 234.

he prioritises formal logic and conceptual analysis over the importance of experience and social context.[137]

> The life of the law has not been logic: it has been experience. The seed of every new growth within its sphere has been a felt necessity. The form of continuity has been kept up by reasonings purporting to reduce every thing to a logical sequence; but that form is nothing but the evening dress which the new-comer puts on to make itself presentable according to conventional requirements. The important phenomenon is the man underneath it, not the coat; the justice and reasonableness of a decision, not its consistency with previously held views. No one will ever have a truly philosophic mastery over the law who does not habitually consider the forces outside of it which have made it what it is. More than that, he must remember that as it embodies the story of a nation's development through many centuries, the law finds its philosophy not in self-consistency which it must always fail in so long as it continues to grow, but in history and the nature of human needs. As a branch of anthropology, law is an object of science; the theory of legislation is a scientific study; but the effort to reduce the concrete details of an existing system to the merely logical consequence of simple postulates is always in danger of becoming unscientific, and of leading to a misapprehension of the nature of the problem and the data.

In this passage, Holmes contrasts his 'bottom-up' theory with Langdell's 'top-down' approach to adjudication.[138] Whereas Langdell had sought to demonstrate that the common law had unfolded logically from common law doctrine, Holmes argues that the common law is built upon the shifting sands of social context: '[t]he felt necessities of the time, the prevalent moral and political theories, intuitions of public policy, avowed or unconscious, even the prejudices which judges share with their fellow men'.[139]

When Holmes was appointed to the Massachusetts Supreme Court in 1882, he approached judicial review in much the same pragmatic vein. While he did not encounter many constitutional cases during his 20-year stint on the Supreme Judicial Court of Massachusetts, his general attitude was 'consistently deferential'.[140] In *Commonwealth v Perry*, Holmes took pains to write a dissenting opinion upholding legislation which prohibited employers from deducting employees' wages for product imperfections. He states that any restraint on legislation 'must be found in the words of the Constitution, either expressed or implied upon a fair and historical construction'; and while he acknowledges 'that the power to make reasonable laws impliedly prohibits the making of unreasonable ones', he says that 'I should not be willing or think myself authorised to overturn legislation on that ground, unless I thought that an honest difference of opinion was impossible, or

[137] ibid.

[138] Oliver Wendell Holmes, Jr, *The Common Law* (Boston MA, Little, Brown and Company, 1949).

[139] ibid 1.

[140] White, *Justice Oliver Wendell Holmes* (n 102 above) 281.

pretty nearly so'.[141] Two years later, when Thayer sent Holmes a copy of his essay on the origin and scope of constitutional law, Holmes replied 'I agree with it heartily and it makes explicit the point of view from which implicitly I have approached the Constitutional questions upon which I have differed from some of the other judges'.[142]

When Holmes was appointed to the US Supreme Court in 1902, he encountered constitutional challenges more frequently. In *Otis v Parker*, he wrote a majority opinion upholding California legislation which prohibited share transfers on margin, saying:[143]

> It is true, no doubt, that neither a state legislature nor a state constitution can interfere arbitrarily with private business or transactions, and that the mere fact that an enactment purports to be for the protection of public safety, health or morals is not conclusive upon the courts ... But general propositions do not carry us far. While the courts must exercise a judgment of their own, it by no means is true that every law is void which may seem to the judges who pass upon it excessive, unsuited to its ostensible end, or based upon conceptions of morality with which they disagree. Considerable latitude must be allowed for differences of view as well as for possible peculiar conditions which this court can know but imperfectly, if at all. Otherwise a constitution, instead of embodying only relatively fundamental rules of right, as generally understood by all English-speaking communities would become the partisan of a particular set of ethical or economical opinions, which by no means are held *semper ubique et ab omnibus*.

In this passage Holmes sums up his thoughts about judicial review, which are essentially similar to Thayer's. Because the interpretation of constitutional values is subject to reasonable disagreement, and legislative assemblies have legitimate authority to interpret the Constitution in light of local circumstances, judges should generally defer to legislation. Thus, in his famous *Lochner* dissent he stated, 'I strongly believe that my agreement or disagreement has nothing to do with the right of a majority to embody their opinions in law', so that legislation should be upheld 'unless it can be said that a rational and fair man necessarily would admit that the statute proposed would infringe fundamental principles as they have been understood by the traditions of our people and our law'.[144] And in his private correspondence, Holmes wrote that judicial review of utility rates 'is determining a line between grabber and grabbee that turns on the feeling of the community'[145]

[141] *Commonwealth v Perry* 155 Mass 117, 124 (1891).

[142] Letter from Holmes to James Thayer 2 November 1893 in Mark DeWolfe Howe, *Research materials relating to life of Oliver Wendell Holmes, Jr, 1858–1968: General Correspondence, General, Group II: Box 18, Folder 1.*

[143] *Otis v Parker* 187 US 606, 608–9 (1902).

[144] *Lochner* (n 19 above) 75–76.

[145] Letter from Holmes to Harold Laski 23 October 1926 in Mark DeWolfe Howe, *The Correspondence of Mr Justice Holmes and Harold J Laski 1916–1925*, vol 2 (Cambridge MA, Harvard University Press, 1953) 888.

so that 'if the rate-making power will only say I have considered A. B. & C., all the elements enumerated, we accept the judgment unless it makes us puke'.[146]

At this point, it seems that Holmes J's position of judicial restraint collapses into submissive deference towards legislative and executive decisions. Further evidence for this assessment can be found in *Moyer v Peabody*.[147] In that case, the Governor of Colorado, James Peabody, declared a state of emergency and called out the State militia to break mining unions which were agitating for legislative reform and better working conditions. During this period, the State militia detained the president of the Western Federation of Miners, Charles Moyer, on dubious grounds of 'military necessity'.[148] When Moyer secured a writ of habeas corpus, the State Attorney General refused to honour the writ.[149] It was only when Moyer brought a motion before the US Court of Appeal for the 8th Circuit two and a half months later that Peabody relented, declared an end to the state of emergency, and released Moyer from prison.[150]

After his release, Moyer sued Peabody for false imprisonment and violating his constitutional rights. However, the lawsuit foundered when it reached the Supreme Court, where Holmes J wrote a majority opinion striking the claim. While Holmes J recognises that Moyer had been deprived of his liberty, he observes that the claimant's constitutional right to due process 'varies with the subject-matter and the necessities of the situation'.[151] Nevertheless, he held that Peabody was the exclusive arbiter of whether the circumstances amounted to a state of emergency, saying

> [w]hen it comes to a decision by the head of the State upon a matter involving its life, the ordinary rights of individuals must yield to what he deems the necessities of the moment. Public danger warrants the substitution of executive process for judicial process.[152]

But in some of his later opinions, Holmes J suggests that he thought the legitimacy of collective decisions depends to some extent on whether basic rights were protected. This shift in Holmes J's thinking can be traced in his opinions regarding freedom of speech. In *Patterson v Colorado*, Holmes J upheld a newspaper publisher's conviction for contempt of court in relation to a series of editorials and cartoons criticising the Colorado Supreme Court. At the time, Holmes J stated that the right of free speech only prohibited

[146] ibid.
[147] *Moyer v Peabody* 212 US 78 (1909).
[148] George Suggs, *Colorado's War on Militant Unionism: James H Peabody and the Western Federation of Miners* (Detroit MI, Wayne State University Press, 1972) 166–67.
[149] ibid 168–70.
[150] ibid 175.
[151] *Moyer* (n 147 above) 84.
[152] ibid 85.

prior restraint, which meant that any speech 'deemed contrary to the public welfare' could be sanctioned.[153] In *Schenck v United States*, which was decided in the spring of 1919, Holmes J reaffirmed his position by stating that the scope of free speech 'depends upon the circumstances in which it is done' so that it 'would not protect a man in falsely shouting fire in a theatre and causing a panic'.[154] Because the evidence showed that Schenk intended to distribute pamphlets advising conscripts to resist enlistment, he saw no reason to question the jury's verdict, saying that '[w]hen a nation is at war many things that might be said in time of peace are such a hindrance to its effort that their utterance will not be endured'.[155] And in a companion case, *Debs v United States*, he upheld the jury's verdict to convict even though the defendant had only expressed sympathy for workers who had spoken out against conscription.[156]

However, in *Abrams v United States*—a case handed down only eight months after *Schenk*—Holmes J adopts a more robust conception of the right to free speech. As in *Schenck*, the defendants were prosecuted for publishing pamphlets critical of the government's military policy. While the majority cites *Schenk* as its basis for upholding the convictions, Holmes J dissents on the ground that the defendants had been deprived of their constitutional rights. While he reaffirms the 'clear and present danger' test from *Schenk*, he augments it by saying that 'only the present danger of an immediate evil or an intent to bring it about' could justify a conviction under the *Espionage Act*. Later in his reasons, he states that 'we should be eternally vigilant against attempts to check the expression of opinions that we loathe' so that state interference is only warranted if 'an immediate check is required to save the country'.[157] This shift marks a significant moment in Holmes J's constitutional jurisprudence.[158] Prior to his *Abrams* dissent, Holmes J asserted that legislatures, executive officials, and juries are the exclusive arbiters of whether the public interest justifies a restraint on speech. After *Abrams*, he asserts that the First Amendment is a constitutional value which

[153] *Patterson v Colorado* 205 US 454, 462 (1907). See also *Fox v Washington* 236 US 273 (1915).

[154] *Schenck v United States* 249 US 47, 52 (1919).

[155] ibid. See also *Frohwerk v United States* 249 US 204 (1919).

[156] *Debs v United States* 249 US 211 (1919). Later that year, one of Holmes J's personal correspondents, Zechariah Chafee, suggested that even though Holmes J harboured reservations about the conclusion in *Debs*, he confessed that he 'could not have gone behind the jury verdict'. David Rabban, 'The Emergence of Modern First Amendment Doctrine' (1982) 50 *University of Chicago Law Review* 1205, 1315 quoting Letter from Zechariah Chafee to Judge Charles Amidon, 30 September 1919.

[157] *Abrams v United States* 250 US 616, 630 (1919).

[158] For a more detailed historical account outlining the development of Holmes J's views regarding the First Amendment, see White, *Justice Oliver Wendell Holmes* (n 102 above) ch 12; Edward White, 'Justice Holmes and the Modernization of Free Speech Jurisprudence: the Human Dimension' (1992) 80 *California Law Review* 391; David Rabban, *Free Speech in Its Forgotten Years* (Cambridge, Cambridge University Press, 1997) ch 8.

entitles judges to assess whether the evidence in fact justifies state limitation of individual rights. Thus, when Holmes J examines the contents of the pamphlets and the surrounding circumstances in *Abrams*, he concludes that

> nobody can suppose that the surreptitious publishing of a silly leaflet by an unknown man, without more, would present any immediate danger that its opinions would hinder the success of the government arms or have any appreciable tendency to do so.[159]

Far from adopting a submissive posture, Holmes J scrutinises the government's rationale and finds it lacking.

II. JUDICIAL RESTRAINT AND ADMINISTRATIVE LAW

A. Contextual Constitutionalism and the Administrative State

Only one other Justice, Brandeis J, concurred with Holmes J's opinion in *Abrams*. Brandeis was Holmes's friend and shared similar beliefs about the role of the judiciary. In fact, when Republicans raised concerns about his stance on judicial review during his confirmation hearing, Louis Brandeis informed one of his attorneys that '[m]y views in regard to the constitution are as you know very much those of Mr. Justice Holmes'.[160] Throughout the 1920s Brandeis and Holmes JJ joined forces to criticise judicial overreach. Their dissents are noteworthy because, unlike the conservative majority on the Court during the *Lochner* era, Brandeis and Holmes JJ advocated judicial restraint when reviewing governmental decisions which had a negative impact on property rights and economic interests, but strict scrutiny in cases concerning personal liberty and free speech.

Despite their similarities, Brandeis and Holmes JJ often arrived at the same conclusion for different reasons. Holmes J had a philosophical disposition and was generally sceptical about the efficacy of legislative reforms, but his scepticism nevertheless led him to defer to democratic decisions because he doubted whether any alternative decision-making process could prevent political disagreement from devolving into a Hobbesian state of nature. By contrast, Brandeis J had an empirical disposition, was generally optimistic that progressive reforms could improve individual well-being and social welfare, and embraced the democratic process (in law, industrial relations, and administration) as a matter of principle. Thus, while Holmes and Brandeis JJ were both pragmatists, Brandeis J's contextual sensitivity

[159] *Abrams* (n 157 above) 628. See also *Gitlow v New York* 268 US 652, 672–73 (1925) (Holmes J dissenting).

[160] Letter from Brandeis to Thomas Watt Gregory, 14 April 1916 in Melvin Urofsky and David Levy (eds), *Letters of Louis D Brandeis*, vol IV (Albany NY, State University of New York, 1971) 165.

and commitment to deliberative democracy complemented Holmes J's more philosophical approach. Furthermore, Brandeis J's experience in the progressive reform movement gave him opportunities to explore how judicial review could be reformed in order to accommodate the modern administrative state.[161]

Brandeis's experience as a law student was dramatically different from Holmes's. After Langdell was appointed Dane Professor of Law in 1870, the Harvard law faculty moved away from the traditional mode of instruction (based on lectures and rote learning) towards the case method accompanied by Socratic dialogue. Langdell's aim was to enable students to trace the development of doctrine, and consider how to apply precedent 'to the ever-tangled skein of human affairs'.[162] Two years later, Brandeis graduated at the top of his class with an average of 97, earning perfect marks of 100 in three subjects.[163]

After a year of graduate studies at Harvard and a brief stint in St Louis, Brandeis returned to Boston to practise law with his old Harvard roommate, Samuel Warren, who had previously worked at Shattuck, Holmes & Munroe.[164] Brandeis met Holmes through Warren, and the two established a friendship that would span the rest of their lives.[165] Brandeis was also a close associate of Thayer, whom Brandeis called 'my best friend among the instructors' at Harvard.[166] Brandeis helped Thayer compile materials for his constitutional law course, and when Thayer travelled to England on sabbatical in 1882, Brandeis taught Thayer's evidence course at Harvard.[167]

Like Holmes, Brandeis believed in a 'bottom-up' theory in which law emerges from its social context. However, Brandeis was a more rigorous, empirically-minded pragmatist than Holmes.[168] In his 1905 address to the

[161] Daniel Farber, 'Reinventing Brandeis: Legal Pragmatism for the Twenty-First Century' [1995] *University of Illinois Law Review* 163.

[162] CC Langdell, *A Selection of Cases on the Law of Contracts* (Boston MA, Little, Brown, and Company, 1871) vi.

[163] James Landis, 'Mr Justice Brandeis and the Harvard Law School' (1941) 55 *Harvard Law Review* 184.

[164] Melvin Urofsky, *Louis D Brandeis: A Life* (New York, Schoken Books, 2009) 42.

[165] ibid 79. When the Harvard law faculty attempted to lure Holmes into academia, Brandeis persuaded one of his clients to donate the necessary funds. See also Francis Biddle, 'The Friendship of Holmes and Brandeis' (1965) 216 *Atlantic Monthly* 86.

[166] Melvin Urofsky and David Levy (eds), *Letters of Louis D Brandeis*, vol I (Albany NY, State University of New York, 1971) 92–93; Letter from Louis D Brandeis to James Thayer 1889 in James Bradley Thayer Papers (Cambridge MA, Harvard Law Library) Box 24, Folder 2.

[167] ibid; Urofsky, *Brandeis* (n 164 above) 78–79. Thayer's son, Ezra (who would later go on to become Dean of Harvard Law School) began his legal career working in Brandeis's firm: Landis, 'Brandeis' (n 163 above) 189.

[168] Holmes himself recognised this point. Writing to Felix Frankfurter, Holmes noted that Brandeis 'always desires to know all that can be known about a case whereas I am afraid that I wish to know as little as I can safely go on. He loves facts and I hate them except as the necessary peg to hang generalizations on'. Robert Mennel and Christine Compston (eds), *Holmes & Frankfurter: Their Correspondence, 1912–1934* (Hanover NH, University Press of New England, 1996) 194.

Harvard Ethical Society, Brandeis argued that a lawyer's training 'fits him especially to grapple with the questions which are presented in a democracy', because:[169]

> The lawyer's processes of reasoning, his logical conclusions are being constantly tested by experience. The facts are running up against him at every point. Indeed it is a maxim of law: Out of the facts grows the law; that is, propositions are not considered abstractly, but always with reference to facts.

Brandeis was also a committed democrat who, like Thomas Jefferson, believed 'in the ability of the common people to understand and to act wisely on even complex issues if only they had the facts at hand'.[170] In this respect, Brandeis believed that the lawyer's primary function was to bring relevant facts to light and facilitate public deliberation about justice.[171]

Brandeis's pragmatic approach to the legal process is illustrated by his argumentative strategy in *Muller v Oregon*, a case in which he was retained to defend maximum work-hours legislation for female workers. In that case, Brandeis shifted the Court's gaze away from abstractions like freedom of contract towards the social, economic, and political context of the case. Thus, at the outset of his famous brief he notes that '[t]he decision in this case will, in effect, determine the constitutionality of nearly all the statutes in force in the United States, limiting the hours of adult women',[172] highlighting the fact that 19 States had introduced similar legislation.[173] He summarises the relevant legal principles in a scant two pages, noting that it is 'well established' in cases like *Lochner* that the States can only restrain freedom of contract if the law has a real or substantial connection to public health, safety or welfare. The remainder of the brief, which spans over 100 pages, details legislation from foreign jurisdictions, factory reports,

[169] Louis Brandeis, 'The Opportunity in the Law' (1905) 39 *American Law Review* 555, 556.

[170] Urofsky, *Brandeis* (n 164 above) 87. See also letter from Thomas Jefferson to William Charles Jarvis, 28 September 1820 in Paul Ford (ed), *The Writings of Thomas Jefferson*, vol 10 (New York, GP Putnam's Sons, 1899) 161: 'I know no safe depository of the ultimate powers of the society but the people themselves; and if we think them not enlightened enough to exercise their control with a wholesome discretion, the remedy is not to take it from them but to inform their discretion by education. This is the true corrective of abuses of constitutional power'.

[171] Melvin Urofsky notes that Brandeis eschewed the characterisation of the lawyer as a zealous advocate, and instead conceived his role as 'counsel to the situation' who mediated conflict between conflicting interest groups: Urofsky, *Brandeis* (n 164 above) xi, 48.

[172] 'Brief for the Defendant in Error in *Muller v Oregon* 208 US 412 (1908)' reprinted in P Kurland and G Casper (eds), *Landmark Briefs and Arguments of the Supreme Court of the United States: Constitutional Law*, vol 16 (Arlington VA, University Publications of America, 1975) 63, 66.

[173] ibid 66–73. Massachusetts, Rhode Island, Louisiana, Connecticut, Maine, New Hampshire, Maryland, Virginia, Pennsylvania, New York, Nebraska, Washington, Wisconsin, North Dakota, South Dakota, Oklahoma, New Jersey, Colorado and South Carolina had all passed legislation establishing maximum hours for female workers.

medical testimony, and sociological data all buttressing the claim that the Oregon statute was justifiable on public health grounds. He employed this strategy repeatedly throughout his legal career, engaging in pragmatic dialogue between various stakeholders on life insurance reform, workers' compensation, unemployment insurance, employee participation in workplace management, consumer protection, utility and railway rates, and the regulation of monopolies.[174] Whereas Holmes and Roscoe Pound theorised about sociological jurisprudence, Brandeis practised it.[175]

A few weeks before his nomination to the Supreme Court, Brandeis articulated his conception of law in an address to the Chicago Bar Association.[176] He begins by stating that 'the American ideal of government' has been 'greatly modified' over the course of history: in the wake of the American Revolution, it was '[a] government of laws and not of men'; during Reconstruction it was '[a] government of the people, by the people and for the people'; but the motto for the Progressive era was 'Democracy and social justice'.[177] In keeping with his contextual orientation, he notes that 'no law, written or unwritten, can be understood without a full knowledge of the facts out of which it arises, and to which it is to be applied'.[178] He points out that '[s]ince the adoption of the federal constitution ... we have passed through an economic and social revolution which affected the life of the people more fundamentally than any political revolution known to history'.[179] However, he argues that judges failed to keep pace with these developments. In a poignant passage, he asserts that:[180]

> Early 19th century scientific half-truths like 'The survival of the fittest,' which translated into practice meant 'The devil take the hindmost,' were erected by judicial sanction into a moral law. Where statutes giving expression to the new social spirit were clearly constitutional, judges, imbued with the relentless spirit of individualism, often construed them away. Where any doubt as to the constitutionality of such statutes could find lodgement, courts all too frequently declared the acts void.

While Brandeis concedes that 'the law has everywhere a tendency to lag behind the facts of life', he warns that the trend towards judicial activism

[174] Urofsky, *Brandeis* (n 164 above) chs 6–10, 12–13.

[175] Holmes, 'The Path of Law' (n 126 above); Roscoe Pound, 'Mechanical Jurisprudence' (1908) 8 *Columbia Law Review* 605.

[176] Louis Brandeis, 'The Living Law' (1916) 10 *Illinois Law Review* 461.

[177] ibid.

[178] ibid 467.

[179] ibid 463. In 1860, there was 30,600 miles of railroad track in the United States; by 1916, there was 254,000 miles. The population of the United States had tripled between 1860 and 1916, the number of people employed in manufacturing had increased fivefold, and investment capital in manufacturing had multiplied 22 times. See David Levy, 'The Lawyer as Judge: Brandeis' View of the Legal Profession' (1969) 22 *Oklahoma Law Review* 374.

[180] ibid 464.

is pernicious 'because constitutional limitations were invoked to stop the natural vent of legislation'[181] resulting in 'waning respect for law'.[182]

Nevertheless, Brandeis remains optimistic that legal practice could be reformed in order to simultaneously curb judicial activism and restore public confidence in the administration of justice. Responding to Theodore Roosevelt's proposal to recall judges and overturn decisions like *Lochner*,[183] Brandeis argues '[w]hat we need is not to displace the courts, but to make them efficient instruments of justice; not to displace the lawyer, but to fit him for his official or judicial task'.[184] The way to accomplish a 'living law'—one which harmonises the theoretical and practical dimensions of legal analysis—is to train lawyers 'not only for the exercise of strictly judicial functions, but also for the exercise of administrative functions, quasi-judicial in character'.[185] In other words, Brandeis advocates a post-Langdellian revolution, whereby law students would learn 'economics and sociology and politics which embody the facts and present the problems of today'.[186]

Similar themes pervade Brandeis's judicial opinions. Like Holmes J, Brandeis J generally adopts a restrained attitude when reviewing legislation regulating property or economic interests. However, whereas Holmes J's opinions proceeded from a sceptical appraisal of abstractions like freedom of contract, Brandeis J's perspective is rooted in a belief that judges should not pronounce upon the constitutionality of legislation until they understood the context of the case. Thus, when the Supreme Court struck down Nebraska's standard bread weight law under the Fifth Amendment, Brandeis J penned a dissenting opinion very similar to his brief in *Muller v Oregon*.[187] He begins by noting that the Court previously upheld similar municipal legislation fixing standard bread weights. While he could have rested his dissent on this point, he proceeds to examine the context of the case to highlight the rational basis for the legislation. Thus, he states that the Court should

> determine whether the prohibition of excess weights can reasonably be deemed necessary; whether the prohibition can reasonably be deemed an appropriate means of preventing short weights and incidental unfair practices; and whether compliance with the limitation prescribed can reasonably be deemed practical.[188]

[181] ibid.
[182] ibid 461.
[183] Theodore Roosevelt, Address at Philadelphia, Pennsylvania: Recall of Judges and Referendum of Decisions (10 April 1912), available at: www.theodore-roosevelt.com/trspeechescomplete.html.
[184] Brandeis, 'The Living Law' (n 176 above) 468.
[185] ibid 469.
[186] ibid 470.
[187] *Burns Baking Co v Bryan* 264 US 504 (1924).
[188] ibid 519.

In order to make these assessments, Brandeis J looks beyond formal doctrine, saying:[189]

> The determination of these questions involves an enquiry into the facts. Unless we know the facts on which the legislators may have acted, we cannot properly decide whether they were (or whether their measures are) unreasonable, arbitrary or capricious. Knowledge is essential to understanding; and understanding should precede judging … [I]n this case, we have merely to acquaint ourselves with the art of breadmaking and the usages of the trade; with the devices by which buyers of bread are imposed upon and honest bakers or dealers are subjected by their dishonest fellows to unfair competition; with the problems which have confronted public officials charged with the enforcement of the laws prohibiting short weights, and with their experience in administering those laws.

He then outlines how common experience led bakers, consumers, and public officials throughout the United States to the conclusion that the impugned regulation was in the public interest. Thus, Brandeis J concludes that the legislation's objectives (ensuring fair competition and fair dealing) were reasonable and its means proportionate.[190] Even though much of this evidence could not be found on the record, Brandeis J asserts that judges can take notice of relevant facts in order 'to perform the delicate judicial task' of assessing 'whether the provision as applied is so clearly arbitrary or capricious that legislators acting reasonably could not have believed it to be necessary or appropriate for the public welfare'.[191]

The importance of context runs through many of Brandeis J's famous opinions on experimental federalism,[192] constitutional avoidance,[193] and diversity jurisdiction.[194] Brandeis J consistently counselled judicial restraint

[189] ibid 520.

[190] ibid 527–33.

[191] ibid 533–34.

[192] *New State Ice Co v Liebmann* 285 US 262, 311 (1932): 'It is one of the happy incidents of the federal system that a single courageous State may, if its citizens choose, serve as a laboratory; and try novel social and economic experiments without risk to the rest of the country'.

[193] *Ashwander v Valley Authority* 297 US 288, 346–48 (1936). The doctrine of constitutional avoidance provides that the Court should exercise restraint when (1) a constitutional lawsuit is the product of collusion between the parties, (2) the Court is invited to anticipate constitutional questions not raised on the facts, (3) the Court is invited to formulate a constitutional principle broader than is necessary in a particular case, (4) the Court can decide the case on non-constitutional grounds, (5) the plaintiff has failed to show that he has been injured by the operation of the statute, (6) the plaintiff has availed himself of benefits under the impugned legislation, and (7) the Court can fairly construe the legislation so as to avoid raising questions about its constitutionality.

[194] *Erie Railroad Co v Tompkins* 304 US 64, 78 (1938). In *Erie*, Brandeis J wrote the majority opinion holding that neither Congress nor federal courts had authority under the Constitution to 'declare substantive rules of common law applicable in a state', which meant that federal courts were bound by statutes by local legislatures and common law rules established by State courts. By doing so, Brandeis J overturned over a century of case law, which held that federal courts had discretion to choose which common law rules should apply in diversity jurisdiction lawsuits.

on all these matters, because he believed that Congress, State legislatures, and local courts were better equipped to mediate the tension between broadly-worded constitutional values and an ever-changing social milieu.

However, Brandeis J's attitude was very different in cases concerning freedom of speech[195] and the right to privacy.[196] As already noted, Brandeis J concurred in the *Abrams* dissent, where Holmes J held that the Court should be 'eternally vigilant against attempts to check the expression of opinions that we loath' so that only speech which constitutes an 'imminent' threat on the facts could be prohibited.[197] But Brandeis J espouses a more robust reading of the First Amendment, so that even speech which is 'likely to result in some violence or in the destruction of property is not enough to justify its suppression'.[198] Thus, when considering the constitutionality of legislation prohibiting the dissemination of communism, Brandeis J asserts that the legislation 'creates merely a rebuttable presumption' which means that the Court is entitled to inquire whether the regulation was justified on the facts.[199] Furthermore, he states that the evidentiary threshold for sustaining the legislation is extremely high: nothing short of proof that the defendant's speech would result in a state of emergency would suffice to uphold the constitutionality of the legislation.[200] Given his restrained attitude on economic matters but more demanding approach to freedom of speech, Brandeis J's analysis foreshadows the different levels of judicial scrutiny outlined in *United States v Carolene Products Co*—a case in which the Court held that the constitutionality of 'regulatory legislation affecting ordinary commercial transactions' should be presumed unless it lacks a 'rational basis', but that legislation which 'appears on its face to be within a specific prohibition of the Constitution', 'restricts those political processes which can ordinarily be expected to bring about repeal of undesirable legislation', or discriminates 'against discrete and insular minorities' should be 'subjected to more exacting judicial scrutiny'.[201]

The idea of different levels of judicial scrutiny also crops up in Brandeis J's administrative law opinions.[202] Brandeis J's chief contribution in these

[195] *Whitney v California* 274 US 357, 378 (1927).
[196] *Olmstead v United States* 277 US 438 (1928).
[197] Above nn 154–55 and accompanying text.
[198] *Whitney* (n 195 above) 378.
[199] ibid 378–79.
[200] ibid.
[201] *United States v Carolene Products Co* 304 US 144, 152–53 (1938). Brandeis J concurred with Stone J's opinion in *Carolene Products*, and Stone J cited Brandeis J's opinion in *Whitney* as supporting his rationale for a doctrine setting different levels of judicial scrutiny. See Edward Purcell, Jr, 'Brandeis, *Erie*, and the New Deal "Constitutional Revolution"' (2001) 26 *Journal of Supreme Court History* 257.
[202] Louis Jaffe, 'The Contributions of Mr Justice Brandeis to Administrative Law' (1932–33) 18 *Iowa Law Review* 213; G Edward White, 'Allocating Power Between Agencies and Courts: The Legacy of Justice Brandeis' (1974) 23 *Duke Law Journal* 195.

cases was to explain why courts should defer to administrative agencies.[203] Brandeis J's rationale for judicial deference to administrative decisions echoes his rationale for deference to legislation—courts should generally exercise restraint because they often lack relevant knowledge about the social context surrounding the decision. Thus, when a shipper sought to circumvent the ICC's jurisdiction by suing the railway in the Supreme Court of Minnesota to recover excessive rates, Brandeis J held that the ICC had primary jurisdiction over the dispute. In reaching his conclusion, he stated 'the courts may not be resorted to until the administrative question has been determined by the Commission',[204] because the dispute 'presents an administrative question, one of perhaps considerable complexity' which 'may rest either upon the peculiar circumstances of a particular case or upon a general practice'.[205] Later, in a dissenting opinion upholding the constitutionality of West Virginia legislation establishing a commission to regulate the production of natural gas, Brandeis J expands on this point by saying '[i]n no other field of public service regulation is the controlling body confronted with factors so baffling as in the natural gas industry; and in none is continuous supervision and control required in so high a degree'.[206] Thus, the issue regarding what quantities of natural gas should be exported for profit, calls 'for the informed judgment of a board of experts' who are better equipped to ascertain existing and untapped reserves, estimate local demand, and review the business practices of gas suppliers.[207]

But in cases where an administrative decision-maker had acted unfairly in rendering its decision, Brandeis J held that parties could bring their dispute before the courts. In *Skinner & Eddy Corp v United States*, a shipper challenged an ICC rate order issued without a hearing.[208] After filing repeated requests for a hearing, the shipper asked a federal district court to enjoin the ICC from enforcing its order. Writing for the Court, Brandeis J held that if the shipper 'had sought relief against a rate or practice alleged to be unjust because unreasonably high or discriminatory, the remedy must have been sought primarily by proceedings before the Commission', and the Commission's decision 'would have been conclusive, unless there was lack of substantial evidence, some irregularity in the proceedings, or some error in the application of rules of law'.[209] However, in his view the shipper was not claiming that the order was unreasonable, but rather that 'the Commission has exceeded its statutory powers'.[210] Brandeis J concluded that, in cases

[203] White, 'Allocating Power' (n 202 above) 207–15.
[204] *Northern Pacific Railway Co v Solum* 247 US 477, 484 (1918).
[205] ibid 482–83.
[206] *Pennsylvania v West Virginia* 262 US 553, 621 (1923).
[207] ibid 622–23.
[208] *Skinner & Eddy Corporation v United States* 249 US 557 (1919).
[209] ibid 562.
[210] ibid.

concerning such issues 'the courts have jurisdiction of suits to enjoin the enforcement of an order, even if the plaintiff has not attempted to secure redress in a proceeding before the Commission'.[211]

In other cases, Brandeis J emphasised that the intensity of judicial review was proportionate to the impact of the decision. In this respect, Brandeis J's approach to judicial review varies greatly between rate-setting decisions and decisions which limited personal liberty.[212] In *Ohio Valley Water Company v Ben Avon Borough*, a majority of the Court held that the due process clause of the Fourteenth Amendment gave the Ohio Valley Water Company the right to a de novo judicial reassessment of the rate.[213] In an opinion which gave judges a broad licence to engage in correctness review, McReynolds J held that if a property owner claims that an administrative decision is confiscatory, 'the State must provide a fair opportunity for submitting that issue to a judicial tribunal for determination upon its own independent judgment as to both law and facts'.[214] Writing in dissent, Brandeis J argued that the majority had overstepped its role, pointing out that the Company had been given a fair hearing before the Commission.[215] In his view, the Commission's decision hinged upon 'pure matters of fact', and was therefore entitled to a presumption 'in favour of the conclusion of an experienced administrative body reached after a full hearing'.[216]

By contrast, in immigration decisions 'Brandeis tended to scrutinize executive action more carefully and to interpret the fact–law distinction more strictly'.[217] Thus, in *Ng Fung Ho v White*, a case in which an immigration commissioner in San Francisco decided to deport two individuals who claimed to be American citizens,[218] Brandeis J wrote a unanimous opinion concluding that they were entitled to a de novo judicial reassessment of their claims. In his view, citizenship was 'an essential jurisdictional fact', which meant that the commissioner could not conclusively determine the outcome.[219] Brandeis J explained that:[220]

> To deport one who so claims to be a citizen, obviously deprives him of liberty … It may result also in loss of both property and life; or of all that makes life worth living. Against the danger of such deprivation without the sanction afforded by

[211] ibid.

[212] White, 'Allocating Power' (n 202 above).

[213] *Ohio Valley Water Company v Ben Avon Borough* (n 20 above), 289. See also *Crowell v Benson* 285 US 22 (1932).

[214] *Ohio Valley Water* (n 20 above) ibid.

[215] ibid 292.

[216] ibid 297. See also *Crowell* (n 214 above) 65–95 (Brandeis J, dissenting); Louis Jaffe, 'Constitutional and Jurisdictional Fact' (1957) 70 *Harvard Law Review* 953.

[217] White, 'Allocating Power' (n 202 above) 226.

[218] *Ng Fung Ho v White* 259 US 276 (1922). See also *Milwaukee Publishing Co v Burleson* 255 US 407, 421–36 (1921) (Brandeis J, dissenting).

[219] *Ng Fung Ho* 284.

[220] ibid.

judicial proceedings, the Fifth Amendment affords protection in its guarantee of due process of law.

The different levels of scrutiny which Brandeis J employed when reviewing administrative decisions track the approach he employed when reviewing the constitutionality of legislation. With very few exceptions, Brandeis J employed a relatively forgiving, 'rational basis' standard when dealing with governmental decisions affecting property and economic interests, but a strict form of de novo scrutiny when reviewing decisions constraining speech or physical liberty. He summed up his views on this point shortly before retiring from the Court by saying '[a] citizen who claims that his liberty is being infringed is entitled, upon habeas corpus, to the opportunity of a judicial determination of the facts' but 'that when dealing with property a much more liberal rule applies'.[221]

B. Functionalism, Due Process, and Administrative Law

Even though Holmes and Brandeis JJ were famous dissenters, their ideas foreshadowed a profound change in American constitutional law. While their nominations to the Supreme Court had provoked reactions ranging from backhanded compliments[222] to hostile criticism,[223] they were lionised by politicians, journalists, and legal academics as 'professional and cultural heroes' by the time Brandeis retired on 13 February 1939.[224] One individual in particular, Felix Frankfurter, was influential in popularising Holmes and Brandeis JJ's ideas through his law journal articles[225] and political essays.[226] And when he was appointed to the Supreme Court two weeks

[221] *St Joseph Stock Yards Co v United States* 298 US 38, 77 (1936).

[222] At the time of his appointment, Holmes was described variously as 'lacking intellectual strength' and being 'more "brilliant" than sound'. See White, *Oliver Wendell Holmes* (n 103 above) 305–6.

[223] During the hotly contested nomination hearings preceding his appointment, the subcommittee of the Senate judiciary committee received a petition signed by several prominent citizens of Massachusetts, including the President of Harvard, declaring that Brandeis was unethical and lacked 'judicial temperament'. Brandeis's nomination was ultimately confirmed by a Senate vote of 47 to 22, which split strictly along partisan lines. See Urofsky, *Brandeis* (n 164 above) ch 18.

[224] G Edward White, 'The Canonization of Holmes and Brandeis: Epistemology and Judicial Reputations' (1995) *New York University Law Review* 576, 577. See also Brad Snyder, 'The House that Built Holmes' (2012) 30 *Law and History Review* 661.

[225] See, eg Felix Frankfurter, 'The Constitutional Opinions of Justice Holmes' (1916) 29 *Harvard Law Review* 683; Felix Frankfurter, 'Twenty Years of Mr. Justice Holmes' Constitutional Opinions' (1923) 36 *Harvard Law Review* 909; Felix Frankfurter, 'Mr. Justice Holmes and the Constitution' (1927) 41 *Harvard Law Review* 121; Felix Frankfurter, Review of *The Dissenting Opinions of Mr Justice Holmes* (1930) 16 *Virginia Law Review* 743; Felix Frankfurter, 'Mr. Justice Brandeis and the Constitution' (1931) 45 *Harvard Law Review* 33.

[226] See, eg Felix Frankfurter, 'Press Censorship by Judicial Construction', *New Republic* (30 March 1921) 124; Felix Frankfurter, 'Mr Justice Holmes', *New Republic* (20 December

before Brandeis J retired, Frankfurter J became the leading proponent of judicial restraint.

Felix Frankfurter was born 15 November 1882 in Vienna, the son of middle-class Jewish parents.[227] He emigrated to New York with his family in 1894 and, after graduating from the City College of New York in 1902, enrolled at Harvard Law School where he excelled as a student.[228] He 'made' the *Harvard Law Review*, graduated at the top his class, and was a research assistant for Holmes's close personal friend, John Chipman Gray.[229] On 4 May 1905, one year before he received his law degree, Frankfurter attended a lecture by Louis Brandeis on 'The Opportunity in the Law'.[230] In the lecture, Brandeis deplored the declining ethical standards of legal professionals, saying 'lawyers have, to a large extent, allowed themselves to become adjuncts of great corporations and have neglected their obligation to use their powers for the protection of the people'.[231] In order to counteract this trend, he stated that '[t]he great opportunity of the American bar is and will be to stand again as it did in the past, ready to protect … the interests of the people'.[232]

After graduation, Frankfurter took a job with a Wall Street firm, but quit after he got an offer from Henry Stimson, the US Attorney for the Southern District of New York. Although he had to take a considerable pay cut, Frankfurter relished the opportunity because it enabled him to 'practise law without having a client'.[233] When Stimson became War Secretary, he took Frankfurter with him to the Bureau of Insular Affairs.[234] But before leaving for Washington, Frankfurter acquired a letter of introduction from his old professor, Gray, addressed to Holmes.[235] Frankfurter visited Holmes frequently, and Holmes returned the favour by dining with Frankfurter at the

1922) 84; Felix Frankfurter, 'Mr Justice Holmes', *New Republic* (17 March 1926) 89; Felix Frankfurter, 'Brandeis and the Shoe Machinery Company', *New Republic* (4 March 1916) 117; Felix Frankfurter, 'The Nomination of Mr Justice Brandeis', *New Republic* (5 February 1916) reprinted in Philip Kurland (ed), *Felix Frankfurter on the Supreme Court: Extrajudicial Essays on the Court and the Constitution* (Cambridge, Belknap Press, 1970) 43.

[227] Melvin Urofsky, *Felix Frankfurter: Judicial Restraint and Individual Liberties* (Boston MA, Twayne Publishers, 1991) 1.

[228] Frankfurter's positive experience as a student at Harvard formed the basis of his meritocratic outlook throughout his life. As he later put it, Harvard exposed him to an atmosphere in which 'excellence in your profession' was prized over social status or race. Harlan Phillips, *Felix Frankfurter Reminisces* (New York, Reynal & Company, 1960) 26–27.

[229] Phillips, *Felix Frankfurter Reminisces* (n 228 above) chs 1–2. Gray's jurisprudence was very similar to Holmes's. See John Chipman Gray, *The Nature and Sources of Law* (New York, Columbia University Press, 1909); Michael Parrish, *Felix Frankfurter and His Times: The Reform Years* (New York, The Free Press, 1982) 20.

[230] Brandeis, 'The Opportunity in the Law' (n 169 above).

[231] ibid 559.

[232] ibid.

[233] Phillips, *Felix Frankfurter Reminisces* (n 228 above) 39.

[234] Urofsky, *Frankfurter* (n 227 above) 4.

[235] Phillips, *Felix Frankfurter Reminisces* (n 228 above) 58.

'House of Truth', a sarcastic moniker for Frankfurter's boarding house.[236] Over the next three years, Frankfurter cultivated friendships with influential lawyers, politicians, academics, artists, and journalists by hosting dinner parties at the House of Truth, which developed a reputation as 'the nation's capital's foremost intellectual and political salon'.[237] Walter Lippmann and Herbert Croly, the founding editors of *The New Republic*, were frequent visitors,[238] and Louis Brandeis dined there when he was in Washington.[239]

Frankfurter corresponded regularly with both Holmes[240] and Brandeis.[241] In his letters to Holmes, Frankfurter expressed 'an exuberant filial devotion approaching deification',[242] punctuated by references to his own reform projects[243] or fulsome praise for one of Holmes's recent opinions.[244] Holmes responded more formally: he welcomed Frankfurter's flattery, dispensed career advice,[245] expressed scepticism about the progressive reforms,[246] and opined on his own philosophical[247] and jurisprudential views.[248] When Brandeis was nominated to the Supreme Court, Frankfurter mobilised support and rebutted conservative criticism during the confirmation hearings.[249] After Brandeis was sworn in, Frankfurter assumed Brandeis's role as the 'people's attorney',[250] frequently defending legislation before the Supreme Court by filing fact-laden Brandeis briefs.[251] Brandeis, who privately considered his protégé to be 'half brother, half son'[252] as well as 'the most useful lawyer in the United States',[253] encouraged Frankfurter to

[236] Jeff O'Connell and Nancy Dart, 'The House of Truth: Home of the Young Frankfurter and Lippmann' (1985) 35 *Catholic University Law Review* 79.

[237] Snyder, 'The House that Built Holmes' (n 224 above) 664.

[238] ibid.

[239] ibid 88–89. See also Urofsky, *Brandeis* (n 164 above) 336–38.

[240] Mennel and Compston (eds), *Holmes & Frankfurter* (n 168 above).

[241] David Levy and Melvin Urofsky (eds), *Half-Son, Half-Brother: The Letters of Louis D Brandeis to Felix Frankfurter* (Norman OK, University of Oklahoma Press, 1991).

[242] Mennel and Compston, *Holmes & Frankfurter* (n 168 above) xv.

[243] See, eg ibid 85–86, 123–24.

[244] See, eg ibid 25–26 (praising Holmes J's dissent in *Coppage* (n 19 above) and *Adair* (n 19 above)) and 75 (praising Holmes J's dissent in *Abrams* (n 157 above)).

[245] See, eg ibid 12–13. Holmes discouraged Frankfurter from accepting an academic position at Harvard, saying 'academic life is but half life—it is a withdrawal from the fight in order to utter smart things that cost you nothing except the thinking them from a cloister'.

[246] See, eg ibid 53–56, 103, 188–89.

[247] See, eg ibid 3–5, 24–25, 35–36, 215–16, 236–37.

[248] See, eg ibid 19–20, 78, 99–100.

[249] See, eg Urofsky, *Brandeis* (n 164 above) 442; Levy and Urofsky (eds), *Letters of Louis D Brandeis*, vol V (Albany NY, State University of New York, 1978) 129–30, 140–41.

[250] Urofsky, *Frankfurter* (n 227 above) 8–9.

[251] Urofsky, *Brandeis* (n 164 above) 592–96. Frankfurter appeared as counsel for the National Consumers' League in *Bunting v Oregon* 243 US 426 (1917); *Stettler v O'Hara* 243 US 639 (1917); and *Adkins* (n 19 above).

[252] Letter from Louis Brandeis to Felix Frankfurter 24 September 1925 in Urofsky and Levy (eds), *Half-Son, Half-Brother* (n 241 above) 212.

[253] Urofsky and Levy, *Letters of Louis D Brandeis*, vol V (n 249 above) 364.

take up a teaching position at Harvard[254] and provided him with an annual stipend to defray costs associated with his various law reform projects.[255]

When Frankfurter returned to Harvard in 1914, he immediately nailed his colours to Thayer's mast.[256] In his first essay in the *Harvard Law Review*, Frankfurter critiqued a series of court rulings in an attempt to turn the tide in favour of judicial restraint.[257] He concluded his argument by paraphrasing Thayer (whom he called 'a great teacher of constitutional law'), saying that 'responsibility for mischievous or inadequate legislation' should be 'sharply brought home where it belongs,—to the legislature and to the people themselves'.[258] Even though Thayer died the year before Frankfurter enrolled at Harvard, Thayer's ideas loomed largely in Frankfurter's mind. Shortly before his own death in 1963, Frankfurter confessed that[259]

> both Homes and Brandeis influenced me in my constitutional outlook, but both of them derived theirs from the same source from which I derived mine, namely, Professor James Bradley Thayer, with whom both had personal relations but whose views influenced me only through his writing, as was indirectly true of the man who taught me constitutional law at Harvard Law School, namely, Professor Wambaugh, a pupil of Thayer. Moreover, Thayer's views were in the air at the Law School while I was there and I undoubtedly imbibed that atmosphere.

Throughout his career, Frankfurter repeatedly invoked Thayer's famous article,[260] which he regarded as 'the great guide for judges … of what the place of the judiciary is in relation to constitutional questions'.[261]

While Frankfurter's general assessment of the Supreme Court was critical, its decision in *Adkins v Children's Hospital* cut him deeply.[262] The case

[254] Phillips, *Felix Frankfurter Reminisces* (n 228 above) 78.

[255] Levy and Urofsky (eds), *Letters of Louis D Brandeis* (n 160 above) 266–67. Between 1916 and 1939, Brandeis gave Frankfurter US$50,000 for his law reform projects, which was a considerable sum at the time. David Levy and Bruce Murphy, 'Preserving the Progressive Spirit in a Conservative Time: The Joint Reform Efforts of Justice Brandeis and Professor Felix Frankfurter, 1916–1933' (1980) 78 *Michigan Law Review* 1252; Urofsky, *Brandeis* (n 164 above) 504.

[256] See generally Brad Snyder, 'Frankfurter and Popular Constitutionalism' (2013) 47 *University of California Davis Law Review* 343.

[257] Felix Frankfurter, 'The Present Approach to Constitutional Decisions on the Bill of Rights' (1915) 28 *Harvard Law Review* 790.

[258] ibid 792–93.

[259] 'Letter from Felix Frankfurter to Arthur Schlesinger, 18 June 1963' in Max Freedman (ed), *Roosevelt and Frankfurter: Their Correspondence 1928–1945* (Boston MA, Little, Brown & Company, 1967) 25.

[260] See also Felix Frankfurter, 'A Note on Advisory Opinions' (1924) 37 *Harvard Law Review* 1002, 1008; Felix Frankfurter and James Landis, 'The Compact Clause of the Constitution—A Study in Interstate Adjustments' (1925) 34 *Yale Law Journal* 685, 728; Felix Frankfurter, *The Commerce Clause Under Marshall, Taney and Waite* (Chapel Hill NC, University of North Carolina Press, 1937); Felix Frankfurter and Henry Hart, Jr, 'The Business of the Supreme Court at October Term, 1933' (1934) 48 *Harvard Law Review* 238, 281.

[261] Phillips, *Felix Frankfurter Reminisces* (n 228 above) 300; Parrish, *Felix Frankfurter and His Times* (n 229 above) 21.

[262] *Adkins* (n 19 above).

concerned a Fifth Amendment challenge to legislation establishing a minimum wage commission for the District of Columbia. Frankfurter filed a brief in support of the legislation in which he argued that the Court's decision in *Muller v Oregon* had convincingly debunked the liberty of contract doctrine.[263] In his oral submissions, Frankfurter hammered home the argument that legislation should be upheld unless it could be shown 'beyond a rational doubt' to infringe the Constitution, that similar legislation had been 'uniformly sustained by the courts' as being justified by the public interest, and both Congress and the Senate had overwhelmingly approved the measure after thorough discussion and debate.[264]

Nevertheless, the Court struck down the enabling legislation. In his majority opinion, Sutherland J held that 'the right to contract about one's affairs ... is settled by the decisions of this Court and is no longer open to question'.[265] While he acknowledged that liberty of contract was not 'absolute', he asserted that it was 'the general rule and restraint the exception; and the exercise of legislative authority to abridge it can be justified only by the existence of exceptional circumstances'.[266] Holmes J protested that '[w]hen so many intelligent persons, who have studied the matter more than any of us can, have thought that the means are effective and are worth the price, it seems to me impossible to deny that the belief reasonably may be held by reasonable men'.[267] While Brandeis J did not participate in the decision (his daughter worked for the Minimum Wage Board at the time), it can safely be surmised that he would have concurred with Holmes J's dissent.[268]

The *Adkins* decision shattered Frankfurter's faith in the judiciary.[269] His personal correspondence with Holmes and Brandeis JJ revealed machinations amongst the justices which diminished the Court's prestige in his eyes.[270] But shortly after the Court rendered its decision in *Adkins*, Frankfurter confessed to his friend, Learned Hand, that 'the possible gain isn't worth the cost of having five men without any reasonable probability that they are qualified for the task, determine the course of social policy for the states and the nation'.[271] Later, in an unsigned editorial in the

[263] In one of his earliest articles, Frankfurter argued that *Muller* constituted a turning point in which the point of emphasis had shifted away from '*a priori* theories' towards '[o]rganized observation, investigation, and experimentation produced facts'. Felix Frankfurter, 'Hours of Labor and Realism in Constitutional Law' (1916) 29 *Harvard Law Review* 353, 364.

[264] *Adkins* (n 19 above), 526–35.

[265] ibid 545.

[266] ibid 546.

[267] ibid 568.

[268] Urofsky, *Brandeis* (n 164 above) ch 24.

[269] Snyder, 'Frankfurter and Popular Constitutionalism' (n 256 above) 363. See also Parrish, *Felix Frankfurter and His Times* (n 229 above) 165.

[270] ibid.

[271] Constance Jordan, *Reason and Imagination: The Selected Correspondence of Learned Hand: 1897–1961* (Oxford, Oxford University Press, 2013) 118.

New Republic, Frankfurter argued that 'no nine men are wise enough and good enough to be entrusted with the power which the unlimited provisions of the due process clauses confer', prompting him to conclude that '[t]he due process clauses ought to go'.[272] He would never argue another case in front of the Supreme Court.[273]

Instead, he channelled considerable energy towards the political arena. Frankfurter was attracted to the progressive movement because it had the potential to achieve constitutional change through political engagement.[274] While living at the 'House of Truth', he became enthralled with the 'Wisconsin' idea—the notion that politics could be guided by university-trained experts;[275] he supported the presidential bids of progressives like Theodore Roosevelt, Robert La Follete, Al Smith, and Franklin Roosevelt;[276] and was instrumental in placing like-minded men in high ranking public offices, often with Brandeis J's advice.[277] In 1916, Frankfurter began teaching courses on public utility regulation and administrative law, a course which was 'inextricably bound up with constitutional law',[278] and each year he selected his best students to serve as law clerks for Holmes and Brandeis JJ. Many of these students went on to become influential scholars in constitutional[279] and administrative law[280] or served in Franklin Roosevelt's administration.[281]

[272] Felix Frankfurter, 'The Red Terror of Judicial Reform' *The New Republic* (1 October 1924) reprinted in Kurland (ed), *Felix Frankfurter on the Supreme Court* (n 226 above) 142, 166–67.

[273] Snyder, 'Frankfurter and Popular Constitutionalism' (n 255 above) 363.

[274] Urofsky, *Frankfurter* (n 227 above) 38, fn 20.

[275] Parrish, *Felix Frankfurter and His Times* (n 229 above) 62; Felix Frankfurter, 'Democracy and the Expert' *Atlantic Monthly* (November 1930) 649. In a letter addressed to his friend, Learned Hand, Frankfurter declared 'I have long thought that juristically, the Wisconsin idea should be nationalised, and that it was up to the Law School to do it.' Letter from Frankfurter to Learned Hand 23 September 1912 reprinted in Sanford Levinson, 'The Democratic Faith of Felix Frankfurter' (1973) 25 *Stanford Law Review* 430, 433.

[276] Snyder, 'Frankfurter and Popular Constitutionalism' (n 256 above) 358–60.

[277] Urofsky, *Brandeis* (n 164 above) ch 20; Urofsky, *Frankfurter* (n 227 above) ch 3.

[278] Felix Frankfurter, 'The Task of Administrative Law' (1927) 75 *University of Pennsylvania Law Review* 614, 618.

[279] See eg, Henry Hart, 'The Power of Congress to Limit the Jurisdiction of Federal Courts: An Exercise in Dialectic' (1953) 66 *Harvard Law Review* 1362; Henry Hart and Herbert Wechsler, *The Federal Courts and the Federal System* (New York, Foundation Press, 1953); Henry Hart and Albert Sacks, *The Legal Process: Basic Problems in the Making and Application of Law, William Eskridge and Philip Frickey*(Westbury, Foundation Press, 1994).

[280] See, eg James Landis, *The Administrative Process* (New Haven CT, Yale University Press, 1938); Louis Jaffe, *Judicial Control of Administrative Action* (Boston MA, Little, Brown and Company, 1965); Louis Jaffe and Nathaniel Nathanson, *Administrative Law: Cases and Materials*, 4th edn (Boston MA, Little, Brown and Company, 1976).

[281] Urofsky, *Frankfurter* (n 227 above) 37. See also G Edward White, 'Felix Frankfurter, the Old Boy Network, and the New Deal: The Placement of Elite Lawyers in Public Service in the 1930's' (1986) 29 *Arkansas Law Review* 631.

In 1930, Frankfurter delivered the Dodge Lectures at Yale,[282] in which he outlined his vision of a government guided by expert administrators.[283] Like Brandeis, he emphasises how rapid social and economic change had revolutionised the nature of American government.[284] Speaking at the onset of the Great Depression, Frankfurter notes that '[g]overnment is no longer merely to keep the ring, to be a policeman, to secure the observance of elementary decencies',[285] because the demands of justice require 'wholly new interactions between citizen and government'.[286] Thus, he argues that State governments should be given 'the amplest scope for energy and individuality in dealing with the myriad problems created by our complex industrial civilization',[287] stating that '[o]pportunity must be allowed for vindicating reasonable belief by experience'.[288]

Alluding to *Adkins*, Frankfurter notes that constitutional interpretation 'should be freely tested by its results and not be erected into a religious dogma intrusted to the zealous keeping of any church'.[289] On this point, he characterises the Supreme Court's 'veto power' over socio-economic legislation as:[290]

> the most destructive and the least responsible: the most destructive, because judicial nullification on grounds of constitutionality stops experimentation at its source, and bars increase to the fund of social knowledge by scientific tests of trial and error; the least responsible, because it so often turns on the fortuitous circumstances which determine a majority decision and shelters the fallible judgment of individual Justices, in matters of fact and opinion not peculiarly within the special competence of judges, behind the impersonal dooms of the Constitution. The inclination of a single Justice or two, the tip of his mind or of his fears, may determine the opportunity of a much needed social experiment to survive, or may frustrate for a long time intelligent attempts to deal with a social evil.

By advocating a pragmatic interpretation of the Constitution, which gives the politically accountable branches of government the latitude to test hypotheses for improving social welfare, Frankfurter seeks to neutralise judicial decisions which obstruct legislative and administrative initiatives.[291]

[282] Felix Frankfurter, *The Public and Its Government* (New Haven CT, Yale University Press, 1930).

[283] Michael Silverstein, *Constitutional Faiths: Felix Frankfurter, Hugo Black, and the Process of Judicial Decision-Making* (Ithaca NY, Cornell University Press, 1984) 79.

[284] Frankfurter, *The Public and Its Government* (n 282 above) 9.

[285] ibid 24.

[286] ibid 27.

[287] ibid 48.

[288] ibid 49.

[289] ibid 42.

[290] ibid 50.

[291] ibid 63.

However, Frankfurter's assessment was not uniformly negative. He acknowledges that the Constitution contains important procedural rights—the right to a jury trial, protection from self-incrimination and unreasonable searches, freedom of speech, and freedom of assembly—which reflect 'the experience of early American statesmen as to the abuses of arbitrary power'.[292] Thus, he urges his audience at Yale in 1930 to heed 'the procedural wisdom of the Bill or rights',[293] stating 'that the history of liberty is to a large extent the history of procedural observances'.[294]

Nevertheless, Frankfurter believed judicial review was not the only safeguard for preserving liberty, nor was it the most important one. Echoing Thayer, he emphasises that the 'ultimate protection' against administrative overreach 'is to be found in ourselves, our zeal for liberty, our respect for one another and for the common good'.[295] But in order for the democratic process to function effectively, other safeguards are required, such as[296]

> very high standards of professional service, an effective procedure (remembering that 'in the development of our liberty insistence upon procedural regulatory has been a large factor'), easy access to public scrutiny and a constant play of alert public criticism, especially by an informed and spirited bar.

Thus, Frankfurter asserts that, while an enlarged administrative state carries the risk of arbitrary governmental decisions, the responsibility for 'final determinations of large policy' should remain with the 'direct representatives of the public' as opposed to administrative officials or judges.[297]

While on the Supreme Court, Frankfurter struggled to reconcile respect for broad delegations of power to expert officials with constitutional standards of fair process. Like Brandeis J, Frankfurter J adjusted the level of scrutiny he employed to fit the context of the case. These subtle variations in Frankfurter J's approach are apparent in two lines of cases—one concerning due process rights, the other concerning the administrative duty to give reasons.

In the first line of cases, Frankfurter J held that rate-making agencies should have considerable latitude to adapt their decision-making processes to their statutory mandate. In *United States v Morgan* Frankfurter J wrote a majority opinion upholding a decision of the Secretary of Agriculture, even though the Secretary employed bureaucratic rather than judicial fact-finding techniques.[298] In April 1930, the Department of Agriculture commenced proceedings under the Packers and Stockyards Act to set rates that could

[292] ibid 58.
[293] ibid 61.
[294] ibid 60.
[295] ibid 159.
[296] ibid.
[297] ibid.
[298] *United States v Morgan* 313 US 409 (1941).

be charged by livestock marketing agencies. Three years later, the Secretary of Agriculture issued an order, which was promptly challenged by marketing agencies on the ground that it violated their constitutional right to due process and the Supreme Court directed a trial of the issue.[299] At the trial, the Secretary and his administrative staff testified at length about whether he had personally considered the evidence, consisting of 13,000 pages of testimony and 1,000 pages of exhibits.[300] While the Secretary admitted that he relied upon preliminary findings made by the Bureau of Animal Industry, he testified that his order was based on his independent assessment of those findings. Nevertheless, the Supreme Court struck down the order because the Secretary had failed to give the marketing agencies a 'full hearing', because he had not allowed them to cross-examine his administrative staff.[301] The case was remitted back for another determination, but when the Secretary rendered his decision the marketing agencies launched another due process challenge.

By the time the matter reached the Supreme Court for the fourth time, President Roosevelt had appointed five new Justices—Frankfurter, Hugo Black, William Douglas, Frank Murphy, and Stanley Reed—who had either supported the New Deal or had served in administrative agencies. Frankfurter J, writing for the Court, begins by observing that the dispute had languished in federal courts for 11 years and that the Secretary's authority had been subjected to unprecedented scrutiny.[302] Furthermore, he notes that the case concerned 'a task of striking a balance and reaching a judgment on factors beset with doubts and difficulties, uncertainty and speculation'.[303] Because Congress had delegated rate-making authority to the Secretary, he held that the Court should not 'convert a contest before the Secretary into one before the courts',[304] stating that '[o]ur duty is at an end when we find, as we do find, that the Secretary was responsibly conscious of conditions at the market' and that 'he duly weighed them'.[305] In an admonition directed to lower courts, he states that 'although the administrative process has had a different development and pursues somewhat different ways from those of courts, they are to be deemed collaborative instrumentalities of justice and the appropriate independence of each should be respected by the other'.[306]

By contrast, in *Knauff v Shaughnessy*, Frankfurter J held that when an individual's liberty is at stake, the intensity of judicial scrutiny is augmented.[307]

[299] *Morgan v United States* 298 US 468 (1936).
[300] *Morgan v United States* 23 F Supp 380, 382 (1937) (Mo DC).
[301] *Morgan v United States* 304 US 1 (1938).
[302] *United States v Morgan* (n 298 above) 413–14.
[303] ibid 417.
[304] ibid.
[305] ibid 420.
[306] ibid 422. See also *Federal Communications Commission v Pottsville Broadcasting Co* 309 US 134, 143 (1940); *Federal Communications Commission v National Broadcasting Co* 319 US 239 (1943) (Frankfurter J, dissenting).
[307] *Knauff v Shaughnessy* 338 US 537 (1950).

The case concerned a decision by the United States Attorney General, who refused to admit the German wife of an American soldier into the United States on the basis of confidential information. Upon her arrival, she was detained at Ellis Island and two months later an immigration commissioner recommended her removal without a hearing. She subsequently brought a *habeas corpus* application claiming that wartime amendments to the War Brides Act, which enabled the Attorney General to exclude aliens on the basis of confidential information, were unconstitutional.

After noting that the claimant had no legal right to enter the country, a majority of the Court held that the Attorney General's decision was 'a fundamental act of sovereignty',[308] which was 'not within the province of any court, unless expressly authorized by law'.[309] In light of the broad powers given to the Attorney General, the Court concluded that '[i]n such a case we have no authority to retry the determination of the Attorney General'.[310] However Frankfurter J, writing in dissent, protests 'that the deepest tie that an American soldier could form may be secretly severed on the mere say-so of an official, however well-intentioned'.[311] In his view, the majority had failed to consider both the impact of the decision and the general purposes underlying the enabling legislation, which were to preserve and promote family relationships. Therefore, he concludes that '[l]egisation should not be read in such a decimating spirit unless the letter of Congress is inexorable',[312] because '[i]t is not to be assumed that Congress gave with a bountiful hand but allowed its bounty arbitrarily to be taken away'.[313]

The second line of cases concerns the duty to give reasons. While Frankfurter J thought that courts should generally defer to the judgments of administrative experts, he also held that administrators had to earn that respect by providing a rational justification for their decisions.[314] For instance, in *Phelps Dodge Corp v National Labor Relations Board* Frankfurter J held that while the National Labor Relations Board's remedial powers were broad enough to grant the award, the case ought to be remanded to the Board for further explanation.[315] The case concerned an allegation that

308 ibid 542.

309 ibid 543.

310 ibid 546.

311 ibid 548.

312 ibid 548.

313 ibid 549. But see *Korematsu v United States* 323 US 214, 224–25 (1944), a decision in which Frankfurter J wrote a concurring opinion upholding the validity of an executive order issued by the US Army, which directed the internment of American citizens of Japanese ancestry. In that case, Frankfurter J held that 'the validity of action under the war power must be judged wholly in the context of war. That action is not to be stigmatized as lawless because like action in times of peace would be lawless'.

314 See, eg *Eastern-Central Association v United States* 321 US 194, 215 (1944) (Frankfurter J, dissenting).

315 *Phelps Dodge Corp v National Labor Relations Board* 313 US 177 (1944).

an employer had committed an unfair labour practice by refusing to hire two union men. After concluding that the employer had violated the statute, the Board ordered the company to offer the men jobs and compensate them for lost wages even though they had subsequently found alternative employment. The company sought judicial review, claiming that the statutory provision which directed the Board 'to take such affirmative action, including reinstatement of employees ... as will effectuate the policies of this Act' did not contemplate such an order.[316]

Frankfurter J held that the enabling legislation should be interpreted generously so as to provide the Board with sufficient remedial powers to achieve its policy objectives. He states that '[a]ttainment of a great national policy through expert administration in collaboration with limited judicial review must not be confined within narrow canons for equitable relief'.[317] Nevertheless, he concluded that the case ought to be remitted back to the Board for further explanation of its decision. While he recognised that the Board had the power to reinstate the men, he did not think the Board had adequately explained the rationale underlying its decision.[318] Frankfurter J emphasises that, in requiring the Board to explain its rationale, the Court was bolstering the legitimacy of the administrative process, saying:[319]

> The administrative process will best be vindicated by clarity in its exercise. Since Congress has defined the authority of the Board and the procedure by which it must be asserted and has charged the federal courts with the duty of reviewing the Board's orders ... it will avoid needless litigation and make for effective and expeditious enforcement of the Board's order to require the Board to disclose the basis of its order. We do not intend to enter the province that belongs to the Board, nor do we do so. All we ask of the Board is to give clear indication that it has exercised the discretion with which Congress has empowered it. This is to affirm most emphatically the authority of the Board.

Frankfurter J reaffirms this same principle in *SEC v Chenery Corp*, saying that 'the orderly functioning of the process of review requires that the grounds upon which the agency acted be clearly discussed and adequately sustained'.[320] In doing so, he planted the seeds of the 'hard look' doctrine, which imposes a duty upon administrative agencies to provide a transparent and reasonable justification for decisions which have a considerable impact on a litigant's interests.[321]

[316] National Labor Relations Act, ch 372, 49 Stat 449 (1935), §10(c).

[317] *Phelps Dodge Corp* (n 315 above) 188.

[318] ibid 197.

[319] ibid.

[320] *Securities & Exchange Commission v Chenery Corp* 318 US 80, 94 (1943).

[321] *Greater Boston Television Corp v Federal Communications Commission* 444 F 2d 841, 851 (DC Cir 1970); *Citizens to Preserve Overton Park v Volpe* 401 US 402, 419–20 (1971); Harold Leventhal, 'Environmental Decisionmaking and the Role of the Courts' (1974) 122 *University of Pennsylvania Law Review* 509; *Motor Vehicle Manufacturers' Association v State Farm Mutual Automobile Insurance Co* 463 US 29 (1983); Cass Sunstein, 'Deregulation

Thus, it is apparent that while Frankfurter J thought judges should generally respect administrative decisions, he did not believe they should defer submissively to them. In cases concerning economic interests, he thought that administrative officials should be given substantial latitude in developing their own decision-making processes, and believed that judges should interpret enabling legislation in a permissive manner so as to enable administrative agencies to pursue policy objectives in the manner they saw fit. But in cases where a decision curtailed civil liberties, he thought that the requirements of due process demanded strict judicial scrutiny.

III. CONCLUSION

When Frankfurter J retired from the Supreme Court in 1962, the law concerning judicial review of administrative decisions was governed by two conflicting lines of authority.[322] The first line of cases rests upon premises essentially similar to Diceyan constitutionalism: the legislature creates the law, the judiciary interprets the law, and administrative officials implement the law enacted by the legislature and interpreted by judges. Furthermore, because this line of cases portrays the administrative state as an incorrigible threat to negative liberty, it asserts that 'a court must independently examine an administrative agency's claimed authority ... just as it would assess the legal authority of a private entity to do so'.[323] Thus, these cases conclude that judges should review administrative decisions on a correctness standard.[324]

The second line of cases suggests an alternative constitutional paradigm which can be traced back to the work of Thayer, Holmes, Brandeis, and Frankfurter. Unlike Dicey, this line of cases holds that no person, institution,

and the Hard-Look Doctrine' [1983] *The Supreme Court Review* 177, 181–84; Matthew Warren, 'Active Judging: Judicial Philosophy and the Development of the Hard Look Doctrine in the DC Circuit' (2002) 90 *Georgetown Law Journal* 2599; Steven Breyer, Richard Stewart, Cass Sunstein and Adrian Vermeule, *Administrative Law and Regulatory Policy: Problems, Text, and Cases*, 6th edn (New York, Aspen Publishers, 2006) 349; Gary Lawson and Stephen Kam, 'Making Law Out of Nothing at All: The Origins of the *Chevron* Doctrine' (2013) 65 *Administrative Law Review* 1, 12–13.

[322] Nathaniel Nathanson, 'Administrative Discretion in the Interpretation of Statutes' (1950) 3 *Vanderbilt Law Review* 470; Colin Diver, 'Statutory Interpretation in the Administrative State' (1985) 133 *University of Pennsylvania Law Review* 549; Lawson and Kam, 'Making Law Out of Nothing at All' (n 321 above); *Pittston Stevedoring Corp v Dellaventura* 544 F 2d 35, 49 (2d Cir 1976); *Natural Resources Defense Council, Inc v US EPA* 725 F 2d 761, 767 (DC Cir 1984).

[323] Diver, 'Statutory Interpretation in the Administrative State' (n 322 above) 551.

[324] See, eg *Social Security Board v Nierotko* 327 US 358, 369–70 (1946); *Hardin v Kentucky Utilities Co* 390 US 1, 14 (1968) (Harlan J, dissenting); *FTC v Colgate-Palmolive Co* 380 US 374, 385 (1965); *Barlow v Collins* 397 US 159, 166 (1970); *Federal Election Commission v Democratic Senatorial Campaign Commission* 454 US 27, 32 (1981).

or class of officials has a monopoly over legal interpretation. Instead, the task of interpreting the law is shared by a broader range of governmental decision-makers—including administrative officials—but these decision-makers are held accountable for their decisions through both the political process and judicial review. Because administrative officials are better equipped to arbitrate interpretive disputes about their enabling legislation, by virtue of their experience and expertise, these cases conclude that judges should show 'great deference to the interpretation given the statute by the officers or agency charged with its administration'.[325]

These two lines of authority collide in *Chevron USA Inc v Natural Resources Defense Council*,[326] a decision which has acquired almost mythical status.[327] In reviewing a decision of the Environmental Protection Agency, Stevens J attempts to straddle the two lines of cases by saying:[328]

> First, always, is the question whether Congress has directly spoken to the precise question at issue. If the intent of Congress is clear, that is the end of the matter; for the court, as well as the agency, must give effect to the unambiguously expressed intent of Congress. If, however, the court determines Congress has not directly addressed the precise question at issue, the court does not simply impose its own construction on the statute, as would be necessary in the absence of an administrative interpretation. Rather, if the statute is silent or ambiguous with respect to the specific issue, the question is whether the agency's answer is based on a permissible construction of the statute.

On its face, the *Chevron* formula simultaneously endorses correctness review with respect to questions clearly addressed by Congress and a more restrained form of reasonableness review when legislation is silent or ambiguous regarding the question at issue.

One reason why the *Chevron* formula has become such a lightning rod is that it restates rather than resolves the dilemma posed by these two lines of authority. On top of these problems, the Supreme Court has added others. Most notably, in *United States v Mead* the Court held that an administrative decision will not qualify for *Chevron* deference unless Congress expressly or impliedly delegates authority 'to make rules carrying the force of law',[329]

[325] See, eg *Gray* (n 24 above); *Dobson* (n 24 above); *National Labor Relations Board v Hearst* (n 24); *Udall v Tallman* 380 US 1 (1965); *Ford Motor Credit Co v Milhollin* 444 US 555, 568 (1980); *Public Service Commission v Mid-Louisiana Gas Co* 463 US 319 (1982).

[326] *Chevron* (n 25 above).

[327] Lawson & Kam, 'Making Law Out of Nothing at All' (n 321 above).

[328] *Chevron* (n 25 above) 842–43.

[329] In *United States v Mead Corp* 533 US 218, 234 (2001), the Court introduced what has become known as *Chevron*'s 'Step Zero' by deciding that judicial deference only comes into play if Congress intends for an administrative institution 'to make rules carrying the force of law'. Thus, it held that if an administrative agency has been given the power to adjudicate or engage in notice-and-comment rulemaking, its decisions may qualify for deference. By contrast, decisions in the form of administrative policy statements, manuals, guidelines and classification rulings would only be entitled to such respect as they deserved on their merits. For further commentary see Cass Sunstein, '*Chevron* Step Zero' (2006) 92 *Virginia Law Review* 187.

but that an administrative decision not eligible for *Chevron* deference might nevertheless merit judicial respect commensurate with the 'thoroughness evident in its consideration, the validity of its reasoning, its consistency with earlier and later pronouncements, and all those factors which give it power to persuade, if lacking power to control'.[330]

But if one looks beyond *Chevron*'s famous two-step formula, Stevens J also gestures toward a framework for judicial review which marginalises the quest for original intent and instead emphasises practical justifications for respecting administrative decisions. Towards the end of his judgment, in which he held that the Court should defer to the EPA's interpretation of its enabling legislation, Stevens J supports his conclusion by saying:[331]

> In these cases the Administrator's interpretation represents a reasonable accommodation of manifestly competing interests and is entitled to deference: the regulatory scheme is technical and complex, the agency considered the matter in a detailed and reasoned fashion, and the decision involves reconciling conflicting policies. Congress intended to accommodate both interests but did not do so itself on the level of specificity presented by these cases. Perhaps that body consciously desired the Administrator to strike the balance at this level, thinking that those with great expertise and charged with responsibility for administering the provision would be in a better position to do so; perhaps it simply did not consider the question at this level; and perhaps Congress was unable to forge a coalition on either side of the question, and those on each side decided to take their chances with the scheme devised by the agency. For judicial purposes, it matters not which of these things occurred.
>
> Judges are not experts in the field, and are not part of either political branch of the Government. Courts must, in some cases, reconcile competing political interests, but not on the basis of the judges' personal policy preferences. In contrast, an agency to which Congress has delegated policymaking responsibilities may, within the limits of that delegation, properly rely upon the incumbent administration's views of wise policy to inform its judgments. While agencies are not directly accountable to the people, the Chief Executive is, and it is entirely appropriate for this political branch of the Government to make such policy choices—resolving the competing interests which Congress itself either inadvertently did not resolve, or intentionally left to be resolved by the agency charged with the administration of the statute in light of everyday realities.

This passage outlines a democratic, pragmatic, contextual and functional case for judicial deference—it eschews a 'top-down' conception of administrative law in which judges determine the limits of administrative jurisdiction by speculating about legislative intent, and instead adopts a 'bottom-up' conception of administrative law which highlights values and practical reasons why judges should respect administrative decisions in the first place.

[330] *Skidmore* (n 24 above), 139–40.
[331] *Chevron* (n 25 above) 865–66.

According to this framework, the primary assumption is that administrative officials have legitimate authority to interpret the law in light of broadly worded legal values, objectives, and principles.[332]

In the next chapter, I will examine how a similar framework has emerged in Canada. As we will see, this framework builds upon the idea of judicial restraint championed by Thayer, Holmes, Brandeis, and Frankfurter. As a result, the Diceyan model of judicial review which Canadian administrative lawyers inherited from the United Kingdom gradually gave way to a pragmatic and functional assessment of administrative decisions. But because that shift has been achieved incrementally through the common law method, it remains plagued by quixotic quests for legislative intent much like the *Chevron* doctrine.

[332] Matthew Stephenson and Adrian Vermeule, '*Chevron* Has Only One Step' (2009) 95 *Virginia Law Review* 597; John Manning, 'Constitutional Structure and Judicial Deference to Agency Interpretations of Agency Rules' (1996) 96 *Columbia Law Review* 612; Cass Sunstein, 'Is Tobacco a Drug? Administrative Agencies as Common Law Courts' (1998) 47 *Duke Law Journal* 1013; Mark Seidenfeld, 'A Syncopated *Chevron:* Emphasizing Reasoned Decisionmaking in Reviewing Agency Interpretations of Statutes' (1994) 73 *Texas Law Review* 83.

5

From Formalism to Reasonable Justification: The Transformation of Canadian Administrative Law

WHEN COMPARING THE law concerning judicial review of administrative decisions in Canada with its British and American counterparts, one immediately encounters a variety of constitutional similarities and differences. Like the United States, Canada is a federal state with a written Constitution which includes an entrenched bill of rights; however, Canadian constitutionalism also been shaped by its colonial and common law ties to the United Kingdom. Canada's founding constitutional document, the British North America Act, was originally an Act of the Westminster Parliament delineating the powers of Parliament and the provincial legislatures;[1] and because the Judicial Committee of the Privy Council was Canada's court of last resort until 1949, its decisions laid the interpretive groundwork for the BNA Act and installed the doctrine of jurisdictional error as the analytical framework for judicial review of administrative decisions. The power of the judiciary was bolstered in 1982 with the proclamation of the Canadian Charter of Rights and Freedoms, which enables judges to strike down legislation and administrative decisions that infringe individual rights to liberty and equality.[2] In short, judges have played a prominent role in shaping contemporary Canadian administrative law, but because they could rely upon a written Constitution, one might expect that the practice of judicial review in Canada today would be more interventionist than in the United Kingdom.

Therefore, it is surprising that the doctrine of judicial deference towards administrative decisions has become so influential over the past 40 years. While it has no textual basis in the Constitution, the idea was borrowed from American jurisprudence and transplanted into the Canadian common

[1] Prior to the patriation of the Canadian Constitution in 1982, this document was referred to as the British North America Act 1867 (UK), 30 & 31 Vict, c 3. I will refer to this document as the BNA Act throughout.

[2] Canadian Charter of Rights and Freedoms, Part I of the Constitution Act 1982, being Schedule B to the Canada Act 1982 (UK), c 11.

law of judicial review. As in the United States, the doctrine of deference highlights important reasons why judges should respect administrative decisions, provided they are fair and reasonable, instead of subjecting them to correctness review.

In this chapter, I will examine the transition from jurisdictional error to judicial deference by carving up Canadian legal history into three periods of doctrinal development. In Section I, I will examine the era of formal and conceptual analysis, which extends from Confederation in 1867 until 1978. During this period, the law pertaining to judicial review was inspired by a formal conception of the separation of powers, which posited analytically distinct roles for the legislative, judicial, and executive branches of government. This formalist nature of this approach derives from the fact that the separation of powers was conceived as a means of ensuring that the different branches of government perform analytically distinct roles rather than a means for advancing constitutional values like liberty or equality.[3] However, this approach to judicial review often frustrated the empowerment and enlargement of the Canadian administrative state, because judges assumed that the Constitution prohibited the delegation of legislative or judicial powers to administrative officials. In addition, because the law of judicial review was based on the doctrine of jurisdictional error, which trades upon a similar analytical distinction between law and politics, Canadian case law during this period displays the same confusion and instability which I identified in Chapters two and three (particularly the way in which jurisdictional analysis vacillates between submissive deference and correctness oversight).

Concerns regarding the legitimacy of the formalist approach prompted judges like Ivan Rand and Bora Laskin to develop an alternative account of judicial review which recognises the legitimacy of administrative law. This alternative approach had been percolating in American legal culture since the end of the nineteenth century, and reached a boiling point in 1937—the year when Franklin President Roosevelt tabled his court-packing plan in Washington and the Privy Council in London struck down the Canadian version of the New Deal. While Rand and Laskin did not expressly invoke American sources in aid of their argument for judicial restraint, both of them had studied at Harvard Law School which was the intellectual epicentre for James Thayer, Oliver Wendell Holmes, Louis Brandeis, and Felix Frankfurter. Thus, while there is no direct evidence indicating that Rand's and Laskin's views regarding judicial restraint were drawn from American jurisprudence, there is a strong circumstantial case to support this inference.

In Section II, I will chart the transition to the pragmatic and functional approach to judicial review, which took place between 1978 and 2000.

[3] David Dyzenhaus, 'Formalism's Hollow Victory' [2002] *New Zealand Law Review* 525.

This transition is marked by three landmark cases which were either written or strongly influenced by Laskin during his tenure as Chief Justice of the Canadian Supreme Court: *Nicholson v Haldimand-Norfolk Police Commissioners*,[4] *CUPE v New Brunswick Liquor Corp*,[5] and *Crevier v Attorney General (Québec)*.[6] Each of these cases represents a distinct element within this framework. In *Nicholson*, the Court rejected the idea that administrative officials are only bound by principles of natural justice when they perform 'judicial' or 'quasi-judicial' functions, and replaced it with a broader, contextualised duty of procedural fairness which arises whenever an administrative decision impacts an individual's 'rights, interests, property, privileges, or liberties'.[7] In *CUPE* the Supreme Court questioned the idea that judges should have the last word on 'jurisdictional' issues or questions of law, and replaced it with a principle of judicial deference which holds that judges should respect administrative interpretations of law considering the relative expertise of administrative officials and their democratic mandate. Thus, the Court concluded that the purpose of judicial review is to ensure that administrative decisions are substantively reasonable rather than to superimpose judicial interpretations of law. Finally, in *Crevier* the Supreme Court rejected the formal conception of the separation of powers, and replaced it with the idea that individuals have a constitutional right to judicial review which cannot be extinguished by statute.

At bottom, this trilogy of cases recognises that the modern administrative state cannot be made to conform to the formal conception of the separation of powers. Thus, instead of conceiving judicial review as a means for ensuring that the legislature, judiciary, and executive perform distinct constitutional functions, the purpose of judicial review is construed as a means of sustaining fundamental values like procedural fairness and ensuring that governmental decisions are reasonably justifiable. Through this transition, the Canadian Supreme Court embraced the idea that administrative officials have legitimate authority to interpret the law, but nevertheless insisted that judges have a constitutional duty to maintain the legitimacy of administrative law.

However, because this transition was achieved incrementally through the common law method, it has often been marred by confusion due to lingering attachments to formal and conceptual analysis. In Section III, I will review some of the more significant difficulties which have arisen when judges revert to a formalist approach to judicial review. I will conclude with a brief overview of the law pertaining to judicial review in Canada in order

[4] *Nicholson v Haldimand-Norfolk Regional Police Commissioners* [1979] 1 SCR 311.

[5] *Canadian Union of Public Employees, Local 963 v New Brunswick Liquor Corporation* [1979] 2 SCR 227.

[6] *Crevier v Québec (Attorney General)* [1981] 2 SCR 220.

[7] *Martineau v Matsqui Disciplinary Board* [1980] 1 SCR 602, 622–23.

to highlight nagging questions which a theory of judicial deference should address.

I. THE FORMAL AND CONCEPTUAL ERA

At the beginning of the twentieth century, the law of judicial review in Canada closely resembled its analogue in the United Kingdom. This is unsurprising, considering that most Canadian lawyers at the time had been educated in the United Kingdom, cut their teeth on British textbooks in Canadian law schools, or apprenticed with a lawyer who had been trained abroad.[8] And because the Privy Council was the Court of last resort for Canada until 1949, two cases discussed in the Chapter three—*Colonial Bank of Australasia v Willan* and *Rex v Nat Bell Liquors Ltd*—were considered to be controlling authorities in Canadian courts.[9] As a result, the normative instability embedded in those decisions, rooted in the simultaneous endorsement of both correctness review and judicial submission to administrative decisions, was also symptomatic of judicial review in Canada during this period.

However, judicial review was also influenced by a formal conception of the separation of powers, one which assumed that the Constitution assigned analytically distinct roles to the legislative, judicial, and executive branches of government. So instead of constructing a moral argument relating to role of judicial review in sustaining constitutional values like liberty or equality, judges erected a series of formal or conceptual distinctions to maintain distinct institutional roles.[10] Thus, if an administrative decision was deemed to be 'legislative' or 'judicial' in nature, the enabling legislation could be struck down in order to vindicate the separation of powers.[11] And, as in

[8] G Blaine Baker, 'Legal Education in Upper Canada 1785–1889: The Law Society as Educator' in David H Flaherty (ed), *Essays in the History of Canadian Law*, vol 2 (Toronto, University of Toronto Press, 1983) 49.

[9] *Colonial Bank of Australasia v Willan* (1874) LR 5 PC 417 (JCPC); *R v Nat Bell Liquors Ltd* [1922] 2 AC 128 (JCPC). As in previous chapters, I will focus primarily upon decisions rendered by the court of last resort in order to identify general doctrinal trends. Since I have already discussed *Willan* and *Nat Bell Liquors* in Chapter 3, my discussion will focus upon Supreme Court of Canada decisions after 1949.

[10] H Wade MacLaughlan, 'Judicial Review of Administrative Interpretations of Law: How Much Formalism Can We Reasonably Bear?' (1986) 36 *University of Toronto Law Journal* 343; Frederick Schauer, 'Formalism' (1988) 97 *Yale Law Journal* 509; John Willis, 'Three Approaches to Administrative Law: The Judicial, the Conceptual, and the Functional' (1935) 1 *University of Toronto Law Journal* 53.

[11] AV Dicey, *Introduction to the Study of the Constitution*, 10th edn (London, MacMillan & Co, 1959); John Willis, 'Statute Interpretation in a Nutshell' (1938) 16 *Canadian Bar Review* 1; John Willis, 'Administrative Law and the British North America Act' (1939) 53 *Harvard Law Review* 251; John Willis, 'Section 96 of the British North America Act' (1940) 18 *Canadian Bar Review* 517; Harry Arthurs, 'Rethinking Administrative Law: A Slightly Dicey Business' (1979) 17 *Osgoode Hall Law Journal* 1.

the United Kingdom, if an administrative decision involved 'jurisdictional' issues, it was assumed that judges were entitled to intervene in order to preserve parliamentary sovereignty or a Diceyan conception of the rule of law. By contrast, if an administrative decision was deemed to be 'administrative' or involve 'non-jurisdictional' issues, judges tended to submit to it even if the person affected by the decision had not been granted a hearing or reasons for the decision.[12] The upshot was an all-or-nothing approach to judicial review which jealously scrutinised the implementation of economic policy, but turned a blind eye towards executive decisions during wartime. While judges invoked the separation of powers, freedom of contract, and property rights to frustrate collective bargaining regimes,[13] they were reluctant to deploy similar constraints to defend civil liberties or question draconian war measures.[14]

A. The Constitution and the Administrative State

The constitutional validity of the Canadian administrative state was tested in two waves of cases. The first wave impugned federal enabling legislation on the ground that it invaded the exclusive domain of provincial legislatures under section 92 of the BNA Act; the second wave challenged the constitutionality of both federal and provincial enabling legislation on the basis it delegated either legislative or judicial powers to administrative officials.

The first wave of cases is illustrated by decisions from the Privy Council and Canadian Supreme Court at the turn of the twentieth century, which juxtaposed a narrow construction of the federal residual power under section 91 of the BNA Act 'to make Laws for the Peace, Order and good Government of Canada' with a broad interpretation of provincial jurisdiction over 'Property and Civil Rights' under section 92(13).[15] Judicial reasoning

[12] David Dyzenhaus, 'The Politics of Deference: Judicial Review and Democracy' in Michael Taggart (ed), *The Province of Administrative Law* (Oxford, Hart Publishing, 1997) 279, 286.

[13] See, eg *Toronto Electric Commissioners v Snider* [1925] AC 396 (JCPC); *John East Iron Works Ltd v United Steel Workers of America, Local 3493* [1948] 1 DLR 652 (Sask CA); *In re Ontario Labour Relations Board: Toronto Newspaper Guild, Local 87 v Globe Printing Company* [1953] 2 SCR 18.

[14] See, eg *In re George Edwin Gray* (1918) 57 SCR 150; *Reference Re: Persons of the Japanese Race* [1946] SCR 248; *Co-operative Committee on Japanese Canadians v Canada (Attorney General)* [1947] AC 87 (JCPC).

[15] See, eg *Citizens Insurance Co v Parsons* (1881) 7 AC 96 (JCPC); *Liquidators of the Maritime Bank of Canada v Receiver-General of New Brunswick* [1892] AC 437 (JCPC); *Ontario Liquor License Case* [1896] AC 348 (JCPC); *Workmen's Compensation Board v Canadian Pacific Railway Company* [1920] AC 184 (JCPC). See also FR Scott, 'Centralization and Decentralization in Canadian Federalism' (1951) 29 *Canadian Bar Review* 1095; RB Haldane, 'Lord Watson' (1899) 11 *Juridical Review* 278 at 280–81; Viscount Haldane, 'The Work for the Empire of the Judicial Committee of the Privy Council' (1922) 1 *Cambridge Law Journal* 143 at 150; John Saywell, *The Lawmakers: Judicial Power and the Shaping of Canadian Federalism* (Toronto, University of Toronto Press, 2002) chs 6–7.

in these cases often rested upon a laissez-faire rationale, which characterised attempts to establish a national welfare state as a threat to civil liberties.[16] For example, in the *Board of Commerce* case, a unanimous Privy Council decision which struck down federal legislation establishing post-war price controls, Viscount Haldane stated:[17]

> It is to the Legislatures of the Provinces that the regulation and restriction of their civil rights have in generally been exclusively confided, and as to these the Provincial Legislatures possess quasi-sovereign authority. It can, therefore, be only under necessity in highly exceptional circumstances, such as cannot be assumed to exist in the present case, that the liberty of the inhabitants of the Provinces may be restricted by the Parliament of Canada, and that the Dominion can intervene in the interests of Canada as a whole in questions such as the present one.

Thus, the Privy Council concluded that Parliament's residual power under section 91 of the BNA Act to legislate for 'the Peace, Order, and good Government of Canada' could only be invoked during a national emergency, and that provincial jurisdiction over property and civil rights immunised broad swathes of economic activity from federal regulation. Similar themes crop up in *Toronto Electric Commissioners v Snider*, a case in which the Privy Council held that legislation establishing a federal agency for resolving industrial disputes was unconstitutional because there was no evidence of an 'emergency putting the national life of Canada in unanticipated peril'.[18]

While some cases did diverge from this general trend,[19] the Privy Council's narrow construction of Parliament's residual jurisdiction ultimately spelled the doom of the Canadian New Deal during the Great Depression. In 1935 the Prime Minister of Canada, RB Bennett, introduced a package of legislation, which signalled an abrupt end to laissez-faire economic policy.[20]

[16] Legal historians have offered two different explanations for this line of cases. The first explanation is that judicial interpretations of Canadian federalism were influenced by the idea that local legislatures were better suited to strike the appropriate balance between individual rights and the public interest. The second explanation is that judicial opinion was heavily influenced by laissez-faire ideology, which skewed doctrinal analysis relating to the division of power between Parliament and provincial legislatures. Regardless of which explanation better captures the judges' subjective motives, the end result was the undoing of Parliament's attempt to construct a welfare state at the national level. See Bernard Hibbits, 'A Bridle for Leviathan: The Supreme Court and the Board of Commerce' (1989) 21 *Ottawa Law Review* 65; Richard Risk and Robert Vipond, 'Rights Talk in Canada in the Late Nineteenth Century: "The Good Sense and Right Feeling of the People"' (1996) 14 *Law & History Review* 1; David Schneiderman, 'Harold Laski, Viscount Haldane, and the Law of the Canadian Constitution in the Early Twentieth Century' (1998) 48 *University of Toronto Law Journal* 521.

[17] *In re the Board of Commerce Act, 1919, and the Combines and Fair Prices Act, 1919* [1922] 1 AC 191, 197–98 (JCPC). See also *In re Board of Commerce* (1920) 60 SCR 456, 488–89 (Idington J).

[18] *Snider* (n 13 above) 415–16.

[19] See, eg *Fort Frances Pulp and Paper Co v Manitoba Free Press Company* [1923] AC 695 (JCPC); *In re Regulation and Control of Aeronautics in Canada* [1932] AC 54 (JCPC); *In re Regulation and Control of Radio Communication in Canada* [1932] AC 304 (JCPC).

[20] Saywell, *The Lawmakers* (n 15 above) 203–4.

The package included farm credit and bankruptcy legislation, a national marketing act, an industrial dispute resolution mechanism, and a federal unemployment insurance scheme. However, the Privy Council struck down nearly every piece of legislation—only the farm credit legislation survived—as encroaching upon provincial jurisdiction over property and civil rights.[21] At the time, Lord Atkin declared that '[w]hile the ship of state now sails on larger ventures ... she still retains the water-tight compartments which are an essential part of her original structure',[22] which meant that the BNA Act was set against the establishment of a national welfare state.[23] These decisions provoked an outcry of critical commentary,[24] one which strongly resembles the reaction to *Lochner v New York* south of the border, and ultimately prompted the Canadian Parliament to abolish appeals to the Privy Council in 1949.[25]

The second wave of cases concerned the Canadian version of the non-delegation doctrine which triggered President Roosevelt's court-packing plan in the United States.[26] While there is no express reference to the separation of powers in the BNA Act, the Canadian version of the non-delegation doctrine emerged from a series of obiter comments from the Privy Council and Canadian courts. These comments suggested that, while provincial legislatures retained sovereign authority within their constitutional bailiwicks, they could not delegate legislative powers to administrative officials.[27] Despite these statements, neither the Canadian Supreme Court nor the Privy Council questioned the constitutionality of the War Measures Act 1914 which delegated sweeping powers to the federal Cabinet during wartime. The Act empowered the Governor-in-Council 'to do and authorize such acts ... orders and regulations as he may, by reason of real or apprehended war, deem necessary or advisable for the security, defence, peace, order and welfare of Canada'.[28] It further stated that the power of the Cabinet extended to censorship and suppression of the press, detention and deportation of individuals, and expropriation of private property. Even though the

[21] See *Attorney General Canada v Attorney General Ontario* [1937] AC 326 (JCPC); *Attorney General British Columbia v Attorney General Canada* [1937] AC 377 (JCPC).

[22] *Attorney General Canada v Attorney General Ontario* (n 21 above) 354.

[23] Saywell, *The Lawmakers* (n 15 above) 228–37.

[24] See, eg WPM Kennedy, 'The British North America Act: Past and Future' (1937) 15 *Canadian Bar Review* 394; FR Scott, 'The Consequences of the Privy Council Decisions' (1937) 15 *Canadian Bar Review* 485.

[25] Richard Risk, 'Canadian Law Teachers in the 1930s: "When the World was Turned Upside Down"' (2004) 27 *Dalhousie Law Journal* 2, 30.

[26] *Panama Refining Co v Ryan* 293 US 388 (1935); *Schecter Poultry Co v United States* 295 US 495 (1935); Willis, 'Administrative Law and the British North America Act' (n 11 above).

[27] See, eg *In re the Initiative and Referendum Act* [1919] AC 935, 945 (JCPC), where Viscount Haldane stated that a provincial legislature cannot 'create and endow with its own capacity a new legislative power not created by the [BNA Act]'.

[28] The War Measures Act, 1914, SC 1914, c 2.

Court conceded that the legislation gave the executive branch 'unlimited powers',[29] it held the legislation was constitutional because Parliament retained the power to repeal the War Measures Act. Therefore, even though Cabinet had summarily repealed the claimant's statutory exemption from military service, Fitzpatrick CJ upheld the constitutionality of the order in council. While the remaining judges cautioned that Parliament could never 'abandon'[30] or 'abdicate'[31] its sovereignty, they held that the powers granted under the War Measures Act were valid because Parliament retained (at least in theory) the power to reverse Cabinet decisions.[32]

But while the non-delegation doctrine did not restrain delegations of unlimited legislative powers to the executive in wartime, it was invoked frequently to prevent provincial legislatures from delegating 'judicial' powers to administrative officials in order to advance domestic economic policy.[33] This restraint was inferred from section 96 of the BNA Act, which gives federal government the power to 'appoint the Judges of the Superior, District and County Courts in each province'.[34] The original purpose of this provision was to insulate superior court judges from local political influence, but during the formative years of the Canadian administrative state the provision was invoked repeatedly to frustrate the delegation of authority to administrative officials.

The basic idea was that 'administrative' or 'ministerial' functions were deemed to be political functions which could be delegated to administrative officials, while the delegation of 'judicial' functions to administrative officials was unconstitutional because it infringed upon the exclusive constitutional status of superior courts. However, the test for determining whether a particular power was judicial or administrative was blatantly anachronistic: the question was whether an analogous function had been exercised by superior courts prior to Confederation in 1867. If the impugned function had been exercised by a superior court prior to 1867, any attempt by the legislature to delegate that function to administrative officials was constitutionally suspect; but if an administrative tribunal or 'inferior' court performed a similar function prior to 1867, the regulatory scheme was presumed to be constitutionally valid. The nature of this test prompted John Willis to observe that

[29] *In re Gray* (n 14 above) 159.

[30] ibid 170.

[31] ibid 176.

[32] ibid 170. Twenty years later, the Privy Council employed a similar rationale in upholding provincial legislation in *Shannon v Lower Mainland Dairy Products Board* [1938] AC 708, 722 (JCPC).

[33] See, eg *Toronto v York Township* [1937] OR 177 (Ont CA); *Kazakewich v Kazakewich and Attorney-General for Alberta* [1936] 1 DLR 548 (Alta CA); *Roskiwich v Roskiwich* (1932) 26 Alberta LR 137 (Alta CA); *Re McLean Gold Mines Ltd and Ontario* (1923) 54 OLR 573 (Ont CA); *Burk v Tunstall* (1890) 2 BCR 12 (BCSC).

[34] BNA Act (n 1 above) s 96.

judicial interpretation of section 96 'inevitably degenerates into the amusing spectacle of a group of judges attempting conscientiously to determine which of a series of pre-1867 functions the functions before them are least unlike'.[35]

The Privy Council addressed this issue in the context of utility rate regulation in *Toronto v York*.[36] In 1916, the City of Toronto entered into an agreement to supply water to the Town of York, and in 1936 the provincial legislature passed legislation which incorporated the agreement and gave the Ontario Municipal Board the power to vary the applicable water rate in the future.[37] The Act further stated that the Board 'shall have all such powers, rights and privileges as are vested in the Supreme Court', including the power to compel 'attendance and examination of witnesses, production and inspection of documents, entry on and inspection of property, enforcement of its orders and all other matters necessary or proper therefor'.[38] York later applied to the Board for a variation of the rate and, in the course of the proceedings, the Board made a series of orders directing the City of Toronto to disclose documents, allow inspection of its waterworks, and direct its Commissioner of Works to attend an examination under oath. Rather than complying with the Board's requests, Toronto city lawyers challenged the constitutionality of the enabling legislation.

While the Court upheld the Board's powers of 'examination, inspection and discovery of documents' on the basis they 'were consistent with the powers of an administrative body',[39] it stated that the legislation was unconstitutional to the extent that it invested the Board with judicial functions. Lord Atkin, writing for the Court, stated that the Board 'is not validly constituted to receive judicial authority' because 'to entrust these duties to an administrative Board appointed by the Province would be to entrust them to a body not qualified to exercise them'.[40]

In later cases, both the Canadian Supreme Court and the Privy Council continued to equivocate about whether and to what extent administrative officials could wield judicial power. In *Reference re Adoption Act*, the Supreme Court of Canada assessed the constitutional validity of provincial legislation concerning alimony, adoption, and the welfare of children[41] and held that so long as the legislation did not fundamentally undermine the jurisdiction of superior courts, provinces could delegate new powers to administrative officials. Duff CJ advocated a holistic, rather than a piecemeal, assessment because the intermingling of administrative and judicial

[35] Willis, 'Section 96 of the British North America Act' (n 11 above) 534.
[36] *Toronto Corporation v York Corporation* [1938] AC 415 (JCPC).
[37] The Township of York Act, 1936, SO 1936, c 88.
[38] The Ontario Municipal Board Act, 1932, SO 1932, c 27, s 45.
[39] *Toronto Corporation* (n 36 above) 428.
[40] ibid.
[41] *Reference re Adoption Act* [1938] SCR 398.

functions was inevitable in a modern society. Thus, he concluded that as long as the scheme broadly conformed to powers exercised by inferior courts and provincial magistrates prior to Confederation, the administrative scheme would be constitutionally valid.[42]

Duff CJ's holistic approach was later endorsed by the Privy Council in *Labour Relations Board of Saskatchewan v John East Iron Works Ltd*.[43] In that case, an employer had dismissed six employees who were union members, and the union alleged that the employer had unlawfully discriminated against the employees. The provincial Labour Board found that the dismissals were discriminatory, and ordered the employer to reinstate the employees with compensation for lost wages. The employer sought judicial review, even though The Trade Union Act declared that the Board's 'proceedings, orders and decisions shall not be reviewable by any court of law'.[44] The Saskatchewan Court of Appeal held that the Board's order was tantamount to the remedy of specific performance and, since this remedy was exercised exclusively by superior courts prior to Confederation, the remedial provisions of The Trade Union Act were unconstitutional.[45]

The Privy Council reversed the Court of Appeal's decision. Lord Simonds, who wrote the leading opinion, argued that the appropriate question was not whether the Board exercised judicial powers per se, but whether the totality of those powers rendered the Board tantamount to a superior court.[46] On the facts, Lord Simonds thought that the Board's function was administrative, because it was created to advance the legislature's policy objective of promoting peaceful industrial relations rather than to adjudicate on contractual rights at common law.[47] Since the policy objective was, from Lord Simond's perspective, both alien and distinguishable from the common law's focus on private interests, the enabling legislation did not infringe section 96. But he also stated there was no reason to assume that a bi-partisan board was incapable of discharging its function judicially, because 'wide experience has shown that, though an independent president of the tribunal may in certain cases be advisable, it is essential that its other members should bring an experience and knowledge acquired extra-judicially to the solution of their problems'.[48]

However, Lord Simonds also raised a question about the constitutionality of the privative clause excluding judicial review. On this point, he held that section 96 prohibited the legislature from excluding judicial review entirely,

[42] *Toronto Corporation* (n 36 above) 415.

[43] *Labour Relations Board of Saskatchewan v John East Iron Works Ltd* [1949] AC 134 (JCPC).

[44] The Trade Union Act, 1944, SS 1944, c 69, s 15.

[45] *John East Iron Works Ltd v United Steel Workers of America, Local 3493* (n 13 above).

[46] *John East Iron Works* (n 43 above) 145–49.

[47] ibid 150.

[48] ibid 151.

because a privative clause 'would not avail the tribunal if it purported to exercise a jurisdiction wider than that specifically entrusted to it by the Act'.[49] This line of reasoning foreshadows how judicial interpretation of section 96 began to shift away from the formal separation of powers rationale towards a rationale based upon a constitutional right to judicial review.

B. Jurisdictional Error

While the doctrine of jurisdictional error does not refer explicitly to a formal conception of the separation of powers, it also assumes a similar analytical distinction between judicial and administrative functions. Thus, if an administrative decision involves the exercise of judicial power, the decision-maker is legally bound to provide a hearing and comply with the principles of natural justice; however, if a decision involves the exercise of an administrative power, the decision-maker is under no procedural obligations. Similarly, if an administrative decision concerns a question of law, a reviewing court can intervene if it disagrees with the substantive reasoning in the decision because the judiciary retains a monopoly on legal interpretation; however, if an administrative decision concerns a non-jurisdictional issue, the court will refrain from intervening, on the basis that the responsible decision-maker is exercising a discretionary political power to determine the outcome.

This framework is apparent in *Toronto Newspaper Guild v Globe Printing*, the first major decision from the Supreme Court of Canada regarding jurisdictional error after appeals to the Privy Council were abolished.[50] The dispute concerned a certification application by a trade union. The Ontario Labour Relations Act gave the Labour Relations Board broad powers to ascertain the scope of the bargaining unit, whether an employee was a union member, and whether there was sufficient support amongst existing employees to warrant union certification.[51] In support of its application, the union submitted a confidential stack of membership cards that had been signed by employees. The union argued that because a majority of employees—58 out of approximately 92 total employees—in the circulation department had signed union cards, it should be certified as the bargaining agent.

At the hearing, the employer's lawyer urged the Board to refuse certification until union representatives could be cross-examined so as to ensure that the employees who had signed union cards had not renounced their union memberships prior to the hearing. This allegation likely had an ulterior motive, because employers frequently resorted to subtle and not-so-subtle strategies like demoting, suspending or terminating employees who were

[49] ibid 152.
[50] *Globe Printing* (n 13 above).
[51] The Labour Relations Act, 1948, SO 1948, c 51, ss 3–4.

union sympathisers in order to thwart certification drives. The chairman of the Board refused, simply stating that he saw no relevance to employee resignations.[52] However, the implicit rationale for the Board's decision was to avoid setting a precedent which would enable employers to cajole or intimidate employees in advance of a certification hearing.[53]

When the employer sought judicial review, Gale J quashed the Board's decision, saying that the Board had been 'entrusted with judicial functions'[54] but had failed to act judicially by refusing to allow the employer's lawyer to cross-examine union officials.[55] On this point, Gale J concluded that 'the Company was improperly excluded from a cardinal privilege which it enjoys under our jurisprudence; that exclusion, of itself, was tantamount to a denial of basic justice'.[56] But because the Board's decision was insulated by a privative clause, Gale J also had to consider whether the Board's procedural ruling was 'jurisdictional'. On this point, he concluded that 'it becomes apparent that the phrase "want of jurisdiction" is extremely flexible and has been extended to include imperfections which ordinarily might not be regarded as pertaining to jurisdiction at all'.[57] Thus, Gale J concluded that the failure to allow cross-examination fell within the broad meaning of jurisdictional error set out in *Willan*.

While the Supreme Court of Canada affirmed Gale J's decision, it framed the issue slightly differently. Instead of asking whether the Board had breached the principles of natural justice, the majority simply asked whether the Board had refused or exceeded its jurisdiction during the course of the hearing. Kerwin J noted that '[i]n England and in Canada the decisions have been uniform that a Superior Court is invested with the power and the duty of seeing that such a tribunal as the Ontario Labour Relations Board

[52] *Re Toronto Newspaper Guild, Local 87, American Newspaper Guild (CIO) and Globe Printing Company* [1951] OR 435, 437.

[53] In a subsequent article, Paul Weiler explained the rationale for the Board's decision to disregard the employer's allegation: 'One can sense three underlying policy factors in the Board's decision. First, the administration of the Act required some cut-off point at which membership was to be determined and efficiency of administration required that it be some time before a Board hearing. Second, it was vital that the employer not learn at this stage who had joined the union, even though this might hamper its full presentation of its case, because of the dangers of job discrimination against union members. Third, the Board wanted dissident employees to present their own case against majority union membership in order that it ensure that resignations, petitions, etc. had not been employer-inspired. The Board, at this time, early in the administration of the statute, was just beginning to articulate these considerations for itself and it received very little help from the very vague language then used in the statute—"member in good standing"': Paul Weiler, 'The "Slippery Slope" of Judicial Intervention: The Supreme Court and Canadian Labour Relations 1950–1970' (1971) 9 *Osgoode Hall Law Journal* 1, 19–20.

[54] *Re Toronto Newspaper Guild* (n 52 above) 441.

[55] ibid.

[56] ibid 455.

[57] ibid 464.

does not act without jurisdiction'.[58] In his view, the Board had exceeded its jurisdiction by refusing to verify whether some employees had renounced their memberships.[59] Kellock J echoed Kerwin J's reasoning, but concluded that 'it was impossible for the board to determine whether any one of the persons ... was in fact a member in good standing if the board refused to enter upon the question'.[60] While Kerwin and Kellock JJ differed on whether the Board had 'exceeded' or 'declined' its jurisdiction, they both invoked a form of correctness review—having concluded that the Board was exercising a judicial function, they both inferred that the Board had a duty abide by fact-finding processes traditionally employed by common law courts; and because the Board had refused to allow the publisher's lawyer to cross-examine the union secretary, its decision was invalid. Thus, Kellock J concluded that while the privative clause 'prohibits the court from questioning any decision which has been come to within the structure of the statute itself', he held that it did not 'endow the board with the power to make arbitrary decisions'.[61]

The pliable nature of jurisdictional error is apparent in Cartwright J's dissenting opinion, which suggests that judges should simply submit to administrative decisions protected by a privative clause. In his view, the Board's refusal to allow the employer's lawyer to cross-examine the union's secretary was not reviewable, because the enabling legislation gave the Board a discretionary power to determine its own hearing process. He argued that, even if the Board had erred in refusing to allow cross-examination, at most the error was 'a wrongful refusal to receive evidence and not a declining of jurisdiction'.[62] Thus, he concluded that the Court's supervisory role was constrained by 'the provisions of the Statute which render the decision of the Board final and forbid its review'.[63]

However the other dissenting opinion in *Globe Printing*, written by Rand J, stakes out a middle ground. Unlike most of his colleagues on the Court, Ivan Rand had received his law degree from Harvard in 1912 and his approach to judicial review resonates with the culture of judicial restraint I examined in Chapter four.[64] Instead of asking whether the issue in dispute was jurisdictional, Rand J held that the Board had legitimate authority to

[58] *Globe Printing* (n 13 above) 23.
[59] ibid.
[60] ibid 35.
[61] ibid 38.
[62] ibid 39.
[63] ibid.
[64] See generally, William Kaplan, *Canadian Maverick: The Life and Times of Ivan C Rand* (Toronto, University of Toronto Press, 2009). The other member of the Court with a Harvard law degree, Estey J, concurred with Kellock J's opinion in *Globe Printing*.

find facts and interpret the law, but that the legality of its decision depended on whether it was reasonable.[65]

> The Board is admittedly a body with a limited jurisdiction, but a jurisdiction that, in many cases, depends upon the determination of questions of law as well as of fact. There is nothing in the Act expressly giving to the Board exclusive power to decide questions of law; but the writ of certiorari and other special remedies, for centuries the means provided for controlling unauthorized action by inferior bodies exercising the power of law, are forbidden ... The real controversy lies in the determination of the boundaries of that contemplated scope; and when, as today, administrative bodies are regulating civil relations which formerly were not within the cognizance of law at all, by what rule or standard are we to test the jurisdictional validity of their decisions? Certainly where the Board is at liberty to inform itself of matters of fact by any means, as it is here, and where it can act if 'satisfied' of certain things and where its findings are declared to be final and judicial review excluded, I doubt that the test can be anything less than this: is the action or decision within any rational compass that can be attributed to the statutory language?

This passage is notable in at least three different respects. First, Rand J acknowledges that, while the Board's jurisdiction is limited, he concedes that the Board has authority to decide 'questions of law as well as of fact'. Thus, Rand J rejects the assumption that judges have exclusive authority over legal interpretation. Second, Rand J recognises that the privative clause requires judicial restraint—but not abdication—when reviewing the Board's decision. Finally, instead of asking whether the Board's decision is correct, he invokes language virtually identical to James Bradley Thayer's rule of administration[66] in asking whether the decision is 'within any rational compass that can be attributed to the statutory language'.[67] Thus, the question was not whether the Board's decision could be strapped onto a Procrustean bed of judicially conceived legal standards, but whether its decision was rationally defensible in light of the policies and principles which animate the enabling legislation as a whole.

Rand J's approach to judicial review, while in need of further refinement, outlines provides a more complex understanding of the relationship between administrative officials and the judiciary.[68] Instead of assuming that judges have a monopoly over legal interpretation, Rand J suggests that the primary question is whether an administrative decision is reasonably justifiable in

[65] *Globe Printing* (n 13 above) 30.

[66] See ch 4 of this volume. Rand J had learned constitutional law from Eugene Wambaugh, who had been Thayer's pupil and introduced Felix Frankfurter to Thayer's views regarding judicial review.

[67] See also *British Columbia (Labour Relations Board) v Canada Safeway Ltd* [1953] 2 SCR 46, 54–55: 'The task of evaluating all these considerations has been committed by the legislature to the Board; and so long as its judgment can be said to be consonant with a rational appreciation of the situation presented, the Court is without power to modify or set it aside'.

[68] Weiler, 'The "Slippery Slope" of Judicial Intervention' (n 53 above) 17–34.

light of the enabling legislation. However, because Rand J did not elaborate on this standard of review, his account still seems to teeter on the brink of judicial submission. Thus, in *Globe Printing* he opined that 'in the simple matter of finding facts, it must be little short of an act of bad faith that can justify a court's interference'.[69] If the reasonableness standard is construed so loosely, there seems to be little difference between Cartwright J's approach (which regards administrative decisions as being immune from judicial scrutiny on matters of process and substance) and Rand J's approach (which only warrants judicial review where an administrative decision is tainted by bad faith).

But in his other opinions, Rand J's understanding of reasonableness review is clearly more demanding. In *Smith & Rhuland Ltd v Nova Scotia*, a Supreme Court decision issued on the same day as *Globe Printing*, Rand J wrote a majority opinion which quashed a decision by the Nova Scotia Labour Relations Board.[70] In that case, the Board held that although the union had satisfied statutory criteria for certification, its application should be rejected on the ground that the union's provisional secretary was a communist sympathiser. However, unlike the Board in *Globe Printing*, the Board in *Smith & Rhuland* issued detailed reasons for its decision. Those reasons stated that certification 'would confer legal powers to affect vital interests of employees and employers upon persons who would inevitably use those powers primarily to advance Communist aims and policies rather than for the benefit of employees'.[71] The union sought judicial review, arguing that the Board had declined its jurisdiction by acting on irrelevant considerations, committed an error of law on the face of its decision, or had breached the principles of natural justice by failing to verify the allegations against the provisional secretary.

As in *Globe Printing*, the Supreme Court quashed the Board's decision. However, in his lead opinion for the majority, Rand J did not ask whether the Board exercised a 'judicial' function, nor did he characterise the central issue as 'jurisdictional'. The main issue for Rand J was whether the Board's decision was reasonably justifiable. On this point, he notes '[t]here is no law in this country against holding such views'[72] and that the Board had approved two other applications by the same union, notwithstanding the fact that the secretary 'held the same office and adhered to the same views as found against him'.[73] Thus, instead of simply asking whether the issue before the Board was jurisdictional and conformed to the Court's interpretation of

[69] *Globe Printing* (n 13 above) 29.
[70] *Smith & Rhuland Ltd v Nova Scotia* [1953] 2 SCR 95.
[71] ibid 104.
[72] ibid 98–99.
[73] ibid.

the enabling statute, Rand J examined whether the reasons given by the Board were defensible in light of credible evidence and existing law, which included both the enabling legislation and previous Board decisions.

Six years later, Rand J employed this same approach in *Roncarelli v Duplessis*, his most famous judicial opinion.[74] The case concerned a decision by the Quebec Liquor Commissioner to cancel a liquor licence held by Frank Roncarelli, who owned a popular restaurant in Montreal. Beginning in 1945, the provincial government began prosecuting Jehovah's Witnesses for distributing pamphlets that offended a majority of Quebec residents who were Catholic. While Roncarelli was a Jehovah's Witness, he did not distribute any pamphlets himself. However, he posted bail in approximately 380 cases where other Jehovah's Witnesses had been charged. When the Premier of Quebec, Maurice Duplessis, was informed of Roncarelli's involvement, he directed the Liquor Commissioner to cancel Roncarelli's liquor licence '*definitivement et pour toujours*'. Shortly afterward, police raided the restaurant during lunch hour and seized CAN$5,000 of liquor. Six months later, Roncarelli's restaurant went under. Roncarelli subsequently sued Duplessis in delict for the wrongful exercise of public authority under the Quebec Civil Code. In order for his claim to succeed, Roncarelli had to satisfy the court that Duplessis's conduct was not an 'act done by him in the exercise of his [public] functions' within the meaning of article 88.[75]

While the Supreme Court ultimately held in Roncarelli's favour, Cartwright J again dissented on the ground that it was inappropriate for the court to scrutinise the Commission's discretionary decision. After reviewing the enabling legislation, which gave the Commission broad authority to issue and revoke liquor permits, Cartwright J stated 'I am unable to find that the Legislature has, either expressly or by necessary implication, laid down any rules to guide the commission'.[76] Later in his reasons, he stated that because 'the function of the commission in making that decision is administrative and not judicial'[77] that 'the Legislature intended the commission "to be a law unto itself"'.[78]

By contrast, Rand J said that the decision to cancel Roncarelli's liquor licence was legally unjustifiable. Unlike Cartwright J, Rand J held that the decision to terminate the licence had to be supported by reasons which

[74] *Roncarelli v Duplessis* [1959] SCR 121.

[75] Article 88 CCP provided that: 'No public officer or other person fulfilling any public function or duty can be sued for damages by reason of any act done by him in the exercise of his functions, nor can any verdict or judgment be rendered against him, unless notice of such action has been given him at least one month before the issue of the writ of summons'. For a more detailed discussion of this aspect of the case, see Robert Leckey, 'Complexifying *Roncarelli*'s Rule of Law' (2010) 55 *McGill Law Journal* 721.

[76] *Roncarelli* (n 74 above) 166–67.

[77] ibid 167.

[78] ibid 168.

were compatible with the declared purpose of the enabling legislation. In a famous passage, Rand J stated:[79]

> In public regulation of this sort there is no such thing as absolute and untrammelled 'discretion', that is that action can be taken on any ground or for any reason that can be suggested to the mind of the administrator; no legislative Act can, without express language, be taken to contemplate an unlimited arbitrary power exercisable for any purpose, however capricious or irrelevant, regardless of the nature or purpose of the statute. Fraud and corruption in the Commission may not be mentioned in such statutes but they are always implied as exceptions. 'Discretion' necessarily implies good faith in discharging public duty; there is always a perspective within which a statute is intended to operate; and any clear departure from its lines or objects is just as objectionable as fraud or corruption.

Later in his judgment, Rand J held that good faith meant 'carrying out the statute according to its intent and purpose; it means good faith in acting with a rational appreciation of that intent and purpose'.[80] In his view, judicial review was not limited to cases involving particularly egregious abuses of executive power (as he had suggested in *Globe Printing*), but also ensured that an administrative decision is reasonably justifiable in light of the purposes, values, and principles which animate the regulatory scheme.

While Rand J's conception of judicial review stands out in retrospect, it did not attract other adherents during this period. Instead, most judges continued to apply the doctrine of jurisdictional error. If an administrative decision hinged on a jurisdictional issue, a reviewing judge could engage in correctness review; however, if the issue was deemed non-jurisdictional, the judge would uphold the administrative decision on the basis that the decision-maker exercised unreviewable discretionary power. And, as in the United Kingdom, the case law regarding the distinction between jurisdictional and non-jurisdictional issues was so fraught with confusion that the judiciary could expand or retract the scope of judicial review in an ad hoc manner.[81] Thus, in *Metropolitan Life Insurance Co v International Union*

[79] ibid 140.

[80] ibid 143.

[81] Weiler, 'The "Slippery Slope" of Judicial Intervention' (n 53 above) 32–33. In this regard, there are two different classes of cases from the Supreme Court. The first class includes *British Columbia (Labour Relations Board) v Traders' Services Ltd* [1958] SCR 672 [privative clause grants exclusive jurisdiction to the Labour Board over findings of fact]; *Farrell v British Columbia (Workers'/Workmen's Compensation Board)* [1962] SCR 48 [privative clause grants exclusive jurisdiction to administrative decision-maker and precludes judicial review]; *Re Kinnaird and Workmen's Compensation Board* [1963] SCR 239 [privative clause gives administrative decision-maker unlimited discretion not subject to appeal or judicial review]; *Commission des Relations Ouvrières de Québec v Burlington Mills Hosiery Co of Canada* [1964] SCR 342 [privative clause bars judicial review provided that the administrative decision-maker exercises discretion in good faith]; *Galloway Lumber Co v British Columbia (Labour Relations Board)* [1965] SCR 222 [review on the merits precluded by privative clause]; *Bakery and Confectionary Workers International Union of America Local 468 et al v White*

of Operating Engineers, Local 796 the Supreme Court followed the House of Lords' ruling in *Anisminic* by stating that although a Labour Board might have jurisdiction in the 'narrow' sense, it could lose jurisdiction in the 'wider' sense by interpreting the law differently than a reviewing court.[82]

Despite the Court's decision in *Metropolitan Life*, there was mounting frustration within the academic community regarding the practice of judicial review.[83] When Paul Weiler surveyed the Supreme Court's jurisprudence in 1971, he criticised the Court for being 'oriented towards the disposition of a specific dispute, rather than ... intelligently developing a coherent fabric of general law'.[84] In a similar vein, Noel Lyon argued that the law of judicial review had become a 'conceptual morass':[85] the concept of jurisdiction was both too narrow (in the sense that it encouraged judges to adopt a positivistic understanding of statutory texts and legislative intent) and too malleable (in the sense that the concept of jurisdictional error was so elastic that judges characterised virtually any legal question as reviewable).

However, neither Weiler nor Lyon argued that judicial review should be abandoned. Rather, they followed Rand J's lead in suggesting that judges should adopt a more restrained approach. Weiler noted that Rand J had 'formulated an intermediate attitude to reviewability' in *Globe Printing*, but concluded that his approach required further elaboration. Lyon argued that section 96 of the BNA Act preserved the rule of law by giving citizens

Lunch Ltd et al [1966] SCR 282 [Board free to act or not to act on evidence before it, since its decision is made final and conclusive by statute]; *Komo Construction Inc v Commission des Relations de Travail du Québec v Canadian Ingersoll-Rand Co Ltd* [1968] SCR 695 [no duty of *audi alteram partem* implied where the dispute concerns only a question of law] and *Noranda Mines Ltd v The Queen* [1969] SCR 898 [privative clause excludes judicial review for all non-jurisdictional errors of law or fact]. The second class includes *Alliance des Professeurs Catholiques de Montreal v Quebec Labour Relations Board* [1953] 2 SCR 140 [duty of *audi alteram partem* implied in spite of privative clause]; *Saltfleet (Township) Board of Health v Knapman* [1956] SCR 877 [implied duty to act judicially in spite of privative clause]; *Jarvis v Associated Medical Services Inc* [1964] SCR 497 [privative clause will not protect Board decision which is at odds with the true construction of the Act]; and *Bell v Ontario (Human Rights Commission)* [1971] SCR 756 [privative clause cannot grant administrative decision-maker exclusive jurisdiction to interpret jurisdictional limits].

82 *Metropolitan Life Insurance Co v International Union of Operating Engineers, Local 796* [1970] SCR 425, 433–35.

83 See, eg Willis, 'Three Approaches to Administrative Law' (n 10 above); John Willis, 'Statute Interpretation in a Nutshell' (n 11 above); John Willis, 'Correspondence: More on the Nolan Case' (1951) 29 *Canadian Bar Review* 580; John Willis, 'The McRuer Report: Lawyers' Values and Civil Servants' Values' (1968) 18 *University of Toronto Law Journal* 351; BL Strayer, 'The Concept of 'Jurisdiction' in Review of Labour Relations Board Decisions' (1963) 28 *Saskatchewan Bar Review* 157; Ken Norman 'The Privative Clause: Virile or Futile?' (1969) 34 *Saskatchewan Law Review* 334, 337; J Pink, 'Judicial "Jurisdiction" in the Presence of Privative Clauses' (1965) 23 *University of Toronto Faculty Law Review* 5.

84 Weiler, 'The 'Slippery Slope' of Judicial Intervention' (n 53 above) 18.

85 Noel Lyon, 'Case Comment' (1971) 49 *Canadian Bar Review* 365. See also David Mullan, 'The Jurisdictional Fact Doctrine in the Supreme Court of Canada—A Mitigating Plea' (1972) 10 *Osgoode Hall Law Journal* 440.

a right of judicial review.[86] But he also recognised that the Supreme Court had undermined important legislative initiatives in the past by reading a formalist conception of the separation of powers into section 96. Given this history, Lyon argued that legislatures were entitled to delegate judicial powers to administrative officials, so long as 'governments and their agents must, when called upon in a court of law to do so, show legal authority for all their acts and decisions'.[87] Accordingly, Lyon argued that 'the function of the courts in policing the rule of law in administrative decision is to establish parameters of legal tolerance rather than superimposing legally "correct" answers'.[88]

II. THE PRAGMATIC AND FUNCTIONAL ERA

Beginning in 1978, almost 20 years after Rand J retired, the Canadian Supreme Court began to gradually overhaul administrative law doctrine in the manner he had suggested. In three landmark decisions, the Canadian Supreme Court, led by Bora Laskin CJ, replaced the formal and conceptual framework for judicial review with a pragmatic and functional approach to judicial review.[89]

Like Rand, Laskin's university training played an important role in shaping his ideas; however unlike Rand, Laskin was able to forge a coalition amongst other members of the Supreme Court, especially Brian Dickson, who would later succeed him as Chief Justice. While most lawyers entering the legal profession in Ontario during the 1930s received vocational training in law at Osgoode Hall, a finishing school for apprenticing lawyers operated by the Law Society of Upper Canada, Laskin received an undergraduate law degree from the University of Toronto. While the fledgling law department at the University of Toronto only had three full-time professors, its aim was to provide students with an opportunity 'to study law as a living entity, intimately connected to the resolution of modern social problems'.[90] This mandate, which echoes Louis Brandeis's plea for a 'living law',[91] made a lasting imprint on Laskin. In a personal interview he recalled that, unlike his contemporaries at Osgoode Hall, 'I knew something about Holmes and Brandeis and Cardozo'.[92]

[86] Noel Lyon, 'Is Amendment of Section 96 Really Necessary?' (1987) 36 *University of New Brunswick Law Journal* 79.

[87] Noel Lyon, 'Case Comment' (1980) 58 *Canadian Bar Review* 646, 657.

[88] Noel Lyon, 'Case Comment' (n 85 above) 379.

[89] *UES, Local 298 v Bibeault* [1988] 2 SCR 1048, 1088.

[90] Philip Girard, *Bora Laskin: Bringing Law to Life* (Toronto, University of Toronto Press, 2005) 47.

[91] Louis Brandeis, 'The Living Law' (1916) 10 *Illinois Law Review* 461.

[92] Bora Laskin interview with Robin Harrison, 1976, quoted in Girard, *Bora Laskin* (n 90 above) 49.

After graduation, Laskin enrolled in the LLM programme at Harvard, where he completed his dissertation under the supervision of Felix Frankfurter, who had also supervised John Willis.[93] That same year, the Privy Council struck down the Canadian New Deal and President Franklin Roosevelt introduced his court-packing plan in the United States, which precipitated an abrupt end to *Lochner* era jurisprudence. In his LLM thesis, Laskin charted 'the growth of administrative control in Canada', using the Ontario Municipal Board as a case study.[94] He argued that the Canadian non-delegation doctrine, which prohibited legislatures from delegating judicial powers to administrative officials, 'is of little utility unless one is prepared to support the proposition that ... it is feasible for courts and administrative boards to keep within their respective, allotted areas and not trespass on one another's field'.[95] Instead, he portrayed the Canadian Constitution as a 'living tree',[96] which was capable of adapting to 'the dictates of everyday life'.[97] In this respect, Laskin echoes Frankfurter's plea for a pragmatic understanding of the separation of powers to facilitate the emergence of a modern, intelligent administrative state staffed by experts with rule-making and adjudicative authority.[98]

While Laskin's jurisprudential perspective defies easy categorisation, it encapsulates what Philip Girard calls a 'modernist' theory of law inspired by the work of Oliver Wendell Holmes, Roscoe Pound, Felix Frankfurter, and Benjamin Cardozo.[99] Generally speaking, Laskin argued that judicial review should be restrained and that judges should respect administrative expertise.[100] In 1952, one year before the Supreme Court issued its decision in *Globe Printing*, Laskin (who was then a law professor at the University of Toronto) wrote a scathing critique of the doctrine of jurisdictional error.[101] While he praised legislative reform in the realm of industrial relations—especially the introduction of a compulsory collective bargaining regime administered by a bi-partisan board—he noted that judges routinely 'flouted' the enabling legislation.[102] Even though Labour Board decisions

[93] Bora Laskin, 'The Ontario Municipal Board' (LLM thesis, Harvard University, 1937).
[94] ibid 1.
[95] ibid 224.
[96] The metaphor derives from *Edwards v Attorney General Canada* [1930] AC 124, 136 (JCPC).
[97] Laskin, 'The Ontario Municipal Board' (n 93 above) 252.
[98] Felix Frankfurter, *The Public and Its Government* (New Haven CT, Yale University Press, 1930) ch 3.
[99] Girard, *Bora Laskin* (n 90 above) 96–102.
[100] Bora Laskin, 'Picketing: A Comparison of Canadian and American Doctrines' (1937) 15 *Canadian Bar Review* 10; Bora Laskin, 'The Labour Injunction in Canada: A Caveat' (1937) 15 *Canadian Bar Review* 270.
[101] Bora Laskin, 'Certiorari to Labour Boards: The Apparent Futility of Privative Clauses' (1952) 30 *Canadian Bar Review* 986.
[102] ibid 987.

were protected by privative clauses, Laskin observed that 'courts have found it expedient to exercise the same supervisory role over these administrative agencies as they would in the absence of any privative clause'.[103] By stretching the idea of jurisdictional error—a concept Laskin derided variously as a 'comforting conceptualism',[104] a 'semantic device',[105] and (quoting Frankfurter J) 'a verbal coat of too many colours'[106]—judges arrogated interpretive authority over public policies which were better administered by officials with personal experience negotiating and resolving industrial disputes.[107] In a stinging rebuke, Laskin stated:[108]

> By circumventing the privative clause, courts needlessly and gratuitously involve themselves in issues of policy. It may be urged, with justification, that all judicial work exhibits such involvement; but evasion of privative clauses through specious interpretation and unsupported assumptions is a trespass on the policy functions of another agency ... In the face of such enactments, judicial persistence in exercising a reviewing power involves an arrogation or authority only on the basis of constitutional principle (and there is no such principle) or on the basis of some 'elite' theory of knowing what is best for all concerned.

Like Frankfurter, Laskin believed that administrative accountability was best secured through the democratic process. Accordingly, he argued that privative clauses should be construed 'as an expression of legislative policy that the legislature will supervise or correct board misbehaviour'.[109]

After Laskin was appointed to the Bench, his ideas about the scope and purpose of judicial review continued to develop.[110] His perspective remained pragmatic, in the sense that he rejected the assumption that the parameters of judicial review could be deduced directly from the statutory text or conceptual analysis. Instead, he argued that the judicial role was to facilitate the intelligent resolution of interpretive disputes regarding the realisation of policy objectives outlined in the enabling legislation. Laskin's pragmatic orientation dovetailed with his functionalist belief that interpretive authority should be distributed so that experts with experiential knowledge would be primarily responsible for adjudicating disputes regarding social policy.[111] Therefore, Laskin believed that judges should respect expert interpretations of law even when they might otherwise disagree with the merits of those decisions.

[103] ibid 988.
[104] ibid 994.
[105] ibid 996.
[106] *United States v LA Tucker Truck Lines Inc* 344 US 33, 39 (1952).
[107] Laskin, 'Certiorari to Labour Boards' (n 101 above) 989–90.
[108] ibid 991.
[109] ibid 1000.
[110] Denise Réaume, 'The Judicial Philosophy of Bora Laskin' (1985) 35 *University of Toronto Law Journal* 438.
[111] See, eg Bora Laskin, 'The Function of Law' (1973) 11 *Alberta Law Review* 118.

But while Laskin stood by his pragmatic and functional beliefs, he nevertheless shared Frankfurter's conviction that judges should uphold fundamental values like fair process through judicial review.[112] Laskin's vision of judicial review has three interlocking components. The first component is that judges should ensure that administrative officials act fairly, even when that duty is not expressly set out in legislation or an administrative official is not exercising a 'judicial' power, so that persons affected by an administrative decision are entitled to participate meaningfully in the decision-making process. The second component is that judges should adopt a respectful attitude when reviewing the substance of an administrative decision: instead of asking whether an administrative decision conforms to the court's interpretation of the law, Laskin asserted that judges should only intervene when an administrative decision was substantively unreasonable. The third, and final component, was that individuals have a constitutional right to judicial review, even in cases where an administrative decision was protected by a broadly-worded privative clause. Thus, while Laskin's pragmatic and functional judicial philosophy resonates with many of the themes he voiced as an academic, it differs from his academic writings in one important respect—instead of arguing that judges should retreat altogether from the field of administrative law, he sought to rehabilitate the practice of judicial review so that it conveyed respect for the considered judgments of administrative officials while still upholding fundamental legal values.

A. Procedural Fairness

Laskin's commitment to procedural fairness is outlined in *Nicholson v Haldimand-Norfolk Regional Police Commissioners*, a case concerning a decision of a police board to dismiss a police constable.[113] Arthur Nicholson was hired on 1 March 1973 by the Town of Caldonia, and was promoted to second class constable after he had completed his one-year probationary period. However, three months after being promoted he was dismissed after he had called regional headquarters to ask for instructions on submitting an overtime slip. Nicholson's superior officer regarded the request as insubordination, and suspended him indefinitely. Six days later, Nicholson was dismissed by the Board of Police Commissioners.

Nicholson sought judicial review, arguing that the Board's decision was invalid because it had failed to notify him of the reasons for his dismissal or provide him with an opportunity to state his case. However, his lawyer could not rely upon the enabling statute to advance this claim. While The

[112] Girard, *Bora Laskin* (n 90 above) chs 15 and 21.
[113] *Nicholson v Haldimand-Norfolk Regional Police Commissioners* [1979] 1 SCR 311.

Police Act did provide a right to a hearing for senior police officers, it stated that 'nothing herein affects the authority of a board ... to dispense with the services of any constable within eighteen months of his becoming a constable'.[114] This provision was a major stumbling block for the Court of Appeal, which held that 'the Legislature has expressly required notice and hearing for certain purposes and has by necessary implication excluded them for other purposes'.[115] Thus, the Court concluded that 'the board may act as it was entitled to act at common law, ie without the necessity of prior notice of allegations or of a hearing'.[116]

While the Supreme Court's decision to quash the Board's decision in *Nicholson* is now considered a landmark, the decision divided the Court in 1978. In the years immediately preceding *Nicholson*, both Laskin CJ and Dickson J had written dissenting opinions, arguing that a duty of fairness should be imposed on administrative officials whenever individual interests were seriously affected by an administrative decision.[117] However, the majority opinions in those same cases asserted that the principles of natural justice only applied where an administrative official exercised 'judicial' powers, which meant that many administrative decisions entailed no procedural rights if the decision was deemed to be 'administrative'.

While the Court split in *Nicholson*, the majority sided with Laskin CJ's expansive understanding of procedural fairness. Martland J, who wrote the dissenting opinion, held that neither the statute nor the common law required the Board to provide Nicholson with either notice or a hearing. Like the Court of Appeal, Martland J concluded that the statute only gave senior police officers the right to either a hearing or a reasoned decision, which meant the Board could dismiss a junior officer like Nicholson for any reason at all. To support his conclusion, Martland J quoted a passage from *Ridge v Baldwin* in which Lord Reid had stated 'where an office is simply held at pleasure the person having the power of dismissal cannot be bound to disclose his reasons'.[118] Hence, Martland J concluded that

> [t]he only interest involved was that of the Board itself. Its decision was purely administrative. This being so, it was under no duty to explain to the appellant why his services were no longer required, or to give him an opportunity to be heard.[119]

Laskin CJ, who wrote the majority opinion on behalf of Dickson J and three other members of the Court, held that the Board was bound by a duty

114 The Police Act, RSO 1970, c 351, s 27(b).

115 *Re Nicholson and Haldimand-Norfolk Regional Board of Commissioners of Police* (1976) 12 OR (2d) 337, 347 (CA).

116 ibid 346.

117 *Howarth v National Parole Board* [1976] 1 SCR 453; *Martineau and Butters v The Matsqui Institution Inmate Disciplinary Board* [1978] 1 SCR 118.

118 *Ridge v Baldwin* [1964] AC 40, 66 (HL).

119 *Nicholson v Haldimand* (n 113 above) 335.

of fairness. The fact that the Board wielded statutory authority entailed a duty to conduct a hearing unless the enabling legislation expressly prohibited one. Therefore, the question was not whether Nicholson had the same statutory rights as more senior police officers, but whether the legislature had unequivocally stated that junior officers could be dismissed without notice. Laskin CJ noted that 'although the appellant clearly cannot claim the procedural protections afforded to a constable with more than eighteen months' service, he cannot be denied any protection. He should be treated "fairly" not arbitrarily'.[120] Furthermore, Laskin CJ rejected the notion that the duty of fairness applied only to powers which could categorised as 'judicial' or 'quasi-judicial' in the abstract—what mattered were the practical consequences of the decision.[121] In his words, 'to endow some with procedural protection while denying others any at all would work injustice when the results of statutory decisions raise the same serious consequences for those adversely affected, regardless of the classification of the function in question'.[122] Thus, after noting that 'the consequences to the appellant are serious indeed', Laskin CJ concluded that Nicholson 'should have been told why his services were no longer required and given an opportunity, whether orally or in writing ... to respond'.[123]

Laskin CJ's opinion in *Nicholson* marks a shift away from formal and conceptual analysis (in which the right to fair process is contingent upon legislative intent or a metaphysical distinction between judicial and administrative powers) towards a pragmatic, contextualised understanding of procedural fairness (in which decision-making processes are conceived as a means of facilitating principled and intelligent inquiries to resolve social problems in light of experience). In the year following *Nicholson*, the Court extended the duty of procedural fairness to another type of administrative decision which had traditionally been exempt from the principles of natural justice: penitentiary discipline. In his concurring opinion in *Martineau v Matsqui Disciplinary Board*, Dickson J noted that 'the application of a duty of fairness ... does not depend upon proof of a judicial or quasi-judicial function' so that the duty applies 'whenever a public body has power to decide a matter affecting the rights, interests, property, privileges, or liberties of any person'.[124] Thus, even though he thought that 'the disciplinary board was not under an express or implied duty to follow a judicial type of procedure', Dickson J held it had a duty to act fairly because 'the board's decision had the effect of depriving an individual of his liberty by committing him to a "prison within a prison"'.[125]

[120] ibid 324.

[121] Geneviève Cartier, 'Procedural Fairness in Legislative Functions: The End of Judicial Abstinence' (2004) 53 *University of Toronto Law Journal* 217, 225.

[122] *Nicholson* (n 113 above) 325.

[123] ibid 328.

[124] *Martineau v Matsqui Disciplinary Board* (n 7 above) 622–23.

[125] ibid 623.

However, this understanding of procedural fairness did not simply expand the scope of judicial review so that decisions which had previously been characterised as 'administrative' were automatically bound to conform to processes employed by the judiciary. For instance in *Kane v Governors, University of British Columbia*, a case involving a decision to suspend a university professor, the Court held that the university Board of Governors had breached its duty of fairness by questioning a witness in the professor's absence. In a line reminiscent of *Nicholson*, Dickson J stated that '[a] high standard of justice is required when the right to continue in one's profession or employment is at stake',[126] which meant that the Board's ex parte interview was unfair. But he also pointed out that '[i]t is the duty of the courts to attribute a large measure of autonomy of decision to a tribunal' so that the Board of Governors 'is free, within reason, to determine its own procedures, which will vary with the nature of the inquiry and the circumstances of the case'.[127]

B. Judicial Deference

The second component in Laskin's model, which counsels judicial respect for the substance of administrative decisions, is set out in *CUPE v New Brunswick Liquor Corporation*.[128] That case arose in the context of a labour dispute, in which a union alleged that the employer's practice of using management personnel to operate retail liquor outlets during a strike violated section 102(3)(a) of The Public Service Labour Relations Act. That provision declared that 'the employer shall not replace the striking employees or fill their position with any other employee'.[129] The Labour Board agreed with the union, and ordered the employer to cease using managers as replacement employees. The employer sought judicial review, arguing that the Board had misinterpreted the statute.

The Supreme Court of Canada unanimously upheld the Board's decision. While Dickson J wrote on behalf of the Court, legal historians claim the judgment 'is one Laskin should have written',[130] because it echoes Laskin's academic scholarship which highlighted 'the comprehensive nature of the responsibilities given to labour boards and their experience and expertise in both fact-finding and determining questions of law'.[131] In this respect,

[126] *Kane v Board of Governors of the University of British Columbia* [1980] 1 SCR 1105, 1113.
[127] ibid 1112.
[128] *CUPE* (n 5 above).
[129] Public Service Labour Relations Act, RSNB 1973, c P-25.
[130] Girard, *Bora Laskin* (n 90 above) 486.
[131] Hudson Janisch, 'Bora Laskin and Administrative Law: An Unfinished Journey' (1985) 35 *University of Toronto Law Journal* 557, 567.

Laskin's views were essentially similar to Felix Frankfurter's and John Willis's.[132]

In *CUPE*, Dickson J began by noting that the provision in dispute 'bristles with ambiguities'.[133] This fact alone might have been sufficient to dispose of the case, because the Court could simply have stated that it agreed with the Board's interpretation of the statute. However, Dickson J went further by expressing more general doubts about the doctrine of jurisdictional error. The problem, in his view, was that the distinction between jurisdictional and non-jurisdictional issues was 'very difficult to determine', which often led judges to overreach by assuming they should have the final word on how the law should be interpreted. In order to remedy this problem, Dickson J declared that 'courts, in my view, should not be alert to brand as jurisdictional, and therefore subject to broader curial review, that which may be doubtfully so'.[134]

Instead of asking whether the issue was jurisdictional, Dickson J identified important reasons why the Court should respect the Board's decision. He pointed out that the statute contained a privative clause, which declared that the Board's decisions 'shall not be questioned or reviewed in any court'.[135] Furthermore, he stated that the privative clause had a policy rationale which was 'straightforward and compelling': the Board had acquired relevant expertise and experience in administering the Act.[136] So instead of speculating about the meaning of section 102(3)(a) in the abstract, Dickson J explained why the Court should respect the Board's understanding of the statute. Thus, Dickson J concluded that the Court could only intervene where the Board's decision was 'so patently unreasonable that its construction cannot be rationally supported by the relevant legislation'.[137]

However, despite expressing general doubts about the doctrine of jurisdictional error, Dickson J conflated the unreasonableness standard with the catalogue of errors set out by the House of Lords in *Anisminic*.[138] Thus, instead of following Rand J's method for assessing the substantive reasonableness of an administrative decision, Dickson J stated that unreasonable decisions are ones which are tainted by bad faith, are based on extraneous factors, fail to consider relevant factors, breach principles of natural justice, or answer the wrong question.[139]

[132] Towards the end of his judicial career, Laskin CJ admitted he was 'an unabashed admirer of John Willis'. Bora Laskin, 'Foreword' (1982–83) 7 *Dalhousie Law Journal* 3. See also Bora Laskin, 'John Willis: An Appreciation' (1972) 22 *University of Toronto Law Journal* 3.

[133] *CUPE* (n 5 above) 230.

[134] ibid 233.

[135] Public Service Labour Relations Act (n 129 above) s 101(1).

[136] *CUPE* (n 5 above) 235–36.

[137] ibid 237.

[138] ibid. See also *Service Employee's International Union v Nipawin Union Hospital* [1975] 1 SCR 382, 389.

[139] *CUPE* (n 5 above) 237.

As a result, two persistent problems marred post-*CUPE* case law. The first problem concerned the threshold question regarding whether a court should review an administrative decision according to a standard of correctness or patent unreasonableness. Because Dickson J did not abolish the doctrine of jurisdictional error outright, jurisdictional analysis popped up frequently. The second issue concerns whether and to what extent the patent unreasonableness standard was distinguishable from correctness review. Because Dickson J conflated patent unreasonableness with the catalogue of errors set out in *Anisminic*, judges continued to conflate reasonableness review with a quixotic quest for jurisdictional error.

The first problem is illustrated by cases like *Syndicat des employés de production du Québec & de l'Acadie v Canada (Labour Relations Board)*, a case in which the Supreme Court revived the broad notion of jurisdictional error in quashing a Canada Labour Relations Board decision to refer a labour dispute to arbitration.[140] While the author of the majority opinion, Beetz J, acknowledged *CUPE*'s admonition to avoid casting a large net for jurisdictional error, he thought there was 'no doubt' that the Board's decision to refer the dispute to an arbitrator involved a jurisdictional question.[141] In language reminiscent of *Anisminic*, he declared that a jurisdictional issue was 'one which describes, limits and lists the powers of an administrative tribunal' and could arise at any point in administrative proceedings 'whether at the start of the hearing, during it, in the findings or in the order disposing of the matter'.[142] In effect, the doctrine of jurisdictional error retained much of its vigour in the decade following *CUPE*, even though the Court frequently paid lip service to *CUPE*'s critique of that practice.[143]

The second problem is illustrated by a schism which emerged on the Supreme Court in the early 1990s.[144] One camp, led by Sopinka J, took the view that in order to determine whether an administrative decision was reasonable, the Court should first determine the correct outcome on the merits and then ask whether the administrative decision was sufficiently proximate to the Court's conclusion. Thus, in his concurring judgment in *CAIMAW v Paccar of Canada Ltd*, Sopinka J stated that '[c]urial deference does not enter the picture until the Court finds itself in disagreement with the tribunal. Only then is it necessary to consider whether the error (so found) is within or outside the boundaries of reasonableness'.[145] This approach

[140] *Syndicat des employés de production du Québec & de l'Acadie v Canada (Labour Relations Board)* [1984] 2 SCR 412.

[141] ibid 437.

[142] ibid 420.

[143] See, eg *UES, Local 298 v Bibeault* (n 89 above).

[144] See David Mullan, 'Of Chaff Midst the Corn: *American Farm Bureau Federation v Canada (Canadian Import Tribunal)* and Patent Unreasonableness Review' (1991) 45 *Admin LR* 264; Margaret Allars, 'On Deference to Tribunals With Deference to Dworkin' (1995) 20 *Queen's Law Journal* 163.

[145] *CAIMAW v Paccar of Canada Ltd* [1989] 2 SCR 983, 1018.

is problematic, because it assumes that judicial interpretation of the law is correct, even though an administrative official has been given primary legal responsibility over the matter and may have relevant expertise or experience which a reviewing court lacks. Moreover, even if the court decides to defer to the administrative decision, it will seem as though the court is perpetuating an incorrect determination of an individual's legal rights.[146]

By contrast, the opposing camp led by Wilson J took the position that *CUPE* had fundamentally changed the law of judicial review. She argued there were cogent reasons to defer to an administrative decision, even in situations where the legislation did not include a privative clause, because administrative decision-makers are better equipped to answer questions left open by the legislature.[147] Thus, she thought that Sopinka J's approach undermined efficient and expert modes of legal interpretation. Instead, she asserted that a reviewing court should refrain from declaring how it would have assessed the merits, saying that so long as an administrative decision was not patently unreasonable there was no need for judges to reveal how they would have decided the matter in its absence.

C. A Constitutional Right to Judicial Review

The third component in Laskin's model concerns a constitutional right to judicial review. Given his academic critique of judicial review, this aspect is difficult to reconcile with the general tenor of his argument for judicial restraint. But while Laskin's support for a constitutional right to judicial review seems like 'an ironic twist',[148] a closer look at Laskin's writings suggests that his primary concerns were to neutralise the formal conception of the separation of powers and establish a constitutional right to judicial review which nevertheless conveyed respect for administrative decisions.[149]

Earlier in this chapter, I reviewed a series of decisions in which both the Privy Council and the Supreme Court of Canada interpreted section 96 of the BNA Act as entrenching a formal conception of the separation of powers. The principal idea, which was vigorously contested by academic commentators during the Great Depression, was that section 96 prohibited provincial legislatures from delegating judicial functions to administrative officials.[150] However, the subsidiary idea in these cases was that legislatures could delegate judicial functions to administrative officials so long as their decisions remained subject to judicial review.

[146] See David Mullan, 'Of Chaff Midst the Corn' (n 144 above).

[147] *National Corn Growers Association v Canada (Import Tribunal)* [1990] 2 SCR 1324, 1336–40 (Wilson J dissenting).

[148] Janisch, 'Bora Laskin and Administrative Law' (n 131 above) 572.

[149] Girard, *Bora Laskin* (n 90 above) 498–502.

[150] See Willis, 'Administrative Law and the British North America Act' (n 26 above); Willis, 'Section 96 of the British North America Act' (n 35 above).

While Laskin rejected the formal conception of the separation of powers, he still thought administrative law could be reconciled with some form of judicial review. In *Attorney General Québec v Farrah*, Laskin CJ distanced himself from the formal conception of the separation of powers, saying:[151]

> First, it is open to a Province to endow an administrative agency, which has adjudicative functions, with power to determine questions of law in the exercise of its authority under a valid provincial regulatory statute such as the one involved in the present case. Indeed, it is difficult to appreciate how such an agency can operate effectively if it is precluded from interpreting and applying the statute under which it exercises its jurisdiction. Second, it is also open to a Province to establish an administrative tribunal as part of a valid regulatory statute and to invest such a tribunal with power to make decisions on questions of law in the course of exercising an appellate authority over decisions of the primary agency. … Applying the foregoing considerations to the present case, it would, in my view, be competent for the Province to invest the Transport Tribunal with power to decide questions of law in the course of hearing appeals from decisions of the Transport Commission. Although such a power involves the exercise of a judicial function, it is not on that account alone beyond the constitutional authority of a Province to repose in a provincially appointed board.

Nevertheless, Laskin CJ held that the enabling legislation in *Farrah* was unconstitutional, because it purported to extinguish judicial review altogether. Thus, Laskin CJ claimed that, while administrative officials had legitimate authority to decide questions of law, the Constitution required some degree of judicial oversight.[152]

This subtle shift in the Supreme Court's section 96 jurisprudence also explains *Crevier*, a case in which the Supreme Court examined the constitutionality of privative clauses.[153] In *Crevier*, two optometrists were found guilty of professional misconduct. Both of them appealed to the Professions Tribunal, a general appellate tribunal for all professional disciplinary committees operating under the Professional Code.[154] The Tribunal overturned the convictions, but the prosecutor challenged the Tribunal's statutory powers under section 96 of the BNA Act.[155] The Court of Appeal held that the Code did not violate section 96 because (1) historically speaking, professional discipline was not an exclusive function of superior courts; and (2) the privative clause in the Code did not prohibit review for jurisdictional error.[156]

[151] *Farrah v Quebec (Attorney General)* [1978] 2 SCR 638, 642–43.

[152] ibid 647.

[153] *Crevier v Québec (Attorney General)* [1981] 2 SCR 220.

[154] Professional Code, RSQ 1977, c C-26. The Code applied to a variety of professional corporations including doctors, dentists pharmacists, optometrists, veterinarians, lawyers, notaries, social workers, architects, engineers, accountants, etc.

[155] As in *Farrah* (n 151 above), this provision purported to exclude judicial review under the provisions of the Quebec Code of Civil Procedure.

[156] *Procureur Général de Québec c Crevier* [1979] CA 333.

In his judgment for a unanimous Court declaring the privative clause unconstitutional, Laskin CJ completely ignored the formal separation of powers argument.[157] Instead, he focused primarily on the constitutionality of the privative clause. He stated that 'where a provincial Legislature purports to insulate one of its statutory tribunals from any curial review of its adjudicative functions, the insulation encompassing jurisdiction, such provincial legislation must be struck down as unconstitutional'.[158] However, in arriving at this conclusion Laskin CJ stated that superior courts retained the ability to correct jurisdictional errors, but qualified this point by saying '[t]here may be differences of opinion as to what are questions of jurisdiction but, in my lexicon, they rise above and are different from errors of law, whether involving statutory construction or evidentiary matters'.[159]

This raises an important question: why did Laskin CJ, who had generally opposed judicial overreach throughout his academic career, declare the entire statutory regime unconstitutional when he could have preserved a right to judicial review through less drastic measures?[160] The most plausible interpretation of Laskin CJ's judgment is that, like Frankfurter, he believed in judicial restraint but also thought judicial review was a constitutional guarantee. Fifteen years later L'Heureux-Dubé J would adopt this reading of *Crevier* in *Pasienchyk v Canada Labour Relations Board* by saying that 'as a matter of constitutional law, a legislature may not, however clearly it expresses itself, protect an administrative body from review on matters of jurisdiction'.[161] While Laskin CJ likely thought that the idea of jurisdictional error should be cabined or defined narrowly, he nevertheless thought individuals had a constitutional right to test the legality of an administrative decision in the courts.

D. Deference and Constitutional Rights

When Laskin CJ died on 26 March 1984, the law of judicial review was still in the throes of transition. The Constitution, which now included the Canadian Charter of Rights and Freedoms, was patriated on 17 April 1982 and gave Canadian courts a powerful new tool for scrutinising legislation and administrative decisions. However, Laskin CJ had succeeded in laying the foundation for a framework for judicial review which counselled judicial

157 On this point, compare the historical analysis of judicial functions employed in *Re Residential Tenancies Act, 1979* [1981] 1 SCR 714. See also David Mullan, 'The Uncertain Constitutional Position of Canada's Administrative Appeal Tribunals' (1982) 14 *Ottawa Law Review* 239, 254–55.

158 *Crevier* (n 153 above) 234.

159 ibid 236.

160 Mullan, 'Administrative Appeals Tribunals' (n 157 above) 248–50.

161 *Pasienchyk v Canada Labour Relations Board* [1996] 1 SCR 369, [55].

restraint so long as administrative decisions were rendered in a fair and reasonable manner. In the years that followed, the Supreme Court continued to build upon the foundation laid in *Nicholson*, *CUPE*, and *Crevier*, but lapsed frequently into the formal and conceptual analysis which had been employed previously.

For example on procedural matters, the Supreme Court continued to assert a broad duty of fairness, but excluded decisions which were categorised as 'legislative' or 'preliminary' in nature. Thus, in *Knight v Indian Head School Division*, L'Heureux-Dubé J noted that '[t]here is no longer a need ... to distinguish between judicial, quasi-judicial, and administrative decisions' in order to ascertain whether an administrative official had a duty to act fairly.[162] Rather, 'the duty to act fairly ... stems from the fact that the employer is a public body whose powers are derived from statute'.[163] Furthermore, she stated that 'the concept of procedural fairness is eminently variable and its content is to be decided in the specific context of each case'.[164] Nevertheless, she carved out some categorical exceptions to the general rule by saying 'not all administrative bodies are under a duty to act fairly', noting that '[d]ecisions of a legislative and general nature' as well as 'preliminary' decisions did not require a hearing.[165]

Similar mixed messages cropped up in substantive review of administrative decisions. While the Court emphasised the functionalist rationale for deferring to administrative expertise in *Pezim v British Columbia (Superintendent of Brokers)* and *Canada (Director of Investigation and Research) v Southam*, this message was often undercut by the suggestion that administrative interpretations of law were generally subject to correctness review.[166] Thus, in *Pezim* Iacobucci J held that 'considerable deference is warranted ... notwithstanding the fact that there is a statutory right of appeal and there is no privative clause',[167] a conclusion he repeated in *Southam* by stating that administrative expertise 'is the most important of the factors that a court must consider in settling on a standard of review'.[168] However, he undercut the functionalist rationale for deference in *Southam* by stating that administrative decisions on questions of law should be assessed on a correctness standard, although he noted that the distinctions between questions of law, fact, and mixed law and fact were difficult to ascertain.[169]

[162] *Knight v Indian Head School Division No 19* [1990] 1 SCR 653, [25].
[163] ibid [22].
[164] ibid [46].
[165] ibid.
[166] *Pezim v British Columbia (Superintendent of Brokers)* [1994] 2 SCR 557; *Canada (Director of Investigation and Research) v Southam Inc* [1997] 1 SCR 748.
[167] ibid.
[168] *Southam* (n 166 above) [50].
[169] ibid [45].

This tension between the functionalist rationale for judicial deference and the lingering attachment to correctness review on questions of law is most noticeable in cases involving human rights. When the Supreme Court initially considered whether administrative officials have the power to apply the Charter to their enabling legislation, it held that administrative officials were bound by the Constitution whenever they exercise delegated authority.[170] Thus, in *Douglas/Kwantlen Faculty Association v Douglas College* LaForest J confessed that 'I fail to see why it would be offensive to the judicature provisions of the *Constitution Act, 1867*, and in particular s. 96, for a tribunal to consider other constitutional questions arising in the course of its mandate'.[171] Moreover, he advanced a cogent practical argument for enabling administrative officials to enforce Charter rights—it enabled individuals to assert their constitutional rights directly before administrative officials seised with their case, it obviated the expense and inefficiency of launching parallel court proceedings, and it enriched constitutional discourse by enabling expert administrators to consider how constitutional values should be interpreted and applied in a particular regulatory context.[172] On this last point, LaForest J noted that human rights questions were not 'vastly different from the application of ordinary statutes for which arbitrators are responsible' and that there was 'little difference' between these questions and 'certain provisions of the Human Rights codes which arbitrators may hold to override provisions in collective agreements'.[173]

However, in the same case LaForest J asserts that an administrative official's authority to interpret the Charter does not stem directly from section 52(1) of the Constitution, which states that '[t]he Constitution of Canada is the supreme law of Canada';[174] rather, it is contingent upon whether the legislature intended expressly or impliedly to delegate authority over questions of law to that official.[175] Furthermore, in *Cuddy Chicks Ltd v Ontario (Labour Relations Board)*, LaForest J stated that administrative decisions concerning Charter values are not entitled to deference, which means that judges are entitled to review such decisions on a correctness standard.[176] Finally, LaForest J noted that even if an administrative official concludes that the enabling legislation infringes the Charter, he can refuse to apply the offending statutory provisions but cannot grant a constitutional remedy.[177]

[170] *Douglas/Kwantlen Faculty Association v Douglas College* [1990] 3 SCR 570, 594. See also *Cuddy Chicks Ltd v Ontario (Labour Relations Board)* [1991] 2 SCR 5; *Tétrault-Gadoury v Canada (EIC)* [1991] 2 SCR 22.

[171] *Douglas/Kwantlen* (n 170 above) 599.

[172] ibid 604–5.

[173] ibid 596–97.

[174] Constitution Act, 1982 (n 2 above) s 52(1).

[175] *Douglas/Kwantlen* (n 170 above). See also *Cuddy Chicks* (n 170 above) 14–15; *Tétrault-Gadoury* (n 170 above) 32.

[176] *Cuddy Chicks* (n 170 above) 17.

[177] *Douglas/Kwantlen* (n 170 above). See also *Cuddy Chicks* (n 170 above); *Tétrault-Gadoury* (n 170 above).

All of this leads to a contradictory or conflicted state of affairs: administrative officials have a general duty to interpret and enforce constitutional rights, but the legislature can restrict the scope of this duty and judges can run roughshod over administrative decisions concerning these issues.

What is even more perplexing is that the Supreme Court refused to defer to the decisions of human rights tribunals. Since 1947, Parliament and the provincial legislatures began introducing human rights codes, giving human rights tribunals the power to enforce and interpret code provisions prohibiting discrimination. However, while the Court deferred to labour relations board interpretations of enabling legislation in cases like *CUPE*, it generally reviewed human rights tribunal decisions on a correctness standard.[178] *Canada (Attorney General) v Mossop*, a case in which the Court reviewed a decision by the Canada Human Rights Tribunal, is illustrative of this trend.[179] The dispute arose when Brian Mossop applied for bereavement leave in order to attend the funeral of his partner's father. However, his employer denied the application because the collective agreement only allowed bereavement leave for the death of 'immediate family' members, which was defined in a manner which excluded homosexual relationships. Mossop filed a complaint with the Canadian Human Rights Commission, claiming that he was the victim of discriminatory treatment under the Canadian Human Rights Act. But in order to succeed, Mossop had to convince the Tribunal that his employer had discriminated against him on the basis of his 'family status' under the Act. The Tribunal held in Mossop's favour, saying that the term 'family status' should be interpreted using the same broad and purposive approach employed by the Supreme Court when interpreting human rights provisions under the Charter.[180] However, the Tribunal's decision was overturned by the Federal Court of Appeal on the ground that, since there was no privative clause in the Act, there was no reason for the Court to defer to the Tribunal's decision on a question of law.

Like the Federal Court of Appeal, the Supreme Court held that the Tribunal's decision should be overturned. The two leading judgments for the majority, written by Lamer CJ and LaForest J, both held that the Tribunal was not entitled to deference because it had no expertise regarding human

[178] Alison Harvison Young, 'Keeping the Courts at Bay: The Canadian Human Rights Commission and Its Counterparts in Britain and Northern Ireland: Some Comparative Lessons' (1993) 43 *University of Toronto Law Journal* 65; Alison Harvison Young, 'Human Rights Tribunals and the Supreme Court of Canada: Reformulating Deference' (1993) 13 Admin LR (2d) 206.

[179] *Canada (Attorney General) v Mossop* [1993] 1 SCR 554. See also *Gould v Yukon Order of Pioneers* [1996] 1 SCR 571; *Berg v University of British Columbia* [1993] 2 SCR 353; *Ross v New Brunswick School District No 15* [1996] 1 SCR 827.

[180] The Canadian Human Rights Act, RSC, 1985, c H-6, s 2 at the time read as follows: 'The purpose of this Act is to extend the laws in Canada to give effect ... to the principle that

rights. Even though Lamer CJ recognised that administrative expertise might justify deference in the absence of a privative clause, he nevertheless argued that the Court's interpretation should prevail because the meaning of 'family status' was a straightforward question of statutory interpretation which the Court was entitled to adjudicate.[181] LaForest J went further in his concurring opinion, stating:[182]

> The superior expertise of a human rights tribunal relates to fact-finding and adjudication in a human rights context. It does not extend to general questions of law such as the one at issue in this case. These are ultimately matters within the province of the judiciary, and involve concepts of statutory interpretation and general legal reasoning which the courts must be supposed competent to perform. The courts cannot abdicate this duty to the tribunal. They must, therefore, review the tribunal's decisions on questions of this kind on the basis of correctness, not on a standard of reasonability.

By contrast, L'Heureux-Dubé J, writing in dissent, thought that the Act gave the Commission and the Tribunal 'broad powers in a highly specialised and sensitive area' to investigate human rights complaints, foster public understanding of the Act, undertake research programmes related to the advancement of human rights, develop policy, and to discourage discriminatory practices through both formal and informal means.[183] After reviewing the Tribunal's reasoning, she concluded that the decision was 'in accordance with the proper principles of interpretation of human rights legislation' and therefore should be upheld.[184]

E. Fairness and Reasonable Justification

The capstone case for the pragmatic and functional era is *Baker v Canada (Minister of Citizenship and Immigration)*,[185] a decision which connects the general duty of procedural fairness with judicial deference towards administrative interpretations of law.[186] The case concerned Mavis Baker, who arrived in Canada in 1981 on a temporary visitor's visa but remained in

every individual should have an equal opportunity with other individuals to make for himself or herself the life that he or she is able and wishes to have, consistent with his or her duties and obligations as a member of society, without being hindered in or prevented from doing so by discriminatory practices based on race, national or ethnic origin, colour, religion, age, sex, marital status, family status, disability or conviction for an offence for which a pardon has been granted'.

[181] *Canada (Attorney General) v Mossop* (n 179 above) [25]–[26].
[182] ibid [45].
[183] ibid [86]–[87].
[184] ibid [141].
[185] *Baker v Canada (Minister of Citizenship and Immigration)* [1999] 2 SCR 817.
[186] David Dyzenhaus and Evan Fox-Decent, 'Rethinking the Process/Substance Distinction: *Baker v Canada*' (2001) 51 *University of Toronto Law Journal* 193.

the country for the next 11 years. During this time, she supported herself by working illegally and had four children, all of whom were Canadian citizens. However, after receiving treatment for post-partum depression in 1992, she was ordered to leave the country. After seeking legal advice, Baker applied for a 'humanitarian and compassionate' exemption that would permit her to remain in Canada while her application for permanent residency was being processed. Despite the fact that four of her children were Canadian citizens, her request was denied. When her lawyer requested an explanation for the decision, the Department of Immigration provided the case notes compiled by the investigating officer. The relevant portions of the notes stated:[187]

> The PC is a paranoid schizophrenic and on welfare. She has no qualifications other than as a domestic. She has FOUR CHILDREN IN JAMAICA AND ANOTHER FOUR BORN HERE. She will, of course, be a tremendous strain on our social welfare systems for (probably) the rest of her life. There are not H&C factors other than her FOUR CANADIAN-BORN CHILDREN. Do we let her stay because of that? I am of the opinion that Canada can no longer afford this kind of generosity.

After receiving the notes, Baker applied for judicial review claiming that the decision to deny the exemption was both biased and unreasonable.

When the case came before the Trial Division of the Federal Court, the judge considered the file notes in a peculiar fashion. First, she held that since the decision-maker had not initially given reasons for his decision, she had to *assume* that he had acted in good faith. Secondly, although Simpson J recognised 'that failure to consider the best interests of a child when making a decision about whether to deport a parent would be an error', she held that no error was apparent in Baker's case.[188] She pointed out how the officer referred repeatedly to the children in capital letters and considered evidence showing that the children would suffer if their mother were deported. Thus, Simpson J upheld the decision to refuse the exemption, saying that '[n]o blatant error is to be found in the officer's notes. His expressions of personal opinion were unfortunate, but they do not taint the decision-maker'.[189]

Baker appealed Simpson J's decision on the grounds that neither the decision-maker nor Simpson J had given adequate consideration to the fact that Canada was a signatory to the International Convention on the Rights of the Child, which states that in all government decisions concerning children 'the best interests of the child shall be a primary consideration'.[190] However, when the matter came before the Federal Court of Appeal, Strayer JA adopted an approach to reasonableness review very similar to

[187] *Baker* (n 185 above) [5].
[188] *Baker v Canada (Minister of Citizenship and Immigration)* [1995] 101 FTR 110, [5].
[189] ibid [44].
[190] Convention on the Rights of the Child, 12 January 1992, Can TS 1992 No 3.

the Court below. He noted that, because Simpson J found that the decision-maker had considered the impact on the children, Baker had to demonstrate that 'the best interests of the children must as a matter of law be given more weight than many other factors'.[191] However, Strayer JA rejected the argument that the Convention required the decision-maker to assign any particular weight to the children's interests. He declared that the Convention did not have any domestic legal effect, because it would offend the separation of powers to enable the executive to change the law via a treaty which had not been ratified by Parliament.[192]

Thus, both Simpson J and Strayer JA adopt a similar approach to reasonableness review, one which limits the role of judicial review to ascertaining simply whether the administrative decision-maker has nominally considered relevant facts and principles in the reasons which accompany their decision.[193] So long as the relevant law and facts are put before the decision-maker, it makes no difference how they actually figure in the outcome. Accordingly, the fact that the immigration officers acknowledged that Baker had four Canadian-born children before refusing her request was sufficient. So the fact that the file notes disclose that the officers thought that the children were an *aggravating* consideration which weighed in favour of deporting their mother instead of allowing her to remain the country was not a concern.

Nevertheless, the Supreme Court held that the decision to deny the exemption was both biased and unreasonable. In doing so, the Court recognised, for the first time, that the duty of fairness requires administrative officials to provide a substantive justification for their decisions. Writing for a unanimous court, L'Heureux-Dubé J echoed Laskin's pragmatic understanding of procedural fairness, saying that the point behind requiring administrative officials to act fairly[194]

> is to ensure that administrative decisions are made using a fair and open procedure, appropriate to the decision being made and its statutory institutional, and social context, with an opportunity for those affected by the decision to put forward their views and evidence fully and have them considered by the decision-maker.

Having considered the relevant context of the case, especially the consequences associated with separating Baker from her children, L'Heureux-Dubé J held that an administrative official has an obligation to provide reasons in situations 'where the decision has important significance for the individual'.[195] Based on the facts of the case, she concluded that '[i]t would

[191] *Baker v Canada (Minister of Citizenship and Immigration)* [1997] 2 FC 127 (FCA) [12].
[192] ibid [20].
[193] Evan Fox-Decent, 'The Internal Morality of Administration: The Form and Structure of Reasonableness' in David Dyzenhaus, *The Unity of Public Law* (Oxford, Hart Publishing, 2004) 143.
[194] *Baker* (n 185 above) [22].
[195] ibid [43].

be unfair for a person subject to a decision such as this one which is so critical to their future not to be told why the result was reached'.[196] However, she noted that the extent of this duty was contextual, which meant that it should be interpreted flexibly in light of 'the day-to-day realities and the many ways in which the values underlying the principles of procedural fairness can be assured'. Accordingly, she concluded that Officer Lorenz's informal file notes satisfied the duty to give reasons, because they provided an intelligible explanation for the decision.

However, because the file notes disclosed an outrageous rationale, the Court held that the decision should be quashed even though it was entitled to deference.[197] Despite the fact that the enabling legislation gave the Minister broad discretionary power to grant the exemption, L'Heureux-Dubé J held that the decision could only be upheld if it disclosed a reasonable justification. Thus, she held that it was insufficient for the investigating officer to merely mention the children in his reasons; in order to satisfy the threshold of reasonableness review, the interests of the children had to be given appropriate consideration.[198]

> [F]or the exercise of the discretion to fall within the standard of reasonableness, the decision-maker should consider children's best interests as an important factor, give them substantial weight, and be alert, alive and sensitive to them. That is not to say that children's best interests must always outweigh other considerations, or that there will not be other reasons for denying an H&C claim even when children's interests are given this consideration. However, where the interests of the children are minimized, in a manner inconsistent with Canada's humanitarian and compassionate tradition and the Minister's guidelines, the decision will be unreasonable.

The salient point here is that *Baker* places the reasoning of the administrative decision-maker at the centre of the inquiry. Instead of simply asking whether an administrative decision mirrors how the Court would have decided, all things considered, the Court asks whether the reasons provide an acceptable legal rationale for refusing the exemption—one which demonstrates adequate regard for the values and principles which accompany the delegation of decision-making power. In other words, judicial deference must ultimately be earned by the administrative decision-maker 'by openly demonstrating the justifications for the decisions they have reached and by demonstrating the reasons why their decision is worthy of curial respect'.[199]

[196] ibid.

[197] After conducting a pragmatic and functional analysis of the regulatory context, L'Heureux-Dubé J held that the appropriate standard of review was reasonableness, *simpliciter*: ibid [57]–[62].

[198] *Baker* (n 185 above) [75].

[199] Murray Hunt, 'Sovereignty's Blight: Why Contemporary Public Law Needs the Concept of "Due Deference"' in Nicholas Bamforth and Peter Leyland (eds), *Public Law in a Multi-Layered Constitution* (Oxford, Hart Publishing, 2003) 337, 340.

Because the officer's substantive rationale was inconsistent with relevant legal standards—the declared objectives of the Act, the principles of the international Convention on the Rights of the Child, and the guidelines that had been issued by the Minister of Immigration—the Court concluded that that it was appropriate to intervene and overturn the decision.[200]

III. THE DIS-FUNCTIONAL ERA

The most recent period of doctrinal development, which spans roughly from 2002 until 2009, is characterised by the re-emergence of formal and conceptual analysis. The cases from this period convey weariness and frustration with how complex and conflicted the pragmatic and functional approach had become.[201] Justice LeBel's concurring opinions in *Chamberlain v Surrey School District No 36*[202] and *Toronto (City) v CUPE, Local 79*[203] are illustrative of this reaction. In those opinions, LeBel J rejects the idea that a reviewing court should routinely apply the pragmatic and functional framework in order to ascertain the appropriate standard of review; like Stevens J in *Chevron v USA Inc v Natural Resources Defense Council*,[204] LeBel J asserts that judges can forgo contextual analysis if they conclude that the legislature has answered the question at issue. Hence, in *Chamberlain* LeBel J noted that '[t]he ultimate question remains the legislature's intent', and that an analysis of 'the various factors in the "pragmatic and functional method" is not always the best path to that intention'.[205] In the years following *Chamberlain*, the Court established a catalogue of issues that warrant correctness oversight: constitutional questions,[206] 'true' jurisdictional issues,[207] and general questions of law which are of central importance to the legal system.[208] This trend prompted two leading scholars to

[200] *Baker* (n 185 above) [65].

[201] Laverne Jacobs, 'Developments in Administrative Law: The 2007–2008 Term—The Impact of *Dunsmuir*' (2008) *Supreme Court Law Review* (2d) 1, 8–10.

[202] *Chamberlain v Surrey School District No 36* [2002] 4 SCR 710.

[203] *Toronto (City) v CUPE, Local 79* [2003] 3 SCR 77.

[204] *Chevron USA Inc v Natural Resources Defense Council, Inc* 467 US 837, 842–43 (1984). The two step formula for judicial review in *Chevron* holds that (1) if Congressional intent is clearly expressed, judges must enforce that intent but (2) if Congressional intent is silent or ambiguous, judges may only intervene if an administrative decision is unreasonable.

[205] *Chamberlain* (n 202 above) [194]–[195]. See also *United Taxi Drivers' Fellowship of Southern Alberta v Calgary (City)* [2004] 1 SCR 485.

[206] *Nova Scotia (Workers' Compensation Board) v Martin*; *Nova Scotia (Workers' Compensation Board) v Laseur* [2003] 2 SCR 504.

[207] *United Taxi Drivers'* (n 205 above); *ATCO Gas & Pipelines Ltd v Alberta (Energy & Utilities Board)* [2006] 1 SCR 140.

[208] *Toronto (City)* (n 203 above); *Canada (Deputy Minister of National Revenue) v Mattel Canada Inc* [2001] 2 SCR 100.

point out that contextual analysis 'appears to have given way to a new brand of formalism'.[209]

With respect to assessing the reasonableness of an administrative decision, the Supreme Court retreated from the 'alert, alive, and sensitive' level of scrutiny in *Suresh v Canada (Minister of Citizenship & Immigration)*.[210] The case concerned a discretionary decision by the Minister of Citizenship and Immigration to deport a Convention refugee who had been detained on the suspicion that he was a threat to national security. In addressing whether the Minister's decision was reasonable, the Supreme Court distanced itself from *Baker* by stating that '[i]f the Minister has considered the correct factors, the courts should not reweigh them'.[211] As long as the Minister's decision was not 'unreasonable on its face, unsupported by evidence, or vitiated by failure to consider the proper factors or apply the appropriate procedures—it should be upheld'.[212] So instead of asking whether the decision was substantively justifiable, in the sense that it was supported by reasons which demonstrated an 'alert, alive and sensitive' appreciation of the facts and relevant law (including constitutional values), the Court in *Suresh* stated that an administrative decision should be upheld so long as relevant factors were mentioned on the face of the decision.

In later cases, LeBel J also targeted the woolly distinctions between the different standards of review. The fact that there was not a universal definition of reasonableness meant that the whole enterprise was on shaky ground. Thus, in *Toronto (City) v CUPE, Local 79*, LeBel J noted that 'the patent unreasonableness standard does not currently provide sufficiently clear parameters for reviewing courts to apply in assessing the decisions of administrative adjudicators'.[213] More specifically, he observed that the patent unreasonableness standard 'shaded uncomfortably' into correctness review, and that it was 'increasingly difficult' to distinguish review for patent unreasonableness from reasonableness *simpliciter* review.[214] But despite these mounting concerns, the issue of reasonableness review did not attract much commentary until *Dunsmuir v New Brunswick*.[215]

As in *Nicholson,* the dispute in *Dunsmuir* concerned the dismissal of a public employee. Over the course of two years of employment with the provincial Department of Justice, David Dunsmuir was reprimanded by his employer three times for poor job performance. Shortly after the third

[209] Lorne Sossin and Colleen Flood, 'The Contextual Turn: Iacobucci's Legacy and the Standard of Review in Administrative Law' (2007) 57 *University of Toronto Law Journal* 581, 591.

[210] *Suresh v Canada (Minister of Citizenship & Immigration)* [2002] 1 SCR 3.

[211] ibid [41].

[212] ibid.

[213] *Toronto (City)* (n 203 above) [66].

[214] ibid.

[215] *Dunsmuir v New Brunswick* [2008] 1 SCR 190.

reprimand, the regional director informed Dunsmuir that he would be subject to a performance review. However, a day before the performance review the director sent a termination letter to Dunsmuir's lawyer. Dunsmuir grieved his dismissal this pursuant to section 100.1 of the Public Service Labour Relations Act, which gave non-unionised public employees the right to challenge any 'discharge, suspension or a financial penalty'.[216] At the hearing, Dunsmuir sought to introduce documents concerning the employment relationship, but the Department objected to the admission of the evidence saying the adjudicator was not entitled to inquire into the reasons for the dismissal. In support of this argument, the Department invoked section 20 of the Civil Service Act, which stated that '[s]ubject to the provisions of this Act or any other Act, termination of the employment of a deputy head or an employee shall be governed by the ordinary rules of contract'.[217]

At the hearing, the adjudicator held that the grievance procedure in the PSLRA entitled him to verify the employer's reasons for the dismissal.[218] Further authority for his conclusion was drawn from a recent Court of Appeal decision,[219] which stated that 'the employer cannot avoid an inquiry into its real reasons for a discharge ... by simply stating that cause is not alleged'.[220] Although the adjudicator ultimately found that Dunsmuir had not been terminated for cause, he also held that the employer had breached its common law duty of fairness by cancelling the performance review. Accordingly, the adjudicator held that the dismissal was unlawful, and ordered the Department to reinstate Dunsmuir.

The Supreme Court quashed the adjudicator's decision, saying that he had erred by inquiring into the reasons for the dismissal and imposing a duty of fairness upon the employer. While the ostensible aim of the Court's decision was to 'to re-examine the foundations of judicial review', the case reveals how the judges attempted to straddle two conflicting approaches to judicial review.[221] One concurring opinion, written by Deschamps J, adheres to formal and conceptual analysis by asserting that

> [a]ny review starts with the identification of the questions at issue as questions of law, questions of fact or questions of mixed fact and law. Very little else needs to be done in order to determine whether deference needs to be shown.[222]

216 Public Service Labour Relations Act RSNB 1973, c P-25, s 100.1.

217 Civil Service Act SNB 1984, c C-5.1, s 20.

218 Section 97(2.1) of the PSLRA (n 216 above) states: 'Where an adjudicator determines that an employee has been discharged or otherwise disciplined by the employer for cause and the collective agreement or arbitral award does not contain a specific penalty for the infraction that resulted in the employee being discharged or otherwise disciplined, the adjudicator may substitute such other penalty for the discharge or discipline as to the adjudicator seems just and reasonable in all the circumstances'. This provision expressly applies to non-unionised employees by virtue of s 100.1(5) of the Act.

219 *Dr Everett Chalmers Hospital v Mills* (1989) 102 NBR (2d) 1 (CA).

220 *New Brunswick (Board of Management) v Dunsmuir* (2005) 293 NBR (2d) 5, [13] (QB).

221 *Dunsmuir* (n 215 above) [24].

222 ibid [158].

Another concurring opinion, written by Binnie J, rejects formal and conceptual analysis by saying that judicial review 'has lately become unduly burdened with law office metaphysics'.[223] Instead, he suggests there should be a general presumption of deference, and that the court should focus its attention on developing a method for assessing the reasonableness of an administrative decision in light of its context. Thus, he argues that 'the reasonableness assessment will vary with the relevant circumstances' and that 'what is required ... is a more easily applied framework into which the judicial review court and litigants can plug in the relevant context'.[224]

The tension between formalism and reasonable justification also pervades the majority's attempt to 'reconsider both the number and definitions of the various standards of review, and the analytical process employed to determine which standard applies in a given situation'.[225] The most prominent revision in *Dunsmuir* is the abolition of the patent unreasonableness standard. After observing that the distinction between patent unreasonableness and reasonableness *simpliciter* was dubious, Bastarache and LeBel JJ stated that 'it would be unpalatable to require parties to accept an irrational decision simply because ... the irrationality of the decision is not clear *enough*'.[226] But despite this change, they were keen to point out that '[t]he move towards a single reasonableness standard does not pave the way for a more intrusive review by courts'.[227]

However, in a further attempt to simplify judicial review, Bastarache and LeBel JJ suggested that judges could circumvent contextual analysis altogether in cases where legislative intent is clear, previous case law already establishes the standard of review, or the case involves issues which presumptively attract correctness oversight. In this respect, they assert that if an administrative decision involves 'true questions of jurisdiction', constitutional issues, questions of law which are of central importance, or 'jurisdictional lines between two or more competing specialised tribunals', an administrative decision should be reviewed according to a correctness standard.[228] By contrast, in cases where an administrative decision is protected by a privative clause, the decision-maker is 'interpreting its own statute or statutes closely connected to its function', or the case involves questions of 'fact, discretion or policy', they argue that the more deferential standard of reasonableness should apply as a matter of course.[229]

The majority concluded that the adjudicator's decision should be reviewed on a reasonableness standard. They pointed out that the decision

223 ibid [122].
224 ibid [150]–[151].
225 ibid [34].
226 ibid [42].
227 ibid [48].
228 ibid [57]–[61].
229 ibid [52]–[55].

was protected by a strong privative clause, which provided 'a strong indication' that judicial deference was warranted.[230] Furthermore, they noted that the adjudicator was interpreting his enabling legislation, which gave rise to the presumption that he had expertise in dealing with these types of disputes. Finally, because the legal issue did not appear to be 'of central importance to the legal system and outside the specialized expertise of the adjudicator', Bastarache and LeBel JJ concluded that the court should exercise restraint.[231] And, in an effort to clarify exactly what reasonableness review entails, they stated that 'reasonableness is concerned mostly with the existence of justification, transparency and intelligibility within the decision-making process'.[232]

Nevertheless, when they considered the merits of the adjudicator's decision, Bastarache and LeBel JJ concluded that '[t]he reasoning process … was deeply flawed'.[233] In their view, the relationship between the parties was governed by the private law of contract, which meant that the employer's reasons for terminating Dunsmuir were irrelevant. The only legal consideration was that if the employer did not allege cause for the dismissal, it had to provide Dunsmuir with adequate notice or payment in lieu of a notice period. Thus, the majority concluded that the adjudicator's decision was 'fatally flawed' because he had given the PSLRA 'an interpretation that allowed him to inquire into the reasons for discharge where the employer had the right not to provide or even have such reasons'.[234]

Similarly, the majority concluded that the adjudicator had erred in holding that the employer owed Dunsmuir a duty of fairness. On this point, Bastarache and LeBel JJ held that the employment contract excluded any procedural rights which might otherwise arise at common law. While they acknowledged that an individual's right to fairness arises whenever a public decision affects his or her 'rights, privileges, and interests', they held that '[w]here a public employee is protected from wrongful dismissal by contract, his or her remedy should be in private law, not in public law'.[235] Hence, they concluded that '[b]y imposing procedural fairness requirements on the respondent over and above its contractual obligations … the adjudicator erred in his application of the duty of fairness'.[236]

In sum, while the majority in *Dunsmuir* set out to establish a 'principled framework that is more coherent and workable', a close reading of the majority opinion suggests that it failed to achieve its objective.[237]

230 ibid [67].
231 ibid [70].
232 ibid [47].
233 ibid [74].
234 ibid.
235 ibid [114].
236 ibid [117].
237 ibid [32].

With respect to the threshold question of judicial deference, the majority resurrects a series of conceptual distinctions, including the problematic notion of jurisdictional error, which reverts to the problematic formal and conceptual approach which prevailed prior to 1978. Thus, the claim by the authors of the majority opinion that they 'neither wish nor intend to return to the jurisdiction/preliminary question doctrine that plagued the jurisprudence in this area for many years' is misleading.[238] Similarly, the claim that 'reasonableness is concerned mostly with the existence of justification, transparency and intelligibility within the decision-making process' is hollow, because they give such short shrift to the adjudicator's explanation for probing the basis for the employer's decision and imposing a duty of procedural fairness. Put simply, the majority opinion in *Dunsmuir* is ironic because it asserts the purpose of judicial review is to ensure 'the existence of justification, transparency and intelligibility within the decision-making process', but concludes that the adjudicator acted unreasonably in requiring the employer to act fairly and provide a transparent justification for his decision.[239]

IV. CONCLUSION

In the years since *Dunsmuir*, the Supreme Court has changed its tack once again.[240] While *Dunsmuir* set out categories of issues which presumptively attract correctness review ('true' questions of jurisdiction, constitutional issues, questions of law which are of central importance to the legal system as a whole, or jurisdictional limits between two or more competing specialised tribunals), it has since held that these categories should either be abolished or construed narrowly. Thus, in *Alberta (Information and Privacy Commission) v Alberta Teachers' Association*, Rothstein J wrote a majority opinion in which he opined that 'it may be that the time has come to reconsider whether … the category of true questions of jurisdiction exists and is necessary to identifying the appropriate standard of review'.[241] Likewise, in *Nor-Man Regional Health Authority v Manitoba Association of Health Care Professionals* the Supreme Court held that judicial deference towards administrative interpretations of common law doctrine was warranted, because 'it hardly follows that arbitrators lack either the legal authority or the expertise required to adapt and apply them in a manner

[238] ibid [59].

[239] ibid [47].

[240] Matthew Lewans, 'Deference and Reasonableness Since *Dunsmuir*' (2012) 38 *Queen's Law Journal* 59.

[241] *Alberta (Information and Privacy Commission) v Alberta Teachers' Association* [2011] 3 SCR 654, [34]. See also *Halifax (Regional Municipality) v Nova Scotia (Human Rights Commission)* [2010] 2 SCR 364.

more appropriate to the arbitration of disputes and grievances in a labour relations context'.[242]

But by far the most interesting shift concerns judicial deference towards administrative decisions concerning human rights. In *Doré v Barreau du Quebec*, the Supreme Court held that administrative decisions concerning constitutional values were entitled to deference.[243] The issue in *Doré* concerned a decision of the Disciplinary Council of the Quebec Bar Association to suspend Gilles Doré's licence to practise law because he had sent a letter to a judge, chastising him for unprofessional conduct. While Doré appeared for a client in a bail hearing, the judge had referred to him and his legal submissions as insolent, impudent, hyperbolic, and totally ridiculous. In a private letter addressed to the judge, Doré stated 'your propensity ... to launch ugly, vulgar, and mean personal attacks ... casts shame on you as a judge'.[244] Doré was subsequently charged under article 2.03 (now article 2.00.01) of the Code of ethics of advocates, which states that a lawyer's conduct 'must bear the stamp of objectivity, moderation and dignity', and the Disciplinary Council decided to suspend his licence for 21 days.[245]

In a unanimous opinion for the Court, Abella J held that administrative decisions concerning constitutional rights should be reviewed according to the reasonableness standard. She began by noting that the Court in *Baker* had established that 'administrative decision-makers are both bound by fundamental values and empowered to adjudicate them', which meant that superior courts had effectively ceded some interpretive authority over constitutional rights to administrative officials.[246] Furthermore, she noted that a posture of deference was warranted on pragmatic and functional grounds: that administrative decision-makers, by virtue of their experience and ability to assess contextual considerations, have a unique and valuable perspective regarding constitutional interpretation which was entitled to judicial respect. Thus, she noted that '[a]n administrative decision-maker exercising a discretionary power under his or her home statute, has, by virtue of expertise and specialization, particular familiarity with the competing considerations at play in weighing *Charter* values',[247] which meant that 'the administrative decision-maker will generally be in the best position to consider the impact of the relevant *Charter* values *on the specific facts of the case*'.[248] These considerations led Abella J to conclude that the deferential standard of reasonableness was appropriate, despite the suggestion

[242] *Nor-Man Regional Health Authority v Manitoba Association of Health Care Professionals* [2011] 3 SCR 616, [44].

[243] *Doré v Barreau du Québec* [2012] 1 SCR 395.

[244] ibid [10].

[245] Code of ethics of advocates RRQ 1981, c B-1, r 1.

[246] *Doré* (n 243 above), [29].

[247] ibid [47].

[248] ibid [54].

in *Dunsmuir* that all constitutional issues should be reviewed on a correctness standard. More recently, the Court has affirmed the holding in *Doré* by stating that when an administrative decision engages Charter rights or values, 'the discretionary decision-maker is required to proportionately balance the *Charter* protections to ensure that they are limited no more than is necessary given the applicable statutory objectives that she or he is obliged to pursue'.[249]

But while the Court seems to be inching toward a presumption of deference, its method of reasonableness review has been all over the map. While the Court in *Dunsmuir* held that 'reasonableness is concerned mostly with the existence of justification, transparency and intelligibility within the decision-making process',[250] it has failed to implement this notion in a principled or consistent manner. For instance, in *Alberta (Information and Privacy Commissioner) v Alberta Teachers' Association* the Court held that even though the decision-maker had not addressed the expiration of a statutory limitation in her reasons, a reviewing court should have given 'respectful attention to the reasons "which could be offered in support of a decision"'.[251] Thus, the Court effectively held that in cases where a decision-maker fails to justify its conclusion, a reviewing court can repair the gap by imagining reasons which might have been sufficient.[252]

At the other end of the spectrum, there are cases in which the Court elides the distinction between correctness and reasonableness review altogether. For instance, while the Court in *Canada (Attorney General) v Mowat* held that the Canadian Human Rights Tribunal's interpretation of its enabling legislation was entitled to deference, it proceeded to assess the reasonableness of that decision by relying upon common law canons of statutory construction which assume that judges have the final word on legal interpretation.[253] Thus, after considering 'the words of the provision in their entire context and according to their grammatical and ordinary sense, harmoniously with the scheme and object of the Act and the intention of Parliament',[254] the legislative history behind the provision, and similar provisions enacted by provincial and territorial legislatures, the Court concluded that the Tribunal's decision was unreasonable because it conflicted with the Court's reading of parliamentary intent.[255]

[249] *Loyola High School v Quebec (Attorney General)* 2015 SCC 12, [4].
[250] *Dunsmuir* (n 215 above), [47].
[251] *Alberta (Information and Privary Commissioner) v Alberta Teachers' Association* (n 241 above), [52].
[252] ibid [53].
[253] *Canada (Attorney General) v Mowat* [2011] 3 SCR 471.
[254] ibid [33].
[255] ibid [64].

The sum total of these developments is that while the Supreme Court has been inching toward a general presumption that administrative decisions are entitled to judicial deference, the Court's understanding of reasonableness review varies dramatically from case to case. Thus, in *Alberta Teachers'* the Court asserts that, even when an administrative decision-maker fails to provide any reasons on an important legal issue, the Court can repair those reasons on its own motion; but in *Mowat*, the Court measures the legality of an administrative decision against its own interpretation of the enabling legislation. This suggests that just because a reviewing court uses the reasonableness standard does not mean that it will defer substantively to an administrative decision. A lot depends on how reasonableness review is implemented in a particular case.

6

Authority, Legitimacy, and Legality in Administrative Law

'[I]n a way beset with those that contend, on one side for too great Liberty, and on the other side for too much Authority, 'tis hard to passe between the points of both unwounded'.[1]

IN THIS CHAPTER, I will examine administrative law from a theoretical perspective. If, as I argued in Chapter two, we reject Dicey's claim that administrative law cannot be reconciled with the rule of law, we must confront a gap in his constitutional theory. I will address this deficit by constructing a theory of administrative law and judicial deference built around three interrelated issues in jurisprudence and political theory: authority, legitimacy, and legality.

All three issues feature prominently in Thomas Hobbes's *Leviathan*, which remains one of the greatest works in political philosophy.[2] Hobbes's main goal in writing *Leviathan* was to articulate a secular justification for political authority, one which could sustain civil order in a pluralistic society without resorting to myth, tradition, or divine right. If individuals are endowed with equal abilities and find themselves in a world of scarce resources,[3] but their reasoning is fallible and frequently distorted by self-interest,[4] they must somehow find a way of escaping chaos to establish a civil society governed by law. As Hobbes puts it, because 'no one man's Reason, nor the Reason of any one number of men, makes the certaintie' individuals must defer to an authority 'to whose sentence they will both stand, or their controversie must either come to blowes, or be undecided, for want of a right Reason constituted by Nature'.[5] The need for authority is pressing, because '[w]here there is no common Power, there is no Law: where no Law, no Injustice'.[6] Put bluntly, the absence of authority allows no opportunity for human industry,

[1] Thomas Hobbes, *Leviathan*, Richard Tuck (ed) (Cambridge, Cambridge University Press, 1996) 3.
[2] ibid.
[3] ibid ch 8.
[4] ibid chs 5–6.
[5] ibid 33.
[6] ibid 90.

agriculture, trade, architecture, innovation, knowledge, history, art, literature, or peaceful interaction because individuals live in 'continuall feare, and danger of violent death'.[7]

However, Hobbes argues that not just any authority will do—it must also be seen as legitimate in the eyes of its subjects. Thus, instead of positing a strongman who can intimidate or manipulate people into submission, Hobbes argues that individuals must be able to reason their way out of the state of nature via a mutually acceptable justification for deferring to the decisions of a sovereign instead of acting according to their own lights. In chapter 14 of *Leviathan*, Hobbes begins to address the issue of legitimacy by introducing two laws of nature: the first is that everyone 'ought to endeavor Peace, as farre as he has hope of obtaining it; and when he cannot obtain it, that he may seek, and use, all helps, and advantages of Warre';[8] the second is that everyone 'be contented with so much liberty against other men, as he would allow other men against himselfe'.[9] From these precepts, Hobbes infers that reasonable persons will contract with each other to respect the decisions of a sovereign so that they might realise the benefits of living in civil society.

While some scholars portray Hobbes's theory as an extended apology for the authoritarian rule of an uncommanded commander, that reading ignores his discussion of legality.[10] Whereas later theorists like John Austin propounded a command theory of law in which compliance is secured by threats of punishment emanating from the sovereign, Hobbes developed a more complex explanation of law's normativity in which a principle of legality buttresses the legitimacy of the legal order. In chapter 15 Hobbes dissects additional laws of nature, a science he refers to as the 'true and onely Moral Philosophy', to elucidate the conditions under which individuals can reasonably accept the decision of an arbitrator to escape the state of nature.[11] Thus, he states that '*if a man be trusted to judge between man and man*, it is a precept of the Law of Nature, *that he deale Equally between them*';[12] that 'no man is a fit Arbitrator in his own cause';[13] and that in resolving disputes the arbitrator must listen impartially to the evidence tendered by witnesses for the parties.[14] While Hobbes acknowledges that his analysis 'may seem too subtile a deduction of the Lawes of Nature, to be taken notice of by all

[7] ibid 89.

[8] ibid 92.

[9] ibid.

[10] David Dyzenhaus, 'Hobbes and the Legitimacy of Law' (2001) 20 *Law and Philosophy* 461; David Dyzenhaus, 'Hobbes on the Authority of Law' in David Dyzenhaus and Thomas Poole (eds), *Hobbes and the Law* (Cambridge, Cambridge University Press, 2012) 186.

[11] Hobbes, *Leviathan* (n 1 above) 110.

[12] Hobbes, *Leviathan* (n 1 above) 108.

[13] ibid 109.

[14] ibid.

men', he suggests it can be distilled into 'one easie sum, intelligible, even to the meanest capacity; and that is, *Do not that to another, which thou wouldest not have done to thy selfe*'.[15]

He returns to the legitimacy of legality again in chapter 26, this time in the context of adjudication in civil society. While he begins by stating 'that Law in general, is not Counsell, but Command',[16] he makes the intriguing observation that '[t]he Law of Nature, and the Civill law, contain each other, and are of equall extent' because 'the Lawes of Nature … are not properly Lawes, but qualities that dispose men to peace, and to obedience'.[17] Thus, while the sovereign 'maketh the Law'[18] by issuing general commands, '[a]ll Laws, written, and unwritten, have need of Interpretation'.[19] However, Hobbes is quick to point out that judges should not project their own private reason onto the civil law 'for then there would be as much contradiction in the Lawes, as there is in the Schooles'.[20] Therefore, he concludes:

> it is not that *Juris prudentia*, or wisedome of subordinate Judges; but the Reason of this our Articifiall Man the Common-wealth, and his Command, that maketh Law: And the Common-wealth being in their Representative but one Person, there cannot easily arise any contradiction in the Lawes; and when there doth, the same Reason is able, by interpretation, or alteration, to take it away. In all Courts of Justice, the Soveraign (which is the Person of the Common-wealth,) is he that Judgeth: the subordinate Judge, ought to have regard to the reason, which moved his Soveraign to make such Law, that his Sentence may be according thereunto; which then is his Sovereaigns Sentence; otherwise it is his own, and an unjust one.

In this passage, Hobbes makes two important points. The first is that judges are not entitled to gainsay the substance of legislation, because such an interpretative strategy would undermine the legitimacy of the legal order they are duty-bound to uphold. This leads to his second point, which is that judges should pursue an 'authentique Interpretation of the Law' guided by the legislator's intent;[21] but in this respect Hobbes says that the legislator's intent 'is always supposed to be Equity: for it were a great contumely for a Judge to think otherwise of the Soveraign'.[22] Accordingly, he argues that 'if the Sovereaign employ a Publique Minister, without written Instructions what to doe; he is obliged to take for Instructions the Dictates of Reason',[23] and 'if the Words of the Law doe not fully authorise a reasonable Sentence' a judge ought to 'supply it with the Law of Nature; or if the case be difficult, to

[15] ibid 109–10.
[16] ibid 183.
[17] ibid 185.
[18] ibid 184.
[19] ibid 190.
[20] ibid 187.
[21] ibid 190.
[22] ibid 194.
[23] ibid 188.

respite Judgement till he have received more ample authority'.[24] Therefore, Hobbes recommends interpretive strategies which avoid contradictions,[25] are rationally connected to the legislator's objectives,[26] based upon the evidence and legal submissions tendered by the parties,[27] and produce reasonable decisions.[28]

Hobbes's insights about the interrelationship between authority, legitimacy, and legality remain highly relevant in our own time. If anything, the need for authority is even more pressing today, because we must tackle a broader array of complex social issues—human rights, immigration, national security, climate change, economic policy, occupational health and safety, public access to health care and education, etc—about which there is deep disagreement. And we cannot hope to address these issues intelligently without harnessing the experience, expertise, and efficiency the modern administrative state provides. Nevertheless, we want to ensure that the operation of the administrative state is legitimate, both in the sense that it is democratically accountable and can be seen to comply with rule of law standards. But it is difficult to even conceptualise, let alone implement, the institutional arrangements and legal principles required to address the thorny issues of authority, legitimacy, and legality in administrative law. As Hobbes notes in the epigraph, we often find ourselves caught between the Scylla and Charybdis of 'those who contend, on one side for too great Liberty, and on the other side for too much Authority', but need a better map to navigate the dilemma.

At first glance, it might seem odd to turn to modern jurisprudence for such a map because legal philosophers tend to discuss these issues separately instead of following Hobbes's suggestion that they are inextricably linked. Thus, when leading philosophers like Joseph Raz and Jeremy Waldron develop theories of legitimate authority, those accounts are hived off from their accounts of legality. So while they develop highly sophisticated arguments about whether an authority's legitimacy derives from its ability to determine sound outcomes or the fairness of its decision-making process, and whether the rule of law should be understood in purely formal terms or as upholding the dignity of individuals through fair legal process, it can be difficult to assess the broader implications of those arguments in the context of the modern administrative state. Among other things, I will argue that by re-examining the linkages between authority, legitimacy, and legality from a jurisprudential perspective, we can gain important insights about how the practice of judicial review can both respect and sustain the legitimacy of administrative law.

[24] ibid 194.
[25] ibid 187.
[26] ibid 191.
[27] ibid 195.
[28] ibid 192.

I. LEGITIMATE AUTHORITY AND THE ADMINISTRATIVE STATE

One way to get our initial bearings is to think through an example. Recall that in *Chevron USA v Natural Resources Defense Council*,[29] the Environmental Protection Agency (EPA) was empowered by statute to set national air quality standards.[30] While the enabling legislation set out broadly worded principles and policy objectives to guide the EPA's deliberations, those terms of reference did not purport to determine the outcome in relation to any particular case. Instead, disputes regarding what the particular air quality standards should be were left for the EPA to decide on a case-by-case basis by interpreting the law in light of the facts before it.[31] Therefore, when the Supreme Court reviewed the EPA's interpretation of the term 'stationary source' in its enabling legislation, it concluded that it ought to defer to the EPA's decision because it was not 'arbitrary, capricious, or manifestly contrary to the statute'.[32]

From this brief synopsis, we can infer that: (1) the EPA is constituted by law to decide what should be done by interpreting and applying more general legal standards in a particular case, (2) the law provides reasons for legal subjects to respect the EPA's authority regarding that case, in the sense that they have an obligation to comply with its decision even if they disagree with its merits, and (3) the law also provides reasons for other legal officials, including judges exercising the power of judicial review, to respect the EPA's decision in a similar sense. These propositions provide a broad outline of the account of administrative law I wish to pursue in this chapter: that administrative officials are entitled to interpret the law, and their decisions warrant the respect of both subjects and other legal officials who share responsibility for upholding the rule of law.

This outline can be fleshed out a bit by probing these basic propositions. First, by asserting that administrative legal authority is constituted by law, I am claiming that administrative officials cannot bootstrap themselves into

[29] *Chevron USA Inc v Natural Resources Defense Council, Inc* 467 US 837 (1984). The legal structure of administrative authority is more or less the same in all common law jurisdictions. For instance, in *Canadian Union of Public Employees, Local 963 v New Brunswick Liquor Corporation* [1979] 2 SCR 227, the Labour Relations Board was empowered by statute to foster peaceful industrial relations by interpreting broadly worded provisions concerning the use of replacement employees during a strike, and its decisions were insulated by a privative clause which prohibited judicial review; and in *Anisminic Ltd v Foreign Compensation Commission* [1969] 2 AC 147 (HL), the Foreign Compensation Commission was empowered by to decide whether and to what extent an applicant was legally entitled to receive government compensation, and its decisions were insulated by a privative clause which prohibited judicial review.

[30] Clean Air Act Amendments of 1977 Pub L No 95-95, 91 Stat 685.

[31] Thomas Merrill, 'The Story of *Chevron USA Inc v Natural Resources Defense Council, Inc* (1984): Sometimes Great Cases Are Made Not Born' in William Eskridge, Philip Frickey and Elizabeth Garrett (eds), *Statutory Interpretation Stories* (New York, Foundation Press, 2011) 164.

[32] *Chevron* (n 29 above) 844–45.

a position of authority by simply imposing their will on would-be subjects and other officials.[33] The central or paradigmatic case[34] of administrative authority involves a delegation of power via some combination of enabling legislation or executive order, but there are borderline cases as well—it might be established by common law doctrine (in situations where prerogative powers are being exercised) or by contract (in situations where the provision of public services has been privatised or an arbitrator adjudicates contractual disputes). However, even in these borderline cases administrative legal authority is derivative rather than original, because it is grounded by more basic laws which are intelligible, publicly accessible, and prospective in their operation.

A second, related point is that just because an administrative official or institution claims authority under enabling legislation does not meant that they are, in fact, entitled to it. An account of administrative legal authority should provide adherents with both authoritative guidance *and* a lucid basis for assessing the legitimacy of particular administrative decisions.[35] As Jeremy Waldron puts it, 'a theory of authority is not just a list of the conditions under which an authority claim is justified: it must also illuminate the *justificandum*'.[36] Among other things, this proviso suggests a reciprocal relationship between those who wield administrative authority and those who are duty-bound to respect that authority's decisions. It also underlines a fundamental tension, namely that enabling laws serve the dual purposes of explaining why administrative decisions ought to be respected, and providing standards by which the legitimacy of those decisions can be scrutinised and assessed by others.[37]

[33] Despite the array of interesting debates in analytical jurisprudence, there is broad consensus amongst legal theorists on this point. HLA Hart employs it to debunk John Austin's command theory of law and replace it with a legal theory premised upon a rule of recognition; Lon Fuller appeals to it when he argues there is an 'inner morality' to law which shapes the manner in which authority is exercised; and it is implicit in Ronald Dworkin's theory of interpretation in which true legal propositions are determined by the best moral justification of a community's political and legal practices. See Hans Kelsen, *Pure Theory of Law* (Berkeley CA, University of California Press, 1967); HLA Hart, *The Concept of Law*, 2nd edn (Oxford, Clarendon Press, 1994); Lon Fuller, *The Morality of Law* revised edn(New Haven CT, Yale University Press, 1969); Ronald Dworkin, *Law's Empire* (London, Fontana, 1986).

[34] On central case analysis, see John Finnis, *Natural Law and Natural Rights*, 2nd edn (Oxford, Oxford University Press, 2011) 9–11.

[35] CJ Friedrich, 'Authority, Reason and Discretion' in CJ Friedrich (ed), *NOMOS I: Authority* (Cambridge, Cambridge University Press, 1958) 35; Joseph Raz, *The Authority of Law* (Oxford, Clarendon Press, 1979) 5–7.

[36] Jeremy Waldron, 'Authority for Officials' in Lukas Meyer, Stanley Paulson and Thomas Pogge, *Rights, Culture, and the Law: Themes from the Legal and Practical Philosophy of Joseph Raz* (Oxford, Oxford University Press, 2003) 45, 49.

[37] David Dyzenhaus refers to this aspect of administrative authority as a 'paradox of rationality', because when someone recognises the rationality of deferring to an administrative authority, she simultaneously measures that practice against her own standards of rationality. See David Dyzenhaus, *The Constitution of Law* (Cambridge, Cambridge University Press, 2006) 126–29.

Thirdly, an account of administrative authority should explain the normativity of administrative decisions—their capacity to generate binding legal rights and obligations in a particular case. There are many ways to describe the normative dimension of administrative authority: we might variously refer to subjects as deferring, respecting, accepting, obeying, complying, surrendering, or submitting to an administrative decision in ways they would not in its absence. While there are important differences between these terms for the internal perspective prompted by an administrative decision, it is not necessary to draw more fine-grained distinctions between them at this point. Suffice it to say that the issuance of an administrative decision provides reasons which render a de novo assessment and substitution of one's own interpretation of the law under the circumstances inappropriate.

Finally, the normativity of administrative authority operates *between legal officials and institutions* in addition to eliciting the respect of those who are subject to an administrative decision.[38] This inter-institutional aspect is of crucial importance when attempting to explain and justify judicial deference towards administrative decisions; but it is also a bit tricky, because 'it is usually not possible to understand the relation between one official or institution and another without understanding the relation between officials in general and those over whom officialdom ultimately rules'.[39] Returning to our example, if the EPA has legitimate legal authority, it is capable of providing both subjects and judges with reasons to adjust their practical reasoning regarding what should be done under the circumstances. Of course, there may be conflicting opinions on how the EPA ought to decide a particular case: one of the main reasons why Congress established the agency in the first place was to settle such disputes. But if judges behaved as though they were entitled to casually disregard the EPA's decisions, they would be ignoring an important normative aspect of this institutional arrangement.

While this initial account of administrative legal authority needs to be fleshed out in greater detail, it is important to point out that it differs fundamentally from the concept of administrative jurisdiction which I examined in Chapter three. The common law concept of administrative jurisdiction cannot explain the phenomenon of administrative law for two simple reasons. First, it assumes that all questions of law or 'jurisdictional' questions are determined exclusively by the judiciary, so it fails to recognise that administrative officials possess any *legal* authority at all. Rather, it assumes that an administrative interpretation of law is merely ephemeral because judges are entitled to quash whenever they disagree with its substance. Secondly, while the concept of administrative jurisdiction does suggest that administrative officials retain the discretionary power to determine policy

[38] Waldron, 'Authority for Officials' (n 36 above).

[39] ibid 45.

matters which arise within their jurisdictional remit, it assumes that this power is a law unto itself and therefore can be exercised arbitrarily without any prospect of judicial redress.

By contrast, the account of administrative law I am pursuing is motivated by the intuition that administrative institutions do possess legitimate interpretive authority over questions of law which warrants the respect of subjects, judges, and other officials. Nevertheless, it rejects the notion that administrative legal authority boils down to the exercise of inscrutable or unconstrained political discretion. Later in this chapter, I will explore how such an account of administrative law might sharpen our understanding of the constitutional relationship between the judiciary and the administrative state. But at this point, I want to further elucidate it by drawing insights about legitimate authority from the most influential account of authority in analytical jurisprudence.[40]

A. Law and Legitimate Authority

For Joseph Raz, one of law's essential features is that it claims to have legitimate authority, and his conception aims to illuminate the conditions which can rationally justify deferring to an authority. Raz grounds his theory firmly in the liberal tradition by pointing out that any claim to authority requires justification because otherwise deference to authority would be an unwarranted abdication of personal autonomy or 'one's right and duty to be responsible for one's action and to conduct oneself in the best light of reason'.[41] Three interrelated theses form the foundation of Raz's theory: the normal justification thesis, the dependence thesis, and the preemption thesis. These theses explain (1) the conditions which legitimate or justify a claim to authority in general, as well as legal authority in particular, (2) the considerations which should generally guide the actions of persons in authority, and (3) how authoritative directives impact on subjects' practical reasoning.

Raz begins with the premise that deference to an authority is not irrational if compliance with that authority's decisions is likely to enhance one's ability to conform to reason. For example, a patient is justified in deferring to the therapeutic judgement of her doctor, because she is more likely to conform to reasons regarding her physical well-being by deferring to the doctor's advice instead of deciding the question directly for herself. This intuition

[40] Joseph Raz, 'Authority and Justification' (1985) 14 *Philosophy and Public Affairs* 3; Joseph Raz, *The Morality of Freedom* (Oxford, Oxford University Press, 1986) chs 2–4; Raz, *The Authority of Law* (Oxford, Clarendon Press, 1979) chs 1 and 11; Joseph Raz, 'The Rule of Law and its Virtue' (1977) 93 *Law Quarterly Review* 195.

[41] Raz, *The Authority of Law* (n 40 above) 4. See also Heidi Hurd, 'Challenging Authority' (1991) 100 *Yale Law Journal* 1611.

regarding the necessary conditions for legitimate authority leads Raz to the normal justification thesis, which holds that:[42]

> the normal and primary way to establish that a person should be acknowledged to have authority over another person involves showing that the alleged subject is likely better to comply with reasons which apply to him (other than the alleged authoritative directives) if he accepts the directives of the alleged authority as authoritatively binding and tries to follow them, rather than by trying to follow the reasons which apply to him directly.

Although Raz acknowledges that this is not the only way to justify all types of authority, he does argue that it is 'the normal and primary one'.[43] So while he acknowledges 'secondary' justifications for deferring to an authority (eg as a means of expressing membership within a political community), he argues that these are not sufficient to render that authority legitimate independently of the normal justification thesis.[44] In his view, such secondary justifications can only serve 'to lower the burden of proof' required to satisfy the normal justification thesis, but 'cannot by themselves establish the legitimacy of an authority'.[45] Thus, if a legal institution does not satisfy the normal justification thesis with respect to a particular question for a particular subject, no amount of respect for the political process which authorises that institution would justify an attitude of deference towards its decisions.

Next, Raz argues that the normal justification thesis implies the dependence thesis, which states that[46] '[a]ll authoritative directives should be based, in the main, on reasons which already independently apply to the subjects of the directives and are relevant to their action in the circumstances covered by the directive'.

Returning to the doctor/patient example, this means that the doctor's therapeutic judgement should be based primarily (although not exclusively) upon reasons which are relevant to the patient's physical or mental well-being. If this were not generally the case, the patient would not construe her doctor's advice as authoritative because in all likelihood it would not advance her interests. This does not, however, entail that an authoritative directive is binding only if it *correctly* reflects all of the reasons that apply to its subjects in a particular case. If that were true, Raz notes, authorities would make no difference in our practical reasoning, because they would merely direct us to do what we ought to be doing in any event. But he argues

42 Raz, 'Authority and Justification' (n 40 above) 18–19.

43 ibid 19.

44 For examples of such secondary arguments, see Dworkin, *Law's Empire* (n 33 above) ch 6; Ronald Dworkin, 'The Partnership Conception of Democracy' (1998) 86 *California Law Review* 453; Jeremy Waldron, *Law and Disagreement* (Oxford, Clarendon Press, 1999) chs 1 and 5.

45 Raz, 'Authority and Justification' (n 40 above) 19.

46 ibid 14.

that even if a doctor's medical advice is mistaken or misguided in a particular case, it would nevertheless be authoritative so long as it satisfies the conditions set by the normal justification thesis. As Raz puts it, 'general success usually falls short of success in every case'.[47] Thus, authorities can make a practical difference, provided that their decisions have content-independent force even when they do not correctly assess the reasons which apply in a particular case. Taken together, the normal justification thesis and the dependence thesis comprise what Raz calls the service conception of authority, which asserts that the primary function of a legitimate authority is to serve its subjects by helping them to act on reasons which apply to them.

Finally, in order to explain the content-independent normative dynamics of authoritative guidance, Raz argues that directives issued by legitimate authorities provide a special type of reason which subjects accept as a reason not to undertake their own assessment of otherwise relevant reasons for action. This is the preemption thesis:[48]

> [t]he fact that an authority requires performance of an action is a reason for its performance which is not to be added to all other relevant reasons when assessing what to do, but should exclude and take the place of some of them.

Raz argues that when the patient follows her doctor's advice, she does not merely assign weight to the doctor's advice so as to compare it alongside other background reasons which are apparent to her. Rather, she takes the fact that the doctor prescribes treatment *x* as a reason to undergo the treatment without re-weighing all the reasons which apply to her situation. If she did not do this, she would risk forgoing the opportunity to be guided by medical expertise by entertaining her less-educated guess on the matter. Thus, the doctor's advice has the ability to provide the patient with a pre-emptive reason for displacing otherwise relevant practical considerations, and that pre-emptive reason allows the patient to reap the benefits of submitting to medical expertise insofar as her physical well-being is concerned.[49]

For Raz, the pre-emption thesis explains the normative impact of authoritative directives: they are *exclusionary* in the sense that subjects take an authoritative directive as a reason which excludes or pre-empts actions based upon their own assessment of otherwise eligible reasons for action.[50]

[47] Joseph Raz, 'Comments and Responses' in Meyer, Paulson and Pogge (eds), *Rights, Culture and the Law* (n 36 above) 260.

[48] Raz, 'Authority and Justification' (n 40 above) 13.

[49] ibid 23–25.

[50] On the nature of exclusionary reasons, see Joseph Raz, *Practical Reason and Norms* (Oxford, Oxford University Press, 1999) ch 1. Within Raz's account of practical reasoning, exclusionary reasons are second-order reasons, which function differently than ordinary first-order reasons. Whereas conflicts between first-order reasons are resolved by their relative weight, conflicts between exclusionary second-order reasons and first-order reasons are subject to a general principle of practical reasoning which holds that exclusionary reasons prevail. However, this general principle remains qualified by two exceptions: an exclusionary reason

An authority's decision is not just another reason to be weighed against all the others. Rather, it is 'meant to be based on the other reasons, to sum them up and to reflect their outcome'.[51] In doing so, an authority's directive replaces some set or subset of otherwise relevant reasons for action. Therefore, the normativity of authoritative directives are content-independent, in the sense that they are facts that exert normative influence in virtue of some feature besides their substantive merit.[52] This is demonstrated by the fact that the doctor's advice still has exclusionary force even when that advice is mistaken or incorrectly reflects the balance of reasons. So long as the authority generally satisfies the normal justification thesis, subjects are justified in deferring to its directives. In Raz's words, 'an authority is legitimate only if there are sufficient reasons to accept it, that is, sufficient reasons to follow its directives regardless of the balance of reasons on the merits of such action'.[53]

B. Democratic Legitimacy and Legislative Authority

How does Raz's picture of authority compare with the provisional account of administrative authority I sketched out at the beginning of this section? One significant difference concerns the normal justification of administrative authority. While instrumental rationales like relative expertise or institutional competency are often cited as an eligible justification, the fact that some person or institution is more likely to render a sound decision on a particular legal issue is not sufficient to endow them with administrative authority.[54] Furthermore, while the service conception of authority is well-suited to explaining piecemeal relationships between doctors and patients or stockbrokers and investors, it is ill-suited to explaining the authority of administrative institutions whose decisions might give rise to a million legal obligations. A more promising lead is that the legitimacy of administrative authority involves an analysis of the process by which administrative institutions are established, because claims to administrative authority usually depend upon a legal delegation of power from a democratically accountable branch of government.

This criticism is inspired by an objection to the Razian account which claims that it cannot account for the legitimate authority of decisions

may not prevail where (1) it is subject to a 'nullifying condition' or (2) incorporates considerations which limit the scope of the first-order reasons it excludes.

[51] Raz, 'Authority and Justification' (n 40 above) 9.

[52] Raz, *The Morality of Freedom* (n 40 above) 35.

[53] Raz, 'Authority and Justification' (n 40 above) 8.

[54] Waldron, 'Authority for Officials' (n 36 above) 63; Scott Hershovitz, 'The Role of Authority' (2011) 11 *Philosophers' Imprint* 1, 6–10.

achieved through the democratic process.[55] The nub of the problem is that although members of a community might agree on the need to adopt a common decision, that decision must be forged amidst deep disagreement about what political morality requires under the circumstances. Waldron calls this predicament 'the circumstances of politics', and argues that it poses a serious challenge for the service conception of authority.[56] If there is pervasive, substantive disagreement in a pluralistic society about what justice requires that disagreement extends a fortiori to disputes regarding which official or institution can satisfy the normal justification thesis in relation to that issue. Therefore, we must settle for another means of arriving at a common decision. And in order to grapple effectively with the circumstances of politics, that alternative mechanism must be capable of satisfying something like the pre-emption thesis—it must be capable of generating content-independent reasons for compliance so that members of the community will coalesce around a common decision instead of holding out for their preferred outcome on the merits.

Democratic proceduralists provide such an alternative—they argue that a fair, democratic decision-making process provides sound reasons for citizens to respect legislation even when they disagree with its content. On this view, the authority of legislation stems from its ability to convey respect for the persons who are subject to it. First, the democratic decision-making process respects 'differences of opinion about justice and the common good' by not pretending or purporting that everyone agrees with the substance of legislation that they might, in fact, reject.[57] Waldron's argument on this point does not appeal to moral relativism—he does not reject the possibility of objectivity in moral discourse about justice,[58] nor does he reject the idea that individuals have moral rights which sometimes should be prioritised over the common good.[59] His point is rather that '[r]espect has to do with how we treat each other's *beliefs* about justice in circumstances where none of them is self-certifying'[60] so that 'whatever the state of my confidence about the correctness of my own view … it is not unexpected, unnatural, or irrational to think that reasonable people would differ'.[61]

Secondly, the democratic decision-making process conveys respect because 'it attempts to give each individual's view the greatest weight

[55] See Waldron, *Law and Disagreement* (n 44 above) chs 1 and 5; Thomas Christiano, 'The Authority of Democracy' (2004) 12 *Journal of Political Philosophy* 266; Scott Hershovitz, 'Legitimacy, Democracy, and Razian Authority' (2003) 9 *Legal Theory* 201; Samantha Besson, 'Democracy, Law and Authority' (2005) 2 *Journal of Moral Philosophy* 89.

[56] Waldron, *Law and Disagreement* (n 44 above) 101–3.

[57] ibid 111.

[58] ibid ch 8.

[59] Jeremy Waldron, 'A Right-Based Critique of Constitutional Rights' (1993) 13 *Oxford Journal of Legal Studies* 18.

[60] Waldron, *Law and Disagreement* (n 44 above) 111.

[61] ibid 111–12.

possible compatible with an equal weight for the views of each of the others'.[62] Unlike flipping a coin or submitting blindly to the decision of a philosopher king, the democratic process gives positive decisional weight to each individual's input, on the condition that her input is weighed equally alongside the views of the other members of the community. Put simply, the democratic decision-making process has normative purchase because it determines the outcome by responding fairly to the views of those who are bound by the decision.

Against this backdrop, Waldron argues that the normal justification thesis is neither a necessary nor sufficient condition for justifying a claim to authority. It is perfectly reasonable to regard the decision of a despot as fundamentally lacking legitimacy, even when compliance with the despot's decisions might enhance our ability to conform to reason in the long run. By the same token, it is perfectly reasonable to regard democratic legislation as having legitimate authority, even when those decisions are substantively inferior or concern issues which we believe we might be better equipped to decide for ourselves.[63] These intuitions also explain why broadening the reach of the normal justification thesis (ie by recognising the capacity of an authority to solve coordination problems) is not an adequate response to the democratic objection,[64] because even if a despot is capable of resolving coordination problems one could still impugn his legitimacy on non-instrumental grounds.[65]

While assigning legitimate authority to democratic decisions often conjures up the spectre of majoritarian excess, it is a mistake to assume that it implies casual disregard for individual rights. On the contrary, Waldron's whole proceduralist argument is premised on the political values which underwrite individual rights—values like freedom, equality, autonomy, dignity, and responsibility.[66] Thus, he argues that 'there is a natural congruence between rights and democracy', because '[t]he identification of someone as a bearer of rights expresses a measure of confidence in that person's moral capacities—in particular his capacity to think responsibly about the relation between his interests and the interests of others'.[67] Therefore, we should be

[62] ibid 114.

[63] Christiano, 'The Authority of Democracy' (n 55 above) 277–80; Hershovitz, 'Legitimacy, Democracy, and Razian Authority' (n 55 above) 216–17.

[64] Raz, 'Authority and Justification' (n 40 above) 16–18.

[65] Waldron, *Law and Disagreement* (n 44 above) ch 5. More recently, Andrei Marmor has argued that the legitimacy of practical authority 'rests on a combination of the soundness of its decision *and* the fairness of the process which has led to it', but assumes that considerations of fairness remain secondary or auxiliary to the normal justification thesis as a ground of legitimacy. Andrei Marmor, 'Authority, Equality and Democracy' (2005) 18 *Ratio Juris* 315, 317.

[66] Waldron, 'A Right-Based Critique of Constitutional Rights' (n 59 above); Jeremy Waldron, 'The Core of the Case Against Judicial Review' (2006) 115 *Yale Law Journal* 1346.

[67] Jeremy Waldron, 'Judicial Review and the Conditions of Democracy' (1998) 6 *Journal of Political Philosophy* 335, 341.

wary of facile assumptions that decisions regarding individual rights should be somehow quarantined or hived off from the democratic decision-making process.[68] To assert that decisions regarding the tradeoffs between rights and the public interest are beyond the scope of the democratic process is deeply ironic, because it assumes that while ordinary legal subjects are endowed with dignity and autonomy as rational beings they cannot be trusted to deliberate responsibly about such matters.[69] Moreover, while it is tempting to assume a neat distinction between issues involving matters individual rights and public policy,[70] that distinction is unworkable in practice because matters of public policy usually implicate individual rights and vice versa.[71]

Nevertheless, while Waldron rejects the normal justification thesis, he seems to employ a variation of the pre-emption thesis in order to explain the normative dynamics of democratic decisions. In order to establish a common decision in the face of reasonable disagreement, Waldron argues that members of a community 'must design and construct a procedure for selecting common policies without reference to any independent criterion for the right result'.[72] Borrowing a term from John Rawls, he suggests that we regard the problem as one of 'pure procedural justice', meaning that whatever substantive outcome is produced by fair process should be accepted as authoritative.[73] This same point is easily convertible to Razian terms: a democratically produced decision provides exclusionary reasons for not acting on our substantive assessment regarding the merits of that decision. As Waldron puts it:[74]

> When something is enacted as law or as a source of law, I believe it makes on us a demand not to immediately disparage it, or think of ways of nullifying it or getting around it, or mobilizing the immune system of the *corpus juris* so as to resist its incorporation. This must be stated carefully, for systems like ours also make available generous structures like appeal, constitutional amendment, legislative reversal, judicial review, periodic elections, and so on; so, in a sense, no one is ever required to accept a legal or political defeat as final or irreversible. However, the demand that interests me operates in the logical space between defying or ignoring a statute or other legal decision and working responsibly for its repeal or reversal. It is a demand for a certain sort of recognition and, as I said, respect—that *this,*

[68] ibid.

[69] Waldron, 'A Right-Based Critique of Constitutional Rights (n 59 above) 27–36; Waldron, 'The Core of the Case Against Judicial Review' (n 66 above) 1365–66.

[70] See, eg Ronald Dworkin, *Taking Rights Seriously* (London, Duckworth, 1977) 91.

[71] Murray Hunt, 'Against Bifurcation' in David Dyzenhaus, Murray Hunt and Grant Huscroft (eds), *A Simple Common Lawyer: Essays in Honour of Michael Taggart* (Oxford, Hart Publishing, 2009) 98, 105–6; Dimitrios Kyritsis, 'Principles, Policies and the Power of Courts' (1007) 20 *Canadian Journal of Law and Jurisprudence* 379.

[72] Jeremy Waldron, 'Legislation, Authority, and Voting' (1996) 84 *Georgetown Law Journal* 2185, 2208.

[73] ibid.

[74] Waldron, *Law and Disagreement* (n 44 above) 100.

> for the time being, is what the community has come up with and that it should not be ignored or disparaged simply because some of us propose, when we can, to repeal it.

Waldron's elaboration on this point is illuminating, because it brings to the surface a point of agreement with Raz. The pre-emption thesis does not entail that subjects are somehow prevented from considering the balance of reasons displaced by an authority's decision. As noted earlier, Waldron persuasively argues that one of the virtues of the democratic decision-making process is that it respects the substantive views of dissenting subjects, so it would be contradictory for him to claim that subjects are somehow prohibited from disputing the merits of legislation. Rather, he argues that subjects must simply accept a democratic decision for the time being instead of acting on their own assessment of its merits.

C. Legislative Authority and Institutional Settlement

More recently, Waldron has enlarged his critique of Raz's model from the perspective of inter-institutional authority.[75] Waldron's account of inter-institutional authority is inspired by the principle of institutional settlement developed by Henry Hart and Albert Sacks. Hart and Sacks posit that 'human societies are made up of human beings striving to satisfy their respective wants under conditions of interdependence, and ... this common enterprise inevitably generates questions of common concern which have to be settled one way or another'.[76] In order to deal with this predicament, they advance a principle of institutional settlement whereby 'decisions which are the duly arrived at result of duly established procedures ... ought to be accepted as binding upon the whole society unless and until they are duly changed'.[77] Thus, if a question of common concern is assigned by law to the judiciary, it entails that 'other officials ought to be prepared to swallow hard and refrain from issuing contrary directives'[78] even if they disagree with a court's decision, or believe they are more competent to decide the matter.[79] The same principle applies if the question has been legally assigned to the legislature—judges should exercise restraint and respect the legislature's decision instead of issuing conflicting directives.

Waldron argues that the principle of institutional settlement is perspicuous, because it shows how the public interest in settling questions of

[75] Waldron, 'Authority for Officials' (n 36 above).

[76] Henry Hart and Albert Sacks, *The Legal Process: Basic Problems in the Making and Application of Law*, William Eskridge Jr and Philip Frickey (eds) (Westbury, Foundation Press, 1994) 4.

[77] ibid.

[78] Waldron, 'Authority for Officials' (n 36 above) 69.

[79] ibid 48.

common concern shapes interactions between co-ordinate legal institutions and officials. Waldron points out that the service conception of authority focuses upon whether the normal justification thesis is satisfied in pair-wise relationships between legal officials and subjects; however, he argues that it cannot explain inter-institutional authority, because it fails to account for public-regarding reasons which guide interactions between officials who fulfill distinct, but complementary, roles in complex constitutional arrangements. Those reasons underline that a variety of legal institutions have been established to resolve questions of common concern,[80] and that the purpose of these arrangements would be frustrated or undone if officials acted as though they were free to disregard each other's decisions.[81]

This insight applies with equal force in the context of judicial review of administrative decisions. There are good reasons why legislatures invest administrative officials with decision-making authority. While a legislative assembly might be able to forge sufficient consensus on broadly worded objectives as a platform for future action, it might reasonably conclude that interpretive disputes regarding those objectives outstrip the capacity of the legislative process; it might conclude that these disputes are better resolved by experts or officials with theoretical or experiential knowledge regarding a particular question of policy or principle; or it might conclude that the administrative process provides a more accessible or contextually sensitive process for resolving interpretive disputes about the law.[82] The basic point is that appointing administrative officials to decide questions about justice on behalf of the community is rational, intelligent, and practically unavoidable when dealing with even modestly complex social issues which cannot be addressed effectively within the legislative process or through litigation of private interests in the common law courts.[83]

This suggests that the primary justification for administrative authority is not exclusively instrumental,[84] but rests on an amalgam of 'institutional' reasons concerning the legitimate distribution of authority in a constitutional democracy. Put differently, questions regarding administrative authority should not be addressed by attempting to discern which

[80] ibid 52–53.

[81] ibid 59–70.

[82] *Chevron* (n 29 above) 865–66; *Canadian Union of Public Employees* (n 29 above).

[83] Henry Richardson, *Democratic Autonomy* (Oxford, Oxford University Press, 2002) ch 8.

[84] For arguments that judicial deference towards administrative decisions is exhausted by an instrumental rationale, see Ivan Hare, 'The Separation of Powers and Judicial Review for Errors of Law' in Christopher Forsyth and Ivan Hare (eds), *The Golden Metwand and the Crooked Cord: Essays on Public Law in Honour of Sir William Wade QC* (Oxford, Clarendon Press, 1998) 113, 137; Jeffrey Jowell, 'Judicial Deference and Human Rights: A Question of Competence' in Paul Craig and Richard Rawlings (eds), *Law and Administration in Europe: Essays in Honour of Carol Harlow* (Oxford, Oxford University Press, 2003) 67, 72–73; Jeffrey Jowell, 'Judicial Deference: servility, civility or institutional capacity?' [2003] *Public Law* 592; David Feldman, 'Human Rights, Terrorism and Risk: The Roles of Politicians and Judges' [2006] *Public Law* 364, 374–77.

institution possesses de facto expertise on a particular policy issue, but must also address which institution has ex officio authority for that issue.[85] This means that subjects and judges are not justified in ignoring or interfering with an administrative decision merely because they disagree with its substance or think they are better equipped to assess the reasons which apply under the circumstances, all things considered. Such casual disregard for administrative decisions has been a chronic problem in the history regarding the relationship between the judiciary and the modern administrative state. During much of the twentieth century, common law judges routinely flouted administrative decisions and erected doctrines regarding the separation of powers which frustrated the development of administrative law. Moreover, even though these decisions frequently undermined the realisation of constitutional values like liberty and equality, they were nevertheless supported by public law theorists who harboured deep suspicions regarding the expansion of the franchise, democratic decision-making, and the redistribution of wealth.

Waldron addresses this problem by arguing that the principle of institutional settlement grounds a claim for something more complex than straight-forward compliance on the part of other officials—it demands a type of respect which 'requires that a duly enacted decision be treated *as a settlement*, and not as something which is of no consequence, leaving open for us the question it purports to address'.[86] Waldron defines the normative impact of institutional settlement by saying:[87]

> If there is an essential core to the idea of respect in the context of institutional settlement—the *concept* of respect, perhaps, as opposed to particular conceptions of it—it is this. First, one must acknowledge that what is at stake here is a question of common concern; second, one must recognize the presence of established arrangements for producing answers to such questions; third, one must ascertain whether such arrangements have actually produced a decision that answers the question; and fourth, if they have, one must play one's part in the social processes that are necessary to sustain and implement such decision as a settlement.

While this precludes judges from gainsaying substantive decisions rendered by administrative officials,[88] Waldron waffles somewhat on what exactly it means to 'play one's part' in this context. At the very least, he argues (consistently with the pre-emption thesis) that it 'involves setting aside the reasons and reasoning one might use if there were no authority or if it had not issued any applicable decision', but he stops short of saying that the decision should be accepted or enforced come what may. Thus, Waldron

[85] Antonin Scalia, 'Judicial Deference to Administrative Interpretations of Law' (1989) 38 *Duke Law Journal* 511, 514.

[86] Waldron, 'Authority for Officials' (n 36 above) 56.

[87] ibid.

[88] ibid 56–57.

worries that if an official's idea of respect is 'too abbreviated', he might submit blindly to the responsible official's decision instead of being guided by public-regarding, institutional reasons for supporting it.[89] As we will see, Waldron's conclusion leaves us hanging, because it stops just short of the point at which fundamental values begin to shape the process and substance of administrative law.

D. Reciprocity and Democratic Legitimacy

If we follow Waldron's flight from substance towards a purely procedural account of legitimate authority, we are left with a positivist theory of law similar to Jeremy Bentham's—one in which a democratically elected legislature converts data regarding individual interests into a *Pannomion* or complete code of rules which aims to determine the outcome in particular cases.[90] To the extent that judges or administrative officials have any measure of power, that power is limited to finding facts which trigger the application of statutory rules.[91] Thus, Bentham excoriated the common law method of adjudication: he called it 'dog-law', because it enabled judges to legislate ex post facto;[92] he resisted Hobbes's suggestion that '[a]ll Laws ... have need of Interpretation',[93] because he thought judges would abuse their interpretive licence to pervert the substance of legislation and undermine social welfare;[94] and he had no truck or trade with the notion of natural rights. He called natural rights an 'anarchical fallacy' because '[s]ociety is held together only by the sacrifices that men can be induced to make of the gratifications they demand: to obtain these sacrifices is the great difficulty, the great task of government'.[95]

[89] ibid 60–63.

[90] See, eg Ross Harrison, *Democracy* (London, Routledge, 1993) ch 6; David Dyzenhaus, 'Recrafting the Rule of Law' in David Dyzenhaus (ed), *Recrafting the Rule of Law: The Limits of Legal Order* (Oxford, Hart Publishing, 1999) 1, 2.

[91] Michael Lobban, *The Common Law and English Jurisprudence 1760–1850* (Oxford, Clarendon Press, 1991) ch 5.

[92] Jeremy Bentham, '*Truth v Ashhurst*' in John Bowring (ed), *The Works of Jeremy Bentham*, 11 vols (Edinburgh, W Tait, 1843) vol 5, 235: 'Scarce any man has the means of knowing a twentieth part of the law he is bound by. Both sorts of law are kept most happily and carefully from the knowledge of the people: statute law by its shape and bulk; common law by its very essence. It is the judges (as we have seen) that make the common law. Do you know how they make it? Just as a man makes laws for his dog. When your dog does anything you want to break him of, you wait till he does it, and then beat him for it. This is the way you make laws for your dog: and this is the way the judges make law for you and me'.

[93] Hobbes, *Leviathan* (n 1 above) 190.

[94] Jeremy Bentham, *Of Laws in General*, HLA Hart (ed) (London, Athlone Press, 1970) 163.

[95] Jeremy Bentham, 'Anarchical Fallacies: Being an Examination of the Rights of the Man and the Citizen decreed by the Constituent Assembly in France' in John Bowring (ed), *The Works of Jeremy Bentham* (Edinburgh, William Tait, 1843) 497.

The springboard for Bentham's project was his scathing critique of William Blackstone's anti-positivist theory of law.[96] Unlike Bentham, Blackstone extolled the virtues of *leges non scripta*—he claimed that the authority of the common law was 'not set down in writing, as acts of parliament are, but ... receive their binding power, and the force of laws, by long and immemorial usage, and by their universal reception throughout the kingdom'.[97] Because the content of the common law was anchored by political morality,[98] he argued that judges (whom he called the 'living oracles' of the common law)[99] were entitled to construe legislation in light of the common law's commitment to liberty, which he thought was 'the very end and scope of the constitution'.[100] Thus, he argued that whenever possible legislation should be construed compatibly with common law principles, penal statutes should be construed strictly, and legislation which was contradictory or impossible to perform should be deemed invalid.[101] More controversially, he claimed that legislation could not derogate from a subject's natural rights, because 'no human legislature has power to abridge or destroy them unless the owner shall himself commit some act that amounts to forfeiture'.[102] However, as Bentham was keen to point out, Blackstone's theory had a decidedly conservative cast—whereas judicial decisions were to be 'held in the highest regard' legislation was to be regarded with suspicion because it threatened the 'symmetry' and 'majestic simplicity' of the common law.[103]

This schism between positivists and anti-positivists crops up continuously in jurisprudence and constitutional theory. In Chapter two I argued that Dicey's constitutional theory is dialectical, because its two main tenets—parliamentary sovereignty and the rule of law—were borrowed from Bentham and Blackstone, respectively. While Dicey recognised that the principles of parliamentary sovereignty and the rule of law 'appear to stand in opposition to each other, or to be at best only counterbalancing forces', he argued that this impression was 'delusive' because the substance of parliamentary legislation would ultimately be determined by judges.[104] Thus, he escaped the dialectic by employing Blackstone's strategy: he argued that '[t]he principle that Parliament speaks only through an Act of Parliament

[96] Jeremy Bentham, *A Fragment on Government*, JH Burns and HLA Hart(eds) (Cambridge, Cambridge University Press, 1988).

[97] William Blackstone, *Commentaries on the Laws of England* (London, Garland, 1978) *64.

[98] ibid *73–74.

[99] ibid *69.

[100] ibid *6.

[101] ibid *58–62, 87–92.

[102] ibid *54.

[103] ibid *9.

[104] AV Dicey, *Introduction to the Study of the Law of the Constitution*, 10th edn (London, Macmillan, 1959) 406.

greatly increases the authority of the judges'[105] because 'from the moment Parliament has uttered its will as lawgiver, that will becomes subject to the interpretation put upon it by the judges of the law'.[106] Furthermore, he argued that the judiciary's monopoly over legal interpretation 'constantly hampers (and sometimes with great injury to the public) the action of the executive'.[107] Similar antipathy towards the administrative state can be found in judicial opinions throughout the common law world during the first half of the twentieth century, particularly (but by no means exclusively) during the *Lochner* era in American constitutional law.[108]

This same rift is apparent in contemporary debates regarding the legitimacy of 'strong' judicial review—the judicial power to strike down or refuse to apply a statute in order to protect individual rights.[109] On the one hand, Waldron follows Bentham in advancing a theory of law that is procedural, democratic, and positivist in its orientation. He argues that judicial review 'is inappropriate as a mode of final decisionmaking in a free and democratic society', because it undermines expressions of popular will;[110] and he lampoons the notion that judges are somehow uniquely qualified to provide us with correct answers to questions about justice.[111] On the other hand, Dworkin advances a theory of law which is substantive, liberal, and anti-positivist. He argues that individual rights are 'trumps' which outweigh collective decisions, and devises an heuristic device for revealing their true content—'a lawyer of superhuman skill, learning, patience, and acumen' named Hercules.[112] Hercules, Dworkin argues, is uniquely qualified to arrive at the correct outcome in hard cases where there is reasonable disagreement about what the law requires. He arrives at the correct outcome by developing a substantive moral argument which both fits past institutional decisions—constitutional provisions, legislation, and common law precedent—and articulates the best justification for them.[113]

But despite their differences, there are points at which Waldron and Dworkin seem to share some common ground. For instance, when Waldron responds to Dworkin's moral reading of the Constitution, he states that 'a theorist of democracy should not affect a pure proceduralist's nonchalance about the fate of individual rights', and concedes that Dworkin is 'correct

105 ibid 407.
106 ibid 413.
107 ibid 411.
108 See chs 3–5.
109 Ronald Dworkin, *Freedom's Law: The Moral Reading of the American Constitution* (Cambridge MA, Harvard University Press, 1996); Ronald Dworkin, *Justice for Hedgehogs* (Cambridge MA, Harvard University Press, 2011) ch 18; Waldron, 'Judicial Review and the Conditions of Democracy' (n 67 above); Waldron, 'The Core of the Case Against Judicial Review' (n 69 above).
110 Waldron, 'The Core of the Case Against Judicial Review' (n 69 above) 1348.
111 ibid 1353.
112 Dworkin, *Taking Rights Seriously* (n 70 above) 105.
113 Dworkin, *Law's Empire* (n 33 above).

when he insists that we are not entitled to appeal to any *fundamental* opposition between the idea of democracy and the idea of individual rights as a basis for criticizing judicial review'.[114] And when he sets out his case against strong judicial review in greater detail, he carefully notes that his objection depends on some pretty big assumptions about the quality of the deliberative process which accompanies the enactment of legislation: he assumes that legislative debates 'are informed by a culture of democracy, valuing responsible deliberation and political equality';[115] that there is 'a well-established and politically independent judiciary ... set up to hear lawsuits, settle disputes, and uphold the rule of law';[116] and that members of society 'keep their own and others' views on rights under constant consideration and lively debate'.[117] All of this suggests that the legitimacy of legislation has both a procedural and substantive dimension to it.[118] Waldron admits as much when he says that '[w]hat we see, on the participatory side, is not what Rawls called a claim of pure procedural justice, but something like imperfect procedural justice', because there are both substantive and procedural criteria for assessing the legitimacy of the outcome.[119]

While Dworkin's climb down is more tentative, he nevertheless acknowledges that '[m]any institutional arrangements are compatible with the moral reading', including those that do not give judges the power to strike down legislation;[120] that judges, like legislators, are fallible interpreters of constitutional values;[121] and concedes that '[e]ven if the experts always improved the legislation they rejected—always stipulated fairer income taxes than the legislature had enacted, for example—there would be a loss in self-government which the merits of their decisions could not extinguish'.[122] What matters is that political power is distributed and exercised in a manner which conveys equal concern and respect for each member of the community, and in this respect Dworkin makes the relatively modest proposal that judicial review is just one available strategy for enhancing the legitimacy of governmental decisions.[123] And in his earlier work, Dworkin argued that the legitimacy of a governmental decision is conditioned by substantive constraints which guard against arbitrariness, but fall short of more demanding Herculean

[114] Waldron, 'Judicial Review and the Conditions of Democracy' (n 67 above) 341.

[115] Waldron, 'The Core of the Case Against Judicial Review' (n 66 above) 1361.

[116] ibid 1363.

[117] ibid 1365.

[118] See, eg Thomas Christiano, 'The Authority of Democracy' (n 55 above); Joshua Cohen, 'Procedure and Substance in Deliberative Democracy' in Seyla Benhabib (ed), *Democracy and Difference: Contesting the Boundaries of the Political* (Princeton NJ, Princeton University Press, 1996) 120.

[119] Waldron, 'The Core of the Case Against Judicial Review' (n 66 above) 1378.

[120] Dworkin, *Freedom's Law* (n 109 above) 7.

[121] ibid 33.

[122] ibid 32.

[123] Dworkin, *Justice for Hedgehogs* (n 109 above) 385.

standards: he argued that governmental decisions cannot be justified by reasons based on prejudice, visceral reactions, or factual assumptions which fall short of minimal standards of evidence.[124]

If we reject Waldron's procedural argument as ignoring necessary substantive conditions for the legitimacy of legislative authority, and Dworkin's substantive argument in favour of strong judicial review because it provides judges with too broad a licence to interfere with democratic decisions, we must attempt to stake out the middle ground between them more precisely or run the risk of vacillating impulsively between these two poles. As we saw in Chapter three, when our constitutional commitments require respect for both legislation and fundamental rights, there is a persistent tendency for judges to provide convenient rationalisations instead of principled justifications for either upholding an administrative decision or upsetting it.

Instead of assigning exclusive legal authority to legislatures, judges, or administrative officials, our account of administrative law must incorporate procedural and substantive principles which sustain the legitimacy of decisions made on behalf of the community by different legal institutions. This concern motivates the regulatory principle of reciprocity which lies at the heart of Amy Gutmann's and Dennis Thompson's work in democratic theory.[125] Like Hobbes and Waldron, Gutmann and Thompson begin with the irreducible fact of moral disagreement in politics, and they develop a conception of legitimate democratic authority for 'people who are mutually motivated to find fair terms of social cooperation among political equals'.[126] But their conception of deliberative democracy transcends the impasse between democratic proceduralists and liberal constitutionalists by asserting that the legitimacy of collective decisions is conditioned by both procedural principles (reciprocity, publicity, and accountability) and constitutional values (basic liberty, basic opportunity, and fair opportunity).[127] However, their procedural principles have more substantive bite than proceduralists like Waldron prefer to admit, and the content of constitutional values remains subject to democratic decision-making in ways that make liberal constitutionalists like Dworkin uncomfortable.[128] In the end, Gutmann and

[124] Ronald Dworkin, 'Lord Devlin and the Enforcement of Morals' (1966) 75 *Yale Law Journal* 986.

[125] Amy Gutmann and Dennis Thompson, *Democracy and Disagreement* (Cambridge, Belknap Press, 1996); Amy Gutmann and Dennis Thompson, 'Deliberative Democracy Beyond Process' (2002) 10 *Journal of Political Philosophy* 153; Amy Gutmann and Dennis Thompson, *Why Deliberative Democracy?* (Princeton NJ, Princeton University Press, 2004); Amy Gutmann and Dennis Thompson, 'Moral Disagreement in a Democracy' in Matt Zwolinski (ed), *Arguing About Political Philosophy* (New York, Routledge, 2009).

[126] Gutmann and Thompson, *Democracy and Disagreement* (n 125 above) 1–52.

[127] Gutmann and Thompson, *Why Deliberative Democracy?* (n 125 above) 23–26, chs 3 and 5.

[128] ibid ch 1; Gutmann and Thompson, 'Deliberative Democracy Beyond Process' (n 125 above) 153–55.

Thompson's theory of deliberative democracy outlines a procedural form for democratic deliberation in which all governmental institutions share responsibility for the realisation and advancement of constitutional values and are held to account publicly for their decisions.

In order for a collective decision to be seen as legitimate, Gutmann and Thompson argue that the decision must be supported by reasons acceptable to free and equal persons seeking fair terms of cooperation.[129] The basis for this requirement is that '[p]ersons should be treated not merely as objects of legislation, as passive subjects to be ruled, but as autonomous agents who take part in the governance of their own society, directly or through their representatives'.[130] Hence, it is not sufficient for a democratic legislature to stipulate an outcome—its decision must be supported by reasons which are intelligible, publicly accessible, and based upon evidence or beliefs which can be assessed by the demos. Furthermore, while Gutmann and Thompson agree that responsibility for collective decisions can be delegated to experts, '[c]itizens are justified in relying on experts if they describe the basis for their conclusions in ways that citizens can understand; and if the citizens have some independent basis for believing the experts to be trustworthy'.[131] By ensuring that common decisions are open to public scrutiny and responsive to citizen's concerns, decision-makers can be held to account for their decisions in elections, formal debate in a legislative assembly, the political press, judicial review, etc. Finally, while a governmental decision supported by adequate reasons might be sufficient to suspend the deliberative process temporarily while the decision is implemented, the decision remains provisional in the sense that it is open to revision if the balance of reasons changes due to new arguments and evidence or new interpretations of old arguments and evidence.[132]

The upshot of Gutmann and Thompson's theory is an ethical way of life[133] or culture of justification[134] which legitimates all governmental authority—legislative, judicial, and administrative. All of these institutions share the implicit aim of arriving at collective, provisional decisions which are mutually acceptable with the understanding that those decisions

[129] Gutmann and Thompson, *Why Deliberative Democracy?* (n 125 above) 3.

[130] ibid.

[131] ibid 5.

[132] Gutmann and Thompson, 'Deliberative Democracy Beyond Process' (n 125 above) 165.

[133] See, eg John Dewey, 'The Ethics of Democracy' in John Dewey, *The Early Works, 1882–1898* (Carbondale, Southern Illinois University Press, 1969) 240–41: 'To say that democracy is *only* a form of government is like saying that home is a more or less geometrical arrangement of bricks and mortar; that the church is a building with pews, pulpit and spire. It is true; they are certainly so much. But it is false; they are infinitely more ... Democracy, in a word, is a social, that is to say, an ethical conception, and upon its ethical significance is based its significance as governmental. Democracy is a form of government only because it is a form of moral and spiritual association'.

[134] See, eg Cheryl Misak, 'A Culture of Justification: The Pragmatist's Epistemic Argument for Democracy' (2008) 5 *Episteme* 94.

are unlikely to attract universal consensus. As they put it, mutual acceptability 'falls between impartiality, which requires something like altruism, and prudence, which demands no more than enlightened self-interest': it involves an exchange of reasons which enables subjects to advance towards a mutually acceptable agreement or, alternatively, assess whether a collective decision is worthy of respect even though it might be morally incorrect in their eyes.[135] Thus, decisions which: are not supported by reasons, are based upon prejudice or blind self-interest, appeal to divine or secular revelation, ignore relevant facts, or deny basic opportunities like equal suffrage or essential health care, fundamentally lack legitimacy no matter how fair the democratic decision-making process might otherwise be.[136] Conversely, if a decision provides generalisable reasons which articulate a morally defensible conception of the public interest, respond meaningfully to citizens' concerns, and explain how the decision can be reconciled with constitutional values, it has legitimate authority even if some citizens might regard it as incorrect or mistaken.

II. LEGALITY AND THE LEGITIMACY OF ADMINISTRATIVE LAW

Up to this point, I have focused on second order or 'institutional' reasons that ground respect for administrative institutions in a general way.[137] While second order reasons for respecting administrative authority are often conflated with first order reasons regarding the merits of a particular decision, it is important to distinguish between these two dimensions because it helps us better understand the character of administrative law and the role it plays in a constitutional democracy. Institutional reasons provide a principled response to the question 'who should answer this question on behalf of the political community?'. In the previous section, I argued that when a democratically responsible branch of government empowers an administrative official to decide a question of common concern, that legal instrument provides both subjects and judges with good reasons for respecting an administrative decision. Subjects and judges should take the administrative decision seriously, meaning it would be inappropriate for them to pursue their preferred outcome or speculate about what ruling they would have imposed if an administrative official had not pronounced a decision.[138]

[135] Gutmann and Thompson, *Democracy and Disagreement* (n 125 above) 2 and ch 2.

[136] ibid; Gutmann and Thompson, 'Deliberative Democracy Beyond Process' (n 125 above).

[137] For further elaboration regarding the distinction between the first and second order assessment, see Gutmann and Thompson, *Why Deliberative Democracy?* (n 125 above) 13; Aileen Kavanagh, 'Deference or Defiance?' in Grant Huscroft (ed), *Expounding the Constitution: Essays in Constitutional Theory* (Cambridge, Cambridge University Press, 2008) 184, 190.

[138] David Dyzenhaus, 'The Politics of Deference' in Michael Taggart (ed), *The Province of Administrative Law* (Oxford, Hart Publishing, 1997) 279, 303.

However, I also noted that, while democratic decisions generally have normative purchase, they are not conclusive because their legitimacy also depends upon whether the decision-making process and the substantive quality of a decision conveys concern and respect for legal subjects. Are there similar procedural and substantive conditions for the legitimacy of administrative law?

In this section, I want to focus on the relationship between the principle of legality and the legitimacy of administrative law. While we can infer from institutional reasons that correctness review is generally inappropriate, it remains unclear whether we should submit blindly to an administrative decision. I will argue that the legitimacy of administrative law cannot be cinched conclusively by institutional reasons—it also depends upon whether an administrative decision complies with the rule of law by demonstrating concern and respect for subjects via requirements of fair process and reasonable justification.

While there are different formulations of the principle of legality, jurisprudential analysis usually builds upon the foundation laid by Lon Fuller 50 years ago.[139] Fuller unpacked the rule of law by identifying eight desiderata necessary to sustain legal order—generality, publicity, prospectivity, intelligibility, consistency, possibility of compliance, stability, and congruence between official action and declared rule.[140] More controversially, Fuller claimed that these desiderata revealed an inherent connection between law and political morality—in his view they exposed the 'internal morality' of law, which secures 'a baseline for self-directed action'[141] as well as 'reciprocity between government and the citizen with respect to the observance of rules'.[142] He argued that in order for law to sustain a legitimate legal obligation—one whose normativity relies on something other than the threat of brute force to elicit compliance—it must project something more than second order or institutional reasons.[143] Thus, he stated that 'mere respect for constituted authority must not be confused with fidelity to law',[144] because when 'this bond of reciprocity is finally and completely ruptured by government, nothing is left on which to ground the citizen's duty to observe the rules'.[145]

However, because Fuller's account is cast at a relatively abstract level, it can be difficult to pinpoint precisely how the principle of legality shapes administrative law. In his famous critique of Fuller's position, HLA Hart claimed that compliance with the principle of legality was nevertheless

[139] Lon Fuller, *The Morality of Law* (n 33 above) ch 2.
[140] ibid 39.
[141] ibid 210.
[142] ibid 39.
[143] See also HLA Hart, *The Concept of Law* (n 33 above) ch 5.
[144] ibid 41.
[145] ibid 40.

'compatible with great iniquity';[146] and in his response to Fuller's argument that his eight desiderata revealed law's 'inner morality', asserted:[147]

> it perpetrates a confusion between two notions that it is vital to hold apart: the notions of purposive activity and morality. Poisoning is no doubt a purposive activity, and reflections on its purpose may show that it has its internal principles. ('Avoid poisons however lethal if their shape, color, or size is likely to attract notice.') But to call these principles of the poisoner's art 'the morality of poisoning' would simply blur the distinction between the notions of efficiency for a purpose and those final judgments about activities and purposes with which morality in its various forms is concerned.

Therefore, while Hart conceded that abiding by the principle of legality might be valuable insofar as it enables those in positions of authority to achieve their objectives more efficiently, its impact on the exercise of political power was merely formal—it did not impose any moral constraints on governmental decisions in either a procedural or substantive sense.

While Fuller rejected Hart's critique,[148] he nevertheless seemed to equivocate on whether and to what extent the principle of legality impacts process or substance in administrative law. For instance, when attempting to clarify his ideas about law's inner morality, he calls it 'a procedural version of natural law', but proceeds to explain that 'the word "procedural" should be assigned a special and expanded sense so that it would include, for example, a substantive accord between official action and enacted law'.[149] Elsewhere he suggests that the principle of legality has a peculiar substantive bite, because 'when men are compelled to explain and justify their decisions, the effect will generally be to pull those decisions toward goodness, by whatever standards of ultimate goodness there are'.[150]

Similar fault lines between formal, procedural, and substantive conceptions of legality crop up repeatedly in contemporary jurisprudence. While both Raz and Waldron build upon Fuller's model, they draw dramatically different inferences from it. Raz, for example, tacks on additional requirements concerning judicial independence, natural justice, judicial review, and access to the courts; however, like Hart he argues that at most these requirements generate a formal account of legality which is compatible with profound injustice. Therefore, he concludes that there is no necessary connection between the principle of legality and the moral legitimacy of governmental

[146] Hart, *The Concept of Law* (n 33 above) 207. See also HLA Hart, 'Problems of the Philosophy of Law' in Paul Edwards (ed), *Encyclopedia of Philosophy* (New York, Macmillan, 1967) vol 6, 264–76.

[147] HLA Hart, Book Review: 'The Morality of Law' (1965) 78 *Harvard Law Review* 1281, 1286.

[148] Fuller, *The Morality of Law* (n 33 above) 200ff.

[149] ibid 96–97.

[150] Lon Fuller, 'Positivism and Fidelity to Law: A Reply to Professor Hart' (1958) 71 *Harvard Law Review* 630, 636.

decisions.[151] For Raz, the value of legality is purely instrumental—it sets merely content-independent parameters for those who wield political power to achieve their goals, whatever those goals might be.

By contrast, Waldron advances a procedural conception of the rule of law which emphasises 'the importance of the procedural and argumentative aspects of legal practice'.[152] He argues that the principle of legality entails the right to an impartial decision-maker and the right to participate in decisions which affect one's personal interests.[153] Moreover, he argues that these criteria curb the abuse of public power and serve to uphold the dignity of legal subjects in the face of governmental action. Thus, *contra* Raz, Waldron argues that the rule of law is not a morally neutral construct, because it constrains the manner in which political power can be exercised, and those constraints enhance the legitimacy of governmental decisions by providing opportunities for legal subjects to interrogate the manner in which officials wield political power and participate in the discursive enterprise of legal interpretation. Such opportunities, in Waldron's view, have moral value because they demonstrate concern and respect for subjects as rational agents who have something to say about how the law ought to be interpreted. Nevertheless, like Raz, Waldron argues that a procedural conception of legality stops short of imposing substantive constraints on administrative decisions.

As we will see, both the formal and procedural conceptions of legality understate the degree to which it shapes administrative law. I will argue that the value of legality entails procedural and substantive constraints on the manner in which administrative authority is exercised, and that these constraints enhance the moral legitimacy, as opposed to the efficiency or expediency, of administrative law. Moreover, I will argue that judicial review serves to uphold the rule of law by ensuring that administrative officials respond to evidence and arguments tendered by subjects, and render decisions which are transparent, intelligible, and legally justifiable.

Nevertheless, while I will argue that the principle of legality suggests that the legitimacy of administrative law depends partly on its substance, I want to keep the institutional reasons for respecting administrative authority firmly in view. Accordingly, I will argue that, while the principle of legality requires judges to ensure that administrative law is both fair and substantively reasonable, it does not provide either subjects or judges with a plenary licence to engage in correctness review. Rather, it gives them a more limited warrant to verify whether an administrative decision is capable of sustaining a legitimate legal obligation, in the sense that it is something 'we

[151] Raz, 'The Rule of Law and Its Virtue' (n 40 above).

[152] Jeremy Waldron, 'The Concept and the Rule of Law' (2008) 43 *Georgia Law Review* 1, 5.

[153] Jeremy Waldron, 'The Rule of Law and the Importance of Procedure' in James Fleming (ed), *Getting to the Rule of Law* (New York, New York University Press, 2011) 3, 10.

can approve in principle even at the moment when it seems to us to miss its mark'.[154] This idea delineates a more limited role for judicial review, which aims to ensure that subjects are treated with concern and respect in a society where there is reasonable disagreement about what the law requires instead of asserting a monopoly over legal interpretation *tout court*.

A. Formal Legality

Recall that according to Raz's preemption thesis, an authority mediates between subjects and the reasons that apply to them by providing decisions with exclusionary, content-independent normative force.[155] Nevertheless, Raz makes it clear that no authority is capable of providing its subjects with an *absolute* reason for compliance, and whether it constitutes a *conclusive* reason for doing so depends on the circumstances.[156] Besides the conditions set out in the service conception of authority, Raz recognises that the exclusionary impact of a decision may be limited by other parameters.[157]

> Even where an authoritative decision is meant to settle finally what is to be done, it may be open to challenge on certain grounds, for example, if an emergency occurs, or if the directive violates fundamental human rights, or if the authority acted arbitrarily. The nonexcluded reasons and the grounds of challenging an authority's directives vary from case to case. They determine the conditions of legitimacy of the authority and the limits of its rightful power.

This passage raises a series of important questions: How does one verify whether an authority's decision is open to such challenges? How does one determine whether an authority's decision is merely 'mistaken' and therefore binding, as opposed to 'arbitrary' and therefore illegitimate?[158] And how can we reconcile these qualifications with the pre-emption thesis, which asserts that subjects (and other legal officials, perhaps) are excluded or pre-empted from acting upon their own assessment of the reasons summed up by an authority's decision?

[154] Fuller, 'Positivism and Fidelity to Law' (n 150 above) 632. Thus, I aim to justify the authority of an administrative decision situated in what Larry Alexander calls 'the gap' between 'what we have reason to do, all things considered … and what we have reason to have our rules (and the officials who promulgate and enforce them) require us to do': Larry Alexander, 'The Gap' (1991) 14 *Harvard Journal of Law and Public Policy* 695.

[155] Above nn 48–53 and accompanying text.

[156] Joseph Raz, 'Authority, Law, and Morality' in Joseph Raz, *Ethics in the Public Domain: Essays in the Morality of Law and Politics*, revised edn (Oxford, Clarendon Press, 1994) 213.

[157] Raz, 'Authority and Justification' (n 40 above) 14.

[158] For an elaboration of Raz's views on the normativity of mistaken authoritative directives, see Alan Bogg, 'In Defence of Correlativity: Authority, Autonomy and Mistaken Legal Directives' (2002) 15 *Ratio Juris* 84.

Raz anticipates questions of this kind, which suggest that the legitimacy of a second order decision is not determined exclusively on an ex ante basis through an application of the normal justification thesis, but also depends on some kind of ex post assessment of an authority's decision. However, he offers two different answers to these types of questions. The first is that the normative impact of a particular decision will be undermined only if the decision contains a 'clear' or 'jurisdictional' error—an egregious substantive error that can be detected without evaluating the process by which the decision was reached or reweighing the merits of the decision.[159] If we adopt this response, an administrative decision will continue to have exclusionary force even if the decision-maker is biased, fails to provide notice to the parties, withholds relevant information, prohibits the parties from retaining counsel, ignores the parties' submissions or salient facts, flouts the animating purposes of its enabling legislation, issues ex parte edicts, renders its decisions in secret, or simply issues a fiat without supporting reasons.[160] But because Raz's definition of jurisdictional error fails to account for even the most basic legal constraints on the exercise of administrative power, this answer is simply not persuasive because it fails to account for important features of legal practice.

The deficiency of this first response comes into better focus when we compare Raz's narrow definition of jurisdictional error with his second response, which explains how arbitrary political power might be restrained by the rule of law.[161] Although the question of normativity remains central to Raz's analysis of legality, he teases out its normative implications from the internal perspective, by saying 'the law must be capable of guiding the behaviour of its subjects'.[162] From this premise, Raz extrapolates criteria of legality, among them that laws must be clear, prospective, relatively stable, and publicly accessible. Furthermore, he asserts that ephemeral laws (ie administrative decisions) should be 'enacted only within a framework set by general laws which are more durable and which impose limits on the unpredictability introduced by the particular orders'; should be rendered in accordance with the principles of natural justice; and subject to review by an

[159] Raz, 'Authority and Justification' (n 40 above) 25–26: 'Consider a long addition of, say, some thirty numbers. One can make a very small yet clear mistake as when the sum is an integer whereas one and only one of the added numbers is a fraction. One the other hand, the sum may be off by several thousands without the mistake being detectable except by laboriously going over the addition step by step ... Establishing that something is clearly wrong does not require going through the underlying reasoning. It is not the case that the legitimate power of authorities is generally limited by the condition that it is defeated by significant mistakes which are not clear'.

[160] Waldron, 'The Rule of Law and the Importance of Procedure' (n 153 above) 13.

[161] Raz, 'The Rule of Law and its Virtue (n 40 above); Joseph Raz, 'The Politics of the Rule of Law' in Joseph Raz (ed), *Ethics in the Public Domain: Essays in the Morality of Law and Politics* (Oxford, Oxford University Press, 1994) 370.

[162] Raz, 'The Rule of Law and its Virtue' (n 40 above) 214.

independent judiciary.[163] In these respects, Raz argues the rule of law guards against arbitrariness, which he defines in the following terms:[164]

> the exercise of power is arbitrary only if it was done either with indifference as to whether it will serve the purposes which alone can justify use of that power or with belief that it will not serve them. The nature of the purposes alluded to varies with the nature of the power.

Now it is possible that Raz shifts between two different senses of arbitrariness in his work: arbitrariness in a narrow sense which is restricted by 'clear', ex ante analytical limits associated with the service conception of authority, and arbitrariness in a broader, ex post sense which guards against more familiar forms of abuse. However, such a distinction would be strange, considering that Raz argues that the service conception of authority is essential to the concept of law, and that the rule of law is a central attribute of any legal system.

This difficulty raises a further problem, because if we continue to probe the manner in which legality reins in the arbitrary exercise of legal authority it casts some doubt upon the pre-emption thesis. The pre-emption thesis suggests that the normative force of an administrative decision is an all-or-nothing proposition: its exclusionary force is determined in advance by delineating the class of background reasons it excludes, except in cases where the decision-maker commits a jurisdictional error on the face of the decision. By contrast, Raz's conception of the rule of law provides a richer, more nuanced account, in which the impact of an administrative decision also depends upon the observance of morally significant procedural and substantive constraints. According to this version, the internal perspective of subjects and judges includes a critical aspect that is not limited to flagging patently obvious errors, but considers whether administrative decision-makers act fairly, transparently, and render decisions which are substantively justifiable in light of more basic legal standards like constitutional values, statutory provisions, or common law principles.

The difficulty with drawing this thread between legitimate authority, fairness, and substantive reasonableness is that Raz rejects tying legal authority to political morality in precisely this way. While he acknowledges that the rule of law curbs the risk of arbitrary decision-making—thereby protecting the liberty and autonomy of subjects by securing a relatively stable, predictable, and determinate framework of laws which enables them to plan their lives—he argues that these beneficial side effects do not establish any necessary connection between law and morality. Rather, he claims that legality is merely a 'negative virtue', because 'conformity to it does not cause good except through avoiding evil and the evil which is avoided is evil which

[163] ibid 216–17.
[164] ibid 219.

could only have been caused by the law itself'.[165] To clarify the point, he notes that 'conformity to the rule of law also enables the law to serve bad purposes', because compliance with legality 'is not a virtue, just as the fact that a sharp knife can be used to harm does not show that being sharp is not a good-making characteristic for knives'.[166] Thus, a wicked legal system 'based on the denial of human rights, on extensive poverty, on racial segregation, sexual inequalities, and religious persecution may, in principle, conform to the requirements of the rule of law better than any of the more enlightened Western democracies'.[167] The suggestion here seems to be that fastidious compliance with rule of law requirements like the principles of natural justice can actually make the realisation of unjust aims more cost-effective.

B. Legality as Fairness

Raz's tendency to either ignore basic procedural constraints associated with the rule of law or discount how they condition the moral legitimacy of governmental decisions suggests that he cannot adequately explain how the legitimacy of administrative law is evaluated in common law jurisdictions. From the internal perspective of common lawyers, compliance with the principles of natural justice contributes to the legitimacy of administrative decisions, and those constraints often impede (instead of facilitate) the straight-forward achievement of the government's legislative or regulatory agenda. For instance, when Lord Reid declared in *Ridge v Baldwin* that 'an officer cannot lawfully be dismissed without first telling him what is alleged against him and hearing his defence or explanation', he was not suggesting that a hearing would provide a more efficient means for terminating Ridge's employment—he was criticising the local watch committee for failing to treat Ridge with the respect he deserved in a country committed to the rule of law.[168] Similarly, when Louis Brandeis asserted that '[s]unlight is … the best of disinfectants; electric light the most efficient policeman', he was not suggesting that regulatory transparency enables those in positions of power to impose their will more effectively—he meant that publicity provides opportunities for ferreting out insidious forms of injustice in the public domain.[169]

Waldron provides an alternative reading of how compliance with the procedural requirements of legality sustains the moral legitimacy of

[165] ibid 224.
[166] ibid 225. For a similar analogy, see Hart, 'Book Review' (n 147 above) 1286.
[167] ibid 211.
[168] *Ridge v Baldwin* [1964] AC 40, 66 (HL).
[169] Louis Brandeis, 'What Publicity Can Do', *Harper's Weekly* (20 December 1913) 10.

administrative law. Like Raz, Waldron argues that the rule of law is a central aspect of any legal system, but agrees with Fuller that there is an intrinsic connection between the rule of law and political morality. Writing in the Fullerian vein, he rejects Raz's formal conception of legality on the ground that it ignores how the rule of law serves important values like individual liberty, autonomy, dignity, and equality. In light of this connection, Waldron argues the rule of law is 'one of a cluster of ideals constitutive of modern political morality' which elucidates the very concept of law.[170] Furthermore, while Waldron opposes 'strong' judicial review of legislation, he supports judicial review of the executive's decisions as a means of upholding the rule of law.[171] Thus, when considering judicial review of executive decisions, he concedes that 'the executive's elective credentials are subject to the principle of the rule of law', which entails that 'officials may properly be required by courts to act in accordance with legal authorization'.[172]

Nevertheless, Waldron remains wary of a substantive conception of the rule of law,[173] which he says 'calls directly for an end to human rights abuses or ... for free markets and respect for private property rights'.[174] While he prefaces this point by saying there is a 'natural overlap' between substantive and formal elements of the rule of law insofar as the formal account rests partly on its capacity to secure the dignity and liberty of subjects, Waldron seeks to prevent the rule of law from collapsing into a full-blown, contestable conception of justice which would provide subjects and judges with a licence to obstruct democratic decisions in the name of individual rights.[175] And he can point to the excesses of the *Lochner* era, a period in which the United States Supreme Court frustrated the development of the modern administrative state by reading substantive constraints on legislative and administrative action into the Fifth and Fourteenth Amendments, to demonstrate that his concern is neither fanciful nor historically unfounded.[176] As I have noted in Chapters three and five, similar lessons might be drawn from the history of judicial review of administrative decisions in the United

[170] Waldron, 'The Rule of Law and the Importance of Procedure' (n 153 above) 12–14; Jeremy Waldron, 'The Rule of Law as a Theater of Debate' in Ronald Dworkin and Justine Burley (eds), *Dworkin and His Critics: With Replies by Dworkin* (Oxford, Blackwell Publishing, 2004) 319; Jeremy Waldron, 'The Concept and the Rule of Law' (n 152 above) 3; Jeremy Waldron, 'Hart and the Principles of Legality' in Matthew Kramer, Claire Grant, and Antony Hatzistavrou (eds), *The Legacy of HLA Hart: Legal, Political, and Moral Philosophy* (Oxford, Oxford University Press, 2008) 67, 77–79.

[171] Waldron, 'The Core of the Case Against Judicial Review' (n 66 above) 1353–59.

[172] ibid 1354.

[173] See, eg Jeremy Waldron 'Legislation and the Rule of Law' (2007) 1 *Legisprudence* 91.

[174] Waldron, 'The Rule of Law and the Importance of Procedure' (n 153 above) 5. See also Paul Craig, 'Formal and substantive conceptions of the rule of law: an analytical framework' [1997] *Public Law* 467.

[175] Waldron, 'The Rule of Law and the Importance of Procedure' (n 153 above) 5.

[176] See ch 4, ibid.

Kingdom and Canada as well. So while Waldron recognises an intrinsic connection between legality and political morality, he nevertheless wishes to advance a procedural conception of the rule of law which maximises the logical space within which the democratic decision-making processes can operate.

In keeping with this proceduralist orientation, he supplements Fuller's original account by appending a series of guarantees traditionally associated with the concepts of natural justice or procedural due process—the right to a hearing before an impartial and independent tribunal, the right to counsel, the right to understand the case and to respond to it, the right to reasons which 'are responsive to the evidence and arguments', and the right of judicial review.[177] The overarching principle is that 'no one should have any penalty, stigma or serious loss imposed upon him by government'[178] unless they have 'an opportunity to put their case, confront and examine the evidence against them … and make arguments for their freedom, in accordance with what we would say were normal legal procedures'.[179]

After setting out these refinements, Waldron asserts that a purely formal conception of the rule of law—one which overlooks how these procedural safeguards are both an essential feature of a functioning legal system and crucial for maintaining law's moral legitimacy—would 'radically sell short the idea of the Rule of Law'.[180] Thus, he argues that the rule of law ensures that subjects are treated respectfully, in the sense that 'they are listened to by a tribunal that … is bound in some manner to attend to the evidence presented and to respond to the submissions that are made in the reasons it eventually gives for its decisions'.[181] In this respect, Waldron argues that the procedural rights entailed by the principle of legality:[182]

> capture a deep and important sense associated foundationally with the idea of a legal system, that law is a mode of governing people that treats them with respect, as though they had a view or perspective of their own to present on the application of the norm to their conduct and situation. Applying a norm to a human individual is not like deciding what to do about a rabid animal or a dilapidated house. It involves paying attention to a point of view and respecting the personality of the entity one is dealing with. As such, it embodies a crucial dignitarian idea—respecting the dignity of those to whom the norms are applied as *beings capable of explaining themselves*. None of this is present in the dominant positivist account; all of it, I submit, should be regarded as an essential aspect of our working conception of law.

[177] ibid 6.
[178] ibid.
[179] ibid 5.
[180] ibid.
[181] ibid 15.
[182] ibid 16. See also Jerry Mashaw, 'Administrative Due Process: The Quest for a Dignitary Theory' (1981) 61 *Boston University Law Review* 885.

However, while affording subjects opportunities to participate in the decision-making process enhances the legitimacy of a collective decision, Waldron's argument also sets up an interesting tension between the formal and procedural accounts of legality.[183] Whereas the formal account highlights the benefits that legal determinacy and predictability have in terms of enhancing the liberty of legal subjects, the procedural account emphasises the importance of maintaining the legitimacy of the law from the perspective of legal subjects. And because the procedural conception of legality involves an interpretive exercise which is responsive to reason and argumentation,[184] it has the potential to upset the certainty, predictability, determinacy and settlement prized by the formal account.[185] But because this tension is 'largely unavoidable', Waldron argues that one must simply 'own up to the fact that the Rule of Law points, as it were, in both directions'.[186]

C. Legality as Reasonable Justification

Waldron's last point regarding the impact of procedural rights on law's determinacy is suggestive—he draws a connection between procedural rights and the moral legitimacy of collective decisions, and infers that the implementation of procedural rights has an impact on law's content. If fundamental rights like *audi alteram partem* and *nemo judex in sua causa* are moral conditions necessary for law's legitimacy because they convey respect for legal subjects as self-governing moral agents who deserve to be consulted, it stands to reason that legal officials must engage substantively with a legal subject's point of view. Otherwise, the procedural rights which Waldron argues are so crucial for maintaining law's legitimacy would be hollow, because an official could treat them as mere formalities which must be observed for the sake of maintaining appearances instead of having a meaningful impact on the decision. In much the same way as Waldron's point about respecting individuals' dignity in the democratic process has substantive implications, it seems that his point about respecting individuals' dignity via the legal process might also have substantive bite on the content of administrative law.[187] Waldron himself comes close to drawing this connection in his Hamlyn lectures, when he acknowledges that 'certain features of the formal/procedural account may point us in the direction of substantive values, imparting a certain momentum which may carry us in a

[183] Waldron, 'The Rule of Law and the Importance of Procedure' (n 153 above) 18.

[184] Dworkin, *Law's Empire* (n 33 above) 11–15; Ronald Dworkin, 'Hart's Postscript and the Character of Political Philosophy' (2004) 24 *Oxford Journal of Legal Studies* 1.

[185] Waldron, 'The Rule of Law and the Importance of Procedure' (n 153 above) 19–20.

[186] ibid 21.

[187] See section I.D above.

particular substantive direction'.[188] However, he declines to elaborate further on this point.

The most likely explanation for Waldron's reticence is that, while he recognises the value of procedural rights, he worries that their double-edged nature paves a slippery slope towards a contestable, substantive account of justice which would undermine the ability of the democratic decision-making process to resolve reasonable disagreements about what justice entails. And if some of those democratic decisions involve institutional settlements—decisions to assign authority over an issue of common concern to an administrative institution—he worries that judges might run roughshod over administrative decisions in pursuit of some controversial political ideal like substantive due process. Therefore, instead of exploring the extent to which the values that underpin procedural rights also entail substantive constraints on administrative law, he concludes his case cryptically by stating that 'one must play one's part in the social processes that are necessary to sustain and implement' institutional settlements.[189]

In order to explain how the principle of legality constrains the substance of administrative decisions while still managing to convey respect for administrative authority, we need to revisit the principle of institutional settlement.[190] Because members of society are unlikely to agree on matters of justice, the second best alternative is for them to institute a legitimate process for resolving interpretive disputes about the law. One important aspect of this process is the principle of institutional settlement, which demands that 'decisions which are the duly arrived at result of duly established procedures ... ought to be accepted as binding upon the whole society unless and until they are duly changed'.[191] While Waldron employs the principle of institutional settlement to explain the dynamics of inter-institutional authority, he neglects to mention that it is nested within a broader framework for the 'reasoned elaboration' of law.[192] For example, when Hart and Sacks discuss a magistrate's power to adjudicate whether a motorcycle is a 'motor car' for the purposes of a highway traffic statute, they do not argue that the magistrate determines the outcome through the exercise of unconstrained discretion backed by the principle of institutional settlement. Rather, they argue 'the magistrate is obliged to resolve the issue before him on the assumption that the answer will be the same in all like cases', meaning that the magistrate

[188] Jeremy Waldron, *The Rule of Law and the Measure of Property* (Cambridge, Cambridge University Press, 2012) 51.

[189] Waldron, 'Authority for Officials' (n 36 above) 56.

[190] See section I.C above.

[191] Hart and Sacks, *The Legal Process* (n 76 above) 4.

[192] ibid 143–58. See G Edward White, 'The Evolution of Reasoned Elaboration: Jurisprudential Criticism and Social Change' (1973) 59 *Virginia Law Review* 279; William Eskridge and Philip Frickey, 'The Making of Legal Process' (1993) 107 *Harvard Law Review* 2031; Anthony Sebok, 'The Legal Process' (1996) 94 *Michigan Law Review* 1571.

cannot render contradictory, ad hoc decisions.[193] Furthermore, they note that 'the magistrate is obliged to relate his decision in some reasoned fashion to the speed statute',[194] which means that the magistrate must respect the role of the legislature and explain how his decision rationally advances the legislature's objectives.[195] Thus, while the process of reasoned elaboration includes respect for institutional settlements, it also requires the magistrate to provide reasons which are intelligible, generalisable, disinterested, constitutionally justifiable, rationally connected to statutory objectives, and (above all else) publicly accessible.[196] This substantive dimension is what distinguishes a fiat, in which the outcome is determined simply by ascertaining which institution has been invested with authority over the issue, from a legitimate legal decision.[197] Nevertheless, Hart and Sacks argue that the strictures of reasoned elaboration fall short of providing judges with a licence for correctness review, because a judge might reasonably conclude that an administrative decision 'ought not to be upset, even though its own answer would have been different as an original matter'.[198]

Hart and Sacks note that field of administrative law is replete with examples of reasoned elaboration at work.[199] When Congress prohibited 'unfair methods of competition' in the Federal Trade Commission Act of 1914, they noted that the statute 'was obviously too vague to be made self-applying' when it came into force.[200] However, 'as choices were made and justified in terms of the governing standard of the Act and its underlying principles and policies a body of subsidiary guides to meaning began to emerge'—administrative rules, principles, and policy statements which elaborated upon the general purposes of the legal framework which the Commission was charged with overseeing.[201] Thus, Hart and Sacks conclude that administrative law synthesises respect for institutional settlement with 'the internal restraint' of reasonable justification, which enables courts to apply 'the external check of judicial review'.[202]

The notion of reasoned elaboration resonates strongly with Lon Fuller's argument that legality requires congruence between official action and declared rule.[203] This is unsurprising, since there is evidence Hart and Sacks's

[193] Hart and Sacks, *The Legal Process* (n 76 above) 143.
[194] ibid.
[195] ibid 147–48.
[196] ibid 148.
[197] ibid 147.
[198] ibid 149.
[199] ibid 150.
[200] ibid 150.
[201] ibid 151.
[202] ibid 151.
[203] Fuller, *The Morality of Law* (n 33 above) 39.

views about legal process were strongly influenced by Fuller's jurisprudential views:[204] Sacks had been Fuller's student,[205] the contrast between fiat and reasoned judgment was lifted from one of Fuller's early articles,[206] and the argument that adjudication involves the reasonable elaboration of legal principles, policies, and purposes mirrors Fuller's famous response to HLA Hart.[207] That response was premised on the idea that law must be seen as legitimate in order to sustain the internal attitude of respectful compliance or 'fidelity to law'. In Fuller's words, 'it cannot be a simple fiat of power or a repetitive pattern discernible in the behavior of state officials', because the law 'must represent some general direction of human effort that we can understand and describe, and that we can approve in principle even at the moment when it seems to us to miss its mark'.[208] Instead of relying upon brute force to secure compliance, a judge must engage with competing, substantive legal arguments in order to construct a reasonable interpretation of the law—one which is rationally defensible in light of its purposes and responds to subjects' interpretive arguments.[209] Thus, the legal process has substantive bite, because 'when men are compelled to explain and justify their decisions, the effect will generally be to pull those decisions toward goodness, by whatever standards of ultimate goodness there are'.[210]

However, the argument that the process of reasoning and argumentation which is essential to law's legitimacy entails substantive constraints is most clearly articulated in Fuller's posthumously published article on the 'Forms and Limits of Adjudication'.[211] Fuller begins by recognising there is a pressing need for a legitimate means of settling interpretive disputes about law, and he constructs a theory of adjudication to fulfil this role. Like Waldron, Fuller emphasises the procedural aspect of adjudication to explain its legitimacy by saying:[212]

> [T]he distinguishing characteristic of adjudication lies in the fact that it confers on the affected party a peculiar form of participation in the decision, that of presenting proofs and reasoned arguments for a decision in his favor. Whatever heightens the significance of this participation lifts adjudication toward its optimum expression. Whatever destroys the meaning of that participation destroys the integrity of adjudication itself. Thus, participation through reasoned argument loses its meaning if the arbiter of the dispute is inaccessible to reason because he is insane, has been bribed, or is hopelessly prejudiced.

204 Eskridge and Frickey, 'The Making of the Legal Process' (n 192 above); Sebok, 'The Legal Process' (n 192 above).

205 Albert Sacks, 'Lon Luvois Fuller' (1978) 92 *Harvard Law Review* 349.

206 Lon Fuller, 'Reason and Fiat in Case Law' (1946) 59 *Harvard Law Review* 376.

207 Fuller, 'Positivism and Fidelity to Law' (n 150 above).

208 ibid 632.

209 ibid 661–69.

210 ibid 636.

211 Lon Fuller, 'The Forms and Limits of Adjudication' (1978) 92 *Harvard Law Review* 353.

212 ibid 364.

In this vein, Fuller argues that the integrity of the adjudicative process—its ability to sustain the legitimacy of the decision it produces—depends on whether an affected party has access to legal representation and whether the arbiter is impartial, complies with principles of due process, and responds to evidence and arguments presented in the context of a hearing.[213]

But Fuller also emphasises that legitimacy of adjudication also depend on whether these procedural constraints have a substantive impact on the ultimate decision. He notes that

> if the grounds for the decision fall completely outside the framework of the argument, making all that was discussed or proved at the hearing irrelevant—then the adjudicative process has become a sham, for the parties' participation in the process has lost all meaning.[214]

And while he concedes that reasons are not necessarily required in all cases, he argues that 'the fairness and effectiveness of adjudication are promoted by reasoned opinions' because they demonstrate 'that the arbiter has in fact understood and taken into account their proofs and arguments'.[215] This leads Fuller to conclude that adjudication 'assumes a burden of rationality not borne by any other form of social ordering' because '[w]e demand of an adjudicative decision a kind of rationality we do not expect of the results of contract or of voting'.[216]

III. ADMINISTRATIVE LAW AND JUDICIAL DEFERENCE

The analysis in this chapter can be distilled into a response to the question I posed at the outset of the book: do administrative officials have legitimate authority to interpret the law? I have argued that administrative officials do possess legitimate authority if they have been legally empowered by a democratically responsible branch of government to decide a question of law on behalf of the community, and their decision conveys concern and respect for persons affected by their decision in both a procedural and substantive sense. This response is complex, because it aims at developing a theoretical account of administrative law and judicial deference which is democratic, liberal, and anti-positivist in character; but it is also ambitious, because in order to construct such an account, one must navigate the polarising tendencies of jurisprudential debates about the nature of law and legal authority. Thus, any attempt to reconcile administrative law with the rule of law must confront a tension between the desire to maintain a democratic distribution of political authority and the desire to ensure that political authority is exercised in a manner which is fair and justifiable.

213 ibid 381–93.
214 ibid 388.
215 ibid 387–88.
216 ibid 366–67.

The front half of my response asserts that the legitimacy administrative law derives partly from the fairness of the democratic decision-making process, which enables subjects to participate on equal terms in collective decisions to resolve reasonable disagreements about what justice requires. Some of these democratic decisions involve rational and reasonable choices to authorise administrative officials to decide what should be done on behalf of the community in light of existing legal commitments. Thus, I argued that legal instruments which authorise administrative officials to decide questions of law provide subjects and other legal officials with sound reasons for respecting administrative decisions instead of holding out for their preferred outcome on the merits. Furthermore, I argued that the legitimate authority of administrative officials extends to matters of fundamental rights as well as more mundane matters of public policy, because questions of right cannot be neatly distinguished from questions of policy and, in any event, disputes about how to balance individual rights against the public interest is a question of justice which should be amenable to democratic deliberation.

However, I also noted that the legitimacy of democratic decisions is not purely procedural, because their legitimacy is also conditioned by the content of those decisions. More specifically, I argued that the legitimacy of democratic decisions also depends on whether it articulates reasons which are acceptable to 'people who are mutually motivated to find fair terms of social cooperation among political equals'.[217] While this condition does not rule out or restrain the delegation of authority to administrative officials per se, it resonates with a conception of the rule of law which promotes the dignity of legal subjects via principles of procedural fairness and reasonable justification. Thus, procedural principles like *audi alteram partem* and *nemo judex in sua causa* are not mere formalities but vital moral constraints for the legitimate exercise of administrative power, because they treat subjects as self-governing moral agents whose views about how the law ought to be interpreted and applied must be taken into account. Moreover, these procedural constraints have substantive bite on the content of administrative law, because an administrative decision-maker is duty-bound to render decisions which respond to the evidence and arguments tendered by the parties as well as more basic legal standards.[218] Thus, the legitimacy of administrative law depends on whether the decision is justified by reasons which are publicly accessible, intelligible, generalisable, consistent, disinterested, respond to evidence and arguments tendered by the parties, and are rationally connected to statutory objectives and constitutional values.

If my argument holds, then it also has implications for the practice of judicial review in a constitutional democracy. Contrary to Dicey's argument

[217] Gutmann and Thompson, *Democracy and Disagreement* (n 125 above) 1–52.

[218] David Dyzenhaus and Michael Taggart, 'Reasoned Decisions and Legal Theory' in Douglas Edlin (ed), *Common Law Theory* (Cambridge, Cambridge University Press, 2007) 134; Jerry Mashaw, 'Administrative Due Process' (n 182 above).

that judges have a monopoly over legal interpretation, it appears that judges share responsibility for interpreting the law with administrative officials. Therefore, the fact that a judge disagrees with an administrative decision on its merits is not a sufficient justification for judicial intervention, because it disregards or discounts the democratic basis for distributing legal authority to administrative officials in the first place. However, it is also irresponsible for judges to defer to an administrative decision merely on the basis that the original decision-maker was designated by statute to render the decision, because the legitimacy of administrative law depends partly on whether the decision treats people fairly and reasonably. Thus, judges should hone methods for scrutinising administrative decisions, which focus on whether an administrative decision is transparent, intelligible and justifiable, instead of attempting to ascertain whether its substance matches their interpretation of the law all things considered. While the burden of justification should be reasonable or proportionate to the impact of the decision on individual rights, there remains a logical space for administrative law and judicial deference.

Bibliography

Ackerman, Bruce (1998) *We the People: Transformations* (Cambridge, Belknap Press).

Alexander, Larry (1991) 'The Gap' 14 *Harvard Journal of Law and Public Policy* 695.

Allan, TRS (2000) 'The Rule of Law as the Foundation of Judicial Review' in Forsyth (ed), *Judicial Review and the Constitution* (Oxford, Hart Publishing).

—— (2002) 'The Constitutional Foundations of Judicial Review: Conceptual Conundrum or Interpretative Inquiry?' 61 *Cambridge Law Journal* 87.

—— [2003] 'Doctrine and Theory in Administrative Law: An Elusive Quest for the Limits of Jurisdiction' *Public Law* 429.

—— (2004) 'Legislative Supremacy and Legislative Intention: Interpretation, Meaning, and Authority' 63 *Cambridge Law Journal* 685.

—— (2006) 'Human Rights and Judicial Review: A Critique of "Due Deference"' 65 *Cambridge Law Journal* 671.

—— (2010) 'Deference, Defiance, and Doctrine: Defining the Limits of Judicial Review' 60 *University of Toronto Law Journal* 41.

Allars, Margaret (1995) 'On Deference to Tribunals With Deference to Dworkin' 20 *Queen's Law Journal* 163.

Aquinas, Thomas (2009) *Summa Theologica, Treatise on Law*, Alfred Freddoso (trans) (South Bend IN, St Augustine's Press).

Arai-Takahashi, Yutaka (2002) *The Margin of Appreciation Doctrine and the Principle of Proportionality in the Jurisprudence of the ECHR* (Oxford, Intersentia).

Aristotle (2009) *Nicomachean Ethics* (Oxford, Oxford University Press).

Arthurs, HW (1979) 'Rethinking Administrative Law: A Slightly Dicey Business' 17 *Osgoode Hall Law Journal* 1.

—— (1983) 'Protection against Judicial Review' 43 *Revue du Barreau* 277.

—— (1985) *'Without the Law': Administrative Justice and Legal Pluralism in Nineteenth-Century England* (Toronto, University of Toronto Press).

Austin, John (1885) *Lectures on Jurisprudence or the Philosophy of Positive Law*, 5th edn, Robert Campbell (ed) (London, John Murray).

—— (1995) *The Province of Jurisprudence Determined* (Cambridge, Cambridge University Press).

Baker, G Blaine (1983) 'Legal Education in Upper Canada 1785–1889: The Law Society as Educator' in David H Flaherty (ed), *Essays in the History of Canadian Law*, vol 2 (Toronto, University of Toronto Press) 49.

Baker, JH (2002) *An Introduction to English Legal History*, 4th edn (London, Butterworths).

Bamberger, Kenneth and Strauss, Peter (2009) '*Chevron*'s Two Steps' 95 *Virginia Law Review* 611.

Barak, Ahron (2007) 'Proportional Effect: The Israeli Experience' 57 *University of Toronto Law Journal* 369.

Barber, NW (2001) 'The Academic Mythologians' 21 *Oxford Journal of Legal Studies* 369.

Beerman, Jack (2009–10) 'End the *Chevron* Experiment Now: How *Chevron* Has Failed and Why It Can and Should Be Overruled' 42 *Connecticut Law Review* 779.

Bentham, Jeremy (1823) '*Truth v Ashhurst*' in John Bowring (ed), *The Works of Jeremy Bentham*, 11 vols (Edinburgh, W Tait, 1843) vol 5, 235.

—— (1843) 'Anarchical Fallacies; Being an Examination of the Declaration of Rights Issued During the French Revolution' in J Bowring (ed), *The Works of Jeremy Bentham* (Edinburgh, W Tait) 489.

—— (1970) *Of Laws in General*, HLA Hart (ed) (London, Athlone Press) 163.

—— (1988) *A Fragment on Government* (Cambridge, Cambridge University Press).

Berlin, Isaiah (1969) 'Two Concepts of Liberty' in Isaiah Berlin, *Four Essays on Liberty* (Oxford, Oxford University Press) 118.

—— (1998) 'My Intellectual Path', *New York Review of Books* (14 May 1998) 53.

—— (1999) *The First and the Last* (London, Granta).

Besson, Samantha (2005) 'Democracy, Law and Authority' 2 *Journal of Moral Philosophy* 89.

Bickel, Alexander (1986) *The Least Dangerous Branch: The Supreme Court at the Bar of Politics*, 2nd edn (New Haven CT, Yale University Press).

Biddle, Francis (1965) 'The Friendship of Holmes and Brandeis' 216(6) *Atlantic Monthly* 86.

Bingham, Tom [1998] 'Incorporation of the ECHR: The Opportunity and Challenge' 2 *Jersey Law Review* 257.

Blackburn, RW [1985] 'Dicey and the Teaching of Public Law' *Public Law* 679.

Blackstone, William (2001) *Commentaries on the Laws of England* (London, Cavendish Publishing).

Blake, Nicholas [2002] 'Importing Proportionality: Clarification or Confusion', *European Human Rights Law Review* 19.

Bogg, Alan (2002) 'In Defence of Correlativity: Authority, Autonomy and Mistaken Legal Directives' 15 *Ratio Juris* 84.

Bowring, J (ed) (1843) *The Works of Jeremy Bentham* (Edinburgh, W Tait).

Brandeis, Louis (1889) 'The Harvard Law School' 1 *Green Bag* 10.

—— (1889) 'Letter to James Thayer 1889' in James Bradley Thayer Papers (Cambridge MA, Harvard Law Library) Box 24, Folder 2.

—— (1905) 'The Opportunity in the Law' 39 *American Law Review* 555.

—— (1908) 'Brief for the Defendant in Error in *Muller v Oregon* 208 US 412 (1908)' reprinted in P Kurland and G Casper (eds), *Landmark Briefs and Arguments of the Supreme Court of the United States: Constitutional Law*, vol 16 (Arlington VA, University Publications of America, 1975) 63.

—— (1916) 'The Living Law' 10 *Illinois Law Review* 461.

—— (1916) 'Letter to Thomas Watt Gregory, 14 April 1916' in Melvin Urofsky and David Levy (eds), *Letters of Louis D Brandeis*, vol IV, (Albany NY, State University of New York, 1971) 165.

—— (1925) 'Letter to Felix Frankfurter 24 September 1925' in Urofsky and Levy (eds), *Half Brother, Half Son: The Letters of Louis D Brandeis to Felix Frankfurter* (Norman OK, University of Oklahoma Press, 1991).

Bressman, Lisa (2009) '*Chevron*'s Mistake' 58 *Duke Law Journal* 549.

Breyer, Steven, Stewart, Richard, Sunstein, Cass & Vermeule, Adrian (2006) *Administrative Law and Regulatory Policy: Problems, Text, and Cases*, 6th edn (New York, Aspen Publishers).

Butterfield, Herbert (1973) *The Whig Interpretation of History* (Harmondsworth, Penguin).

Cartier, Geneviève (2004) 'Procedural Fairness in Legislative Functions: The End of Judicial Abstinence' 53 *University of Toronto Law Journal* 217.

Christiano, Thomas (2004) 'The Authority of Democracy' 12 *Journal of Political Philosophy* 266.

Cicero, MT (1853) 'On the Commonwealth' in CD Yonge (ed), *The Treatises of M.T. Cicero on the Nature of the Gods; on Divination; on Fate; on the Republic; on the Laws; and on Standing for the Consulship* (London, Henry G Bohn).

Cohen, Felix (1935) 'Transcendental Nonsense and the Functional Approach' 35 *Columbia Law Review* 809.

—— (1937) 'The Problems of a Functional Jurisprudence' 1 *Modern Law Review* 5.

Cohen, Joshua (1996) 'Procedure and Substance in Deliberative Democracy' in Seyla Benhabib (ed), *Democracy and Difference: Contesting the Boundaries of the Political* (Princeton NJ, Princeton University Press) 120.

Collini, Stefan (1991) *Public Moralists: Political Thought and Intellectual Life in Britain 1850—1930* (Oxford, Clarendon Press).

Cooley, Thomas (1868) *A Treatise on the Constitutional Limitations Which Rest upon the Legislative Power of the States of the American Union* (Boston MA, Little, Brown, and Company).

Corwin, Edward (1909) 'The Supreme Court and the Fourteenth Amendment' 7 *Michigan Law Review* 643.

Cosgrove, Richard (1980) *The Rule of Law: Albert Venn Dicey, Victorian Jurist* (London, Macmillan).

Craig, Paul (1990) *Public Law and Democracy in the United Kingdom and the United States of America* (Oxford, Clarendon Press).

—— [1997] 'Formal and substantive conceptions of the rule of law: an analytical framework' *Public Law* 467.

—— (1998) 'Ultra Vires and the Foundations of Judicial Review' 57 *Cambridge Law Journal* 63.

—— [1999] 'Competing Models of Judicial Review' *Public Law* 428.

—— (1999) 'Unreasonableness and Proportionality in UK Law' in Evelyn Ellis (ed), *The Principle of Proportionality in the Laws of Europe* (Oxford, Hart Publishing) 85.

—— (2000) 'Ultra Vires and the Foundations of Judicial Review' in Forsyth (ed), *Judicial Review and the Constitution* (Oxford, Hart Publishing) 61.

—— (2008) *Administrative Law*, 6th edn (London, Sweet & Maxwell).

Cushman, Barry (1998) *Rethinking the New Deal Court: The Structure of a Constitutional Revolution* (Oxford, Oxford University Press).

de Smith, SA (1951) 'The Prerogative Writs' 11 *Cambridge Law Journal* 40.

—— (1955) 'The Right to a Hearing in English Administrative Law' 68 *Harvard Law Review* 569.

—— (1973) *Judicial Review of Administrative Action*, 3rd edn (London, Stevens & Sons Ltd).

de Smith, SA, Lord Woolf, and Jowell, JL (1995) *Judicial Review of Administrative Action*, 5th edn (London, Sweet & Maxwell).

DeWolfe Howe, Mark (ed) (1953) *Holmes-Laski Letters: The Correspondence of Mr Justice Holmes and Harold J Laski 1916–1935*, vol 1 (Cambridge, Harvard University Press).

—— (1963) *Justice Oliver Wendell Holmes: The Proving Years 1870–1882*, vol 2 (Cambridge, Belknap Press).

—— (1969) *Touched With Fire: Civil War Letters and Diary of Oliver Wendell Holmes, Jr 1861–1864* (New York, Da Capo Press).

Dicey, AV (1860) *The Privy Council: The Arnold Prize Essay 1860* (London, Whittaker).

—— (1868) 'The Legal Limits of Liberty' 3 *Fortnightly Review* (NS) 1.

—— (1871) 'Legal Education' 25 *MacMillans* 115.

—— (1874) 'Judicial Policy' 29 *Macmillan's* 473.

—— (1876) 'Modern English Law' 23 *Nation* 273.

—— (1878) 'Bentham' 27 *Nation* 352.

—— (1880) 'The Study of Jurisprudence' 5 *Law Magazine & Review* 382.

—— (1881) 'Sir George Bramwell and the English Bench' 33 *Nation* 468.

—— (1882) 'Fifty Years of Reform in England' 35 *Nation* 49.

—— (1883) *Can English Law be Taught at the Universities?* (London, MacMillan & Co).

—— (1883) 'A Sign of the Times in England' 37 *Nation* 30.

—— (1883) 'The Prevalence of Lawlessness in England' 37 *Nation* 95.

—— (1884) 'The Social Movement in England' 38 *Nation* 29.

—— (1884) 'The Social Movement in England—II' 38 *Nation* 49.

—— (1884) 'The Social Movement in England—III' 38 *Nation* 272.

—— (1885) 'The United States and the Swiss Confederation' 41 *Nation* 297.

—— (1894) 'The Referendum' 23 *National Review* 65.

—— (1899) 'The Teaching of English Law at Harvard' 76 *Contemporary Review* 742.

—— (1901) '*Droit Administratif* in Modern French Law' 17 *Law Quarterly Review* 302.

—— (1909–10) 'Blackstone's Commentaries' 54 *National Review* 653.

—— (1910) 'The Referendum and its Critics' 212 *Quarterly Review* 538.

—— (1915) 'The Development of Administrative Law in England' 31 *Law Quarterly Review* 148.

—— (1920) 'Law-Teaching, Oral and Written' in Herbert Hensley Henson (ed), *A Memoir of the Right Honourable Sir William Anson* (Oxford, Clarendon Press) 84.

—— (1959) *Introduction to the Study of the Constitution*, 10th edn (London, Macmillan & Co).

—— (1962) *Lectures on the Relation Between Law and Public Opinion in England During the Nineteenth Century*, 2nd edn (London, Macmillan & Co Ltd).

Diver, Colin (1985) 'Statutory Interpretation in the Administrative State' 133 *University of Pennsylvania Law Review* 549.

Dworkin, Ronald (1966) Lord Devlin and the Enforcement of Morals' 75 *Yale Law Journal* 986.

—— (1977) *Taking Rights Seriously* (London, Duckworth).

—— (1996) *Freedom's Law: The Moral Reading of the American Constitution* (Cambridge MA, Harvard University Press).

—— (1998) 'The Partnership Conception of Democracy' 86 *California Law Review* 453.

—— (1986) *Law's Empire* (London, Fontana).

—— (2004) 'Hart's Postscript and the Character of Political Philosophy' 24 *Oxford Journal of Legal Studies* 1.

—— (2006) *Justice in Robes* (Belknap Press, Cambridge).

—— (2011) *Justice for Hedgehogs* (Cambridge MA, Harvard University Press).

Dyzenhaus, David (1993) 'Dicey's Shadow' 43 *University of Toronto Law Journal* 127.

—— (1997) 'The Politics of Deference: Judicial Review and Democracy' in Michael Taggart (ed), *The Province of Administrative Law* (Oxford, Hart Publishing) 279.

—— (1998) 'Law as Justification: Etienne Mureinik's Conception of Legal Culture' 14 *South African Journal of Human Rights* 11.

—— (1999) 'Recrafting the Rule of Law' in David Dyzenhaus (ed), *Recrafting the Rule of Law: The Limits of Legal Order* (Oxford, Hart Publishing).

—— (2000) 'Form and Substance in the Rule of Law: A Democratic Justification for Judicial Review?' in Christopher Forsyth (ed), *Judicial Review and the Constitution* (Oxford, Hart Publishing) 141.

—— (2001) 'Hobbes and the Legitimacy of Law' 20 *Law & Philosophy* 461.

—— [2002] 'Formalism's Hollow Victory' *New Zealand Law Review* 525.

—— (2004) 'The Left and the Question of Law' 17 *Canadian Journal of Law and Jurisprudence* 7.

—— (2005) 'The Logic of the Rule of Law: Lessons from Willis' 55 *University of Toronto Law Journal* 691.

—— (2006) *The Constitution of Law: Legality in a Time of Emergency* (Cambridge, Cambridge University Press).

—— (2012) 'Hobbes on the Authority of Law' in David Dyzenhaus and Thomas Poole (eds), *Hobbes and the Law* (Cambridge, Cambridge University Press).

Dyzenhaus, David and Fox-Decent, Evan (2001) 'Rethinking the Process/Substance Distinction: *Baker v Canada*' 51 *University of Toronto Law Journal* 193.

Elliott, Mark (2000) 'The Ultra Vires Doctrine in a Constitutional Setting: Still the Central Principle of Administrative Law' in Christopher Forsyth (ed), *Judicial Review and the Constitution* (Oxford, Hart Publishing).

—— (2001) *The Constitutional Foundations of Judicial Review* (Oxford, Hart Publishing).

Ellis, Evelyn (1999) (ed), *The Principle of Proportionality in the Laws of Europe* (Oxford, Hart Publishing).

Endicott, Timothy (2003) 'Constitutional Logic' 53 *University of Toronto Law Journal* 201.

Engle, Eric (2012) 'The History of the General Principle of Proportionality: An Overview' 10 *Dartmouth Law Journal* 1.

Eskridge, William and Frickey, Philip (1993) 'The Making of Legal Process' (1993) 107 *Harvard Law Review* 2031.

Farber, Daniel [1995] 'Reinventing Brandeis: Legal Pragmatism for the Twenty-First Century' *University of Illinois Law Review* 163.

Feldman, David [2006] 'Human Rights, Terrorism and Risk: The Roles of Politicians and Judges' *Public Law* 364.

Fennell, P (1986) '*Roberts v. Hopwood:* The Rule Against Socialism' 13 *Journal of Law & Society* 401.

Finnis, John (2011) *Natural Law and Natural Rights*, 2nd edn (Oxford, Oxford University Press).

Fisch, Max (1986) 'Justice Holmes, The Prediction Theory of the Law, and Pragmatism' in Kenneth Ketner and Christian Floesel (eds), *Peirce, Semeiotic and Pragmatism* (Bloomington IN, Indiana University Press).

Forbath, William (1991) *Law and the Shaping of the American Labor Movement* (Cambridge MA, Harvard University Press).

Ford, Paul (ed) (1899) *The Writings of Thomas Jefferson*, vol 10 (New York, GP Putnam's Sons, 1899).

Forsyth, Christopher (ed) (2000) *Judicial Review and the Constitution* (Oxford, Hart Publishing).

—— (2000) 'Of Fig Leaves and Fairy Tales: The Ultra Vires Doctrine, the Sovereignty of Parliament and Judicial Review' in Christopher Forsyth (ed), *Judicial Review and the Constitution* (Oxford, Hart Publishing).

—— 'Heat and Light: A Plea for Reconciliation' in Forsyth (ed), *Judicial Review and the Constitution* (Oxford, Hart Publishing).

—— (2007) 'Showing the Fly the Way Out of the Flybottle: The Value of Formalism and Conceptual Reasoning in Administrative Law' 66 *Cambridge Law Journal* 325.

—— *et al* (eds), *Effective Judicial Review: A Cornerstone of Good Government* (Oxford, Oxford University Press).

Forsyth, Christopher and Dring, Emma (2010) 'The Final Frontier: The Emergence of Material Error of Fact as a Ground for Judicial Review' in Christopher Forsyth *et al* (eds), *Effective Judicial Review: A Cornerstone of Good Government* (Oxford, Oxford University Press) 245.

Forsyth, Christopher and Hare, Ivan (eds) (1998) *The Golden Metwand and the Crooked Cord: Essays on Public Law in Honour of Sir William Wade* (Oxford, Oxford University Press).

Fox, William (1889) *Regimental Losses in the American Civil War, 1861—1865* (Albany, Albany Publishing).

Fox-Decent, Evan (2004) 'The Internal Morality of Administration: The Form and Structure of Reasonableness' in David Dyzenhaus, *The Unity of Public Law* (Oxford, Hart Publishing) 143.

Frankfurter, Felix (1912) 'Letter to Learned Hand, 23 September 1912' reprinted in Sanford Levinson, 'The Democratic Faith of Felix Frankfurter' (1973) 25 *Stanford Law Review* 430, 433.

—— (1915) 'The Present Approach to Constitutional Decisions on the Bill of Rights' 28 *Harvard Law Review* 790.

—— (1916) 'The Constitutional Opinions of Justice Holmes' 29 *Harvard Law Review* 683.

—— (1916) 'Brandeis and the Shoe Machinery Company', *New Republic* (4 March 1916) 117.

—— (1916) 'The Nomination of Mr Justice Brandeis', *New Republic* (5 February 1916) reprinted in Philip Kurland (ed), *Felix Frankfurter on the Supreme Court:*

Extrajudicial Essays on the Court and the Constitution (Cambridge, Belknap Press, 1970) 43.

—— (1916) 'Hours of Labor and Realism in Constitutional Law' 29 *Harvard Law Review* 353.

—— (1921) 'Press Censorship by Judicial Construction', *New Republic* (30 March 1921) 124.

—— (1922) 'Mr Justice Holmes', *New Republic* (20 December 1922) 84.

—— (1923) 'Twenty Years of Mr. Justice Holmes' Constitutional Opinions' 36 *Harvard Law Review* 909.

—— (1924) 'A Note on Advisory Opinions' 37 *Harvard Law Review* 1002.

—— (1924) 'The Red Terror of Judicial Reform', *The New Republic* (1 October 1924) reprinted in Philip Kurland (ed), *Felix Frankfurter on the Supreme Court: Extrajudicial Essays on the Court and the Constitution* (Cambridge, Belknap Press, 1970) 142.

—— (1924) 'The American Judge' reprinted in Philip Kurland (ed), *Felix Frankfurter on the Supreme Court: Extrajudicial Essays on the Court and the Constitution* (Cambridge, Belknap Press, 1970) 149.

—— (1926) 'Mr Justice Holmes' *New Republic* (17 March 1926) 89.

—— (1927) 'Mr. Justice Holmes and the Constitution' 41 *Harvard Law Review* 121.

—— (1927) 'The Task of Administrative Law' 75 *University of Pennsylvania Law Review* 614.

—— (1930) Review of *The Dissenting Opinions of Mr Justice Holmes* 16 *Virginia Law Review* 743.

—— (1927) 'The Case of Sacco and Vanzetti' (March 1927) 139 *Atlantic Monthly* 409.

—— (1930) *The Public and Its Government* (New Haven CT, Yale University Press).

—— (1930) 'Democracy and the Expert' *Atlantic Monthly* (November 1930) 649.

—— (1931) 'Mr. Justice Brandeis and the Constitution' 45 *Harvard Law Review* 33.

—— (1937) *The Commerce Clause Under Marshall, Taney and Waite* (Chapel Hill NC, University of North Carolina Press).

—— (1937) 'Letter to Louis Brandeis (26 March 1937)' as quoted in Urofsky, *Felix Frankfurter: Judicial Restraint and Individual Liberties* (Boston MA, Twayne Publishers, 1991).

—— (1963) 'Letter to Arthur Schlesinger (18 June 1963)' in Max Freedman (ed), *Roosevelt and Frankfurter: Their Correspondence 1928–1945* (Boston, MA, Little Brown and Company, 1967) 25.

Frankfurter, Felix and Hart, Henry Jr (1934) 'The Business of the Supreme Court at October Term, 1933' (1934) 48 *Harvard Law Review* 238.

Frankfurter, Felix and Landis, James (1925) 'The Compact Clause of the Constitution—A Study in Interstate Adjustments' 34 *Yale Law Journal* 685.

Freedman, Max (ed) (1967) *Roosevelt and Frankfurter: Their Correspondence 1928–1945* (Boston MA, Little, Brown and Company).

Freund, Ernst (1928) *Administrative Powers Over Persons and Property: A Comparative Survey* (Chicago IL, University of Chicago Press).

Friedman, Barry (1998) 'The History of the Countermajoritarian Difficulty, Part One: The Road to Judicial Supremacy' 73 *New York University Law Review* 333.

—— (2002) 'The History of the Countermajoritarian Difficulty, Part Two: Reconstruction's Political Court' 91 *Georgetown Law Journal* 1.

Friedman, RB (1968) 'An Introduction to Mill's Theory of Authority' in JB Schneewind (ed), *Mill: A Collection of Critical Essays* (London, Macmillan) 379.

Friedrich, CJ (1958) 'Authority, Reason and Discretion' in CJ Friedrich (ed), *NOMOS I: Authority* (Cambridge, Cambridge University Press) 35.

Fuller, Lon (1958) 'Positivism and Fidelity to Law: A Reply to Professor Hart' 71 *Harvard Law Review* 630.

—— (1969) *The Morality of Law*, revised edn (New Haven CT, Yale University Press).

Gabin, Sanford (1976) 'Judicial Review, James Bradley Thayer, and the "Reasonable Doubt" Test' 3 *Hastings Constitutional Law Quarterly* 961.

Galligan, DJ (1982) 'Judicial Review and the Textbook Writers' 2 *Oxford Journal of Legal Studies* 257.

—— (1986) *Discretionary Powers: a legal study of official discretion* (Oxford, Clarendon Press).

Girard, Philip (2005) *Bora Laskin: Bringing Law to Life* (Toronto, University of Toronto Press).

Goodnow, Frank (1893) *Comparative Administrative Law: An Analysis of the Administrative Systems National and Local, of the United States, England, France and Germany* (New York, GP Putnam's Sons).

—— (1905) *The Principles of the Administrative Law of the United States* (New York, GP Putnam's Sons).

Gordon, DM (1929) 'The Relation of Facts to Jurisdiction' 45 *Law Quarterly Review* 459.

—— (1931) 'The Observance of Law as a Condition of Jurisdiction' 47 *Law Quarterly Review* 386.

—— (1933) '"Administrative" Tribunals and the Courts' 49 *Law Quarterly Review* 94.

—— (1933) 'Case Comment' 11 *Canadian Bar Review* 510.

—— (1960) 'Conditional or Contingent Jurisdiction of Tribunals' 1 *University of British Columbia Law Review* 185.

Gordon, Robert (1981) 'Book Review of *Tort Law in America: An Intellectual History* by G Edward White 94 *Harvard Law Review* 903.

—— (2005) 'Willis's American Counterparts: The Legal Realists' Defence of Administration' 55 *University of Toronto Law Journal* 405.

Gray, John Chipman (1909) *The Nature and Sources of Law* (New York, Columbia University Press).

Grey, Thomas (1989) 'Holmes and Legal Pragmatism' 41 *Stanford Law Review* 787.

Griffith, John (1968) 'Judges in Politics: England' 3 *Government and Opposition* 485.

—— (1978) *Administrative Law and the Judges: The Pritt Memorial Lecture 1978* (London, Haldane Society of Socialist Lawyers).

—— (1979) 'The Political Constitution' 42 *Modern Law Review* 1.

—— (1997) *The Politics of the Judiciary*, 5th edn (London, Fontana Press).

—— (2000) 'The Brave New World of Sir John Laws' 63 *Modern Law Review* 160.

Gutmann, Amy and Thompson, Dennis (1996) *Democracy and Disagreement* (Cambridge, Belknap Press).

—— (2002) 'Deliberative Democracy Beyond Process' (2002) 10 *Journal of Political Philosophy* 153.
—— (2004) *Why Deliberative Democracy?* (Princeton NJ, Princeton University Press).
—— (2009) 'Moral Disagreement in a Democracy' in Matt Zwolinski (ed), *Arguing About Political Philosophy* (New York, Routledge).
Haldane, RB (1899) 'Lord Watson' 11 *Juridical Review* 278.
—— (1922) 'The Work for the Empire of the Judicial Committee of the Privy Council' 1 *Cambridge Law Journal* 143.
Hall, James Parker (1909) 'James Bradley Thayer' in William Draper Lewis (ed), *Great American Lawyers* (Philadelphia PA, John C Winston Company) 345.
Halpin, Andrew (2001) 'The Theoretical Controversy Concerning Judicial Review' 64 *Modern Law Review* 500.
Hare, Ivan (1998) 'The Separation of Powers and Judicial Review for Errors of Law' in Christopher Forsyth and Ivan Hare (eds), *The Golden Metwand and the Crooked Cord: Essays on Public Law in Honour of Sir William Wade QC* (Oxford, Clarendon Press) 113.
Harlow, C (1994) 'Changing the Mindset: The Place of Theory in English Public Law' 14 *Oxford Journal of Legal Studies* 419.
Harlow, Carol and Rawlings, Richard (2009) *Law and Administration*, 3rd edn (Cambridge, Cambridge University Press).
Harrison, Ross (1993) *Democracy* (London, Routledge).
Hart, HLA (1958) 'Positivism and the Separation of Law and Morals' 71 *Harvard Law Review* 593.
—— (1965) 'Book Review: "The Morality of Law"' 78 *Harvard Law Review* 1281.
—— (1994) *The Concept of Law*, 2nd edn (Oxford, Clarendon Press).
Hart, Henry (1953) 'The Power of Congress to Limit the Jurisdiction of Federal Courts: An Exercise in Dialectic' 66 *Harvard Law Review* 1362.
Hart, Henry and Sacks, Albert (1994) *The Legal Process: Basic Problems in the Making and Application of Law*, William Eskridge Jr and Philip Frickey (eds) (Westbury, Foundation Press).
Hart, Henry and Wechsler, Herbert (1953) *The Federal Courts and the Federal System* (New York, Foundation Press).
Harvison Young, Alison (1993) 'Keeping the Courts at Bay: The Canadian Human Rights Commission and Its Counterparts in Britain and Northern Ireland: Some Comparative Lessons' 43 *University of Toronto Law Journal* 65.
—— (1993) 'Human Rights Tribunals and the Supreme Court of Canada: Reformulating Deference' 13 Admin LR (2d) 206.
Hayek, FA (1944) *The Road to Serfdom* (London, Routledge).
Henderson, Edith G (1963) *Foundations of English Administrative Law: Certiorari and Mandamus in the Seventeenth Century* (Cambridge MA, Harvard University Press).
Henderson, Gerard (1919) 'Railway Valuation and the Courts' 33 *Harvard Law Review* 902.
Hershovitz, Scott (2003) 'Legitimacy, Democracy, and Razian Authority' 9 *Legal Theory* 201.
—— (2011) 'The Role of Authority' 11 *Philosophers' Imprint* 1.
Hewart, Gordon (1929) *The New Despotism* (London, Ernest Benn Ltd).

Hibbits, Bernard (1989) 'A Bridle for Leviathan: The Supreme Court and the Board of Commerce' 21 *Ottawa Law Review* 65.

—— (1994) 'The Politics of Principle: Albert Venn Dicey and the Rule of Law' 23 *Anglo-American Law Review* 1.

Hickman, Tom (2010) *Public Law after the Human Rights Act* (Oxford, Hart Publishing).

Hobbes, Thomas (1996) *Leviathan*, Richard Tuck (ed) (Cambridge, Cambridge University Press).

Hogg, Peter (1974) 'Judicial Review: How Much Do We Need?' 20 *McGill Law Journal* 157.

Holmes, Oliver Wendell Jr (1864) 'Letter to his parents 16 May 1864' in Mark DeWolfe Howe (ed), *Touched With Fire: Civil War Letters and Diary of Oliver Wendell Holmes, Jr 1861—1864* (New York, Da Capo Press, 1969) 121.

—— (1870) 'Codes, and the Arrangement of the Law' 5 *American Law Review* 1.

—— (1872) 'Book Notice' 6 *American Law Review* 723.

—— (1880) 'Book Notice' 14 *American Law Review* 233.

—— (1895) 'Memorial Day Address, 30 May 1895' in Max Lerner (ed), *The Mind and Faith of Justice Holmes* (Boston MA, Little, Brown and Company, 1946) 18.

—— (1893) 'Letter to James Thayer, 2 November 1893' in Mark DeWolfe Howe, *Research materials relating to life of Oliver Wendell Holmes, Jr, 1858–1968: General Correspondence, General, Group II: Box 18, Folder 1.*

—— (1897) 'The Path of Law' 10 *Harvard Law Review* 457.

—— (1918) 'Natural Law' 32 *Harvard Law Review* 40.

—— (1953) 'Letter to Harold Laski, 28 July 1916' in Mark DeWolfe Howe (ed), *Holmes-Laski Letters: The Correspondence of Mr Justice Holmes and Harold J Laski 1916–1935*, vol 1 (Cambridge MA, Harvard University Press) 8.

—— (1953) 'Letter to Harold Laski, 23 October 1926' in Mark DeWolfe Howe, *The Correspondence of Mr Justice Holmes and Harold J Laski 1916–1925*, vol 2 (Cambridge MA, Harvard University Press) 888.

—— (1928) 'Letter to Arthur Garfield Hays, 20 April 1928', Holmes Papers (Harvard Law School).

—— (1949) *The Common Law* (Boston, MA, Little Brown and Company).

Hood Phillips, Owen [1985] 'Dicey's *Law of the Constitution*: A Personal View' *Public Law* 587.

Hook, Jay (1993) 'A Brief Life of James Bradley Thayer' 88 *Northwestern University Law Review* 1.

Horwitz, Morton (1992) *The Transformation of American Law 1870–1960: The Crisis of Legal Orthodoxy* (Oxford, Oxford University Press).

Hunt, Murray [1999] 'Judicial Review after the Human Rights Act' 2 *Queen Mary Westfield College Law Journal* 14.

—— (2003) 'Sovereignty's Blight: Why Contemporary Public Law Needs the Concept of "Due Deference"' in Nicholas Bamforth and Peter Leyland (eds), *Public Law in a Multi-Layered Constitution* (Oxford, Hart Publishing) 337.

Hurd, Heidi (1991) 'Challenging Authority' 100 *Yale Law Journal* 1611.

Huscroft, Grant (ed) (2008) *Expounding the Constitution: Essays in Constitutional Theory* (Cambridge, Cambridge University Press).

Hutchinson, Michael (1999) 'The Margin of Appreciation Doctrine in the European Court of Human Rights' 48 *International and Comparative Law Quarterly* 638.

Iacobucci, Frank (2002) 'Articulating a Rational Standard of Review Doctrine: A Tribute to John Willis' 27 *Queen's Law Journal* 859.

Issalys, Pierre (1978) 'The Professions Tribunal and the Control of Ethical Conduct among Professionals' 24 *McGill Law Journal* 588.

Jackson, Robert (1959) *The Chief: The Biography of Gordon Hewart Lord Chief Justice of England 1922–40* (London, George G Harrap & Co Ltd).

Jacobs, Laverne (2008) 'Developments in Administrative Law: The 2007–2008 Term—The Impact of *Dunsmuir*' *Supreme Court Law Review* (2d) 1.

Jaffe, L (1932–33) 'The Contributions of Mr Justice Brandeis to Administrative Law' 18 *Iowa Law Review* 213.

—— (1949) 'The Judicial Universe of Mr. Justice Frankfurter' 62 *Harvard Law Review* 357.

—— (1957) 'Judicial Review: Constitutional and Jurisdictional Fact' 70 *Harvard Law Review* 953.

—— (1965) *Judicial Control of Administrative Action* (Boston MA, Little, Brown and Company).

Jaffe, Louis and Nathanson, Nathaniel (1976) *Administrative Law: Cases and Materials*, 4th edn (Boston MA, Little, Brown and Company).

Janisch, Hudson (1985) 'Bora Laskin and Administrative Law: An Unfinished Journey' 35 *University of Toronto Law Journal* 557.

Jefferson, Thomas (1820) 'Letter to William Charles Jarvis, 28 September 1820' in Paul Ford (ed), *The Writings of Thomas Jefferson*, vol 10 (New York, GP Putnam's Sons, 1899) 161.

Jennings, W Ivor (1935) 'In Praise of Dicey' 13 *Public Administration* 123.

—— (1936) 'The courts and administrative law—the experience of English housing legislation' 49 *Harvard Law Review* 426.

—— (1940) 'Book Review of *Introduction to the Study of the Law of the Constitution* by AV Dicey' 3 *Modern Law Review* 321.

—— (1959) *The Law and the Constitution*, 5th edn (London, University of London Press).

Jordan, Constance (2013) *Reason and Imagination: The Selected Correspondence of Learned Hand: 1897–1961* (Oxford, Oxford University Press).

Jowell, Jeffrey [1999] 'Of Vires and Vacuums: The Constitutional Context of Judicial Review' *Public Law* 448.

—— [2003] 'Judicial deference: servility, civility or institutional capacity' *Public Law* 592.

—— (2003) 'Judicial Deference and Human Rights: A Question of Competence' in Paul Craig and Richard Rawlings (eds), *Law and Administration in Europe: Essays in Honour of Carol Harlow* (Oxford, Oxford University Press) 67.

Jowell, Jeffrey and Cooper, Jonathan (2003), 'Introduction' in Jeffrey Jowell and Jonathan Cooper (eds), *Delivering Rights: How the Human Rights Act is Working* (Oxford, Hart Publishing).

Kaplan, William (2009) *Canadian Maverick: The Life and Times of Ivan C. Rand* (Toronto, University of Toronto Press).

Kavanagh, Aileen (2008) 'Deference or Defiance? The Limits of the Judicial Role in Constitutional Adjudication' in Grant Huscroft (ed), *Expounding the Constitution: Essays in Constitutional Theory* (Cambridge, Cambridge University Press) 194.

—— (2009) *Constitutional Review under the UK Human Rights Act* (Cambridge, Cambridge University Press).

—— (2010) 'Defending Deference in Public Law and Constitutional Theory: A Reply to TRS Allan' 126 *Law Quarterly Review* 236.

—— (2010) 'Judicial Restraint in the Pursuit of Justice' 60 *University of Toronto Law Journal* 23.

Kellogg, Frederic (2007) *Oliver Wendell Holmes, Jr., Legal Theory, and Judicial Restraint* (Cambridge, Cambridge University Press).

Kelsen, Hans (1967) *Pure Theory of Law* (Berkeley CA, University of California Press).

Kennedy, WPM (1937) 'The British North America Act: Past and Future' 15 *Canadian Bar Review* 394.

Kens, Paul (1991) 'The Source of a Myth: Police Powers of the States and Laissez Faire Constitutionalism, 1900–1937' 35 *American Journal of Legal History* 70.

Ketner, Kenneth and Floesel, Christian (eds) (1986) *Peirce, Semeiotic and Pragmatism* (Bloomington IN, Indiana University Press).

Kimball, Bruce (2007) 'Langdell on Contracts and Legal Reasoning: Correcting the Holmesian Caricature' 25 *Law and History Review* 346.

King, Jeff (2008) 'Institutional Approaches to Judicial Restraint' 28 *Oxford Journal of Legal Studies* 409.

Kramer, Larry (2004) *The People Themselves: Popular Constitutionalism and Judicial Review* (Oxford, Oxford University Press).

—— (2012) 'Judicial Supremacy and the End of Judicial Restraint' 100 *California Law Review* 621.

Kurland, Philip (ed) (1970) *Felix Frankfurter on the Supreme Court: Extrajudicial Essays on the Court and the Constitution* (Cambridge, Belknap Press).

Kurland, P and Casper, G (eds) (1975) *Landmark Briefs and Arguments of the Supreme Court of the United States: Constitutional Law*, vol 16 (Arlington VA, University Publications of America).

Landis, James (1938) *The Administrative Process* (New Haven CT, Yale University Press).

—— (1941) 'Mr Justice Brandeis and the Harvard Law School' 55 *Harvard Law Review* 184.

Langdell, CC (1871) *A Selection of Cases on the Law of Contracts* (Boston MA, Little, Brown, and Company).

Laski, Harold (1925–26) 'Judicial Review of Social Policy in England: A Study of *Roberts v. Hopwood*' 39 *Harvard Law Review* 832.

Laskin, Bora (1937) 'The Ontario Municipal Board' (LLM thesis, Harvard University).

—— (1937) 'Picketing: A Comparison of Canadian and American Doctrines' 15 *Canadian Bar Review* 10.

—— (1937) 'The Labour Injunction in Canada: A Caveat' 15 *Canadian Bar Review* 270.

—— (1952) 'Certiorari to Labour Boards: The Apparent Futility of Privative Clauses' 30 *Canadian Bar Review* 986.

—— (1972) 'John Willis: An Appreciation' 22 *University of Toronto Law Journal* 3.

—— (1973) 'The Function of Law' 11 *Alberta Law Review* 118.

—— (1982–83) 'Foreword' 7 *Dalhousie Law Journal* 3.

Laws, John (1998) '*Wednesbury*' in Christopher Forsyth and Ivan Hare (eds), *The Golden Metwand and the Crooked Cord: Essays on Public Law in Honour of Sir William Wade* (Oxford, Oxford University Press) 185.

—— (2010) 'Illegality: The Problem of Jurisdiction' in Michael Supperstone, James Goudie, and Sir Paul Walker (eds), *Judicial Review*, 4th edn (London, LexisNexis).

Lawson, FH (1959) 'Dicey Revisited' 7 *Political Studies* 109.

Lawson, Gary and Kam, Stephen (2013) 'Making Law Out of Nothing at All: The Origins of the *Chevron* Doctrine' 65 *Administrative Law Review* 1.

Leckey, Robert (2010) 'Complexifying *Roncarelli*'s Rule of Law' 55 *McGill Law Journal* 721.

Lewans, Matthew (2012) 'Deference and Reasonableness Since *Dunsmuir*' 38 *Queen's Law Journal* 59.

Lerner, Max (ed) (1946) *The Mind and Faith of Justice Holmes* (Boston MA, Little, Brown and Company).

Letwin, Shirley (1965) *The Pursuit of Certainty* (Cambridge, Cambridge University Press).

Leuchtenburg, William (1996) *The Supreme Court Reborn: The Constitutional Revolution in the Age of Roosevelt* (Oxford, Oxford University Press).

Leventhal, Harold (1974) 'Environmental Decisionmaking and the Role of the Courts' 122 *University of Pennsylvania Law Review* 509.

Levinson, Sanford (1973) 'The Democratic Faith of Felix Frankfurter' 25 *Stanford Law Review* 430.

Levy, David (1969) 'The Lawyer as Judge: Brandeis' View of the Legal Profession' 22 *Oklahoma Law Review* 374.

Levy, David and Murphy, Bruce (1980) 'Preserving the Progressive Spirit in a Conservative Time: The Joint Reform Efforts of Justice Brandeis and Professor Felix Frankfurter, 1916–1933' 78 *Michigan Law Review* 1252.

Lewis, William Draper (ed) (1909) *Great American Lawyers* (Philadelphia PA, John C Winston Company).

Lewis, Tom (2007) 'What not to Wear: Religious Rights, the European Court, and the Margin of Appreciation' 56 *International and Comparative Law Quarterly* 395.

Lobban, Michael (1991) *The Common Law and English Jurisprudence 1760–1850* (Oxford, Clarendon Press).

Luban, David (1994) 'Justice Holmes and the Metaphysics of Judicial Restraint' 44 *Duke Law Journal* 449.

Loughlin, Martin (1992) *Public Law and Political Theory* (Oxford, Clarendon Press).

—— (2005) The Functionalist Style in Public Law' 55 *University of Toronto Law Journal* 361.

Lyon, Noel (1971) 'Case Comment' 49 *Canadian Bar Review* 365.

—— (1980) 'Case Comment' 58 *Canadian Bar Review* 646.

—— (1987) 'Is Amendment of Section 96 Really Necessary?' 36 *University of New Brunswick Law Journal* 79.

MacDonald, RA (1983) 'Comment' 17 *University of British Columbia Law Review* 111.

MacLauchlan, HW (1986) 'Judicial Review of Administrative Interpretations of Law: How Much Formalism Can We Reasonably Bear?' 36 *University of Toronto Law Journal* 343.

Maine, Sir Henry (1885) *Popular Government* (London, John Murray).

Manning, John (1996) 'Constitutional Structure and Judicial Deference to Agency Interpretations of Agency Rules' 96 *Columbia Law Review* 612.

Marmor, Andrei (2005) 'Authority, Equality and Democracy' 18 *Ratio Juris* 315.

Mashaw, Jerry (2010) 'Federal Administration and Administrative Law in the Gilded Age' 119 *Yale Law Journal* 1362.

—— (2012) *Creating the Administrative Constitution: The Lost One Hundred Years of American Administrative Law* (New Haven CT, Yale University Press).

McAuslan, P (1978) 'Administrative Law and Administrative Theory: The Dismal Performance of Administrative Lawyers' 9 *Cambrian Law Review* 40.

Menand, Louis (2001) *The Metaphysical Club: A Story of Ideas in America* (New York, Farrar, Strauss and Giroux).

Mendelson, Wallace (1957) 'Mr. Justice Frankfurter on Administrative Law' 19 *Journal of Politics* 441.

—— (ed) (1964) *Felix Frankfurter: A Tribute* (New York, Reynal & Company).

Mennel, Robert and Compston, Christine (eds) (1996) *Holmes & Frankfurter: Their Correspondence, 1912–1934* (Hanover NH, University Press of New England).

Merrill, Thomas (1994) 'Textualism and the Future of the *Chevron* Doctrine' 72 *Washington University Law Quarterly* 351.

Mill, John Stuart (1859) *On Liberty* (London, JW Parker & Son).

Misak, Cheryl (2013) *The American Pragmatists* (Oxford, Oxford University Press).

Moglen, Eben (1993) 'The Transformation of Morton Horwitz' 93 *Columbia Law Review* 1042.

Mommsen, Theodor and Krueger, Paul (eds), Watson, Alan (trans) (1985) *The Digest of Justinian* (Philadelphia PA, University of Pennsylvania Press).

Monaghan, Henry (1983) '*Marbury* and the Administrative State' 83 *Columbia Law Review* 1.

Mullan, David (1972) 'The Jurisdictional Fact Doctrine in the Supreme Court of Canada—A Mitigating Plea' 10 *Osgoode Hall Law Journal* 440.

—— (1982) 'Developments in Administrative Law: The 1980–81 Term' 3 *Supreme Court Law Review* 1.

—— (1982) 'The Uncertain Constitutional Position of Canada's Administrative Appeal Tribunals' 14 *Ottawa Law Review* 239.

—— (1983) 'Developments in Administrative Law: The 1981–82 Term' 5 *Supreme Court Law Review* 1.

—— (1985) 'The Re-emergence of Jurisdictional Error' 14 *Administrative Law Reports* 326.

—— (1987) 'The Supreme Court of Canada and Jurisdictional Error: Compromising *New Brunswick Liquor*' 1 *Canadian Journal of Administrative Law & Practice* 71.

—— (1991) 'Of Chaff Midst the Corn: *American Farm Bureau Federation v Canadian Import Tribunal)* and Patent Unreasonableness Review' (1991) 45 Admin LR 264.

—— (1992) 'A Blast from the Past: A Surreptitious Resurgence of *Metropolitan Life*?' 5 *Administrative Law Reports* (2d) 117.

—— (1999) 'Recent Developments in Administrative Law: The Apparent Triumph of Deference!' 12 *Canadian Journal of Administrative Law & Practice* 192.

—— (2004) 'Deference from *Baker* to *Suresh* and Beyond: Interpreting the Conflicting Signals' in David Dyzenhaus (ed), *The Unity of Public Law* (Oxford, Hart Publishing) 21.

Nathanson, Nathaniel (1950) 'Administrative Discretion in the Interpretation of Statutes' 3 *Vanderbuilt Law Review* 470.

—— (1957) 'Mr. Justice Frankfurter and Administrative Law' 67 *Yale Law Journal* 240.

Nolte, Georg (1994) 'General Principles of German and European Administrative Law—A Comparison in Historical Perspective' 57 *Modern Law Review* 191.

Norman, Ken (1969) 'The Privative Clause: Virile or Futile?' 34 *Saskatchewan Law Review* 334.

Note (2005) '"How Clear is Clear" in *Chevron*'s Step One?' 118 *Harvard Law Review* 1687.

O'Connell, Jeff and Dart, Nancy (1985) 'The House of Truth: Home of the Young Frankfurter and Lippmann' 35 *Catholic University Law Review* 79.

Parris, Henry (1969) *Constitutional Bureaucracy: The Development of British Central Administration since the Eighteenth Century* (London, George Allen & Unwin Ltd).

Parrish, Michael (1982) *Felix Frankfurter and His Times: The Reform Years* (New York, The Free Press).

Peters, Shawn (2000) *Judging Jehovah's Witnesses: Religious Persecution and the Dawn of the Rights Revolution* (Lawrence, University Press of Kansas).

Phillips, Harlan (1960) *Felix Frankfurter Reminisces* (New York, Reynal & Company).

Pierce, Richard Jr (1995) 'The Supreme Court's New Hypertextualism: An Invitation to Cacophony and Incoherence in the Administrative State' 95 *Columbia Law Review* 749.

Pink, J (1965) 'Judicial 'Jurisdiction' in the Presence of Privative Clauses' 23 *University of Toronto Faculty Law Review* 5.

Poole, Thomas (2009) 'The Reformation of English Administrative Law' 68 *Cambridge Law Journal* 142.

Posner, Richard (2012) 'The Rise and fall of Judicial Self-Restraint' 100 *California Law Review* 519.

Pound, Roscoe (1908) 'Mechanical Jurisprudence' 8 *Columbia Law Review* 605.

—— (1964) 'Felix Frankfurter at Harvard' in Wallace Mendelson (ed), *Felix Frankfurter: A Tribute* (New York, Reynal & Company) 137.

Purcell, Edward Jr (2001) 'Brandeis, *Erie*, and the New Deal "Constitutional Revolution"' 26 *Journal of Supreme Court History* 257.

Qvortrup, Mads (1999) 'AV Dicey: The Referendum as the People's Veto' 20 *History of Political Thought* 531.

Rabban, David (1982) 'The Emergence of Modern First Amendment Doctrine' 50 *University of Chicago Law Review* 1205.

—— (1997) *Free Speech in Its Forgotten Years* (Cambridge, Cambridge University Press).

—— (2013) *Law's History: American Legal Thought and the Transatlantic Turn to History* (Cambridge, Cambridge University Press).

Raz, Joseph (1977) 'The Rule of Law and its Virtue' 93 *Law Quarterly Review* 195.
—— (1979) *The Authority of Law* (Oxford, Clarendon Press).
—— (1985) 'Authority and Justification' 14 *Philosophy and Public Affairs* 3.
—— (1986) *The Morality of Freedom* (Oxford, Oxford University Press).
—— (1994) 'Authority, Law, and Morality' in Joseph Raz, *Ethics in the Public Domain: Essays in the Morality of Law and Politics*, revised edn (Oxford, Clarendon Press) 213.
—— (1994) 'The Politics of the Rule of Law' in Joseph Raz (ed), *Ethics in the Public Domain: Essays in the Morality of Law and Politics* (Oxford, Oxford University Press) 370.
—— (1999) *Practical Reason and Norms* (Oxford, Oxford University Press).
—— (2003) 'Comments and Responses' in Lukas Meyer, Stanley Paulson and Thomas Pogge, *Rights, Culture, and the Law: Themes from the Legal and Practical Philosophy of Joseph Raz* (Oxford, Oxford University Press) 260.
Réaume, Denise (1985) 'The Judicial Philosophy of Bora Laskin' 35 *University of Toronto Law Journal* 438.
Richardson, Henry (2002) *Democratic Autonomy* (Oxford, Oxford University Press).
Risk, Richard (2004) 'Canadian Law Teachers in the 1930s: "When the World was Turned Upside Down"' 27 *Dalhousie Law Journal* 2.
Risk, Richard and Vipond, Robert (1996) 'Rights Talk in Canada in the Late Nineteenth Century: "The Good Sense and Right Feeling of the People"' 14 *Law & History Review* 1.
Roach, K (1989) 'The Administrative Law Scholarship of DM Gordon' 34 *McGill Law Journal* 1.
Robson, William (1951) *Justice and Administrative Law*, 3rd edn (London, Stevens & Sons).
Roosevelt, Theodore (1912) 'Address at Philadelphia, Pennsylvania: Recall of Judges and Referendum of Decisions' (10 April 1912), available at www.theodore-roosevelt.com/trspeechescomplete.html.
Rubinstein, Amnon (1965) *Jurisdiction and Illegality* (Oxford, Clarendon Press).
Saywell, John (2002) *The Lawmakers: Judicial Power and the Shaping of Canadian Federalism* (Toronto, University of Toronto Press).
Scalia, Antonin (1989) 'Judicial Deference to Administrative Interpretations of Law' 38 *Duke Law Journal* 511.
Scarman, Leslie (1974) *English Law—the New Dimension* (London, Stevens).
Schauer, F (1987) 'Formalism' 97 *Yale Law Journal* 509.
Schiller, Reuel (2007) 'The Era of Deference: Courts, Expertise, and the Emergence of New Deal Administrative Law' 106 *Michigan Law Review* 399.
Schneewind, JB (ed) (1968) *Mill: A Collection of Critical Essays* (London, Macmillan).
Schneiderman, David (1998) 'Harold Laski, Viscount Haldane, and the Law of the Canadian Constitution in the Early Twentieth Century' 48 *University of Toronto Law Journal* 521.
Schwartz, Bernard (1950) 'The Administrative World of Mr. Justice Frankfurter' 59 *Yale Law Journal* 1228.
—— (1950) 'Mixed Questions of Law and Fact and the Administrative Procedure Act' 19 *Fordham Law Review* 73.

Schwarze, Jürgen (2006) *European Administrative Law* rev'd edn (London, Sweet & Maxwell).

Schweber, Howard (1999) 'The "Science" of Legal Science: The Model of the Natural Sciences in Nineteenth-Century American Legal Education' 17 *Law & History Review* 421.

Scott, FR (1937) 'The Consequences of the Privy Council Decisions' 15 *Canadian Bar Review* 485.

—— (1951) 'Centralization and Decentralization in Canadian Federalism' 29 *Canadian Bar Review* 1095.

Sebok, Anthony (1996) 'The Legal Process' 94 *Michigan Law Review* 1571.

Secretary of State for the Home Department (1997) 'Rights Brought Home: The Human Rights Bill' (Cm 3782).

Seidenfeld, Mark (1994) 'A Syncopated *Chevron:* Emphasizing Reasoned Decisionmaking in Reviewing Agency Interpretations of Statutes' 73 *Texas Law Review* 83.

Silverstein, Michael (1984) *Constitutional Faiths: Felix Frankfurter, Hugo Black, and the Process of Judicial Decision-Making* (Ithaca, Cornell University Press).

Simpson, AWB (1973) 'The Common Law and Legal Theory' in AWB Simpson (ed), *Oxford Essays in Jurisprudence* (Oxford, Clarendon Press, 2nd series) 77.

Singh, S, Hunt, M and Dennetriou, M [1999] 'Is There a Role for the "Margin of Appreciation" in National Law After the HRA?' *European Human Rights Law Review* 15.

Snyder, Brad (2012) 'The House that Built Holmes' 30 *Law and History Review* 661.

—— (2013) 'Frankfurter and Popular Constitutionalism' 47 *University of California Davis Law Review* 343.

Sossin, Lorne and Flood, Colleen (2007) 'The Contextual Turn: Iacobucci's Legacy and the Standard of Review in Administrative Law' 57 *University of Toronto Law Journal* 581.

St Macdonald, R (1993) 'The Margin of Appreciation' in R St Macdonald, F Matscher and H Petzold (eds), *The European System for the Protection of Human Rights* (London, Martinus Nijhoff Publishers) 83.

Stapleton, Julia (1995) 'Dicey and his Legacy' *History of Political Thought* 234.

Stephenson, Matthew and Vermeule, Adrian (2009) '*Chevron* Has Only One Step' 95 *Virginia Law Review* 597.

Stone, Alec and Mathews, Jud (2008) 'Proportionality Balancing and Global Constitutionalism' 47 *Columbia Journal of Transnational Law* 72.

Strauss, Peter (1984) 'The Place of Agencies in Government: Separation of Powers and the Fourth Branch' 84 *Columbia Law Review* 573.

Strayer, BL (1963) 'The Concept of 'Jurisdiction' in Review of Labour Relations Board Decisions' 28 *Saskatchewan Bar Review* 157.

Sugarman, David (1983) 'The Legal Boundaries of Liberty: Dicey, Liberalism and Legal Science' 46 *Modern Law Review* 102.

—— (1986) 'Legal Theory, the Common Law Mind and the Making of the Textbook Tradition' in William Twining (ed), *Legal Theory and Common Law* (Oxford, Blackwell) 26.

Suggs, George (1972) *Colorado's War on Militant Unionism: James H Peabody and the Western Federation of Miners* (Detroit MI, Wayne State University Press).

Sunstein, Cass (1983) 'Deregulation and the Hard-Look Doctrine' *The Supreme Court Review* 177.
—— (1987) 'Lochner's Legacy' (1987) 87 *Columbia Law Review* 873.
—— (1998) 'Is Tobacco a Drug? Administrative Agencies as Common Law Courts' 47 *Duke Law Journal* 1013.
—— (2006) '*Chevron* Step Zero' 92 *Virginia Law Review* 187.
Symposium (1993) 'One Hundred Years of Judicial Review: The Thayer Centennial Symposium' 88 *Northwestern University Law Review* 1.
Taggart, Michael (1996) 'Outside Canadian Administrative Law' 46 *University of Toronto Law Journal* 649.
—— (ed) (1997) *The Province of Administrative Law* (Oxford, Hart Publishing).
—— (2000) 'Ultra Vires as Distraction' in Forsyth (ed), *Judicial Review and the Constitution* (Oxford, Hart Publishing).
—— (2005) 'Prolegomenon to an Intellectual History of Administrative Law in the Twentieth Century: The Case of John Willis and Canadian Administrative Law' 43 *Osgoode Hall Law Journal* 223.
—— [2008] 'Proportionality, Deference, Wednesbury' *New Zealand Law Review* 423.
Thayer, James (1856) 'The Right of Eminent Domain' 9 *The Monthly Law Reporter* (New Series) 241.
—— (1878) *Letters of Chauncey Wright: with some account of his life* (Cambridge, John Wilson and Son).
—— (1884) 'Constitutionality of Legislation: The Precise Question for a Court' 38 *Nation* 314 (10 April 1884).
—— (1887) 'Legal Tender' 1 *Harvard Law Review* 73.
—— (1893) 'The Origin and Scope of the American Doctrine of Constitutional Law' 7 *Harvard Law Review* 129.
—— (1901) *John Marshall* (Boston, Houghton, Mifflin & Company).
Tomkins, Adam (2010) 'The Role of the Courts in the Political Constitution' 60 *University of Toronto Law Journal* 1.
Touster, Saul (1964) 'In Search of Holmes from Within' 18 *Vanderbilt Law Review* 437.
Tulloch, Hugh (1980) 'A.V. Dicey and the Irish Question: 1870–1922' 15 *Irish Jurist* (NS) 137.
Twining, William (ed) (1986) *Legal Theory and Common Law* (Oxford, Blackwell).
United Kingdom (1932) *Committee on Ministers' Powers Report* Cmd 4060 (London, HMSO).
Urofsky, Melvin (1991) *Felix Frankfurter: Judicial Restraint and Individual Liberties* (Boston MA, Twayne Publishers).
—— (2009) *Louis D. Brandeis: A Life* (New York, Schoken Books).
Urofsky, Melvin and Levy, David (eds) (1971) *Letters of Louis D Brandeis*, vol I (Albany NY, State University of New York).
—— (1971) *Letters of Louis D Brandeis*, vol IV (Albany NY, State University of New York).
—— (1978) *Letters of Louis D Brandeis*, vol V (Albany NY, State University of New York).
—— (1991) *Half-Son, Half-Brother: The Letters of Louis D Brandeis to Felix Frankfurter* (Norman OK, University of Oklahoma Press).

Weill, Rivka (2003) 'Dicey was not Diceyan' 62 *Cambridge Law Journal* 474.
Wade, HWR (1951) 'The Twilight of Natural Justice?' 67 *Law Quarterly Review* 103.
—— (1955) 'The Basis of Legal Sovereignty' 13 *Cambridge Law Journal* 172.
—— (1967) *Administrative Law*, 2nd edn (Oxford, Clarendon Press).
—— [1969] 'Constitutional and Administrative Aspects of the Anisminic Case' 85 *Law Quarterly Review* 198.
—— (1970) *Administrative Law*, 3rd edn (Oxford, Clarendon Press).
—— (1980) *Constitutional Fundamentals* (London, Stevens & Sons).
—— (1982) *Administrative Law*, 5th edn (Oxford, Clarendon Press).
Wade, HWR and Forsyth, Christopher (2009) *Administrative Law*, 10th edn (Oxford, Oxford University Press).
Waldron, Jeremy (1993) 'A Right-Based Critique of Constitutional Rights' 13 *Oxford Journal of Legal Studies* 18.
—— (1996) 'Legislation, Authority, and Voting' 84 *Georgetown Law Journal* 2185.
—— (1998) 'Judicial Review and the Conditions of Democracy' 6 *Journal of Political Philosophy* 335.
—— (1999) *Law and Disagreement* (Oxford, Clarendon Press).
—— (2003) 'Authority for Officials' in Lukas Meyer, Stanley Paulson and Thomas Pogge, *Rights, Culture, and the Law: Themes from the Legal and Practical Philosophy of Joseph Raz* (Oxford, Oxford University Press) 45.
—— (2004) 'The Rule of Law as a Theater of Debate' in Ronald Dworkin and Justine Burley, (eds), *Dworkin and His Critics: With Replies by Dworkin* (Oxford, Blackwell) 319.
—— (2006) 'The Core of the Case Against Judicial Review' 115 *Yale Law Journal* 1346.
—— (2007) 'Legislation and the Rule of Law' 1 *Legisprudence* 91.
—— (2008) 'The Concept and the Rule of Law' 43 *Georgia Law Review* 1.
—— (2008) 'Hart and the Principles of Legality' in Matthew Kramer, Claire Grant, and Antony Hatzistavrou (eds), *The Legacy of HLA Hart: Legal, Political, and Moral Philosophy* (Oxford, Oxford University Press) 67.
—— (2011) 'The Rule of Law and the Importance of Procedure' in James Fleming (ed), *Getting to the Rule of Law* (New York, New York University Press) 3.
Warren, Matthew (2002) 'Active Judging: Judicial Philosophy and the Development of the Hard Look Doctrine in the DC Circuit' 90 *Georgetown Law Journal* 2599.
Weiler, Paul (1971) 'The 'Slippery Slope' of Judicial Intervention: The Supreme Court and Canadian Labour Relations 1950–1970' 9 *Osgoode Hall Law Journal* 1.
White, G Edward (1973) 'The Evolution of Reasoned Elaboration: Jurisprudential Criticism and Social Change' 59 *Virginia Law Review* 279.
—— (1974) 'Allocating Power Between Agencies and Courts: The Legacy of Justice Brandeis' 23 *Duke Law Journal* 195.
—— (1986) 'Felix Frankfurter, the Old Boy Network, and the New Deal: The Placement of Elite Lawyers in Public Service in the 1930's' 29 *Arkansas Law Review* 631.
—— (1992) 'Justice Holmes and the Modernization of Free Speech Jurisprudence: the Human Dimension' 80 *California Law Review* 391.
—— (1993) *Justice Oliver Wendell Holmes: Law and the Inner Self* (New York, Oxford University Press).

—— (1993–94) 'Revisiting James Bradley Thayer' 88 *Northwestern University Law Review* 48.

—— (1995) 'The Canonization of Holmes and Brandeis: Epistemology and Judicial Reputations' 70 *New York University Law Review* 576.

—— (2003) 'The Constitutional Journal of "Marbury v Madison"' 89 *Virginia Law Review* 1463.

—— (2005) 'Historicizing Judicial Scrutiny' 57 *South Carolina Law Review* 1.

—— (2007) *The American Judicial Tradition: Profiles of Leading American Judges*, 3rd edn (Oxford, Oxford University Press).

Willis, John (1933) *The Parliamentary Powers of English Government Departments,* (Cambridge MA, Harvard University Press).

—— (1935) 'Three Approaches to Administrative Law: The Judicial, the Conceptual, and the Functional' 1 *University of Toronto Law Journal* 53.

—— (1938) 'Statute Interpretation in a Nutshell' 16 *Canadian Bar Review* 1.

—— (1940) 'Section 96 of the British North America Act' 18 *Canadian Bar Review* 517.

—— (1951) 'Correspondence: More on the Nolan Case' 29 *Canadian Bar Review* 580.

—— (1968) 'The McRuer Report: Lawyers' Values and Civil Servants' Values' 18 *University of Toronto Law Journal* 351.

—— (1974) 'Canadian Administrative Law in Retrospect' 24 *University of Toronto Law Journal* 225.

Woolf, Harry, Jowell, Jeffrey and LeSueur, Andrew (2007) *De Smith's Judicial Review*, 6th edn (London, Sweet & Maxwell).

Yonge, CD (ed) (1853) *The Treatises of M.T. Cicero on the Nature of the Gods; on Divination; on Fate; on the Republic; on the Laws; and on Standing for the Consulship* (London, Henry G Bohn).

Zacharias, LS (2013) 'Reframing the Constitution: Brandeis, "Facts", and the Nation's Deliberative Process' *Journal of Jurisprudence* 327.

Zeppos, Nicholas (1993) 'Deference to Political Decisionmakers and the Preferred Scope of Judicial Review' 88 *Northwestern Law Review* 296.

Index

www.ingramcontent.com/pod-product-compliance
Lightning Source LLC
LaVergne TN
LVHW052304200926
848481LV00002B/456